BIRDFINDI

In Forty National and Grasslands

WHITE MOUNTAIN NATIONAL FOREST, NEW HAMPSHIRE

This Guide was produced in cooperation
between the U.S. Department of Agriculture Forest Service
and the American Birding Association.

AMERICAN BIRDING ASSOCIATION
Colorado Springs
1994

BIRDFINDING in Forty National Forests and Grasslands

U.S.D.A. FOREST SERVICE
Jack Ward Thomas, Chief

AMERICAN BIRDING ASSOCIATION
Daniel T. Williams, Jr., President

PROJECT OFFICERS
Gregory S. Butcher (ABA) ◆ Debra S. Pressman (USFS)

Our book is based on information supplied by the following U.S.D.A. Forest Service personnel:

Rick Alexander ◆ Carrie Anderson ◆ Karen Austin ◆ Steve Babler ◆ Norm Barrett ◆ Gerald Bauer
Dean Beyer ◆ Garvan Bucaria ◆ Dawn Carrie ◆ Tim Charon ◆ Jerry Cline ◆ Paula Crumpton
Sam Cuenca ◆ Cecelia Dargan ◆ Kevin Doran ◆ John Dorio ◆ James Dunn ◆ Betsy Follman ◆ Larry Ford
Tom Fratt ◆ Ricardo Garcia ◆ Steve Gerdes ◆ Greg Goodwin ◆ Patricia Greenlee ◆ D. Clayton Grove
Karen Holtrop ◆ Phil Huber ◆ Matt Hunter ◆ Dennis Lowry ◆ Laura Lowery ◆ Jina Mariani
Clinton McCarthy ◆ Nancy McGarigal ◆ Bob McKinney ◆ Kathleen Milne ◆ Laura Mitchell ◆ Jim Morphew
Doug Munson ◆ Brad Nelson ◆ William Noblitt ◆ Rebecca Oreskes ◆ John Ormiston ◆ Mary Jeanne Packer
Becky Parmenter ◆ Joy Patty ◆ Karen Raftery ◆ Jill Reeck ◆ Susan Reel ◆ Deana Reyher ◆ Kelle Reynolds
Charles Richmond ◆ Leslie Rowse ◆ Greg Schenbeck ◆ Doreen Schmidt ◆ Jerry Schumacher ◆ Chris Schumaker
Bill Shuster ◆ Emily Skelton ◆ Randall Smith ◆ Sally Sovey ◆ Duane Strock ◆ Jody Sutton ◆ Nancy Tankersley
Gary Taylor ◆ Cindy Thompson ◆ Nancy Upham ◆ James Wiley ◆ Richard Williams ◆ Kirie Willimon ◆ Carl Wolf
Brian Woodbridge ◆ Don Yasuda ◆ Susan Yasudo

EDITORIAL STAFF FOR ABA

EDITORIAL DIRECTORS
George G. Daniels ◆ Daphne D. Gemmill

MANAGING EDITOR
Carol S. Lawson

EDITORS
William J. Boyle, Jr. ◆ Roland H. Wauer

CONSULTING EDITORS
Paul J. Baicich ◆ Paul Lehman ◆ Hugh Willoughby

CARTOGRAPHERS
Cindy Lippincott ◆ Thomas Pizer

ILLUSTRATORS
Jonathan Alderfer ◆ Tony Bennett ◆ M. Jean Buschmann (flowers, plants, and trees) ◆ James Coe
Shawneen Finnegan ◆ Carl James Freeman ◆ Kenn Kaufman ◆ Rudolf Koes ◆ Daniel Lane
Gail Diane Luckner ◆ Walter Marcisz ◆ Patricia J. Moore ◆ Michael O'Brien ◆ Jeremy Pearse ◆ David Sibley
Keith Taylor ◆ Mimi Hoppe Wolf ◆ Julie Zickefoose

CONTRIBUTING EDITORS
Robert S. Berman ◆ Cindy Lippincott ◆ Richard C. Rosché ◆ W. Ross Silcock

ABA FIELD CONTRIBUTORS AND FRIENDS
Dennis Abbott ◆ Thaïs Bach ◆ Ebbe Banstorp ◆ Sandy Banstorp ◆ Wes Biggs ◆ Alan Barron ◆ Jim Berry
Steve Bouricius ◆ Jim Carlson ◆ Dan Canterbury ◆ Lois Canterbury ◆ David Chaffin ◆ Joy Chapper ◆ John Coons
Kate Duffy ◆ Kim Eckert ◆ John Eckfeldt ◆ Walter Ellison ◆ Bob Evans ◆ Sally Gaines ◆ Jeff Gilligan ◆ Dave A. Griffiths
Ted Grisez ◆ Barb Haas ◆ Frank Haas ◆ Edward Harper ◆ Jo Heindel ◆ Tom Heindel ◆ Alan Hilton ◆ Roy Houser
Pete Isleib ◆ Greg Jackson ◆ Mayme Johnson ◆ Willard Johnson ◆ Kenn Kaufman ◆ Hugh Kingery ◆ Rick Knight
Aileen Lotz ◆ Robert Moore ◆ Ed Morgan ◆ Harry Nehls ◆ Robert Norton ◆ Karl Overman ◆ Tommie Rogers
Bill Roney ◆ Oliver Scott ◆ Scott Seltman ◆ Mark Simpson ◆ Charles Smith ◆ Doris Smith ◆ Ella Sorenson
Thede Tobish ◆ Carole Toppins ◆ Terry Toppins ◆ Bill Tweit ◆ Ray Vaughn ◆ Kathy Veit
Noel Wamer ◆ Ron Weeks ◆ Nathaniel Whitney ◆ David Wolf ◆ Bill Young

EDITORIAL PRODUCTION
Catherine S. Isham ◆ Susanna v.R. Lawson

EXECUTIVE STAFF FOR ABA
Robert S. Berman, BUSINESS MANAGER ◆ Stanley R. Lincoln, TREASURER
Langdon R. Stevenson, DEVELOPMENT DIRECTOR

CONTENTS
Forty National Forests and Grasslands

CARL JAMES FREEMAN, DRAWING

About This Book

THE PARTNERSHIPS ARE MANY AND VARIED between private organizations and public agencies in the United States. That is one of the great things about American democracy—the joining together of individuals and the whole. Here, with *Birdfinding in Forty National Forests and Grasslands,* we have another such cooperative venture, and a splendid new one at that.

This Guide was produced through the combined efforts of the U.S. Department of Agriculture Forest Service, which manages 191 million acres of public lands, and the American Birding Association, whose 13,500 members are at the core of the country's community of field ornithologists.

Our goals were easy to define. Everybody acknowledges the role of National Forests in logging, mining, and other commercial endeavors; hunters and anglers make ample use of the Forests. But relatively few people fully consider the vast potential of the nation's federal forests and grasslands for low-profile, non-consumptive public use—as places to relax and quietly enjoy the flora and fauna. We decided to encourage birders and their families and friends to make greater use of this inestimable national treasure.

We had a second objective, as well. The bird life of our National Forests has not been well-studied. And in these days of ever-greater concern over the ultimate fate of so many bird species, particularly neotropical migrants, it is extremely important to understand the status of our birds over so vast a domain as the National Forests. Birders can be instrumental in gathering the vital data, and we urge all visitors to pass along their observations to the USFS.

Our project took a lot of time and effort by a lot of dedicated people. Some might even call it a bear of a job—our apologies, Smokey. We started over three years ago, with a plan that drew from the *ABA / Lane Birdfinding Guides* that are so popular with birders. But while those guides focus almost exclusively on avifauna, we wanted the Forest Guide to be interesting and useful to everybody tuned in to the natural world. Thus, we included information on each Forest's history whenever appropriate, on its life zones and scenery, on its diversity of trees, shrubs, grasses, and wildflowers. We explained a little about its animal life, its reptiles and amphibians, and its moths and butterflies. Then, at the end of every entry, we went into what else visitors might enjoy on the Forest, and what they might find appealing in the surrounding area—from National Parks to astronomical observatories and Shakespeare Festivals.

Armed with our plan, a veritable army—have a look at the masthead—of Forest Service people sallied forth to gather the necessary information. Since it was obviously impossible to cover everything, the Forest Service authors used their expert judgment to lay out Birding Routes that would give visitors the richest possible sampling of what each forest has to offer.

After many months, the first write-ups came flooding onto the desks of ABA's editorial team. Requests for clarifications and further information went back to the Forests. Amended versions were researched and written. Consultations about maps were critical. Calls went out for illustrations, and artists and photographers responded eagerly. Here and there, the plan was modified by special considerations; a single set of rules did not fit every situation.

In time, ABA's editors shaped the Forest Service submissions into more or less definitive manuscripts, which then went out for review by top birders living near each Forest. Numerous fresh suggestions were folded into the write-ups. Maps were corrected, routes checked and rechecked; now and again, a completely new route recommended itself to the experts and editors. At last, we were able to send the entries back to the Forests for a final look. And then we went to press.

We all—all 198 of us—wish you good birding and the best of fun.

—THE AUTHORS, EDITORS, AND CONTRIBUTORS

In Thanks

THIS GUIDE could not have been published without the wholehearted support and inspiration of the two men in charge of the American Birding Association and the U.S. Forest Service at the inception of the project and during much of its progress:

Allan R. Keith, President of ABA from 1989 to 1993

F. Dale Robertson, Chief of the USFS from 1987 to 1993,

and without the steady encouragement and careful planning of Robert D. Nelson, Director, USFS Wildlife and Fisheries.

We wish also to thank Nancy Green, a biologist formerly with the USFS, for helping to forge the idea and bring together the partners.

Nor could *Birdfinding in Forty National Forests and Grasslands* have been carried to completion without the most generous financial assistance of the following organizations and individuals:

AMERICAN FOREST AND PAPER ASSOCIATION

BAUSCH & LOMB, SPORTS OPTICS DIVISION

BROWNING–FERRIS INDUSTRIES

INTERNATIONAL PAPER COMPANY

LEICA CAMERA INC. *Leica*

SAMUEL AND IMOGENE JOHNSON

NATIONAL FISH AND WILDLIFE FOUNDATION

OTTENHEIMER PUBLISHERS, INC. Ottenheimer PUBLISHERS, INC

PENTAX CORPORATION **PENTAX**

PHILLIPS PETROLEUM COMPANY

WELDON OWEN PUBLISHING, AUSTRALIA

OTHER ABA PUBLICATIONS

Birding (ABA bimonthly journal); *Winging It* (ABA monthly newsletter)

A Bird's-Eye View (ABA quarterly newsletter for young birders)

ABA Checklist: Birds of the Continental United States and Canada (4th ed., 1990)

Annual Directory of Volunteer Opportunities for Birders

A Birder's Guide to Southern California (rev. ed., 1990)

A Birder's Guide to the Rio Grande Valley of Texas (rev. ed., 1992)

A Birder's Guide to Wyoming (1993)

A Birder's Guide to Florida (rev. ed., 1989)

A Birder's Guide to Southeastern Arizona (rev. ed., 1989)

A Birder's Guide to Colorado (rev. ed., 1988)

A Birder's Guide to the Texas Coast (rev. ed., 1993)

A Birder's Guide to Churchill (rev. ed., 1994)

A Birder's Guide to Eastern Massachusetts (in press, 1994)

General Notes

THIS VOLUME IS SELF-CONTAINED. However, when embarking on a visit to a National Forest, you may wish to stop by or write ahead to the Forest Supervisor's Office listed at the end of each entry. The Forest Offices will be happy to supply you with bird lists, further information on camping, nature trails, and local attractions, along with whatever regulations and precautions might apply. You may also wish to purchase one of the highly-detailed Forest maps available at nominal cost from every Forest Office; they will enhance your explorations when used in conjunction with the trail locator maps and Birding Route mileage directions in the text.

After your visit, the Forest Office is the place to drop off or mail in your bird observations—what species you have seen, in what numbers, with what evidence of nesting, unusual behavior, etc. Please direct your records to the Forest biologists. They will be grateful for your help.

Key to Symbols

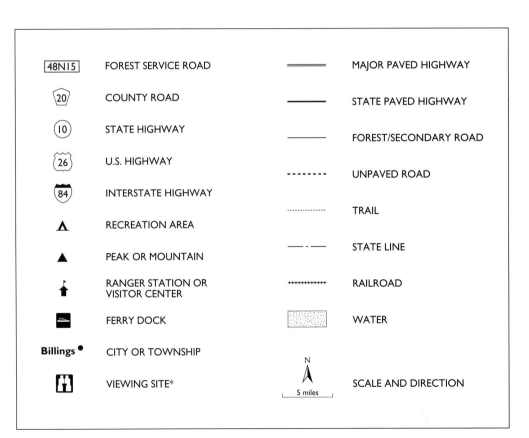

As you travel through the National Forests, you will sometimes see brown-and-white road signs featuring a binocular symbol. These signs identify special wildlife viewing sites, some for birdfinding opportunities, others for seeing mammals, reptiles, amphibians, insects, and such. Some of the individual bird-viewing sites are described in this guide.

Alaska and the West Coast

CHUGACH FOREST
Alaska

HOW TO GET THERE. *Visitors can enter the Forest in two main ways. Access to the 118-mile Seward Scenic Byway is from either Anchorage (Alaska Route 1) or Seward (Alaska Route 9). Cordova, at the start of the 48.8-mile Copper River Highway, can be reached by commercial air service from Anchorage, Juneau, or Seattle. A birdier voyage to Cordova is by the Alaska Marine Highway ferry from Whittier, 50 miles by road and/or railroad shuttle from Anchorage. Those same Marine Highway ferries can take you on mini-pelagic trips as they wend their way around Prince William Sound. A circuitous but scenic route is from Anchorage to Glennallen (Alaska Route 1), thence south to Valdez Alaska Route 4) where connections to the Marine Highway System link Valdez, Cordova, Whittier, and Seward.*

SHOREBIRDS, HARTNEY BAY, COPPER RIVER DELTA

ALASKA'S monumental 5.7-million-acre Chugach National Forest is the second-largest of the nation's Forests, surpassed only by the 16.9-million-acre Tongass National Forest in the southeastern part of the state. Our northernmost Forest stretches southeastward almost 200 miles from Anchorage and Seward to Cordova and Cape Suckling on the Gulf of Alaska, encompassing a vast domain of wetland, fjord, mountain, and glacier, rich with spectacular scenery and bountiful wildlife. It will be a life-rewarding experience to tour either—or both—the Seward Scenic Byway on the Kenai Peninsula at the north-western extremity of the Forest and the Copper River Highway on the southeastern end, reached by way of the Alaska state ferry.

The region's earliest inhabitants spread across the Arctic from Siberia 10,000 years ago. Over time, other sturdy, sea-oriented peoples, perhaps descendants of the first group or later immigrants, occupied these awesome lands. The first Europeans to view Alaska were Russians, members of the Bering and Cherikov expedition, who landed near Cordova in 1741. By then, the region was inhabited by a broad tapestry of native Americans, including Chugach Eski-mos, Eyak Indians, and Dena'ina Athabaskan Indians. The Russians bestowed the name *Ghugatz* or *Tchougatskoi* (their version of the Eskimos' name for themselves) on the vast assemblage of mountains and glaciers marching inland from the coast. Eventually, the Russian terms evolved into "Chugach," by which we now know the area.

It is a place in flux. The slow retreat of the glaciers since the end of the last great advance 10,000 years ago has created a succession of new lands, clothed first by lichens, then by mosses and shrubs. Later came the towering forests and lesser groves of trees. At the edge of Prince William Sound's spectacular marine environment, abundant rain and snow sustain a lush temperate rain forest of huge western hemlock and Sitka spruce, rising as straight as the columns of some ancient temple. Inland, the colder northern sections of the Kenai Peninsula possess vegetation similar to that of central Alaska, with wide tracts of birch, aspen, white spruce, and spindly black spruce. Above 2000 feet lies another world of alpine tundra, snow-free only for a few months in the year. Together, these Chugach National Forest habitats support a profusion of mammals, including Sitka black-tailed deer, moose, caribou, Dall sheep, mountain goat, wolf, coyote, wolverine, porcupine, lynx, black bear and the gargantuan brown bear that ranks as the world's largest carnivore.

Bird Life

More than 250 species of resident and migrant birds have been recorded from the Chugach. Among the specialties are enormous colonies of Black-legged Kittiwakes, Common Murres, and smaller numbers of Horned and Tufted puffins, and Thick-billed Murres on the seaside cliffs. The elusive Marbled Murrelet frequents the fjords and nests in the lichen-festooned trees in the mossy inland forests. Aleutian Terns breed in the Copper River Delta area. Bountiful salmon and other spawning fish attract one of the heaviest congregations of Bald Eagles to be seen anywhere; as many as 3000 birds are on the Forest at all times. All three species of ptarmigan can be found in appropriate habitat: White-tailed and Rock ptarmigans on the alpine tundra and rocky scree of the mountain slopes and Willow Ptarmigan among the willow and alder stands along streams and at the lower edges of alpine tundra.

Spring migration, from April to early June, is nothing short of fantastic. The region's topography, cut with few low-lying passes through the mountains, makes the coastal zone a major corridor for millions of waterfowl, raptors, and passerines

on their way to far northern breeding grounds.

Most spectacular of all are the shorebird concentrations in May. The Bering and Copper river deltas east of Cordova form the major contiguous network of wetlands on the Pacific Coast—approximately 700,000 acres of shallow ponds, intertidal sloughs, braided glacial streams, sedge marshes, tidal flats, and sandy barrier islands. These food-rich areas are key stopovers, where shorebirds can rest and restore fat reserves after their long, dangerous flights from the wintering-grounds. Indeed, the Copper River Delta Shorebird Unit is so important that it was dedicated as a Hemispheric Site by the Western Hemisphere Shorebird Reserve Network in May of 1990.

The migration reaches its zenith during the first two weeks of May; in 1993, approximately 1,200,000 shorebirds were observed in one day along 75 miles of Copper River Delta habitat. Two species predominate, with Dunlin and Western Sandpiper comprising as much as 98 percent of the mass. But 30 species or more are ordinarily present. Among the common shorebirds are Black-bellied Plover, American Golden-Plover, Greater

and Lesser yellowlegs, Whimbrel, Black Turnstone, Surfbird, Sanderling, Spotted, Least, and Pectoral sandpipers, Short-billed and Long-billed dowitchers, Common Snipe, and Red-necked Phalarope.

In addition, a patient birder in appropriate habitats usually will be rewarded by Solitary, Semipalmated, and Baird's sandpipers, and Hudsonian and Marbled godwits, as well as Wandering Tattler, Red Knot, and Ruddy Turnstone. Bar-tailed Godwit, Bristle-thighed Curlew, and White-rumped and Stilt sandpipers have appeared on occasion, and a number of Asian shorebirds are infrequent visitors.

A pageant of waterfowl parades through the Delta and adjacent waters. Arriving in late March or early April, ducks and geese may be found on nearly every one of the hundreds upon hundreds of ponds when open water is available. Tundra and Trumpeter swans and Greater White-fronted, Snow, and Canada geese are prevalent. Dabbling-ducks include Green-winged Teal, Mallard, Northern Pintail, Northern Shoveler, Gadwall, and American Wigeon. Diving-ducks are everywhere: Ring-necked Duck, Canvasback, Redhead, Greater

ALEUTIAN TERNS

HUDSONIAN GODWIT

and Lesser scaups, Common and Red-breasted mergansers, Common and Barrow's goldeneyes, among others. Blue-winged and Cinnamon teals, Eurasian Wigeon, and Hooded Merganser are less common but nevertheless are present most years. Occasionally a vagrant turns up: Whooper Swan, Emperor Goose, Garganey, Tufted and Ruddy ducks, and King Eider have been reported from the area, usually in fall or winter.

Birding Routes

Copper River Delta. The 48.8-mile Copper River Highway combines dazzling scenic vistas with some truly splendid birding—not merely for the above-mentioned shorebirds and waterfowl, but for hawks, owls, and passerines as well. The road follows the route of the old Copper River & Northwestern Railroad, which once did yeoman service transporting copper ore from the Wrangell Mountain mines to Cordova on Orca Inlet. For your convenience, a road guide to the Copper River Highway is available from the Forest Service in Cordova; the road itself is well marked in any case with mile-posts beginning at the Cordova ferry dock.

Start your tour at the ferry dock (mile 0.0). Drive 1.4 miles and turn onto the well-maintained gravel Whitshed Road for a side-trip to Hartney Bay. The road winds through the forest that fringes the bay and the tidal areas frequented by waterfowl and shorebirds. An indigenous goose breeding on the Copper River Delta is the "Dusky" Canada Goose, a large, dark subspecies of our ubiquitous *Branta canadensis* that winters in western Washington and Oregon; keep an eye out also for the midget of the Canada family, the mallard-sized "Cackling" Goose, which migrates through the area in spring and fall. There are further good viewing-spots at mile 6 and mile 7 at the end of the road. The best time for both birding and photography is on rising and high tides when the birds come off the flats to flock tightly together near the beach. Then keep your eye peeled for a Merlin or Peregrine Falcon bursting into the concentrations. Scan the open water for Common and Pacific loons, and for such sea ducks as Harlequin, Oldsquaw, and Surf and White-winged scoters. In fall, winter, and early spring, an observer might spot a Steller's Eider among the other ducks. Watch for Bonaparte's, Mew, Glaucous, Herring, and Glaucous-winged gulls. Caspian Terns are often present, and Northwestern Crows patrol the shoreline.

In spring and fall, you are likely to find American Pipits and Lapland Longspurs along the roadside, while the forest borders are good for Rufous Hummingbird, Steller's Jay, Chest-

OLDSQUAW

nut-backed Chickadee, Winter Wren, Golden-crowned and Ruby-crowned kinglets, Hermit and Varied thrushes, Orange-crowned, Yellow, and Wilson's warblers, American Tree, Savannah, Fox, Song, Lincoln's, White-crowned, and Golden-crowned sparrows, and Pine Siskin. In years of good cone crops, Red and White-winged crossbills may be found feeding in the spruce and hemlock. Continuing on Whitshed Road, stop at the Three-Mile (or Sawmill) Bay turnout for more flocks of shorebirds and waterfowl.

Return to the Copper River Highway. Stands of Sitka spruce and western and mountain hemlock border the road from mile 2.1 to mile 7.5. Breeding birds of this community include Northern Goshawk, Great Horned Owl, and Townsend's Warbler; keep an eye out for Common Raven, Red-breasted Nuthatch, and Lincoln's Sparrow. Watch for Trumpeter Swans on Eyak Lake and at the Eyak River Bridge (mile 5.7). The delta supports 6 percent of the Alaska Trumpeter population of about 13,300 birds, and they often can be seen up close feeding or resting. Aside from the swans and other waterfowl, look for Arctic Tern and Belted Kingfisher, and for American Dipper among the rocks in the river. At mile 7.5, to the left in the distance, look for the massive nest of Bald Eagles.

At mile 10.7 is the Copper River Delta entrance pavilion

with its excellent interpretive display of the area's ecosystem. From June to mid-August, this location is great for both waterfowl and land-birds. The shrub thickets are favorite haunts of Alder Flycatchers, among many other passerines. The small pond with dead trees to the north usually has nesting Mew Gulls on the sedge tussocks, and Tree, Violet-Green, Bank, and Barn swallows course for insects overhead.

The Sheridan Glacier Road (mile 13.7) offers a 4.3-mile side-trip through a newly-exposed glacial landscape with breathtaking views of the retreating blue ice. Drive another few miles along the Highway (mile 17) and you will come to Alaganik Slough Road. This 3-mile gravel road meanders through open sedge meadows, broad expanses of sweetgale and willow shrub, patches of spruce and cottonwood, and around small ponds and sloughs to the edge of Alaganik Slough; wild iris and shooting-stars emblazon the banks in summer. Here, the Pete Isleib Memorial Boardwalk, named for a much-respected Alaskan and stalwart ABA member, leads to elevated views of the wetlands.

Watch for Northern Harrier and Short-eared Owl, as well as moose,

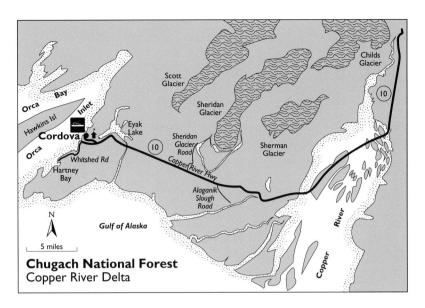

Chugach National Forest
Copper River Delta

which are often seen along the first mile of road. The small ponds and sedge meadows provide nesting-habitat for Red-throated Loon, Horned Grebe, Greater Yellowlegs, Red-necked Phalarope, and Parasitic Jaeger, along with the swans and other waterfowl. Occasionally, Aleutian Terns range inland from the outer sedge meadows. Keep your eye peeled for Northern Goshawk and Peregrine Falcon; should you visit in early spring or late fall, you have a chance for Gyrfalcon at this location.

Return to the highway and proceed to mile 19. Here you will find Haystack Trail, an easy 0.75-mile walk through a rain forest of hemlock and Sitka spruce. You are likely to find Sharp-shinned Hawk, Northern Goshawk, Northern Saw-whet

Owl, Steller's Jay, Chestnut-backed Chickadee, Hermit and Varied thrushes, and American Robin on this "spruce island." The end of the trail offers a splendid view of the encircling wetlands with sightings of moose, bear, coyote, and wolf possible.

Return to the Copper River Highway and drive to the Alaganik Bridge overlook (mile 22), where hundreds of eagles congregate with gulls to feed on smelt in May and June. The overlook also is a fine spot to hear and see Great Horned Owls in late afternoon and evening. The road past mile 22 may be impassable should snow persist into May or June.

From mile 26.8 to mile 38.2, the Highway traverses the Copper River with its braided channels and sandy wooded islands. Here is a good place to see Parasitic Jaeger and perhaps Willow Ptarmigan, which frequent

WILLOW PTARMIGAN

the willow shrub. The larger trees on Long Island (mile 27.3 to mile 33.9) are favored by numerous nesting eagles. Arctic Terns are common over the island ponds, and swans, geese, and ducks ply the waters.

Cottonwood forest borders the road from mile 38.3 to the end at mile 48. Northern Hawk Owl and Merlin nest here some years, and the mammal-watching can be tremendous. With a little luck, you might see a black bear or a huge brown bear crossing the highway. Between mile 41.5 and mile 42.5 focus your binoculars on the Chugach Mountains to the east; you may be rewarded by the sight of mountain goats resting, feeding, or scaling the crags.

From the Million Dollar Bridge, where the Copper River joins the delta, and from the Forest Service viewing-platform there, you can watch Child's Glacier calve off huge slabs of blue ice into the Copper River. Upriver to the east lies a breathtaking view of Miles Lake and Glacier, stretching to the vastness of the Copper River Canyon.

Prince William Sound and Boswell Bay. A boat trip from Cordova Boat Harbor to Boswell Bay near Hinchinbrook Island is the best way to observe nesting seabirds. The boat runs during the annual shorebird festival through

WESTERN SANDPIPER

the second week of May and goes about 11 miles up the tidal channels of Orca Inlet to a large Black-legged Kittiwake colony. Small numbers of Pelagic and Double-crested cormorants, Glaucous-winged Gulls, Pigeon Guillemots, and Tufted Puffins also nest here. Near the entrance to Boswell Bay is Strawberry Channel and Bar, where, especially in June to late July, you are likely to encounter foraging Arctic and Aleutian terns. East of Boswell Bay, across Strawberry Bar, is 17-mile-long Egg Island, home to the world's largest colony of Glaucous-winged Gulls, with more than 10,000 breeding pairs.

While enroute to and from Boswell Bay, watch the rocky shorelines for Black Oystercatchers, Surfbirds, Ruddy and Black turnstones, and late migrant Rock Sandpipers. In calm weather and at low tides, you may observe masses of shorebirds feeding on the extensive mud flats and large rafts of sea and bay ducks pausing on their northward journey.

In addition, boats are available in Cordova and Whittier for chartered pelagic trips around Prince William Sound, but these are fairly expensive. A boat suitable for a party of six, for example, will cost about $500 a day. Fork-tailed Storm-Petrel, Pelagic and Red-faced cormorants, various sea ducks, Black Oystercatcher, Wandering Tattler, Common Murre, Pigeon Guillemot, and Marbled and Kittlitz's murrelets are among the possibilities. Mammals you may see are Steller's sea lion, harbor seal, Dall porpoise, and, possibly, harbor porpoise, humpback, minke, and killer whales, and that engaging comedian, the sea otter.

To bird western Prince William Sound, take local Whittier small-boat charters, or for general viewing take

WANDERING TATTLER

the Alaska Marine Highway ferry from Whittier to Valdez. It passes through some prime areas, with a large kittiwake colony on the steep cliffs to the right as you enter Passage Canal outside of Whittier. Marbled and Kittlitz's murrelets can be found feeding in the areas of merging milky glacial runoff and dark sea water. Offshore, you are likely to find Parakeet Auklets and Tufted and Horned puffins feasting on sandlance and other small fishes. Look for Red-faced Cormorants near the Dutch Island Group in Wells Passage between Whittier and Valdez. Fork-tailed Storm-Petrel has been observed here as well. Numerous gulls, terns, jaegers, and phalaropes complete the experience.

Birdfinding in Forty National Forests and Grasslands

summer Boreal and Saw-whet owls, Spruce Grouse, Rufous Hummingbird, Three-toed Woodpecker, Steller's Jay, Boreal Chickadee, Varied Thrush, Townsend's Warbler, and Pine Grosbeak. The 7-mile Crow Creek Road, a left turn about 2 miles east of the Forest Service office, is a narrow gravel road ending at the Crow Creek Cabin trailhead (1500-ft elevation) for a 27-mile trail into Chugach State Park. By hiking just a half-mile up this trail, you will be in alpine habitat with a chance for Golden Eagle, Rock, White-tailed, and Willow ptarmigans, Townsend's Solitaire, Golden-crowned Sparrow, and Common Redpoll. White-tailed Ptarmigan, Surfbird, and Townsend's Solitaire frequent more exposed, less vegetated rocky ridges and higher areas than those other alpine nesters. Those not wishing to hike may find the same species by continuing on the Alyeska Highway to the Mt. Alyeska ski-resort and taking the lift to the top of the mountain.

The Seward Highway continues southeast along the edge of Turnagain Arm, famous for its 34-foot tides, to Portage. From Portage, one can take the Alaska Railroad shuttle to Whittier, the "Gateway to Prince William Sound," via the Alaska Marine Highway. The Portage Valley Highway, at mile 78.9 of the Seward Highway, leads 7 miles east to the Begich–Boggs Visitor Center. Located on the edge of Portage Lake near the Portage Glacier, the Center offers film-showings and interpretive displays, and, in summer, at a private facility, boat trips to view the glacier. Birds that might be encountered along the way include Harlequin Duck, Solitary Sandpiper, American Dipper, and such passerines as Violet-green, Tree, and Cliff

swallows, Orange-crowned and Yellow warblers, and Song, Fox, Savannah, and Golden-crowned sparrows.

Returning to the Byway, the road leaves the shore and rises up through the mountains and alpine valleys to Turnagain Pass, where you might find many of the warblers and sparrows mentioned above by venturing off the road for a short hike. Tern Lake is located at the intersection of the Seward and Sterling Highways, mile 36.6 of the Scenic Byway. This boggy lake, best known for nesting Arctic Terns, has attracted a wide variety of other species, including many ducks, sandpipers, Common Loon, Red-necked Phalarope, and Mew and Glaucous-winged gulls. The Tern Lake Campground, on the northwest side of the lake and off Sterling Highway a mile from the junction, has nesting Orange-crowned, Yellow, Yellow-rumped, Townsend's, Blackpoll, and Wilson's warblers, and Northern Waterthrush, all arriving by late May. The abandoned Old Sterling Highway near

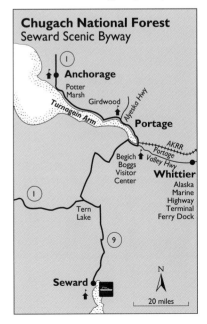

Seward Scenic Byway. In spring and early summer, you will find a somewhat different mix of birds along the Seward Scenic Byway from those on the Copper River Highway. This 118-mile tour, most of which lies within the Glacier and Seward Ranger Districts of the Chugach National Forest, runs from Seward (mile 0.0) on the Kenai Peninsula to Potter Marsh (mile 117.6) on the outskirts of Anchorage. Because most birders will be coming from Anchorage, this description runs north to south.

Turn left at mile 90.3 onto Alyeska Highway for the Glacier Ranger District headquarters at Girdwood. The spruce–hemlock forests of the Girdwood Valley offer in late spring and the entrance to the campground has resident Great Horned, Boreal, and Northern Saw-whet owls, Black-backed, Three-toed, Downy, and Hairy woodpeckers, and nesting Gray-cheeked, Swainson's, Hermit, and Varied thrushes.

Northern Three-toed Woodpecker and Spruce Grouse are occasionally common in the insect-infested woods along the Seward Highway. Check any of the campgrounds and Forest Service trails off the main road. In recent years, the Johnson Pass trailhead, near the Trail Lake Fish Hatchery, has been excellent for woodpeckers and other forest-dwellers.

The Scenic Byway ends at the town of Seward, where the boat harbor provides an opportunity to see a variety of cormorants, ducks, gulls, and alcids, plus the ever-playful sea otter. Several charter companies at the small boat harbor offer excellent daily boat trips around Resurrection Bay (half-day trips) and to the Chiswell Islands (part of the Alaska Maritime National Wildlife Refuge), and to Aialik Bay in Kenai Fjords (full-day trip). Specialties on either of these voyages include Pelagic and Red-faced cormorants, Common and Thick-billed murres, Marbled and Kittlitz's murrelets, and Tufted and Horned puffins. The full-day trip to the Chiswell Islands is better for sea birds and mammals, but all are recommended.

ACCOMMODATIONS ◆ WEATHER ◆ OTHER ATTRACTIONS

FORGET-ME-NOT, ALASKA'S STATE FLOWER

ALASKA BLUEBERRY

ALASKA IRIS

When to visit. Early to mid-May is best for migration, but the Forest and adjacent waters are birdy until late fall, though most migrant insectivores usually depart by early September.

Where to stay. Forest Service rental cabins at Cordova. Forest Service campgrounds along the Seward Scenic Byway and Sterling Highways, as well as hotels, motels, and bed-and-breakfast establishments in Anchorage, Girdwood, Seward, and Cordova.

Weather and attire. Marine influences dominate most of the Forest. Areas nearest the coast are subject to heavy precipitation, and high winds are frequent. Rain-gear and proper footwear (rubber boots) are essential year-round, as is warm clothing. The threat of hypothermia exists for the unwary; be prepared to cope with prolonged exposure to moisture and wind. If you plan to tent-camp, bring along sleeping-bags that will not absorb moisure and tents that repel wind-driven rains. In summer, a 100-percent DEET insect repellent is not just advisable—it is essential.

What Else to Do. Hike Forest trails, fish, sea-kayak, canoe, visit glaciers. Visit Potter Marsh (Anchorage Coastal Wildlife Refuge), known for its variety of waterfowl and gulls and for its numbers of Arctic Terns. A little farther on, the Beluga Point Interpretive site (at mile 110.8 in Chugach State Park) features some of the animals to be seen along the highway, including Dall sheep, beluga whale, killer whale, and Bald Eagle. The entrance to Chugach National Forest is at mile 93.8.

For more information. General information, District Office and State Ferry addresses, maps, bird list, details on campgrounds and cabin rentals, write or telephone the Chugach National Forest, 3301 "C" Street, Suite 300, Anchorage, Alaska 99503-3998; telephone 907/271-2500. For Alaska Railroad schedules, write to AKRR Corporation, 327 Ship Creek Avenue, Anchorage, Alaska, 99501. The Alaska Public Lands Information Center is at 605 W. Fourth Avenue, Suite 105, Anchorage, Alaska 99501; telephone 907/271-2737.

OLYMPIC FOREST
Washington

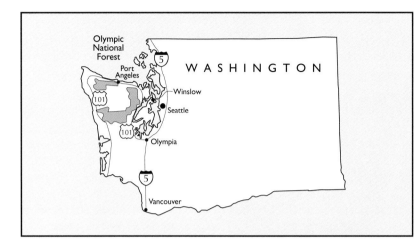

HOW TO GET THERE. *From Olympia, drive north on U.S. Route 101. From Seattle, take the ferry to Winslow and drive north on Washington Route 305 to Poulsbo. Then go north on Washington Route 3 to Washington Route 104, which crosses the Hood Canal Bridge and brings you to U.S. 101. Turn south on U.S. 101.*

MARBLED MURRELET

SHAWNEEN FINNEGAN, DRAWING

THE OLYMPIC PENINSULA, including the 632,000-acre National Forest, is a land of vast natural diversity compressed into a relatively small geographic area. The Peninsula features a rugged coastal shoreline and lush rain forests in its western valleys. The deep and narrow channel of the Hood Canal, a glacier-created inlet, forms much of the Peninsula's eastern edge. The Olympic Mountain ridges that radiate in all directions like the spokes of a gigantic wheel dominate the central Penin-sula with snow-clad peaks rising 8000 feet over the Pacific Ocean and Greater Puget Sound. High meadows carpeted with wildflowers, small lakes nestled in alpine basins, and precipitous cliffs and rocky summits create a breathtaking panorama.

Visitors will revel in the scenic splendor, but getting on intimate terms with it is another matter. The west side coniferous rain forest is one of the world's great wonders, nourished by more than 200 inches of rainfall annually. The mountainous land is carpeted with immense Sitka spruce, western hemlock, western red cedar, and Douglas-fir; beneath lies an understory of vine maple, devil's club, and huckleberry along with a veritable cornucopia of ferns, mosses, and lichens. All forms of animal life flourish in this natural greenhouse. Alas, the area is not easily accessible to automobiles and thus to most vacationers.

The good news, however, is that the eastern side of the peninsula is readily accessible. While much drier (from 15 to 80 inches of rainfall annually), the area has its own scenic beauties and much to offer birders and other visitors.

Bird Life

Overall, 357 species of birds have been recorded on the Forest and surrounding lands and waters. Of particular note to birders and researchers alike is the threatened Marbled Murrelet. This small, zippy seabird can best be found off the coast and within the adjacent bays and estuaries. It nests inland on the broad branches of large old-growth trees, but is extremely secretive at the nest site. As of 1991, researchers had

PRIME MARBLED MURRELET HABITAT, OLYMPIC PENNINSULA

located but a handful of Marbled Murrelet nests in the Pacific Northwest with only three on the Olympic Peninsula.

Among the common breeding birds of the Olympic Forest are Turkey Vulture, Ruffed and Blue grouse, Band-tailed Pigeon, Rufous Hummingbird, Vaux's Swift, Red-breasted Sapsucker, Downy, Hairy, and Pileated woodpeckers, five species of flycatchers (Olive-sided, Willow, Hammond's, Pacific-slope, and Western Wood-Pewee), Chestnut-backed Chickadee, Red-breasted Nuthatch, Brown Creeper, Winter Wren, American Dipper, Townsend's Solitaire, Varied Thrush, four species of vireos (Solitary, Hutton's, Warbling, and the rare Red-eyed), Western Tanager, and Orange-crowned, Black-throated Gray, Townsend's, MacGillivray's, Yellow-rumped, Hermit, and Wilson's warblers.

The east side of the peninsula is one of two major zones of Hermit–Townsend's Warbler intergradation. Intergrades are commonly found, varying in appearance from females that resemble Townsend's with some gray in the back to males with Hermit head-patterns and yellow throat, chest, and flanks. Typical birds of both species are also common. Obviously, they cannot be identified by song in this area.

Breeding raptors here include Bald Eagle, Sharp-shinned, Cooper's, and Red-tailed hawks, Northern Goshawk, Western Screech-Owl, Great Horned, Spotted (rare), and North-ern Saw-whet owls, and Northern Pygmy-Owl. Peregrine Falcons have been sighted on the Forest and nest on the western coast of the Peninsula.

Birding Route

U.S. Route 101 provides an excellent route for finding a wide variety of birds. This highway runs north–south along the coast from California, but also has an inland arm that follows the eastern edge of the Forest along the Hood Canal. The highway traces the shoreline of the canal for 37 miles around the Quilcene, Dosewallips, Hamma Hamma, and Duckabush estuaries, where Pacific salmon spawn. Quilcene Forest Service Visitors Center, a convenient reference-point and source of information, is located about 75 miles north of the junction of I-5 and U.S. 101. The best viewing points for wintering seabirds, waterfowl, shorebirds, and Bald Eagles are Seal Rock Campground and the many pull-offs on U.S. 101. The campground, situated on a shell midden of a Twana Native-American settlement, is located 10.9 miles south of the Quilcene Forest Service Visitors Center on U.S. 101. Follow the signs and park in the beach-access and picnic parking area, which provides a convenient approach to the tidal zone and Seal Rock Interpretive Trail.

HARLEQUIN DUCKS

In winter, look for Red-throated, Pacific, Common, and (with luck) Yellow-billed loons, Pied-billed, Horned, Red-necked, Eared, and Western grebes, and Double-crested, Brandt's, and Pelagic cormorants. Sea ducks are numerous: Greater and Lesser scaups, Harlequin Duck, Black, Surf, and White-winged scoters, Common and Barrow's goldeneyes, Bufflehead, and Red-breasted Merganser. Look for groups of Trumpeter Swans and Brant. The Trumpeter Swans are usually found at the Quilcene and Dosewallips river estuaries. Also, large concentrations of Bald Eagles gather here to feed on spawning Pacific salmon.

Winter is a good time to brush up on your gull identification skills. Hood Canal provides plenty of opportunities, since ten species occur here. In winter, Bonaparte's, Mew, and Glaucous-winged gulls predominate. The careful birder can usually find Thayer's, California, and Ring-billed gulls. Herring and Glaucous gulls can be found in areas where chum salmon are spawning, and Black-legged Kittiwake can sometimes be found after winter storms. In fall, Heermann's Gull, Common Tern, and Parasitic Jaeger can be seen over the canal.

Alcids are a specialty of the Hood Canal area. From August to April, Seal Rock Campground is a good spot to search for Common

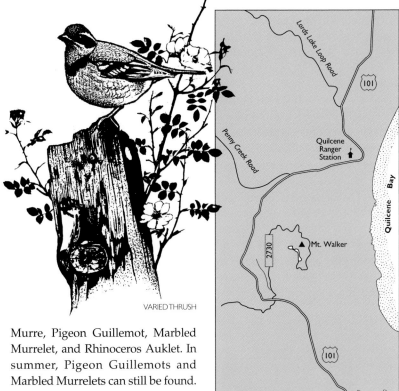

VARIED THRUSH

Murre, Pigeon Guillemot, Marbled Murrelet, and Rhinoceros Auklet. In summer, Pigeon Guillemots and Marbled Murrelets can still be found. Check the shoreline for Black-bellied Plover, Black Turnstone, and Western Sandpipers. For hardy souls, the best way to bird the canal is by kayak or canoe, which can be launched from the campground.

To observe forest-dwelling birds, walk the nature trail or campground roads. Year-round residents include Hairy, Downy, and Pileated woodpeckers, Red-breasted Sapsucker, Chestnut-backed Chickadee, Red-breasted Nuthatch, Winter Wren, Golden-crowned Kinglet, and Orange-crowned and

Olympic National Forest

Yellow-rumped warblers. Summer resident birds include Rufous Hummingbird, Olive-sided, Hammond's, and Pacific-slope flycatchers, Swainson's Thrush, Townsend's, Hermit, MacGillivray's, and Wilson's warblers, Western Tanager, and Black-headed Grosbeak.

To sample the beginning of the rain-forest environment, explore the Mount Walker Trail a short distance beyond the Seal Rock Campground. The trailhead is located 0.25 mile past the entrance gate to Forest Service Road (FS) 2730, which turns right off U.S. 101, 5.4 miles north of the Seal Rock Campground entrance. This 2-

KEITH TAYLOR, DRAWING

DAVID A. SIBLEY, DRAWING

BONAPARTE'S GULLS

mile trail climbs steadily for 2804 feet to the summit of Mount Walker, passing through 100-year-old Douglas-firs, spring-blooming rhododendrons, and a ground cover of Oregon grape.

For the birder who prefers not to walk, Mount Walker is the only peak facing Puget Sound that has a road to its summit. The 4.2-mile FS 2730, however, is steep and narrow and not recommended for trailers or motorhomes. On a clear day, the pull-offs along this road offer spectacular views of the Olympic and Cascade Mountains, Hood Canal, and the city of Seattle. Hike any of the trails from the pull-offs. Watch for Sharp-shinned and Cooper's hawks, North-ern Goshawk, Black Swift, and Hermit and Varied thrushes, plus many of the woodland birds mentioned previously.

You may wish to try two additional routes for forest birds. Dose-wallips Road runs west from U.S. 101 just 0.7 mile south of the entrance to Seal Rock Campground; it ends after 19.8 miles at a popular trailhead in Olympic National Park. Penny Creek Road departs U.S. 101, heading west 0.9 mile southwest of the Quilcene Visitor Center; there are plenty of good stops to bird in the old-growth and second-growth stands in the 3.3 miles before you come to FS 27 (Big Quilcene River Road), where you enter the National Forest. At FS 27, you may continue to several nearby trails, all of which are listed on road-side signs. Two of the most popular are the Lower Big Quilcene and the Big Quilcene trails. To reach the Lower Big Quilcene, which is a relatively easy hike, follow FS 27 for 1.5 miles from the Forest boundary to FS 2700-080. Turn left onto this road and drive 0.5 mile to the trailhead. This trail ends at the trailhead for the Big Quilcene Trail. To reach the Big Quilcene by car, continue on FS 27 for another 5.7 miles to FS 2750. Turn left onto FS 2750 and drive for 4.6 miles to the trailhead. The Big Quilcene Trail is more difficult than the lower trail; it leads into the Buckhorn Wilderness.

FLETTS VIOLET   PIPER'S BELLFLOWER   REDWOOD SORREL

Both the violet and the bellflower are endemic to the Olympic Mountains.

ACCOMMODATIONS ◆ WEATHER ◆ OTHER ATTRACTIONS

When to visit. Winter is best for seabirds and waterfowl, and forest birds are most active in spring and early summer.

Where to stay. Forest Service and Olympic National Park campgrounds available all year; reservations recommended in summer. Motels in various towns along U.S. 101, the nearest in Brinnon and Quilcene.

Weather and attire. Average temperatures range from 40 to 70° F in summer, and from 35 to 50° F in winter. Rain-gear is essential all year, and layers of warm clothes and sturdy shoes are recommended.

What else to do. Hiking, kayaking, canoeing, scuba diving, beachcombing, picnicking, berry-picking, wildflower viewing, photography. Spectacular Olympic National Park lies just next to the Hood Canal. Outside the National Forest are Dungeness National Wildlife Refuge near Sequim, Grays Harbor near Aberdeen for shorebirds and seabirds, Cape Flattery on the northwest tip of the Peninsula near Neah Bay for large concentrations of Red-tailed Hawks and other buteos, accipiters, and eagles (mid-March to mid-April), also nesting Tufted Puffins. Cape Flattery offers great views of migrating Gray Whales offshore in April and May and in December and January.

For more information. General and campground information, District Office addresses, maps, bird list: Olympic National Forest, 1835 Black Lake Boulevard SW, Olympia, Washington 98502-5423; telephone 206/956-2300.

MOUNT HOOD FOREST
Oregon

HOW TO GET THERE. *From Portland take Interstate 84 east approximately 10 miles to Troutdale.*

NORTHERN GOSHAWK

MICHAEL O'BRIEN, DRAWING

TOWERING OVER this 1,063,000-acre national forest is Mt. Hood, 11,235 feet high and one of the truly majestic volcanic peaks of the Cascade Range. The Forest contains two very different ecosystems, a dry eastern section dominated by ponderosa pine, Douglas-fir, and grand fir, and a moist forest of western hemlock and Douglas-fir found west of the Cascade Crest. Within the two systems are mosaics of micro-environments, ranging from ancient cedar forests carpeted with fog-wet mosses to sun-baked talus slopes, river-bottom alder tangles, and high subalpine meadows. Although the Forest does not quite touch the Columbia River, that mighty watercourse describes the Forest's northern boundary for many miles.

Bird Life

Mt. Hood offers a splendid array of Cascade montane species. Typical are Blue Grouse, Band-tailed Pigeon, Spotted Owl, Northern Pygmy-Owl, and Hermit Warbler. Less-common breeding species that warrant filing reports with the Forest Service are Northern Goshawk, Cooper's and Sharp-shinned hawks, Bald and Golden eagles, Spotted and Barred owls, Great Gray Owl, and Harlequin Duck. Alpine and subalpine habitats support Calliope and Rufous hummingbirds, Willow, Hammond's, Dusky, and Pacific-slope flycatchers, Gray Jay, Clark's Nutcracker, Common Raven, American Pipit, Chipping Sparrow, and Gray-crowned Rosy-Finch.

Birding Route

Mount Hood Loop. Most Forest roads are open from May to November, but the birding is good all year. From mid-May to early July, the highest numbers of bird observations can be counted along the well-marked and scenic Mt. Hood loop that runs for more than 200 miles. In addition, several sites along this route are known for interesting fall migrants. You can drive the loop and do a little birding in one long day, but two or three days are optimal and will give you a chance to hike some of the trails. The three major areas are Larch Mountain (4056 feet), Timothy Lake, and Timberline Lodge. The Mt. Hood loop follows Interstate 84 from Troutdale (just east of Portland off I-205) east to Hood River, then south on Oregon Route 35 to Timberline Lodge, and returns to Troutdale via U.S. Route 26 through Gresham.

First stop on the loop is the Forest's Larch Mountain, reached by leaving I-84 at Troutdale (Exit 17). Follow the signs to the Columbia River Scenic Route (it is well marked). Next, follow signs to Multnomah Falls. Watch for the turnoff to Larch Mountain on the right, 2 miles east of Corbett. The road climbs 11 miles from the river-bottom to a parking area in the forest, providing an ideal cross-section of habitats. Watch for Blue Grouse, Western and Mountain bluebirds, Townsend's Solitaire, and Lazuli Bunting in the clearings, and White-crowned Sparrow in the adjacent shrubbery. Forest breeding birds include Olive-sided and Hammond's flycatchers, Stel-

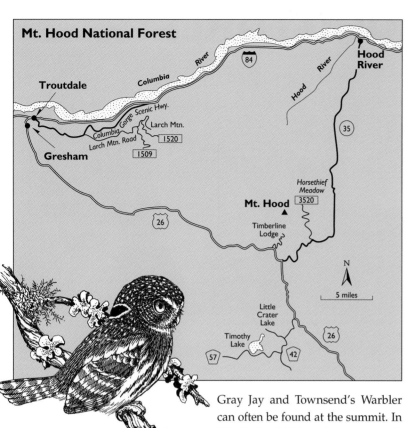

Mt. Hood National Forest

Troutdale

Gresham

Columbia River

84

Hood River

Hood River

Columbia Gorge Scenic Hwy.

Larch Mtn.

Larch Mtn. Road

1520

1509

35

26

Horsethief Meadow 3520

Mt. Hood ▲

Timberline Lodge

N

5 miles

Little Crater Lake

Timothy Lake

57

26

42

NORTHERN PYGMY-OWL

ler's Jay, Chestnut-backed Chickadee, Winter Wren, Hermit and Varied thrushes, Black-throated Gray (at lower elevations), Hermit, and Townsend's warblers, Western Tanager, Pine Siskin, and Evening Grosbeak. Also look and listen for Pileated Woodpecker. Northern Pygmy-Owl is active at dawn and dusk, and Northern Saw-whet Owl calls after dark.

A 0.2-mile trail leads from the northeast corner of the parking lot to Sherard Point, Larch Mountain's summit. A set of steep steps provides access to the craggy summit that offers spectacular views of the surrounding forest and Cascade mountain peaks. Far below and to the north is the Columbia River Gorge National Scenic Area.

Northern Pygmy-Owl (usually found in spring by imitating its call) frequents the wooded canyons, and

Gray Jay and Townsend's Warbler can often be found at the summit. In fall, birds of higher elevations, such as Mountain Chickadee, Mountain Bluebird, and Cassin's Finch, are seen here. The heavy forests east of Larch Mountain contain Spotted and Barred owls; however, they are hard to find. There are trails that wind from Larch Mountain through the Columbia River Gorge, but they are steep and difficult.

Enroute back down the mountain, stop and take a short walk along either Forest Service Road (FS) 1520 or FS 1509 (5 and 6 miles below the parking area, respectively). The patchwork of clearcut and mature forest has created mixed habitats for Mountain Quail (usually found in spring when calling), Blue Grouse, Band-tailed Pigeon, Vaux's Swift, Rufous Hummingbird, Willow and Pacific-slope flycatchers, Common Raven, Bushtit, House Wren, Western Bluebird, MacGillivray's Warbler, and Lazuli Bunting. Dusky Flycatcher has also been reported in this area.

Then continue down the mountain to the Scenic Highway, turn right, and drive 1 mile to Crown Point State Park. This is not on the Forest, but the view of the Columbia River and the gorge is not to be missed. From Crown Point you can see three prime attractions: Multnomah Falls, steep-sided Oneonta Gorge, and the immensity of Bonneville Dam.

Continue on Scenic Highway for 8 miles to Multnomah Falls. The Multnomah Falls viewing area, only a 50-yard walk, provides superb views of the falls that plunge 620 feet over five different basalt flows into a deep pool. The cool mist creates a microclimate favoring ferns, forbs, and mosses that cover the canyon walls. Wildflowers, such as chickweed, monkeyflower, cliff larkspur, and Sitka mist maidens in early May, and round-leaf bluebells and Oregon stonecrop in mid-July, decorate the rocky cliffs. The songs of American Dippers can be heard echoing off the canyon walls from the pool and stream below from April through July.

Three miles beyond Multnomah Falls on the Scenic Highway is the town of Dodson, where you rejoin I-84; Hood River village is 28 miles

F.P. BENNETT, DRAWING

DAVID A. SIBLEY, DRAWING

farther east on I-84. Stop at Lausmann State Park, which lies within the Forest. At the rest stop and trailhead (Exit 58), 23 miles beyond Dodson, you can scan the cliffs and sky for perching or soaring Peregrine Falcons. The Columbia River Gorge provides ample nesting habitat for this magnificent raptor. Other soaring birds to look for here include Turkey Vulture, Osprey, Bald Eagle, and Red-tailed Hawk.

The town of Hood River is 5 miles beyond the rest stop; take Exit 64 onto Rte. 35, which follows the East Fork of the Hood River and eventually leaves the valley, reentering the National Forest about 20 miles south of town. This area is a transition zone between the moist west side Douglas-fir–hemlock forests and the drier east-side pine forests.

Stop at Horsethief Meadows or camp at nearby Robinhood Campground, 20.5 miles beyond the Odell turnoff. Take FS 3520 to your right, just beyond the turnoff to Robinhood Campground. This gravel road continues to the west and north through the meadow. An easy 4-mile trail (No. 650) links Robinhood and Sherwood campgrounds and parallels the East Fork. Before dawn and after dusk, listen for Northern Pygmy-

MT. HOOD WITH BEARGRASS IN FOREGROUND

Owl and Northern Saw-whet Owl in the surrounding forest. Here, too, are Ruffed Grouse, Pacific-slope Flycatcher, Golden-crowned Kinglet, Varied Thrush, Solitary and Warbling vireos, Yellow-rumped and Black-throated Gray warblers, Western Tanager, Black-headed Grosbeak, Red Crossbill, and Pine Siskin.

The junction of Rte. 35 and U.S. 26 is another 7.5 miles to the southwest, beyond the Horsethief Meadows junction. From this junction, turn left on U.S. 26 and follow the signs east toward Madras. In 9 miles, take a right on paved Skyline Road (FS 42) and follow the signs to Timothy Lake. Watch along this road for Northern Goshawk. The area contains abundant prey-species for this reclusive raptor, such as Blue and Ruffed grouse, Northern Flicker,

Pileated Woodpecker, and Gray and Steller's jays. Golden Eagles occur in this area during the fall.

The Pacific Crest Trail crosses Skyline Road (FS 42) just before the junction with FS 57, 17.5 miles from U.S. 26. This international trail connects Mexico, California, the Pacific Northwest states, and Canada, and skirts the treeline of Mt. Hood. You may hike northwest to Timothy Lake and Little Crater Meadows, a total of less than 6 miles one-way from here. To drive to Timothy Lake, turn right onto paved FS 57. Immediately to your left is a meadow formed by the Oak Grove Fork of the Clackamas River. This is a good location for marsh and meadow birds, such as Great Blue Heron, Mallard, Virginia Rail, Sora, Vaux's Swift, Willow Flycatcher, Tree, Violet-green, and Northern Rough-winged swallows, Hermit and Varied thrushes, Yellow Warbler, and Common Yellowthroat.

Just ahead on FS 57 are four Forest campgrounds on the south side of Timothy Lake. The first two, Oak Fork and Gone Creek, afford fine views of the south end of the lake from paved parking lots. This is a good place from late July through

PACIFIC LOONS

PINE SISKIN

November to find migratory species such as Red-throated, Pacific, and Common loons, Pied-billed, Horned, and Western grebes, Double-crested Cormorant, Tundra Swan, Common and Barrow's goldeneyes, California and Sabine's gulls, Forster's Tern, Horned Lark, and Lapland Longspur. Clark's Grebe and Surf and White-winged scoters are occasionally found.

The Timothy Lake Trail (No. 528) connects the campgrounds and winds along the south, west, and northwest forested lakeshore. It also connects to the Pacific Crest Trail on the southeast end of the lake and again on the north end just south of Little Crater Meadows, a total of 8 miles. A summertime hike along this trail should produce Western Grebe, American Wigeon, Hooded and Common mergansers, Rufous Hummingbird, Hairy and Pileated woodpeckers, Hammond's Flycatcher, Steller's Jay, Mountain and Chestnut-backed chickadees, Brown Creeper, Golden-crowned and Ruby-crowned kinglets, Solitary and Warbling vireos, Townsend's and Hermit warblers, Western Tanager, Savannah Sparrow, Purple and Cassin's finches, and Evening Grosbeak. Three-toed and Black-backed woodpeckers inhabit forests with abun-

dant snags along the edge of the meadows.

Afterwards, backtrack to FS 57 and FS 42, and drive 4.3 miles northeast on FS 42 to paved FS 58. Turn left on FS 58 for 2.2 miles (stay right at the junction with FS 4280) to the turnoff with a sign to Little Crater Meadows Campground. Turn left into the campground and continue (stay right) toward the far end to the parking area at the edge of Little Crater Meadows.

This 15-acre wet meadow is crossed by numerous small, riparian corridors, and bordered by marshes. Walk the trail across the meadow. Hidden within a forested island in the center of the meadow is Little Crater Lake, an incredibly clear, turquoise-blue artesian spring. Look here for Nashville Warbler and Common Yellowthroat. Other breeding birds include Spotted Sandpiper, Common Snipe, and Lincoln's and White-crowned sparrows.

Continue west on the meadow trail, past the spring, to the junction with the Pacific Crest Scenic Trail (PCT) and hike for a mile or so through the Douglas-fir and hemlock forest here. Look for Black-backed and Pileated woodpeckers, Red-breasted Nuthatch, and Brown Creeper. Additional species to be expected include Gray and Steller's jays, Mountain Chickadee, Golden-crowned Kinglet, Townsend's Solitaire, Hermit and Varied thrushes, Western Tanager, Chipping Sparrow, Red Crossbill, and Pine Siskin. This also is another place to be on the lookout for Northern Goshawk.

As you bird along, notice the Pacific yew trees in the understory along the edge of the trail. You will

recognize these interesting small conifers by their flat, shiny, dark-green needle-sprays; red, stringy bark; and small, fleshy red cones called arils. The bark is harvested as a source of the cancer-fighting drug taxol, and the strong, flexible limbs were used by Native Americans to make bows.

About one mile from the junction of the PCT and Meadow Trails your route will swing close to the forest edge, and you should see a meadow on your right through the trees. Pick your way carefully through 20 yards of log-strewn forest floor and step out into the meadow. There you will find a small beaver pond and a marsh with Mt. Hood as a backdrop. In spring and summer, look for Sandhill Cranes and their young. Among the rails, Virginia and Sora nest here.

Retrace your route to U.S. 26. Follow U.S 26 west toward Portland beyond the junction with U.S. 35 for 2.5 miles to the turnoff for Timberline Lodge; turn right and drive 6 miles to the lodge. Gray-crowned Rosy-Finch is an uncommon resident bird of the adjacent alpine habitats. The birds are easiest to locate in spring before the snow melts (mid-May or mid-June) and in fall after the first snows in late October and early November. Finding rosy-finches in late spring and early summer requires a hike to the snowline. Follow the many well-trodden, gravel trails behind the lodge for 0.5 mile to the Cloud-Cap–Paradise Park Trail. Hike along the trail, looking for rosy-finches at the edges of snowbanks. Other birds to be found during the nesting season around the lodge and on the trails include Rufous Hummingbird, Horned Lark, Gray Jay, Mountain Bluebird, American Pipit, Townsend's Warbler, Cassin's Finch, Pine Siskin, and Evening Grosbeak. Clark's Nutcrackers are year-round residents as well. Bobcat, mountain lion, pine marten, and even wolverine have been seen near treeline on Mt. Hood. Then there is the scenery. The views are spectacular and the wildflowers stunning in July with masses of sulphur flower, Davidson's penstemon, yarrow, Cascade aster, and arnica.

Return to U.S. 26 and turn right. Along U.S. 26, check Zigzag River and Sandy River for Harlequin Ducks in April, May, and June, and for American Dippers, which are there all year. To complete your tour, continue to Gresham and follow Burnside Avenue straight ahead to the sign indicating the route to I-84, a right turn on 242nd Drive. Continue several miles to Wood Village and the junction of I-84. Then head west on I-84 toward Portland to access I-205 and I-5.

ACCOMMODATIONS ◆ WEATHER ◆ OTHER ATTRACTIONS

When to visit. The Forest is open all year, although most secondary roads are closed during the winter months and many are closed during hunting season– from late September into November. May, early June, and late August to October are best for migratory species, and late May to early June best for rosy-finches.

Where to stay. Developed campgrounds along loop route at Sherwood, Robin Hood, Camp Creek, Frog Lake, Clear Lake, Timothy Lake, and Wildwood. Wilderness camping in the Badger Creek and Mt. Hood Wilderness Areas. Accommodations: Timberline Lodge historic inn at Cloud Cap, hotels in Zig Zag, Government Camp, and Hood River. Deluxe accommodations and dining at Timberline Lodge, where there is also a visitors center open daily, year-round.

Weather and attire. Mountain weather is always unpredictable. A dry season runs from June or early July to October, but rain can be expected in late fall, winter, and spring. Bring rain-gear for all seasons and warmer dress from late fall to spring. Remember to dress in layers with wool or polypropylene long-underwear in winter. Wear sturdy hiking boots or walking shoes for trails, and rubber boots are advised if you intend to visit wet meadows. Sunglasses with ultraviolet protection and a hat with a visor are recommended.

RICE LILY

What else to do. Ski areas within the Forest include Timberline, Mt. Hood Meadows, Ski Bowl/Multorpor, Summit, and Cooper Spur; rafting the Salmon River; world famous windsurfing on the Columbia River at Hood River village. Wineries and microbreweries in Hood River village, fruit orchards at Parkdale. The Mt. Hood Festival of Jazz, each August in Gresham. The town of Rhododendron is known for its June rhododendron blooms.

For more information. General and camping information, District Office addresses, maps, bird checklist: Mt. Hood National Forest, 2955 N.W. Division Street, Gresham, Oregon 97037; or telephone 503/666-0771.

COAST TRILLIUM

SIUSLAW FOREST
Oregon

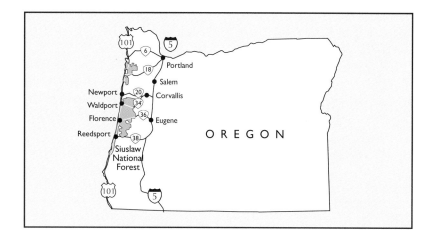

HOW TO GET THERE. *The Siuslaw National Forest is headquartered in Corvallis, Oregon, and can be reached via U.S. Route 20 and Oregon Route 34. Marys Peak lies on Rte. 34 west of Corvallis and Philomath. The Cape Perpetua Scenic Area is on Oregon coastal U.S. Route 101, just 11 miles south of Waldport. The Siltcoos estuary is also on coastal U.S. 101, 8 miles south of the town of Florence.*

COASTLINE AT SIUSLAW NATIONAL FOREST

THE SIUSLAW NATIONAL FOREST rises abruptly from the sea in a series of intricately-carved basaltic headlands and islands, dark prominences crowned with stands of immense Sitka spruce nurtured by the rolling Pacific fogs. The great green trees, some as tall as 200 feet, march inland with the fog for 4 miles—and then the spruce band gradually gives way to the 150-foot hemlock and fir that clothe most of the forest's 625,000 acres.

In stunning contrast, the Siuslaw also boasts the Oregon Dunes National Recreation Area, and here there are no large trees. By a quirk of nature, the land is covered with 32,000 acres of beach, sand dunes, and freshwater ponds; the dunes are perpetually in motion, shifting direction and changing shape at the whim of the winds.

All forms of wildlife thrive in this wonderfully varied region. More than ninety-five mammals, such as river otter, northern flying-squirrel, and beaver, live on the Forest. Larger mammals, including Roosevelt elk, black-tailed deer, black bear, coyote, and bobcat, also dwell here. And off the coastline, up to 10,000 gray whales pass by on their way to Baja California in Mexico in December and January and again from March through May enroute to Alaska for the summer. These majestic creatures often swim less than a mile from shore and can easily be seen with the naked eye. Look for waterspouts or the whales' glistening gray backs as they arc through the water.

Other notable wildlife on the Siuslaw includes the Oregon silverspot butterfly, which inhabits coastal salt-spray meadows. This butterfly is named for the silvery spots on the underside of its 2-inch wings. Only six small populations

BLAINE ULMER, PHOTOGRAPH

of this threatened species exist along the West Coast.

Bird Life

More than 250 bird species have been recorded on the Siuslaw National Forest, and several of these are threatened or endangered: (California) Brown Pelican, Bald Eagle, Peregrine Falcon, "Aleutian" Canada Goose, and Spotted Owl. Two addi-

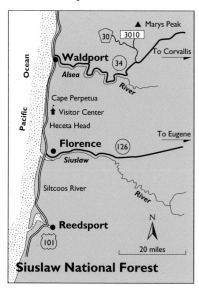

Siuslaw National Forest

tional species, "Western" Snowy Plover and Marbled Murrelet, have been listed as threatened in the contiguous forty-eight states, but they are not listed in Alaska.

Among the birds of the forest and open meadows are Ruffed and Blue grouse, Mountain Quail, Western Screech-Owl, Great Horned and Northern Saw-whet owls, Vaux's Swift, Rufous Hummingbird, Hairy and Pileated woodpeckers, Chestnut-backed Chickadee, Bushtit, and Evening Grosbeak.

Birds of the sea and shore include Red-throated, Common, and Pacific loons, Red-necked, Horned, and Western grebes, Double-crested,

Brandt's, and Pelagic cormorants, Black, Surf, and White-winged scoters, Harlequin Duck, Black Oystercatcher, Snowy Plover, Red-necked Phalarope, Black and Ruddy turnstones, Surfbird, Caspian Tern, and numerous alcids, such as Pigeon Guillemot, Rhinoceros Auklet, Common Murre, Marbled Murrelet, and Tufted Puffin (spring and summer only).

Birding Routes

Marys Peak, the highest point in the Oregon Coast Range at 4097 feet, is the best place to begin your birding tour. To reach Marys Peak, start at the junction of U.S. Route 20 and Oregon Route 34 in Corvallis, which is about 9 miles west of Interstate 5 and 80 miles south of Portland. Continue west on U.S. 20 and Rte. 34 for 6 miles to the town of Philomath, and go one mile beyond town. Turn left onto Rte. 34 when the two highways diverge, then drive 7 miles to Forest Service Road (FS) 30. Turn right onto FS 30, and follow the signs for 9 miles to the parking area and trailhead, bearing right onto FS 3010 after about 6 miles. Marys Peak is usually accessible all year; the road to the parking area is plowed in winter. Hiking, however, can be difficult in mid-winter. Oregon SnoPark permits, available at local Forest Service offices, are required from October through April. A seven-page auto-tour brochure also is available from the Forest Service.

On a clear day, the summit of Marys Peak

MARYS PEAK

offers a fantastic panorama from Mt. Adams in Washington, south to Mt. Thielsen near Crater Lake, and west across the Coast Range to the Pacific Ocean. Marys Peak supports an equally exciting diversity of wildflowers and insects which combine to form a complex ecosystem. Wildflowers include yellow and giant fawn lilies, Oregon anemone, slender bog orchid, twinflower, Cardwell's penstemon, and western false and star-flowered Solomon's seals.

The open grass summit of Marys Peak is surrounded by 1000 acres of noble fir forest. A number of trails wind through open meadows, along a rock garden near the summit, and through the old-growth forest. The 1.2-mile round-trip Summit Trail begins in the parking lot and follows a gravel road to the top; no vehicles are allowed. During spring and summer,

SNOWY PLOVER

American Kestrel, Rufous Hummingbird, Northern Flicker, Tree and Violet-green swallows, Cedar Waxwing, White-crowned Sparrow, and American Goldfinch are usually encountered along the road. Lazuli Buntings are occasionally found at the edges of the meadows. American Pipits are frequent migrants. During winter, Gray-crowned Rosy-Finches often can be found here as well.

Just below the summit lie 15 acres of alpine-like meadow that local botanists refer to as the "rock garden." Here you will find prairie lupine, sulphur buckwheat, and scalloped onion, plants more commonly found on dry, rocky high elevations in the Cascades and Rockies.

From the summit, in spring and fall, Turkey Vulture, Red-tailed Hawk, and American Kestrel are often seen riding the thermals. Rufous Hummingbirds and an occasional Anna's Hummingbird may be found competing with honeybees for nectar among the wildflowers.

The 2-mile Meadow Edge (loop) Trail that also begins at the parking lot passes through an impressive stand of noble fir with a wonderfully green carpet of wood sorrel and fairybells. This trail also skirts meadow habitat and crosses a riparian area at the head of Parker Creek. Year-round resident birds along this trail include

Ruffed and Blue grouse, Great Horned and Northern Saw-whet owls, Northern Pygmy-Owl, Red-breasted Sapsucker, Hairy and Pileated woodpeckers, Chestnut-backed Chickadee, Brown Creeper, Winter Wren, Golden-crowned Kinglet, Varied Thrush, and Hutton's Vireo. During spring and summer, migrants and breeders, such as Hammond's and Pacific-slope flycatchers, Hermit and Swainson's thrushes, Black-throated Gray, Townsend's, and Hermit warblers, and White-crowned Sparrow also are present.

Of special interest to birders are Northern Goshawk, Spotted Owl, and Marbled Murrelet. Murrelets can be heard, mostly at dawn and dusk, giving their piercing, gull-like *keer-keer-keer* call in mature conifer stands during summer. If you are persistent—and very lucky—you may be rewarded with a glimpse of one as it buzzes through the forest at 50 mph enroute to and from nighttime fishing grounds at sea.

Cape Perpetua. After Marys Peak, continue west on Route 34 for 49 miles from FS 30 to U.S. Highway 101 at Waldport, and then drive south on U.S. 101 for 11 miles to the Cape Perpetua Scenic Area. Pelagic Cormorants, Black Oystercatchers, Western Gulls, and Pigeon Guillemots nest on the Cape's rocky cliffs and are frequently seen from a pullout at an Oregon Historic

Marker, 3 miles south of Yachats. The Black Oystercatchers are joined in winter by Black Turnstone, Surfbird, and occasionally Rock Sandpiper. Another 0.3 mile south on U.S. 101 is the Devil's Churn parking area and trailhead. Don't miss this fantastic geological feature: a narrow chasm funnels huge waves that smash against the rock wall, sending a spectacular shower of spray into the air.

At 0.4 mile farther south is the Cape Perpetua Visitor Center, open daily in summer from 9 AM to 5 PM, and in winter on weekends from 10 AM to 4 PM. The visitors center also serves as the trailhead for an extensive network of trails to the ocean and into the forest. Some of the best birding occurs after winter storms when birds congregate close to shore. The numbers and variety can be staggering.

Look for Double-crested, Brandt's, and Pelagic cormorants, Black Oystercatcher (year-round), and Sanderling, Western Sandpiper, and Dunlin in migration. Western and Glaucous-winged gulls are among the full-time residents. Winter birds include Red-throated, Pacific, and Common loons, Red-necked, Horned, and Western grebes, occasional Rock Sandpiper, and Marbled and Ancient (occasional) murrelets. Vagrant pelagic species, such as Leach's and Fork-tailed storm-petrels, may appear after storms.

In the forest, watch for such year-round residents as Steller's Jay, Chestnut-backed Chickadee, Winter Wren, Brown Creeper, Wrentit, Golden-crowned Kinglet, Varied Thrush, and Yellow-rumped Warbler. In spring and summer, Rufous Hummingbird, Swainson's Thrush, and Cedar Waxwing are common.

WOOD DUCK

MIMI HOPPE WOLF, DRAWING

Sandy beaches and the rocky coast are easily accessible on foot from the visitors center. The 1-mile Trail of Restless Waters goes to the Devil's Churn, and the connecting Captain Cook Trail continues to the tidal pools and the Spouting Horn. Both trails pass shell middens from Alsea Indians who camped here for hundreds of years. All of the seabirds mentioned previously are visible from these trails.

The 2-mile Giant Spruce Trail leads from the visitors center into the coastal conifer forest. Breeding species include Pileated Woodpecker, Western Wood-Pewee, Hammond's and Pacific-slope flycatchers, Red-breasted Nuthatch, Brown Creeper, Hutton's Vireo, Black-throated Gray and Hermit warblers, and Western Tanager. Walk down the trail 0.75 mile and listen for Marbled Murrelets at dusk and dawn as they depart and return to their nests on mossy branches of giant Douglas-firs.

The Cape Perpetua View Point can also be reached by road. Drive north on U.S. 101 for 0.25 mile and turn east for 1 mile to the parking area. The 0.25-mile Whispering Spruce Trail leads to the View Point and West Rim Shelter, a stone parapet built in the 1930s by the Civilian Conservation Corps.

Birders hoping for the treat of seeing or hearing a Spotted Owl should hike either the Gwynn Creek Trail, a 7-mile loop that begins

BLACK OYSTERCATCHER

behind the visitors center, or the 10-mile Cummins Creek Loop Trail within the Cummins Creek Wilderness Area. This trail can be reached by driving south 1 mile from the visitors center on U.S. 101.

Grassy meadows lie between the coast and forest. A good example of this habitat is the Rock Creek Meadows along U.S. 101, 6 miles south of the visitors center. Look for Western Meadowlarks and also for the signs to Rock Creek Campground. In spring and summer, Rufous Hummingbirds share airspace with the threatened Oregon silverspot butterflies. Song and White-crowned sparrows and Dark-eyed Juncos frequent the shubbery.

In the stunted pines are Black-capped and Chestnut-backed chickadees, Bushtit, Bewick's Wren, and Orange-crowned, MacGillivray's, and Wilson's warblers.

Eleven miles south of the visitors center are Heceta Lighthouse and Devil's Elbow State Park, an excellent area for viewing Tufted Puffins in May, June, and July. Look closely at the rock crevasses and holes in the rocky sea-stacks where the birds typically make their nests. This area is also good for viewing pelagic birds from shore during migration, including Sooty and Short-tailed shearwaters, Red Phalarope, Black-legged Kittiwake, and Common and Arctic terns.

Oregon Dunes National Recreation Area. Continue south on U.S. 101 past the town of Florence for 8 miles to the Siltcoos River and Estuary. Drive onto Siltcoos Dune and Beach Access Road for 1 mile to the parking area and trailhead for the Stagecoach and Waxmyrtle Trails. Walk the Waxmyrtle Trail for 0.25 mile to a bridge across the Siltcoos River; cross the bridge and follow the

DUNLIN

river on the south side for 0.75 mile to the beach. Among the species frequently visible in the estuary are Common Loon, Western Grebe, Sanderling, and Western Sandpiper from fall to spring, and Wood Duck, Common Merganser, and Snowy Plover in spring and summer. During the spring and fall migration, there is the possibility of Red-throated and Pacific loons, Tundra Swan, Red-breasted Merganser, and Red-necked Phalarope. Brown Pelican and Heermann's Gull are possible from August through October. Band-tailed Pigeons frequent this area in fall. In some falls, this is a good shorebird spot, with Semipalmated Plover, Greater and Lesser yellowlegs,

WRENTIT

Whimbrel, Baird's and Pectoral Sandpipers, Dunlin, and Short-billed Dowitcher.

In spring and summer, the estuary is the domain of at least one family of Ospreys diving for small salmon and

smelt. Northern Harriers frequent the marsh, coursing back and forth in search of mice, voles, frogs, and snakes. Fortunate birders may witness a Bald Eagle pirating food from either the Osprey or harrier. Watchful birders may catch a glimpse of an American Bittern in the marsh.

The shrubbery and forested areas along the trail support a number of nesting birds. Wrentits inhabit the dense shrubs, and Band-tailed Pigeons, Olive-sided Flycatchers, and Bewick's Wrens frequent the forest.

To return to Corvallis, follow U.S. 101 north to Waldport, and then go east on Oregon Route 34 to Philomath.

ACCOMMODATIONS ♦ WEATHER ♦ OTHER ATTRACTIONS

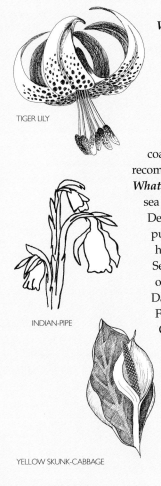

TIGER LILY

INDIAN-PIPE

YELLOW SKUNK-CABBAGE

When to visit. The best birding is during migration and in summer, but winter along the ocean can be very good, as well.

Where to stay. U.S. Forest Service, U.S. Bureau of Land Management, and Oregon State Parks: campgrounds along coastal U.S. 101 and Rte. 34. Motels in Reedsport, Florence, Corvallis, Newport, and Waldport.

Weather and attire. Spring and fall are cool (40 to 50° F) and often rainy. Winter is only slightly cooler but much stormier. Summer temperatures range from the high 60s along the coast to occasional 90s near the Willamette Valley. The coast is almost always breezy. Clothing for wind, cool temperatures, and rain is recommended.

What else to do. Hiking, fishing, beachcombing, exploring tide-pools, canoeing, and sea kayaking. Whale-watching tours and deep-sea fishing originate at Newport, Depot Bay, and Florence. Newport's Hatfield Marine Science Center is open to the public with free admission, and the Oregon Coast Aquarium and Yaquina Lighthouse Marine Bird Sanctuary are located in Newport as well.

Sea Lion Caves and Heceta Head Lighthouse are 11 miles south of Cape Perpetua on U.S. 101. Dean Creek Elk Viewing Area is 4 miles east of Reedsport on Rte. 38. Darlingtonia State Park, featuring endangered pitcher-plants, is 5 miles north of Florence. William L. Finley National Wildlife Refuge, designated to protect Dusky Canada Geese and other waterfowl, is 8 miles south of Corvallis on Oregon Highway 99W. Highway 99, known as "Oregon's winery route," offers tours and wine-tasting at various time of the year.

For more information. General and camping information, District office addresses, maps, bird list: Siuslaw National Forest, 4077 Research Way, Corvallis, Oregon 97333; telephone 503/750-7000. Oregon Dunes National Recreation Area, 855 Highway Ave., Reedsport, Oregon 97467; telephone 503/271-3611.

WILLAMETTE FOREST
Oregon

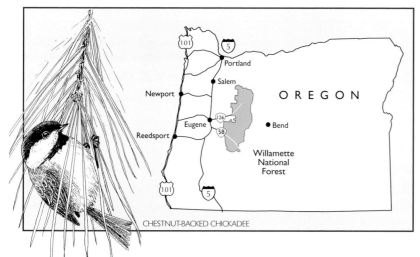

CHESTNUT-BACKED CHICKADEE

CARL JAMES FREEMAN, DRAWING

HOW TO GET THERE.
Gold Lake—leave Interstate 5 at exit 188, about 5 miles south of Eugene, and drive southeast on Oregon 58 for about 63 miles to Forest Service Road 500. Clear Lake—from Eugene, Exit 194 off I-5, take Oregon Route 126 east for about 70 miles. Optional routes include the following: from Salem, take Oregon Route 22 east and south to its intersection with U.S. Route 20/Rt. 126. Turn right and go 4 miles to where U.S. 20 and Rte. 126 diverge; go left on Rte. 126 and drive 3 miles to Clear Lake. From Corvallis, take U.S. 20 east for about 82 miles to the junction with Rte. 126; turn right and drive 3 miles to Clear Lake.

LIKE SO MANY of its sister reserves, the Willamette National Forest owes its name to the native Americans who first inhabited the region. In English corruption, Wallamt became Willamette, and serves as a name for both the broad river that flows into the Columbia and for the forest where the Willamette River has its source.

Centrally located along the western slope of the Oregon Cascades, the forest varies dramatically in elevation from under 1000 feet along the Willamette and McKenzie Rivers to 10,495 feet at the summit of Mt. Jefferson. Dense stands of conifers carpet most of its 1,675,407 acres. At lower elevations, Douglas-fir predominates with lesser numbers of western hemlock, western red-cedar, and Pacific yew. At moderate elevations, Pacific silver and noble firs occur in many areas. In the higher reaches, mountain hemlock, subalpine fir, lodgepole and western white pines, and Engelmann spruce cover the slopes. Patches of whitebark pine are conspicuous on rocky peaks above treeline.

More than a hundred natural lakes nestle into the slopes at mid- and high elevations, while six reservoirs have been built at lower elevations on the western portion of the Forest. Deciduous and mixed habitats generally border these bodies of water, as well as the other openings created by natural meadows, timber harvest, and occasional fire and windstorm. Marsh habitat is comparatively rare, although some does exist.

An impressive fifty-three species of mammals inhabit the forest: Roosevelt elk, black-tailed deer, black bear, mountain lion, and bobcat, as well as beaver, rabbits and hares, squirrels, mice, voles, and shrews. Moist areas host a variety of frogs and salamanders (eight and nine species, respectively), and thirteen species of reptiles are found in drier areas. Cutthroat trout, dace, and sculpin are the most common native fish; thirty-five species have been recorded altogether.

Bird Life
Some 230 species of birds have been found on the Forest, of which more than 100 breed regularly, and another 80 or so either winter or pass through as migrants. One of the Willamette's specialties is the Northern Spotted Owl. The Forest lies in the heart of the Northwest's old-growth Douglas-fir region and is home to more than 1000 of these rare and endangered birds. Forest policy, however, is not to reveal specific locations.

Birding Routes
Two easily accessible areas, Gold Lake and Clear Lake, offer exceptional birding. The lakes are 132 miles apart, but are partially linked by the 58-mile Forest Service Road (FS) 19, also known as Robert Aufderheide Memorial Drive, after a well-remembered Forest supervisor. This route begins in Oakridge on Oregon Route 58 just west of Willamette Pass and crosses through the Forest to Oregon Route 126, east of Blue River.

Gold Lake is situated at 4800-feet elevation near the crest of the Cascades. From Rt. 58, just west of Willamette Pass, turn left (north) onto FS 500, at the sign for the lake, and drive 2 miles to a campground at the south end of the lake; park near the stream outlet at the north end of the campground. The vegetation around the lake is typically coniferous with a thick carpet of fern and shrubs, in-

BLACK SWIFTS

cluding vine maple, rhododendrons, maidenhair and spreading wood ferns, and a variety of wildflowers, such as wild ginger, twinflower, and Sitka columbine.

Walk the trail on the west side of the lake, just across the stream, to the Gold Lake Bog Research Natural Area. The trail to the southwest, on the near side of the stream, goes to nearby Marilyn Lakes (0.5 mile).

Both trails offer excellent birding in late spring and summer. Look for Blue Grouse, Hairy and Pileated woodpeckers, Red-breasted Sapsucker, Olive-sided Flycatcher, Gray and Steller's jays, Clark's Nutcracker, Chestnut-backed Chickadee, Red-breasted Nuthatch, Brown Creeper, Winter Wren, Golden-crowned Kinglet, Hermit and Varied thrushes, Hermit Warbler, Dark-eyed Junco, Pine Siskin, and Evening Grosbeak.

In open areas, you will find Common Nighthawk, Vaux's Swift, Rufous Hummingbird, Tree and Violet-green swallows, and Red-winged and Brewer's blackbirds. Willow Flycatcher and Lincoln's Sparrow haunt the brushy areas. Pied-billed Grebe, Mallard, Barrow's Goldeneye, and Bufflehead occur on the lakes, while Spotted Sandpiper and American Dipper frequent the

shorelines and streams. For several years in the early and mid-1980s, Solitary Sandpipers were found defending territories in the bog. The west side of Gold Lake is one of the best places in Oregon to find Three-toed Woodpeckers. Old-growth Engelmann spruce seems to be the preferred habitat, but the woodpeckers nest in lodgepole pine, mountain hemlock, and western white pine. They often orient their nest-holes toward water or use a natural opening. They have nested right in the campground and also at Marilyn Lakes.

By mid-July, many of the breeding birds are feeding fledglings. Dispersing Great Blue Herons appear and usually remain until the lake freezes in fall. By mid-September, migrant Golden-crowned Sparrows and the darker northern races of Fox Sparrow appear in brushy places and stay for about a month. Also during this period and through October, small mixed flocks (five to twenty birds) of American Robins, Varied Thrushes, Yellow-rumped Warblers, Red Crossbills, and Evening Grosbeaks pass through the area. White-winged Crossbills, Pine Grosbeaks, Williamson's Sapsuckers, Green-tailed Towhees, and other unusual birds have

also been seen in fall migration.

Once the snow flies, usually by late October or November, bird populations dwindle, but the fall scenery is beautiful. A few hardy species remain: Pileated Woodpecker, Common Raven, Gray Jay, Chestnut-backed Chickadee, Brown Creeper, Golden-crowned Kinglet, Red Crossbill, and Pine Siskin. From November 15 to April 30, access to Gold Lake is limited to snowshoes, skis, or snowmobiles. Snow-park permits are required at this time and are available at stores and motels in Oakridge.

Nearby sites off Rt. 58 that offer good birding include Waldo Lake, accessible by FS 5897 about 2 miles west of FS 500; Salt Creek Falls, located 4 miles west of FS 500; and Mule Prairie, a large riparian area upstream from the falls.

Waldo Lake is one of the deepest (420 ft.) lakes in Oregon and is blessed with remarkably clear water. Although bird life is similar to that at Gold Lake, Clark's Nutcrackers are more common. Campgrounds, located 8 and 13 miles north of Rt. 58 on FS 5897 on the east side of Waldo Lake, offer access to the lake and forest trails. Since the late

BOBCAT

Birdfinding in Forty National Forests and Grasslands

1980s, Boreal Owls have been found at night in September and October, about a mile from North Waldo Campground, along Taylor Burn Road that runs northeast from near the campground entrance. This road is rough and is best suited for hiking, horseback, or mountain bikes.

Salt Creek Falls, tumbling 286 feet, is the second-highest waterfall in Oregon and the state's only known nesting-site for Black Swift. These birds nest behind the falls and are most often seen on cloudy days when they forage lower, from late May through August. The best viewing area can be reached by a short, marked trail from the parking area, located just off Rt. 58 on the south side of the road. Vaux's Swift also frequents the locality, so examine the birds with care.

The Mule Prairie riparian area, 1 to 3 miles east of the falls, has breeding Red-breasted Sapsucker, Warbling Vireo, Yellow, MacGillivray's, and Wilson's warblers, Northern Waterthrush (rare), and numerous Lincoln's Sparrows. The walking is difficult, however, since the ground is extremely wet and the

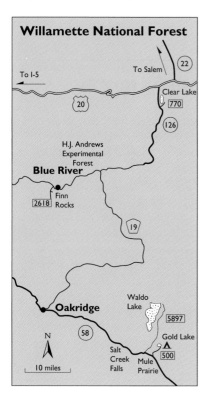

vegetation thick. The edges are most easily accessible along Rt. 58 about a mile east of the entrance to Salt Creek Falls; there is a pull-out just past an open meadow on the south side of the road.

Clear Lake is located between the geologically-recent high Cascades and the older West Cascades. One of the lake's outstanding features is, in fact, the clarity of the water on the north side where springs bubble to the surface. Down in the depths, you can see a forest of snags that have been preserved by the cold temperatures.

To reach Clear Lake from the Gold Lake area, return to Oakridge and turn right on scenic FS 19, which begins just west of town. Follow FS 19 to its intersection with Rt. 126, about 5 miles east of Blue River. You might wish to visit the H.J. Andrews Experimental Forest here; the birding can be excellent in the dense old-growth stands. Afterwards take Rt. 126 northeast for 25 miles. You can begin exploring this area at Coldwater Cove Campground on FS 770, off Rt. 126 at the southeastern end of the lake. Another excellent spot is Clear Lake Resort, on the west side of the lake on FS 775, about 1.5 miles north of FS 770 and 3 miles south of the junction of Rt. 126 with U.S. 20. The resort has rustic cabins, a café, and boat rentals. The 5-mile Clear Lake Loop Trail passes around the lake and through beautiful old-growth forest and volcanic flows.

SPOTTED OWL

In summer, Ospreys and Bald Eagles feed on fishes in the lake. Tree, Violet-green, and Northern Rough-winged swallows can be seen overhead. Forest-dwelling birds include Hairy and Pileated woodpeckers, Steller's and Gray jays, Brown Creeper, Red-breasted Nuthatch, Yellow-rumped Warbler, and Western Tanager. You also should find breeding Red-breasted Sapsucker, Hammond's Flycatcher, Clark's Nutcracker, and Evening Grosbeak. Where the forest abuts the open areas, look for Northern (Red-shafted) Flicker, Olive-sided Flycatcher, Cedar Waxwing, Lazuli Bunting, Chipping Sparrow, Dark-eyed Junco, Brewer's Blackbird, Brown-headed Cowbird, and Evening Grosbeak. Deciduous shrubs along the edge of the lake and in moist areas near streams support nesting Orange-crowned and MacGillivray's warblers and Lincoln's Sparrow. In the contiguous forested areas, search for Golden-

Willamette National Forest

To Salem · 22
To I-5
20
Clear Lake · 770
126
H.J. Andrews Experimental Forest
Blue River
2618 Finn Rocks
19
Waldo Lake · 5897
Oakridge
N
58
Gold Lake · 500
Salt Creek Falls
Mule Prairie
10 miles

HERMIT WARBLER

DAVID A. SIBLEY, DRAWING

crowned Kinglet, Winter Wren, and Swainson's, Hermit, and Varied thrushes.

The Clear Lake Loop-trail joins the 26-mile McKenzie River National Recreation Trail at the junction of Rt. 126 and FS 770, on the south end of the lake near Cold Water Campground. A mile-long hike south on this beautiful route winds through old-growth forests to two magnificent waterfalls, Sahalie and Koosah Falls, where one can find American Dipper.

Also in the vicinity of Clear Lake are Lost Lake, 10 miles east of Rt. 126 on U.S. 20; Trailbridge Reservoir, 7 miles south of Clear Lake on Rt. 126; and Finn Rock Ponds. Aside from the forest birds mentioned above, Lost Lake supports nesting Barrow's Goldeneyes and Olive-sided and Willow flycatchers. The area also is a good bet for Three-toed Woodpeckers. Try Lost Lake Campground, where a pair has nested in recent years. Ospreys are present in summer.

In winter, Trailbridge Reservoir is an excellent place to find Common and, sometimes, Barrow's goldeneyes in beautiful alternate plumage. In mid-to-late April, Harlequin Ducks can often be seen along the river inlet at the north end of the reservoir.

Finn Rock Ponds is an area of low-elevation marsh, deciduous riparian habitat, shrubby areas, and young, mature, and old-growth forest. Nesting species found here that are not often seen at other places on the Forest include Virginia Rail, Common Yellowthroat, Hutton's Vireo, and Black-throated Gray Warbler. Western Wood-Pewee, Pacific-slope Flycatcher, Swainson's Thrush, Warbling Vireo, and Black-headed Grosbeak are common. To reach the ponds, stay on Rt. 126 for 3 miles southwest of Blue River, then turn left (south) on FS 2618 at Finn Rock, cross the bridge, and take the first left on the south side of the bridge. Keep to the right at the only fork and drive approximately 2.5 to 3 miles on the gravel road until you see a cattail marsh. You can walk the road and through the forest adjacent to the ponds, or you can canoe the ponds for close-up viewing. Eugene is probably the closest place to rent a canoe.

ACCOMMODATIONS ◆ WEATHER ◆ OTHER ATTRACTIONS

When to visit. Late May through July is best for songbirds; October and November are best for waterfowl.

Where to stay. Campgrounds at Gold Lake, Odell Lake, Waldo Lake, Coldwater, and elsewhere along U.S. 20 and Rtes. 126 and 22. Lodges at both ends of Odell Lake and cabins at Clear Lake. Motels in Oakridge, Crescent Junction, and McKenzie Bridge.

Weather and attire. Snow is usually on the ground for six months of the year. Spring is mixed with rain and sun, but nights are still cold; summer is warm-to-hot with occasional rain and sometimes cool nights; rain-gear is a necessity, as is a jacket for evenings. Fall brings dry days and cooler temperatures. Insect repellent is highly recommended in spring and summer. If you plan to hike, carry water.

What else to do. Hiking, fishing, boating. Nearby points of interest: Mt. Jefferson, Diamond Peak, and Mt. Washington Wilderness areas. The Dee Wright Observatory on the summit on Rte. 242, for observing recent lava-flows (only open in summer months; access road not recommended for trailers).

For more information. General and campground information, District Office addresses, maps, bird list: Willamette National Forest, 211 E. 7th, Eugene, Oregon 97440; telephone 503/465-6626.

FAIRY SLIPPER ORCHID

KLAMATH FOREST
Oregon and California

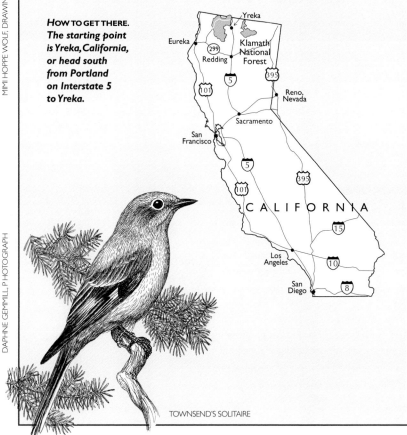

How to get there.
The starting point is Yreka, California, or head south from Portland on Interstate 5 to Yreka.

TOWNSEND'S SOLITAIRE

VIEW ON THE KLAMATH NATIONAL FOREST

FOUR DISTINCT PHYSIOGRAPHIC regions are represented on northern California's magnificent 1,700,000-acre Klamath National Forest: the Klamath Mountains, Cascade Range, the Coast Range, and the Great Basin. The three mountain ranges rise to 8500 feet and are drained by the Klamath River and its tributaries, the Salmon and Scott Rivers and Wooley Creek—all designated as National Wild and Scenic Rivers. East of the Cascades, the Great Basin is characterized by low, rolling terrain and recent volcanic formations.

Plant communities vary from riparian areas and sage-steppe to open chaparral slopes and conifer and mixed forest types. The conifer stands are dominated by Douglas-fir, ponderosa pine, incense cedar, and white fir, while the mixed forests are interspersed with such hardwoods as madrone, black oak, and bigleaf maple. To the east, Basin big sage and Basin wild-rye characterize the Great Basin's Butte Valley National Grassland. Farmlands in the Butte Valley are so rich in prey (small mammals and locusts) that they support the densest breeding population of Swainson's Hawks in California, along with many Golden Eagles and other raptors. Among the denizens of the Forest are several herds of Roosevelt elk, as well as black bear, Pacific fisher, marten, and river otter. Butte Valley habitats support badger, yellow-bellied marmot, mule deer, and some 700 pronghorn.

Bird Life
More than 300 species of birds have been recorded on the Forest. The "most wanted" of these include Mountain Quail and Great Gray, Spotted, and Flammulated Owls.

Knowledge of trees is important in finding the forest owls. Flammulated Owls prefer ponderosa pine; Northern Spotted Owl, old mixed-conifer forest; Northern Pygmy-Owl, Northern Saw-whet Owl, and Western Screech-Owl, oaks; and Great Gray Owl, high-elevation firs. The Klamath is home to White-headed and Lewis's woodpeckers, Calliope Hummingbird, Sage Thrasher, Hermit Warbler, and Sage Sparrow. Old-growth associated birds, such as Vaux's Swift, and Pileated Woodpecker, breed here as well.

Waterfowl and riparian birds abound. In late spring, Wood Ducks and Common Mergansers begin their courtship displays, seemingly oblivious to their surroundings. Lewis's Woodpeckers perform display flights near snags, which they excavate for nests. Ospreys return to their stick nests, and scattered pairs of Bald Eagles nest along the Forest's larger rivers and lakes.

Birding Routes

There are two excellent birding routes on the Forest, the West Side loop and the Butte Valley tour to the east.

The West Side loop, which crosses over the Siskiyou Crest and runs along the Klamath River, takes you through a large variety of habitats with good chances for many high-elevation birds. Key species include Mountain Quail, Calliope Hummingbird, White-headed Woodpecker, and four species of *Empidonax* flycatchers: Hammond's, Dusky, Pacific-slope, and Willow.

The Butte Valley tour is dominated by spectacular views of Mt. Shasta to the south and the Cascade Range to the west. From February to May, up to 150 Bald and Golden eagles frequent the area, often close enough for good photographs. In spring and summer, as many as seventy pairs of Swainson's Hawks breed here, along with numerous Northern Harriers and Red-tailed Hawks. Other grassland birds of interest include Sandhill Crane, Burrowing Owl, Sage Thrasher, and Sage Sparrow.

A note of caution: Truck traffic can be moderately heavy on the main roads; be sure to pull completely off the roadway when stopping.

The West Side Birding Loop is 74 miles long, starting at the Mount Ashland exit off Interstate 5 North (25 miles north of Yreka). The route follows paved roads for about 10 miles, dirt roads for 32 miles, and then turns back to pavement. The dirt roads are suitable for passenger cars but are not advised for trailers. Because of the high elevation, the route is often closed by snow from mid-November through late June; it is then open to cross-country skiing.

Mileage begins at the Mt. Ashland exit (mile 0.0), the first exit in Oregon coming from the south. Turn right and follow the signs for Mt. Ashland and the Siskiyou Summit; pass under the interstate to a second stop-sign. (If you are coming from the north, this is where you will join the tour, at mile 0.2). Turn left toward Mt. Ashland, paralleling I-5 for 0.9 mile, then go right onto Mt. Ashland Road. Continue to mile 2.5, past Colestine Road, to a mixed conifer forest of ponderosa pine, sugar pine, incense cedar, Douglas-fir, and white fir. Pull off to the right; look and listen in late spring and summer for Mountain Quail, Hammond's and Dusky flycatchers, Steller's Jay, Mountain Chickadee, Hermit Thrush, Nashville and MacGillivray's warblers, and Pine Siskin. Also, keep an eye on the sky for soaring Golden Eagles.

Continue to mile 4, where the slope to the right is covered with greenleaf manzanita and chinquapin. Look here for MacGillivray's Warbler and Fox Sparrow. This site also provides a splendid view of 14,162-foot Mt. Shasta to the south.

A wide pull-out at mile 4.3 is a good place for Steller's Jay, Hermit Thrush, Solitary Vireo (Cassin's race, which some ornithologists consider a full species), Hermit Warbler (high in the trees), Fox Sparrow, and Dark-eyed Junco.

At mile 7.8, Ball Gap Snowpark exits to the right. Park near the intersection; look and listen for Hammond's Flycatcher, Red-breasted Nuthatch, and Dark-eyed Junco. You also should hear Hermit Warblers, although they may be hard to see after May when they sing from perches in the tallest conifers. During May they often forage in the lower branches out in the open.

Just ahead, at mile 8.3, you will enter a forest dominated by white fir

MOUNTAIN QUAIL

JONATHAN ALDERFER, DRAWING

and Mt. Shasta red fir. The large Mt. Shasta firs (locally called "silver tips") on the right are favorites for Christmas trees. Bird species utilizing this habitat include Pileated Woodpecker, Olive-sided and Hammond's flycatchers, Townsend's Solitaire, and Hermit Warbler.

At mile 9, just as you drive around a left-hand curve, you can see an observatory and ski-lifts high atop Mt. Ashland. The ski-area parking lot is just ahead. Bird the surrounding forest for Red-breasted Nuthatch, House Wren, Fox Sparrow, and Purple Finch.

Pavement ends at mile 10, where a sign announces that the road ahead is one-lane with pull-outs. Some years the road is not completely open until the first of July, but at other times it is open by mid-May.

At mile 10.3 is the Mt. Ashland Campground; some years it has potable water. Continue on the main road through the campground to mile 11.1, where Forest Service Road (FS) 300 goes to the right to the summit of Mt. Ashland. Continue on the main road (the left fork). Here you can search the surrounding meadows for the Willow Flycatcher—a California state-endangered species.

At mile 11.1, look for Green-tailed Towhees among the surrounding chokecherry shrubs. Also listen for the very low booming of Blue Grouse. To see the bird, walk slowly toward the booming; you may get lucky. Dusky Flycatchers and Fox Sparrows frequent the shrub habitat here. Just beyond, at mile 11.2, you will see a pair of western white pines on

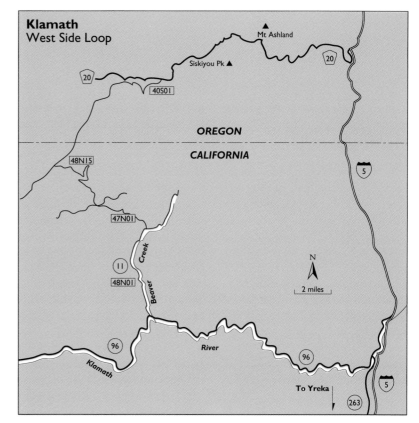

Klamath
West Side Loop

the left; this is a good spot for Calliope Hummingbird, Northern Flicker, Lazuli Bunting, Lincoln's Sparrow, and Pine Siskin. All along this portion of the route are large patches of tubular flowers—scarlet gilia, American bistort, delphinium, and the endemic Mt. Ashland lupine—excellent for Calliope and Rufous hummingbirds.

At mile 12, a road to the left goes 0.25 mile to scenic Grouse Gap

BURROWING OWLS

Shelter, a great picnic spot. At mile 13.2, you will come to a small rocky outcrop where you may find Rock Wrens. Stop at Meridian Overlook (mile 14.2) for unprecedented views of Mt. Shasta and the Oregon Cascades. Here you are likely to find Mountain Quail, Common Raven, Willow Flycatcher, Northern Flicker, Dusky Flycatcher, Red-breasted Nuthatch, Hermit and Varied thrushes, Townsend's Solitaire, and Fox Sparrow. At mile 14.4 is a nice stand of old-growth mountain hemlock and red fir; you can usually find Mountain Chickadee, Brown Creeper, Hermit Warbler, and Fox Sparrow. Continue straight through the intersections with FS 22 at mile 16.8, FS 40S16 at mile 16.9, and FS 40S12 at mile 17.5. Stop at mile 19.9; Dusky Flycatcher, Steller's Jay, Redbreasted Nuthatch, and Rock Wren are likely to be

JULIE ZICKEFOOSE DRAWING

found here. Then continue straight on to Jackson Gap, at mile 23, where you must bear to the left onto FS 40S01.

If you have not yet seen Hammond's Flycatcher, stop at mile 24.1 and look for this species among the mature conifers. Then continue on, ignoring FS 48N21 and FS 40S15, to mile 27.3 and a tree that will welcome you to California. Stay on FS 40S01, heading south, ignoring other roads to the right and left. At mile 28.4 there is a regenerating clearcut where you are likely to find Lincoln's Sparrows.

MOUNTAIN BLUEBIRD

The road begins to descend at mile 29.4. At mile 30.8, you must turn sharply to the left onto FS 48N15. Elevation here is 5500 feet. The route follows West Fork Beaver Creek to Beaver Creek and eventually to the Klamath River. At mile 32.7, pull off to the left where pine-mat manzanita is growing on the cutbank to the left. This is a good place for Mountain Quail, Hammond's Flycatcher, Her-

mit Thrush, Townsend's Solitaire, Nashville and Hermit warblers, and Red Crossbill. During years of good cone crops, flocks of Red Crossbills can be heard *kip-kip*ping and seen flying to and from the conifers.

The small pull-out on the right at mile 32.01 is usually excellent for White-headed Woodpecker, Olive-sided Flycatcher, Red-breasted Nuthatch, the ubiquitous Nashville Warbler, and Pine Siskin. Occasionally, Dusky Flycatcher, Clark's Nutcracker, and Western Tanager can also be seen here.

At mile 32, FS 47N15 goes off to the left, but you should continue straight ahead on FS 48N15 and stop at mile 32.9, where there is a remnant of lovely mature forest. Several interesting birds occur here: White-headed and Pileated woodpeckers, Brown Creeper, Red-breasted Nuthatch, Hermit Warbler, Western Tanager, Dark-eyed Junco, and Pacific-slope Flycatcher.

At mile 37.4, you are likely to find Western Wood-Pewee, Hermit Thrush, Solitary and Warbling vireos, MacGillivray's Warbler, and Lazuli Bunting. If you want another spot for Pacific-slope Flycatcher, stop at mile 38.3.

At mile 38.7, FS 48N18 exits to the left and FS 48N15 ends. Stop on the right and look and listen for Warbling Vireo, Black-headed Grosbeak, and Hermit Warbler. If you walk 100 yards up FS 48N18, a MacGillivray's Warbler is sometimes singing on the left. Continue straight ahead on FS 47N01 and watch for American Dippers along the creek. At mile 42.3, turn right onto paved FS 11 (same as FS 48N01). Here is the main stem of Beaver Creek, an important fishery

on the Forest for rearing young steelhead trout. Just beyond, at mile 42.4, listen for the loud haunting calls of Pileated Woodpeckers. If you are lucky, one may be feeding nearby, but because of their extensive territories, they are not often seen.

At mile 43.1, you will pass Beaver Creek Campground to your left. Look and listen for Northern Pygmy-Owl in the riparian oak habitat. Stop ahead at mile 43.85 for Dusky Flycatchers, Warbling Vireos, and Lazuli Buntings that frequent the manzanita shrubbery on the left. And at mile 46.4 Vaux's Swifts have been seen along with Tree and Violet-green swallows. Also watch for Mountain Quail, Dusky Flycatcher, Nashville Warbler, and Western Tanager.

When you reach mile 47.2, pull off to the left and look for Common Merganser in the creek. Check for Lewis's Woodpecker, Western Wood-Pewee, Bushtit, Warbling Vireo, Yellow Warbler, Yellow-breasted Chat, and Black-headed Grosbeak in the surrounding vegetation.

You will reach California Route 96 and the Klamath River at mile 47.9. Take Rte. 96 to the left and continue the tour. If you are thirsty, hungry, or low on gas, there is a small store, with gasoline, soda, homemade sandwiches, and pie, 0.7 mile downstream on Rte. 96 to the right.

Back on the birding route, stop at mile 53.5 at the pull-out to the right where Western Kingbird, Yellow Warbler, Yellow-breasted Chat, and Song Sparrow should be found in spring and summer. At Skeehan Bar (mile 55.4), the dry slope across the road is a good place for Blue-gray Gnatcatcher. Western Wood-Pewee, Yellow Warbler, Western Tanager, and Northern Oriole occur along the river. There is a telephone and a pit toilet at mile 63.45, also a good spot to find California Quail, Black-throated Gray Warbler, Lazuli Bunting, Brewer's Blackbird, and Northern Oriole.

Stop at mile 66, the pull-off for Tree-of-Heaven Campground, which has full service and good birds. Golden Eagles and Ospreys often cruise by. Purple Martins have been seen between the highway and the campground. In April, large flocks of Vaux's Swifts migrate upsteam with mixed flocks of swallows. Belted Kingfisher, Ash-throated Flycatcher, Blue-gray Gnatcatcher, and Yellow-breasted Chat can also be found here.

Mile 68.7 is the location of the Ash Creek Bridge and the Forest boundary sign. From here, it is 2.9 miles to the turnoff to Yreka (Route 263). Go that way to I-5 if you are headed south. If you wish to go north toward Oregon, continue on Rte. 96 for another 2.4 miles beyond the Yreka turnoff to the I-5 North entrance. Watch for Lewis's Woodpeckers in the roadside oak stands. Flammulated Owl can be seen in the evening along the entire route but probably will require playing a tape.

Butte Valley Tour, on the eastern portion of the Forest, is 40 miles long and crosses state and private lands. This route boasts a wide variety of habitat and bird life that is very different from that found on the West Side loop.

The Butte Valley route begins at the small town of Macdoel, on U.S. 97, 40 miles northeast of Weed, California (which is on I-5 19 miles south of Yreka). On your way, you might want to stop at the Grass Lake Rest Area, 21 miles north of Weed on Rte. 97, for nesting "Greater" Sandhill

Cranes, Bald Eagles, waterfowl, and large numbers of Yellow-headed Blackbirds in a large montane wetland.

The tiny town of Macdoel, 20 miles north of Grass Valley, lies in the center of Butte Valley, which is dominated by a mix of sage-brush flats, juniper woodlands, wetlands, and cultivated fields.

From the post office, drive north on U.S. 97 for 1.1 miles to Sheep Mountain Road and turn right (across the railroad tracks) into the southeastern corner of the Butte Valley National Grassland and adjacent farmland. The next several miles provide some of the best raptor-viewing in the state during winter, spring, and summer. Take Sheep Mountain Road 2.3 miles to an intersection and make the little jog to the right and continue on for another 3 miles. Then turn around and backtrack on Sheep Mountain Road for 0.9 mile to the Macdoel-Dorris Road. Turn right and drive for 1 mile to paved Shady Dell Road and turn right. During winter and early spring, watch for large

groups of Bald and Golden eagles feeding at deer carcasses in fields. Watch for raptors soaring overhead, perching on utility poles, or sitting on the ground consuming Belding's ground-squirrels. In summer, numbers of Swainson's and (Harlan's) Red-tailed hawks, Northern Harriers, Golden Eagles, and Prairie Falcons, as well as Turkey Vultures, should be present.

Continue on Shady Dell Road for 2 miles, then go left on E. Butte Valley Road for 3.1 miles, watching for Mountain Bluebirds and Pinyon Jays along the road. In winter, Ferruginous, Rough-legged, and (Harlan's) Red-tailed hawks and many eagles can be seen along this route. Return to Shady Dell Road, turn right, and drive 5.2 miles back to U.S. 97. Turn right and drive 2.2 miles north, then turn left on paved Sam's Neck Road, onto the Butte Valley National Grassland. Drive 1.7 miles and turn left on a marked red-cinder road. Watch for the raptors listed above; you may also find Burrowing Owl, Gray Flycatcher, Sage Thrasher, Western Blue-

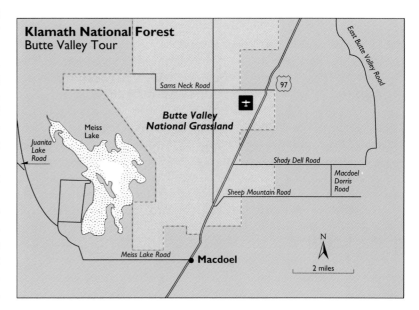

Klamath

31

bird, and Brewer's, Vesper, and Sage sparrows almost anywhere along this segment of the route in spring and summer. To find the owl, it is best to get out of your vehicle and scan areas of short grasses with ground-squirrel burrows. In the evening, watch for Long-eared Owls flying between scattered junipers. Drive 3.1 miles south to U.S. 97, then turn right toward Macdoel.

From U.S. 97, turn right onto Meiss Lake Road (0.5 mile south of Macdoel). Drive 5.1 miles to the Butte Valley Wildlife Area (administered by California Department of Fish and Game) and take the 4.5-mile self-guided auto tour through the refuge. In spring and fall, the area is home to several thousand migrant Canada, Greater White-fronted, and Snow geese, as well as more than a dozen species of ducks. Huge (20,000+) flocks of Greater White-fronted and Snow geese often forage in the farmlands in March and April, and several hundred can be found in the Butte Valley Wildlife Area in summer. A few ducks, American Avocets, and Black-necked Stilts nest here, and American White Pelicans can often be found soaring overhead or in one of the large ponds. When you have completed your Wildlife Area tour, retrace your steps to U.S. 97, completing the route.

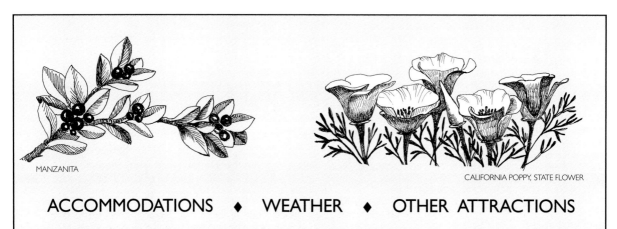

MANZANITA

CALIFORNIA POPPY, STATE FLOWER

ACCOMMODATIONS ◆ WEATHER ◆ OTHER ATTRACTIONS

When to visit. Early spring and late fall best for spectacular flocks of geese and a variety of raptors. Late spring and early summer best for highland birding.

Where to stay. Several campgrounds on the Forest and in adjacent towns. Motels in Yreka, California, Ashland, Oregon, and in many other small towns found around the Forest. If you wish to camp in the area, Juanita Lake Campground can be reached from Meiss Lake Road by continuing past the Wildlife Area Headquarters to Juanita Lake Road; turn left and drive 3 miles to the campground. This campground is adjacent to a man-made lake where a nesting pair of Bald Eagles can often be seen fishing in spring and summer.

Weather and attire. Winters are relatively mild on the west side but with rain at lower elevations and snow above 4000 feet. Summers can be hot with temperatures often in the 90s. Evenings are generally cool, even on the hottest days. Jackets recommended for early spring, and early fall; take thermal underwear as well. Shorts suggested for summer, with jackets essential for higher elevations.

What else to do. Hiking, boating, rafting, fishing, horseback riding, mountain-biking. Lower Klamath and Tule National Wildlife Refuges, for huge numbers of waterfowl and wintering Bald Eagles, are just a few miles east of Butte Valley. The Butte Valley Wildlife Area, administered by California Department of Fish and Game, is on Meiss Lake Road at Macdoel. Crater Lake National Park is just a couple hours drive from Yreka. Visit Ashland, Oregon, 45 minutes north, for a fine Shakespeare Festival, February to October.

The region was a major gold-mining area at the turn of the century. There still are many active mines on the Forest. Try the Siskiyou County Museum, Yreka, for excellent displays on the region's history.

For more information. General and camping information, District Office addresses, maps, bird list: Klamath National Forest, 1312 Fairlane Road, Yreka, California 96097; telephone 916/ 842-6131. There are two Ranger District Offices: Goosenest, 37805 U.S. Route 97, Macdoel, California 96050, telephone 916/ 398-4391; Oak Knoll, 22541 California Route 96, Klamath River, California 96050, telephone 916/ 465-2241.

SHASTA–TRINITY FOREST
California

MIMI HOPPE WOLF, DRAWING

STELLER'S JAY

DAPHNE GEMMILL PHOTOGRAPH

MT. SHASTA GLEAMS AMIDST ITS SURROUNDING NATIONAL FOREST

THE COMBINED SHASTA–TRINITY National Forest lies in the hub of California's Shasta–Cascade recreational wonderland, and it boasts some spectacular landmarks. Shasta Forest is known for Shasta Lake and for Mt. Shasta with a summit rising to 14,162 feet. The great mountain is ringed by no fewer than seven glaciers and is one of the largest volcanoes in the world. Trinity Lake and the rugged granite peaks of the 7500-to-9000-foot Trinity Alps are centerpieces of the Trinity Forest. Nearly one-quarter of the vast 2,100,000-acre domain is wilderness, offering an exceptional variety of habitats, an abundance of wildlife, and an oft-appreciated ration of blessed solitude.

On Shasta–Trinity you will find grasslands and chaparral, where black-tailed deer browse and tiger swallowtail butterflies draw nectar from carpets of golden poppies. There are ponderosa pine forests and great stands of old-growth Douglas-fir, whose cathedral-like silence is broken by sounds of Northern Spotted Owls and Pileated Woodpeckers. Bald Eagles are found at Shasta Lake, where Ospreys and Purple Martins raise their young. There are broad mountain meadows, where heads of lilies nod and stands of sugar and digger pines offer cones to be gathered by wildlife and human alike, oak woodlands, where busy western gray squirrels scamper over showy pink phlox, and alpine glaciers and scree slopes beckon to visiting rosy-finches.

Riparian communities abound on the Forest, with 53,000 acres of lakes and wetlands and 5500 miles of rivers and streams. Large rivers are the spawning-grounds for anadromous steelhead trout and chinook and coho salmons. In spring and summer, Bald Eagles (the largest breeding population in California), Ospreys, Common Mergansers, and American Dippers join western pond turtles, yellow-legged frogs, river otters, and beaver in their aquatic habitats.

The Forests also support a wonderment of mammals. Black-tailed deer, coyote, and gray fox are common; beaver, muskrat, and river otter are less obvious; and black bear are not unusual. The golden-mantled ground-squirrel and Allen's chipmunk are fun to watch scurrying about. Fisher, mink, and ring-tailed cat are elusive, and you would be very lucky to see any of them.

Bird Life

The Forest has accumulated a list of more than two hundred species. There is a profusion of raptors, including Bald Eagle (year-round), Spotted Owl, and Peregrine Falcon, as well as strong populations of Steller's and Scrub jays, Acorn, Downy, Hairy, Nuttall's, and Pileated Woodpeckers, Black-capped, Mountain, and Chestnut-backed chickadees, Western Tanager, and several species of warblers—Black-throated Gray, Hermit, Yellow-rumped, MacGillivray's, and Wilson's. California and Mountain quail, Green-tailed and

California towhees, and Lazuli Bunting, as well as Fox, Golden-crowned (winter and early spring), and White-crowned sparrows, can be found in shrubby areas. At the larger lakes are Western, Eared, and Horned grebes in fall, winter, and spring, along with nineteen species of ducks.

Birding Routes

The best birding is at Lewiston Lake on the Trinity Forest, at McCloud Flats, and the Mt. Shasta Wilderness on the Shasta Forest.

Lewiston Lake. The lake area is particularly good for viewing raptors, riparian birds, and some of the upland-forest species. The forests here are dominated by ponderosa pines interspersed with scattered meadows.

From Redding, drive approximately 30 miles west on California Route 299 to the Lewiston turnoff, then 4 miles north on County Route 105 to Lewiston. The lake is 2 miles beyond Lewiston, a well-preserved Gold Rush town just west of the highway. Begin bird-watching at the Trinity River Fish Hatchery, on the right, about half-way between Lewiston and Lewiston Lake. The hatchery parking area is 1.5 miles north of Lewiston (or 6 miles north of Rte. 299).

Walk below the dam to the riffles on the river and search the surroundings for Wood Duck, Belted Kingfisher, Anna's Hummingbird, Black Phoebe, Bushtit, Bewick's and Winter wrens, Wrentit, Rufous-sided and California towhees, Song Sparrow, and Red-winged Blackbird. All are year-round residents.

Nearby are several trails where you can walk

along the river. Various migrating and breeding warblers are to be found here, including Orange-crowned, Yellow, Black-throated Gray, Yellow-rumped, and MacGillivray's, and Yellow-breasted Chat. In spring and summer, look for Western Wood-Pewee, Pacific-slope, Willow (rare), and Ash-throated flycatchers, Western Kingbird, Violet-green Swallow, Western Tanager, Black-headed Grosbeak, Lazuli Bunting, Northern Oriole, and Lesser Goldfinch. In winter, Golden-crowned Sparrows frequent the area.

Return to Rte. 105, turn right, and drive 1 mile north to Lewiston Lake. Rte. 105 follows the western shoreline and is known as Trinity Dam Boulevard. Drive the 7-mile-long boulevard, stopping now and then to look for birds on the lake and along the marshy shoreline. A stop at Lewiston Lake Vista, near the south end of the lake, is likely to produce soaring Osprey, Bald and Golden eagles, and Sharp-shinned, Cooper's, and Red-tailed hawks. Uncommon raptors include White-tailed Kite, American Kestrel, and Merlin (fall and winter only).

Waterfowl and marsh birds may include Great Blue and Green herons, Great Egret, Canada Goose, Wood Duck, Common Merganser, Killdeer, Spotted Sandpiper, Common Snipe, Belted Kingfisher, and American Dipper. Also watch for elusive Virginia Rails and Soras.

During spring and fall, look for American Wigeon, Canvasback, Greater and Lesser scaups, Common and Barrow's goldeneyes, Bufflehead, and Ruddy Duck. The best viewing sites for waterfowl are Coot's Roost, across from Lakeview Terrace Resort (about 3 miles north of Lewiston Lake Vista), and Pine Cove Fishing Access (another mile beyond). If you want to view birds from the water, boat rentals are available at Pine Cove Marina.

Forest and open-woodland birds can best be found along the road-

ACORN WOODPECKER

SHAWNEEN FINNEGAN, DRAWING

ways and campgrounds; there are no trails. Resident species include five kinds of woodpeckers (Acorn, Nuttall's, and Pileated, Red-breasted Sapsucker, and Northern Flicker), Steller's and Scrub jays, Common Raven, Mountain and Chestnut-backed chickadees, Hutton's Vireo, and House Finch. In summer, one can find Solitary Vireo and Hermit Warbler, while Townsend's Warbler is a common migrant and uncommon winter visitor. Also watch the shrubby areas for California Quail and the more secretive Mountain Quail.

McCloud Flats encompass a gentle rolling upland of 155,000 acres, rimmed on the north, east, and west by the unique volcanic features of Medicine Lake highland, Porcupine Butte lava flows, and Mt. Shasta. The vegetation is about the same as at Lewiston Lake. Lodgepole pines and true firs grow on the ancient lavaflows, volcanic ridges, and buttes. Drive 60 miles north of Redding on Interstate 5 to California Route 89, the McCloud exit. Then take Rte. 89 east 9 miles to the town of McCloud. McCloud Flats is 4 miles farther east along Rte. 89.

Begin your excursion at Upper Falls, Lakin Dam, and Bigelow Meadow in the upper McCloud River area. From the Shell station in McCloud, take Rte. 89 east for 5.4 miles and turn right on Forest Service Road (FS) 39N30 at Fowler's Camp exit. Then drive south 0.6 mile and take the second left on FS 40N44, following signs to Lakin Dam. After 1.3 miles turn right, and go 0.1 mile to the Upper Falls. Nesting American Dippers can usually be seen in the spring and early summer by peering over the edge by the mouth of the waterfall. Watch also for Wood Duck, Spotted Sandpiper, Belted Kingfisher, Western Wood-Pewee, and Black Phoebe. To reach the Lakin Dam marsh area, return to FS 40N44 and take a right after 0.4 mile, turn right on FS 39N134, go 0.3 mile and

turn right on FS 39N134B. The parking and picnic area is 0.2 miles farther. Early spring and early fall are the best times to see Canada Geese, Wood and Ring-necked ducks, Green-winged Teal, and Mallards. You may also see Green Heron, Osprey, Virginia Rail, Sora, Marsh Wren, and Hutton's and Warbling vireos.

Next, follow the trail up the McCloud River course from the south (left) side of the Lakin Dam parking area. In the mile of this gentle-grade trail, you will enjoy views through the forest to Bigelow Meadow. Resident Song and Fox sparrows and Rufous-sided Towhees are normally active in the riparian vegetation. The willow thickets are prime habitats for the rare Willow as well as Western flycatcher and Orange-crowned,

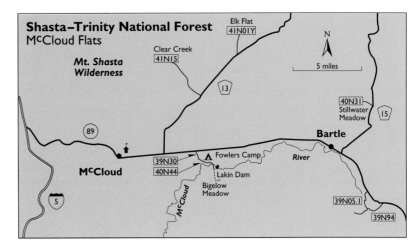

CANADA GEESE

MacGillivray's, and Wilson's warblers. Be alert for Sharp-shinned and Cooper's hawks hunting in the area.

To continue on the McCloud Flats Route, return to Rte. 89 and proceed 10.9 miles east to the town of Bartle, then turn left (north) onto Harris Spring Road (FS 15). Drive north for 4.8 miles, then turn left onto FS 40N31, which is near the junction with FS 49. Within a mile, take a left at the first fork and a right at the T-junction. Follow this road past the culvert. You will then be at Stillwater Meadow, which has several small connected meadows

Shasta–Trinity National Forest
McCloud Flats

Mt. Shasta Wilderness

Elk Flat
41N01Y

Clear Creek
41N15

N

5 miles

13

40N31
Stillwater Meadow
15

Bartle

89

39N30

Fowlers Camp

River

McCloud

40N44

Lakin Dam

Bigelow Meadow

5

39N05.1

39N94

and fenced areas. Park at a convenient spot for birding at the meadow. Willow Flycatchers breed in the willows around the meadows. Female Blue Grouse and chicks actively forage here from late May through June. Northern Goshawks are known to nest nearby. Northern Flicker, Steller's and Gray jays, Golden-crowned and Ruby-crowned kinglets, Townsend's Solitaire, Hermit and Varied thrushes, and Western Tanager forage in the adjacent forest. Here, too, can be found a variety of warblers: Yellow, Yellow-rumped, Hermit, MacGillivray's, and Wilson's. Warbling Vireos may be heard singing during May and June from a white fir or incense cedar.

Mt. Shasta Wilderness lies at elevations above 6000 feet on the southern slope of Mt. Shasta and is your best shot at highland birds. Follow the previous directions to the town of McCloud. Continue east on Rte. 89 from McCloud for about 3 miles, then turn left on Pilgrim Creek Road (FS 13). Proceed northeast 5.2 miles to FS 41N15 and left for 8 miles, following signs, along primitive roads to the Clear Creek trailhead, which is at about 6400 feet. This high-elevation red-fir forest is home to Red-breasted and Williamson's sapsuckers, White-headed Woodpecker, Gray Jay, Clark's Nutcracker, Red-breasted Nuthatch, Red Crossbill, Cassin's Finch, and Evening Grosbeak. For additional exploration and exercise, hike 2 miles higher up the trail into the Wilderness, at about 8000 feet. Watch for American Pipit at the meadows and Rock Wren and Gray-crowned Rosy-Finches feeding at the base of the glacial slopes beyond the meadows. Look for Golden Eagle .

Afterwards, return to Pilgrim Creek Road 13. Turn left and drive 3.8 miles east to FS 41N01Y; turn left, stay right at the fork, and go 1 mile to the east side of Elk Flat. This dry meadow is an excellent place for Mountain Bluebird in spring. The bluebirds nest in tree cavities around the edge and forage over the meadow. Look for Black-throated Gray Warbler, Chipping, Vesper, Lark, and Savannah sparrows, and Lesser and American goldfinches. You may also hear Pileated Woodpeckers within the conifer forest. Watch for Pygmy Nuthatches gleaning insects from tree trunks. During early morning, listen for the *quick three beers* song of the Olive-sided Flycatcher. At dusk or dawn, a fortunate birder may hear a Spotted Owl, and there is also a possibility of Black-billed Magpie.

ACCOMMODATIONS ◆ WEATHER ◆ OTHER ATTRACTIONS

When to visit. Spring, summer, and autumn are the best times for birding. At lower elevations, birders can see Bald Eagles year-round. Winter snow can make some areas inaccessible. Logging traffic can be heavy during spring, summer, and fall, so be careful, especially in the McCloud Flats area.

Where to stay. Campgrounds throughout the Forest. At Lewiston: cabins, RV park, campground, Lakeview Terrace Resort, plus a marina for boat rental. Motels in Lewiston, Weaverville, Dunsmuir, McCloud, and Mt. Shasta. Houseboat and patio-boat rentals at Shasta Lake.

Weather and attire. Spring temperatures are pleasant, but rain and snow can occur early in the season. Summer is dry with temperatures in the 80s. Elevations around Lewiston Lake are 2200 to 2500 feet; most areas on McCloud Flats are at 3700 to 4500 feet. Winter temperatures are usually in the 30s and 40s.

What else to do. Hiking, including portions of the Pacific Crest Trail that stretches from Canada to Mexico, horseback riding, fishing, and boating. The road along Lewiston Lake is part of the Trinity Heritage Scenic Byway that starts in Weaverville, to the south, and ends approximately 110 miles north at Coffee Creek. This is a self-guided auto tour (pamphlet available from the Forest Service) that offers opportunities to learn about the area's history, including the culture of the Wintu Indians, California Gold Rush days, and the lives of early settlers.

For more information. General and camping information, bird lists, District Office addresses, maps: Shasta-Trinity National Forest, 2400 Washington Ave., Redding, California 96001; telephone 916/246-5222.

CALIFORNIA PITCHER-PLANT

WESTERN DOGWOOD

WILD CURRANT

ELDORADO FOREST
California

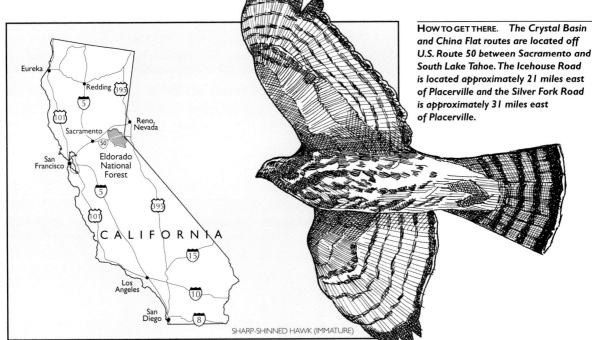

SHARP-SHINNED HAWK (IMMATURE)

GAIL DIANE LUCKNER, DRAWING

HOW TO GET THERE. *The Crystal Basin and China Flat routes are located off U.S. Route 50 between Sacramento and South Lake Tahoe. The Icehouse Road is located approximately 21 miles east of Placerville and the Silver Fork Road is approximately 31 miles east of Placerville.*

THE HORDES OF GOLD-SEEKING forty-niners may long be gone, but the big National Forest rising from the foothills to the snow-capped peaks of the Sierra Nevada Mountains is still an "el dorado" as far as naturalists are concerned. Ranging in elevation from 2500 to 10,000 feet, the Forest boasts such a splendid diversity of habitats—mixed and montane chaparral, oak woodlands, Sierra mixed conifer, red-fir, wet meadows, and subalpine scrub—that no fewer than 1100 species of wildflowers, shrubs, and trees thrive on its 600,000 acres. There are 80 species of mammals, such as mountain lion, black bear, gray fox, raccoon, porcupine, and gray and Douglas squirrels. Reptiles and amphibians abound: western rattlesnake, rubber boa, mountain kingsnake, California newt, and Pacific treefrog, to name only a few. In the spring of some years, large numbers of California tortoise-shell and California sister butterflies migrate through the area.

Bird Life

The bird list for the Eldorado National Forest tops two hundred species and represents some of the best and most varied montane birding in Central California. If you bird the Forest in spring, you will probably find all of the area specialties: Bald Eagle, Osprey, Mountain Quail, White-headed and Pileated woodpeckers, Hammond's and Dusky flycatchers, Townsend's Solitaire, Solitary Vireo, Hermit Warbler, Lazuli Bunting, Green-tailed Towhee, and Fox Sparrow. The much desired Flammulated Owl is also found on this Forest.

Birding Routes

There are many excellent birding areas, but two rate as especially good: on the Pacific Ranger District, the Crystal Basin Recreation Area, and on the Placerville Ranger District, the China Flat area and the South Fork American River. The South Fork of the American River, incidentally, was

where a carpenter named James W. Marshall first found gold on January 24, 1848, thus triggering the greatest mass adventure since perhaps the Crusades.

Crystal Basin Area is home to more than eighty species of breeding birds, most of which you can find along a 70-mile loop that begins on Icehouse Road at the junction of U.S. Route 50 at Riverton. The intersection is approximately 21 miles east of Placerville and 40 miles west of South Lake Tahoe. All roads are paved unless otherwise noted.

As you travel up the Icehouse Road, you will pass through some of the 22,500 acres burned in the 1992 Cleveland fire. This area previously burned in the 1959 Icehouse fire, and the thirty-year-old conifers were just beginning to return the area to a forested habitat. The more recent fire has begun the successional change from brush to trees once again.

Stop first 0.5 mile up Icehouse Road at a wide pull-out on the left.

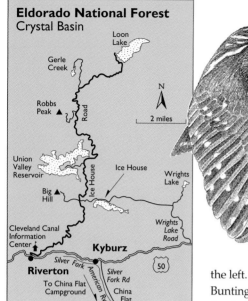

Eldorado National Forest
Crystal Basin

(map) Loon Lake · Gerle Creek · Robbs Peak ▲ · Road · N · 2 miles · Union Valley Reservoir · Ice House · Ice House · Wrights Lake · Big Hill · Wrights Lake Road · Cleveland Canal Information Center · Kyburz · Riverton · Silver Fork · Silver Fork Rd · 50 · To China Flat Campground · American River · China Flat

NORTHERN SAW-WHET OWL

JULIE ZICKEFOOSE, DRAWING

Listen for calling Mountain Quail and look for Barn Swallow, Nashville Warbler, Black-headed Grosbeak, and Rufous-sided Towhee. The Cleveland Corral Information Center is located 2.5 miles farther on Icehouse Road and provides restrooms, drinking water, and an information kiosk and display board. Plan to spend some time here; more than twenty species of birds can be found in this small area. Search behind the picnic grounds in spring and summer for Brown Creeper, House Wren, Solitary Vireo, Black-throated Gray Warbler, Chipping Sparrow, and Purple Finch. Watch, also, for nesting Northern (Bullock's) Orioles near the information center.

Then continue on Icehouse Road for 0.5 mile to a large, open area on the left. This is a good spot for Lazuli Bunting, often found sitting on top of the deer brush. Also look for Calliope Hummingbird among the deer brush and elderberry. The nearby brushy draw is prime habitat for MacGillivray's Warbler. Listen, too, for singing Fox Sparrow.

For the next 6 miles there are many opportunities to pull off the road and explore the adjacent area. Icehouse Road carries moderate traffic, so be sure to drive completely off the pavement into one of the pull-outs.

Upon reaching the top of the ridge, there is a sign for Peavine Ridge Road on the left. Pull off on the right just before the intersection or continue around the corner to the right and use the large pull-out at the next corner. This brushy area is a good place to look for Green-tailed Towhee, Lazuli Bunting, and Fox Sparrow.

Continue up Icehouse Road for 2.5 miles to a small store and café, where gasoline, supplies, restrooms, and a telephone are available in summer. Near the store, you are likely to find Anna's Hummingbird, Downy and Hairy woodpeckers, Cliff and Barn swallows, Red-breasted Nuthatch, American Robin, Brewer's Blackbird, Brown-headed Cowbird, and Dark-eyed Junco.

You will come to a four-way-stop intersection 1.5 miles beyond the store. Turn left toward Big Hill Look-out and drive about 100 yards to a mature stand of old-growth conifers. Some of the gigantic sugar pines here are six hundred years old. Look for Hammond's Flycatcher, Steller's Jay, Mountain Chickadee, Red-breasted Nuthatch, and Western Tanager. Listen for the *quick three beers* of Olive-sided Flycatchers and the low booming of Blue Grouse. This place is excellent for seeing and hearing Pileated Woodpecker; and, in spring, Spotted Owls can often be heard at dusk and dawn. Return to Icehouse Road and turn left toward Union Valley Reservoir. This part of the route passes through a mature mixed conifer forest where Northern Goshawk, White-headed Woodpecker, Hammond's Flycatcher, Golden-crowned Kinglet, Hermit Thrush, Hermit Warbler, and Cassin's Finch breed. Red Crossbill and Evening Grosbeak may also be found, depending upon the cone crop.

Nine miles beyond the intersection turn left off Icehouse Road and drive 0.75 mile to Union Valley Reservoir and Yellowjack Campground, boat-ramp, and parking area. Scan the reservoir for Eared Grebe, Canada Goose, Mallard, Common Merganser, and Belted Kingfisher. Search the shoreline for Killdeer and Spotted Sandpipers. Check the trees along the shore for Bald Eagle and Osprey. In winter, up to a half-dozen Bald Eagles can be expected around the reservoir, and both the eagles and Osprey breed there.

Afterwards, return to Icehouse Road, turn left, and continue another 2 miles to Robb's Peak Summit. Turn right at the sign to Van Vleck Ranch and continue 1.25 miles to a private pond on the right; stay on the road. Wood Duck, Mallard, and Lesser Scaup can often be found here. While returning to Icehouse Road, watch for Pileated Woodpecker, Golden-crowned Kinglet, Townsend's Solitaire, Hermit Thrush, and Cassin's Finch.

HOUSE WREN

MICHAEL O'BRIEN, DRAWING

Back on Icehouse Road, drive another 3.5 miles and turn right at the four-way intersection between Loon Lake and Gerle Reservoir. The 5-mile drive to Loon Lake (6400 feet) is beautiful with open granite slopes overlooking the Rubicon River. Watch for Osprey, Cooper's Hawk, Golden Eagle, Common Raven, Clark's Nutcracker, and Green-tailed Towhee.

Gerle Reservoir is north of the intersection, and Gerle Creek Campground in approximately 4 miles up the road. Park in the day-use area at the end of the campground and scan this small reservoir and inlet. Breeding Great Blue Heron, Canada Goose, Common Merganser, Ruddy Duck, Belted Kingfisher, and American Dipper can usually be found. This campground has restrooms and a wheelchair-accessible fishing pier, and an interpretive trail that explains Native American use of the area.

Backtrack about 18.5 miles to the intersection on Icehouse Road where you turned to reach Big Hill. Go left. Drive 1 mile toward Icehouse Reservoir and Campground and turn left onto Wrights Tie Road, which intersects with Wrights Lake Road. Turn left. Wrights Lake Campground is 6 miles beyond; park at the picnic area inside the campground. Check the area for Northern Goshawk and Sharp-shinned and Cooper's hawks, Mallard, Belted Kingfisher, Hairy and Black-backed woodpeckers, Williamson's Sapsucker, Lincoln's Sparrow, and Cassin's Finch.

To complete the Crystal Basin loop-route, drive south on Wrights Lake Road past the Wrights Tie Road intersection. Check the large meadow at the intersection for a patrolling Red-tailed Hawk. You likely will find Northern (Red-shafted) Flicker in the lodgepole pines in the meadow, also Tree and Violet-green swallows and Western Bluebird.

In the 8-mile return route to U.S. 50, watch for Mountain Quail, Townsend's Solitaire, and Dark-eyed Junco

while driving through the Wrights Fire burn. From U.S. 50, the town of Riverton, where the route began, is 13.5 miles to the right; South Lake Tahoe is 26.5 miles to the left.

The South Fork American River and China Flat area can serve as an extension to the Crystal Basin Route, since it begins just 5 miles from the end of the Wrights Lake Road. From the intersection of Wrights Lake Road and U.S. 50, turn right and drive west for 4.5 miles toward Placerville. Just before the town of Kyburz, take the Silver Fork Road on the left; this is a fairly sharp turn, so use caution. Follow the Silver Fork Road for 3 miles and look for the China Flat Campground sign on the right. Be alert for coveys of Mountain Quail with broods crossing the road along this route.

Walk through the campground and watch for White-headed Woodpecker, Steller's Jay, Red-breasted Nuthatch, Brown Creeper, Golden-crowned Kinglet, American Robin, and Yellow-rumped Warbler. Along the river you will find nesting Yellow and Wilson's warblers among the alder patches. Spotted Sandpipers frequent the islands and banks. You may catch a glimpse of some impressively large brook and rainbow trout in the many pools.

Near the middle of the campground is a bridge. Cross it and walk left into the old-growth patches of mixed conifers. Listen for the drumming of Pileated Woodpecker and watch for Northern Goshawk and Western Tanager. If you stay until dusk, both Spotted and Northern Saw-whet owls may be heard tuning up in spring.

If you are camping, the twenty-

seven-site China Flat campground is an excellent place to stay while birding the area. Where else can you bird, catch fresh fish for dinner, and enjoy the evening, relaxing around a campfire listening to one of the talks put on by the Forest Service?

Leaving China Flat Campground, turn right on Silver Fork Road, and drive 1.25 miles and turn left onto Forest Service Road (FS) 11N18 at the sign for Middle Creek/Long Canyon. Continue up this good dirt road for about a mile until you come to the inter-

GREAT BLUE HERON

section for Middle Creek and Long Canyon. Turn toward Middle Creek; there is a wire gate across this road; be courteous and close the gate after passing through.

The area beyond the gate burned in the early 1930s and again in the 1970s, creating a mosaic of pine and brush stands surrounding the creek. Look for nesting Sharp-shinned Hawks in the wooded areas and Prairie Falcons and Common Ravens soaring overhead. Check the large snags for White-headed Woodpecker, Northern Flicker, Olive-sided Flycatcher, Mountain Chickadee, and Red-breasted Nuthatch. Search the brushy areas for Mountain Quail, Anna's Hummingbird, MacGillivray's Warbler, Rufous-sided Towhee, Fox Sparrow, and the abundant Dark-eyed Junco.

In the early evening, watch for Common Poorwills foraging for moths and insects. This also is a good location, especially in late May and June, to hear Flammulated Owl. Long-eared Owls have been heard in the drainages just across from Middle Creek crossing.

Backtracking to the Silver Fork

CLARK'S NUTCRACKER

GAIL DIANE LUCKNER, DRAWING

Road, you can turn left and go 5 miles to the Silver Fork Campground and continue to bird along the river and more "old-growth" areas. Or you can turn right and return to Highway 50. At Highway 50, turn right and continue 9 miles to the Strawberry Lodge. Follow the frontage road at

the end of the lodge parking lot across the American River about 0.25 mile to Lovers' Leap Campground. This is a small campground, so park carefully off the road around the campground loop while you explore an interesting mix of forest-, brush-, and cliff-dwelling species: Anna's and Calliope hummingbirds, Nashville Warbler, Rufous-sided Towhee, Mountain Quail, Common Raven, and White-headed Woodpecker. Scouring the cliff face with binoculars may reward you with Golden Eagles that occasionally nest here, or a Prairie Falcon.

Return to Highway 50 and continue birding the high-elevation conifer forests the 17 miles from here to South Lake Tahoe, or return 42 miles to Placerville.

ACCOMMODATIONS ◆ WEATHER ◆ OTHER ATTRACTIONS

INDIAN PINK

LUPINE

When to visit. Spring through early summer is best. Snow or extreme fire conditions may make some areas inaccessible at other times of the year.

Where to stay. Numerous campgrounds on the Forest along the two birding routes; some sites accessible to individuals with disabilities. Motels in Pollock Pines and Placerville, and hotels in Placerville and South Lake Tahoe.

Weather and attire. Springtime is variable; daytime temperatures are usually warm, while nights are cold. Summers are warm and pleasant (70 to 90° F). Afternoon thunderstorms are common in fall. Winters are cold with snow typical above 5000 feet from December through May. A warm jacket or sweatshirt and rain-gear are recommended during spring and fall; bring a light jacket for cool nights in summer. In winter and early spring, carry tire chains and be prepared for snow. Some roads are plowed (U.S. 50 and Icehouse Road). Do not park your vehicle on the road during snow-removal conditions.

What else to do. Picnicking, hiking, boating, fishing, rafting, mountain-biking, and cross-country skiing. Nearby are Sly Park Recreation Area and Stumpy Meadows Reservoir. Lake Tahoe is an hour's drive away. Historic gold-mining displays at Coloma, Placerville, and Nevada City. Apple Hill in the Placerville area for fresh fruit in the fall and Christmas tree farms in the winter. Desolation Wilderness and Mokelumne Wilderness areas offer many hiking-trails along the Sierra Nevada crestline and opportunities to view alpine wildflowers and wildlife. Permits required for day use and overnight travel into the Wilderness Area.

For more information. General and camping information, District Office addresses, maps, bird list: Eldorado National Forest, Forest Information Center, 3070 Camino Heights Drive, Camino, California 95709; telephone 916/644-6048.

INYO FOREST
California

KEITH TAYLOR, DRAWING

EARED GREBE

HOW TO GET THERE. *The Mono Basin lies in the eastern central part of California at the junction of U.S. Route 395 and California Route 120. To get there from Los Angeles take Interstate 5 to Route 14 to Route 395. It is about 300 miles. From the San Francisco Bay area you can take Route 120 through Yosemite National Park (this road is closed in winter, usually November through May) or take U.S. Route 50 through South Lake Tahoe and south on U.S. 395, a trip of 250 to 300 miles, depending on the route.*

APPROPRIATELY NAMED after the Paiute Indian word for *dwelling-place of a great spirit,* the 1.96-million-acre Inyo National Forest encompasses large parts of the magnificent Sierra Nevada and the Glass, White, and Inyo mountains. The Forest is long and narrow, stretching 165 miles north-to-south and spreading 4 to 60 miles across. As might be expected, there are sharp contrasts. Elevations range from 3680 feet near Owens Dry Lake to the 14,495-foot summit of Mt. Whitney, highest peak in the contiguous United States. Precipitation varies dramatically. Mammoth Pass, for example, receives an average of 45 inches annually, mostly as snow between November and March; the eastern and lower portions of the Forest are much drier, with the town of Bishop (4140 feet) getting only 6 inches of precipitation yearly.

Plant and animal habitats are equally diverse—desert and wet meadow, forest and alpine tundra. Rugged, barren escarpments stand high above the forested hills, sagebrush flats, and grassy plateaus. Approximately 400 species of terrestrial vertebrates occur on the Forest,

O. TRUMAN HOLTZCLAW, PHOTOGRAPH

AN ANCIENT
BRISTLECONE PINE
ON THE WHITE MOUNTAINS
OF INYO NATIONAL FOREST

PRAIRIE FALCON

including several of special concern. Bald Eagle and Peregrine Falcon are federally regarded as threatened or endangered species and Willow Flycatcher is considered sensitive; among mammal species listed as sensitive are Sierra Nevada bighorn sheep, fisher, pine marten, wolverine, Sierra Nevada red fox, and Northern Goshawk. Of special interest are Tule elk, Nelson bighorn, Golden Eagle, and Prairie Falcon.

The Forest contains 1100 miles of streams and several hundred lakes, the most famous of which is Mono Lake, at an elevation of 6400 feet in the center of the 120,000-acre Mono Basin National Forest Scenic Area. Extending over 60 square miles, the lake was shaped by geological forces more than 700,000 years ago and is the second oldest such body of water in North America, after Lake Tahoe. It has no outlet. Throughout its long existence, salts and minerals have washed into the lake until Mono is now 2.5 times saltier than the ocean and 1000 times more alkaline than

seawater. As Mark Twain once wrote: "Its sluggish waters are so strong with alkali that if you only dip the most hopelessly soiled garment into them once or twice and wring it out, it will be found as clean as if it had been through the ablest of washer woman's hands." A swim is a memorable experience.

Only a few life-forms inhabit Mono Lake, but those that do thrive in astronomical numbers. The half-inch-long brine shrimp Artemia monica can be seen in the lake from April through December; an estimated four trillion individuals throng the waters at the height of summer. Together with the alkali fly Ephydra hyans, the shrimp provide a fabulous food-source for many birds.

Bird Life

A total of 279 species have been identified in the Mono Lake area, and 140 species have been recorded in the high country. Mono Lake has only recently been recognized for its importance in the link of feeding- and resting-sites for migratory birds and is, therefore, designated for protection as an "International Reserve" in the Western Hemisphere Shorebird Reserve Network. On a single day, approximately 100,000 Wilson's and 50,000 Red-necked phalaropes can depend upon Mono Lake during their annual intercontinental migration, and nearly 1,000,000 Eared Grebes pass through the area in the fall. Many water birds spend the winter at Mono, and a surprising number nest on the islands in the

lake or on the alkali flats, including about 400 Snowy Plovers, a California species of special concern.

Birding Routes

The most spectacular birding is at Mono Lake, and three routes are recommended for the lake and its environs: Mono Lake County Park, South Tufa, and Burger's Retreat. To sample other habitats and a different mix of birds, two additional routes are suggested: Crowley Lake and Ancient Bristlecone Pine Forest.

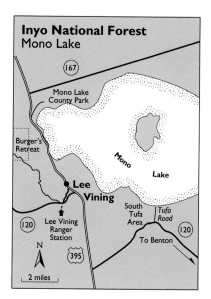

Mono Lake County Park, located on the north shore of the lake, can be reached by driving 4 miles north from Lee Vining on U.S. Route 395 to Cemetery Road; turn right and drive 0.4 mile east to the park entrance. You will want to hurry down to the lake by way of a one-third-mile boardwalk and start enjoying the spectacle. If you hit it on migration, the vast numbers of phalaropes and Eared Grebes will dazzle the eye. Scan, too, for migrant Common Loon, Pied-billed Grebe, Great Blue Heron, Northern Pintail, American Wigeon, Ring-necked and Ruddy ducks, Bufflehead, Western and Least sandpipers, and Long-billed Dowitcher.

Numbers of Ring-necked and Ruddy ducks winter at Mono, along with Tundra Swan, Snow and

WILSON'S PHALAROPE

Birdfinding in Forty National Forests and Grasslands

Canada geese, Canvasback, Lesser Scaup, and Common Goldeneye.

Although the islands themselves are closed April 1 to August 1 each year, you can use your binoculars to look for nesting California Gulls and scan the flats for Snowy Plovers. You should also find Canada Goose, Mallard, Cinnamon Teal, Gadwall, American Coot, Killdeer, Black-necked Stilt, American Avocet, Spotted Sandpiper, Wilson's Phalarope, and Caspian Tern.

The open marshy areas of the Park hold Virginia Rail and Sora, and also Common Snipe. Overhead, watch for Northern Harrier (year-round), Prairie Falcon and Common Nighthawk in summer, and Bald Eagle and Rough-legged Hawk in winter.

One of the beauties of the park is its excellent land-birding. A short walk north of the parking area (across the road) will bring you to a grove of cottonwoods, poplars, and old apple trees. Residents include: Black-billed Magpie, Plain Titmouse (rare summer and uncommon winter resident), Bushtit (rare summer and fairly common winter resident), and Bewick's Wren. This is also a good place to find migrants such as Lewis's Woodpecker (when the fruit is ripe), Calliope and Rufous hummingbirds, and Black-throated Gray, Townsend's, and MacGillivray's warblers. Summer breeders to look for include Red-breasted Sapsucker and Western Wood-Pewee, House Wren, Warbling Vireo, Black-headed Grosbeak, and Brewer's and Vesper sparrows. In winter, you might find an occasional Harris's Sparrow. Several eastern vagrants have been seen here over the years in late spring and in fall, such as Hooded, Black-and-white, and Blackpoll warblers, and Northern Parula.

South Tufa, on the south shore, is an excellent place to observe shorebirds and find sage-brush birds. Watch for

Bald Eagle as you drive south on U.S. 395 from Lee Vining about 5 miles to California Route 120 East, turn left and drive east another 5 miles toward Benton, and turn left at the sign for Mono Lake South Tufa area. From the parking lot, walk the mile-long loop-trail through the sage-brush to the tufa towers and shoreline. The sage-brush flats provide nesting-habitat for Brewer's Sparrow and Sage Thrasher (spring and summer) and for Sage Sparrow. Loggerhead Shrikes also frequent this area in search of insects and lizards. Green-tailed Towhees sing from the tops of shrubs, and Mountain Bluebirds patrol near their nests in the tufa towers. Noisy Pinyon Jays often stray out of the nearby forests, and Common Nighthawks swoop overhead at dusk and dawn. Pinyon Jays may also be seen along California Route 167 on the north side of the lake. In winter, the open country provides good hunting-grounds for Bald Eagles, Rough-legged Hawks, and Prairie Falcons.

As you approach the tufa grove, watch for Say's Phoebes that nest in the towers in spring and summer. The larger and more secluded towers also provide nesting-sites for Great Horned Owls, and Long-eared Owls occasionally are found here, as well.

Burger's Retreat is private property within the Mono Basin National Forest Scenic Area located 2 miles west of Lee Vining off Route 120 West at 8500-feet elevation. Owned by the Dallas Burger family, this 160-acre site has been designated as a wildlife sanctuary, and special care should be taken, especially during the fawning season from mid-June throughout July. One can bird along the road or park on the road and walk (the admonition to stay on the road refers

to vehicles). The road continues beyond Burger's property for several miles, but his property is marked by signs.

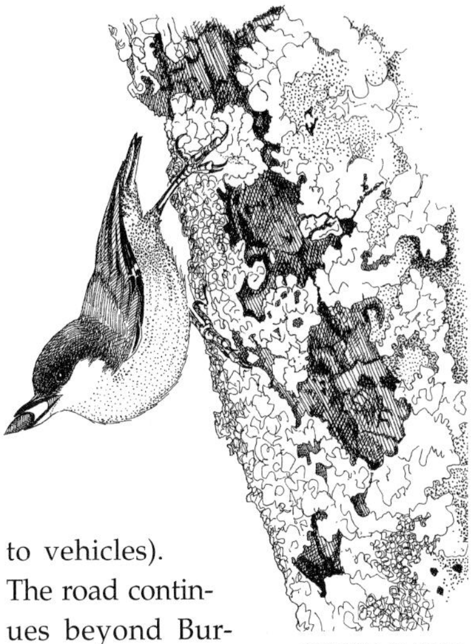

PYGMY NUTHATCH

To reach Burger's Retreat, drive south on U.S. 395 from Lee Vining for about a mile to Rt. 120 West. Turn right and drive about a mile to the Lee Vining Ranger Station on the left. Take the dirt road on the right, opposite the Ranger Station, and you will enter the reserve in about a mile; then continue on to the retreat. The road is steep and winding but passable for most vehicles. Habitats include open meadows, sage-brush, aspens, and pines. The open sage-brush-scrub areas, as well as the margins of the meadows and aspen groves, offer excellent birding.

Blue Grouse, Mountain Quail, Western Wood-Pewee, Dusky Flycatcher, Mountain Bluebird, Warbling Vireo, Orange-crowned Warbler, and Cassin's Finch frequent the open pine forest and sage-brush areas in late spring and summer. Red-breasted Sapsucker, Bewick's Wren, and Townsend's Solitaire prefer the willows and aspen groves. The more heavily wooded riparian areas contain Northern Pygmy-Owl (rare) and Pygmy Nuthatch. Watch, too, for Northern Goshawk (rare) in the dense forest broken by meadow or stream openings. Rock and Canyon wrens inhabit the areas with open boulders

AMERICAN WIGEON

and cliffs. Transient Rufous Hummingbirds, Say's Phoebes, and Western Tanagers can be expected in any of these habitats.

Crowley Lake. In late winter or early spring, there are two active Sage Grouse leks at Crowley Lake, about 25 miles south of Mono Lake. To reach them from U.S. Route 395, go east on Benton Crossing Road at the green church 1 mile south of Convict Lake Road. After 1.2 mile, take the dirt road to the right. When it forks, in about 0.7 mile, turn right and go about half-way to Crowley Lake. A large shortgrass meadow on the right is the only opening in the sage and is marked by signs to the lek. The second lek is reached by continuing east on Benton Crossing Road. Return to the paved road from the first lek, turn right, go 5.5 miles, and cross over the Owens River. The lek is 1.5 mile farther, on the left.

Ancient Bristlecone Pine Forest. In the White Mountains of Inyo National Forest Lake, ancient Bristle-cone Pines (*Pinus aristata*) survive at 11,000-feet altitude. One tree is 4700 years old, perhaps the oldest living thing on earth. Several are more than 4000 years old. Most have been beautifully sculpted over the centuries by elements of nature: fire, wind-blown sand, and ice particles. For this reason they have been referred to as "living driftwood." The trees grow slowly, often less than one inch in diameter every one hundred years. Yet they cling to life so fiercely that some wind-blown specimens have grown parallel to the earth rather than give in to the forces of nature. It is also significant that the cones of many of the oldest trees still produce fertile seeds.

The Ancient Bristlecone Pine Forest can be reached from Big Pine (13 miles south of Bishop, which is approximately 25 miles southeast of Lake Crowley on U.S. 395) by going about 12 miles east on Route 168 through Westgard Pass, where you may find Mountain Bluebird, "Plum-beous" Solitary Vireo, and a few Gray Flycatchers. At Tollhouse Spring (on left 8.4 miles from Big Pine at the 6000-feet elevation sign) there are Chukar, Calliope and Broad-tailed hummingbirds, Pinyon Jay, and Red Crossbill. Turn left at Westgard Pass onto White Mountain Road; travel about 10 miles to the Ancient Bristlecone Pine Forest. At the end of the paved road is the Schulman Grove with two self-guided trail hikes: Discovery Trail, a short walk, and Methuselah Trail, about 4 miles round trip. A few miles before you reach the Grove is the Sierra View vista-point with an utterly spectacular view of the Sierra Nevada. In the sage meadows just across the road from the visitors center, in summer and early fall you may see Sage Grouse. Around the visitors center and on the two trails, you can find Golden Eagle, Clark's Nutcracker, Pygmy Nuthatch, Mountain Bluebird, Green-tailed Towhee, Dark-eyed (Gray-headed) Junco, and Red Crossbill.

ACCOMMODATIONS ◆ WEATHER ◆ OTHER ATTRACTIONS

When to visit. Every season is special in the Mono Basin. In winter, the high country is covered with snow and can best be accessed on skis, snowshoes, or snowmobile. The area around Mono Lake is rarely snow-covered for long. Fall, spring, and summer, when migrants are present, provide the best birding; fewer species can be found in winter, although populations can be extensive.

Where to stay. Forest Service campgrounds in Lee Vining Canyon, county campgrounds in Lee Vining and Lundy Canyons. Convict Lake near Lake Crowley and along California 168. Several motels and an RV park in Lee Vining, Bishop, and Big Pine. If visiting the Ancient Bristlecone Pine Forest, Grandview Campground is about 4 miles from Schulman Grove.

AVALANCHE LILY

Weather and attire. It can snow in summer and be shirt-sleeve weather in winter. Never underestimate the possibilities; changes can be sudden and severe. Temperatures generally range from the 90s in summer to about minus 10° F in winter. Warm clothing is often appropriate in summer, especially in early mornings and evenings. Sunblock or a hat is useful, and insect repellent is recommended, especially in spring.

What else to do. The east entrance to Yosemite National Park is only 12 miles west of Lee Vining on Rte. 120. Bodie State Historic Park, the West's best preserved ghost town, is an hour's drive north of Lee Vining. Each of the larger towns in Owens Valley (Bishop, Big Pine, Independence, and Lone Pine) has a major road leading up the eastern scarp of the Sierra into the unique "rainshadow" forest with other exciting birds like Blue Grouse, Mountain Quail, American Dipper, Townsend's Solitaire, and rosy-finch.

For more information. General and campground information, District Office addresses, maps, bird list: Inyo National Forest, 873 N. Main Street, Bishop, California 93514; telephone 619/837-2400. The Mono Basin Scenic Area Visitors Center is located on U.S. Route 395, 0.5 mile north of Lee Vining; telephone 619/647-3044.

The Rocky Mountains and Arizona

FLATHEAD FOREST
Montana

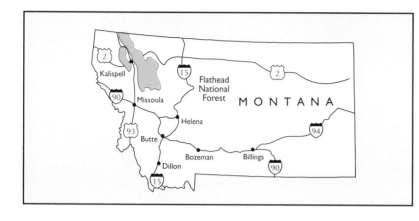

How to get there. *The Flathead National Forest headquarters is centrally located in Kalispell. Kalispell is 120 miles north of Missoula, on U.S. Route 93. District offices are located in Whitefish, Bigfork, Columbia Falls, Hungry Horse, and at Spotted Bear.*

ROAD ON FLATHEAD NATIONAL FOREST

LOCATED IN NORTHWESTERN Montana and named for the Flathead Indians, the 2.3-million-acre Flathead National Forest represents the heart of the northern Rocky Mountain wild lands. Almost half of the Forest area is designated wilderness, stretching across parts of five mountain ranges drained by five major rivers: South Fork, Middle Fork, and North Fork of the Flathead River, and the Stillwater and Swan Rivers. All five flow into the two-hundred-square-mile Flathead Lake, the largest natural freshwater lake in the northwestern U.S.

Elevations range from 3000 feet in the valleys to more than 8000 feet at the mountain summits. Lush forests blanket the mountainsides. Ponderosa, western white, and lodgepole pines, Douglas-fir, western larch, grand fir, and western red-cedar thrive on the slopes; whitebark pine and alpine larch grow in the higher valleys; and subalpine fir and Engelmann spruce occur on the high ridges.

The Forest remains one of the last strongholds of grizzly bears in the Lower Forty-Eight. Gray wolves are here as well, recolonizing from

Canada. Both the grizzly and the wolf are secretive and difficult to find. Mountain lions, bobcats, and pine martens are other unobtrusive inhabitants of the forest, along with elk and white-tailed and mule deer. River otters, beaver, muskrats, and moose can be found along rivers and streams.

Bird Life

More than two hundred species of birds have been recorded on the Flathead's diversity of lakes and rivers, streams and wetlands, coniferous forests, and alpine communities.

Lakes and rivers provide habitat for breeding Common Loons, Red-necked Grebes, Great Blue Herons, Ospreys, Bald Eagles, Canada Geese, Barrow's Goldeneyes, and Common Mergansers. Watch along streams and wetlands for Mallard, Wood, Ring-necked, and Harlequin ducks, Spotted Sandpiper, and American Dipper. During the spring and fall migration, open water areas often teem with a variety of waterfowl, as many as 100,000 birds, representing 24 species, including Tundra Swan.

Flathead's coniferous forest community

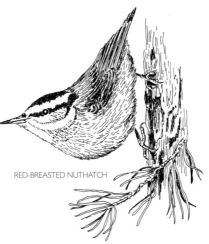
RED-BREASTED NUTHATCH

supports Vaux's Swift, Hammond's Flycatcher, Black-capped and Mountain chickadees, Red-breasted Nuthatch, Brown Creeper, Swainson's and Varied thrushes, Yellow-rumped Warbler, and Pine Siskin. The higher spruce–fir forests contain several specialty birds, such as Blue and Spruce grouse, Boreal Owl, Three-toed Woodpecker, and Pine Grosbeak, and the higher alpine habitats provide habitat for White-tailed Ptarmigan, Clark's Nutcracker, Gray-crowned Rosy-Finch, and White-crowned Sparrow, but are difficult to reach. A few species, such as Black-backed Woodpecker and Mountain Bluebird, prefer recently burned sites, but Black-backed Woodpecker will not be found reliably forever—once the bark insects are gone, the bird leaves. One such burn site occurs along the

Flathead National Forest
Tally Lake Route

North Fork of the Flathead River, located along U.S. Route 93 between Olney and Stryker.

Birding Routes

A variety of Forest birds can be found at two locations: Tally Lake provides excellent lowland birding, while Jewel Basin offers good highland birding.

Tally Lake. This site is located about 20 miles northwest of Kalispell. From the intersection of U.S. 93 and Montana Route 35, drive north 1 mile on U.S. 93 to Reserve Street, and west on Reserve Street for 4 miles to the Farm-to-Market Road. Turn right (north) onto the Farm-to-Market Road and drive 9 miles (past Kuhn's Wildlife Management Area, a good place to see Ruffed Grouse and possibly Wild Turkey) to Forest Service Road (FS) 913. Then turn left onto FS 913 (at times narrow and winding) and follow it for 8 miles to Tally Lake Campground. This road is impassable from November to early May due to snow and ice.

At the campground, park at the picnic area next to the swimming-beach, a good place to find Gray Jay, Black-capped Chickadee, Red-breasted Nuthatch, Brewer's Blackbird, Black-headed Grosbeak,

GRIZZLY BEAR

PATRICIA J. MOORE, DRAWING

MIMI HOPPE WOLF, DRAWING

GREAT HORNED OWL

Hairy and Pileated woodpeckers, and Northern (Red-shafted) Flicker. Watch for nesting Ruby-crowned Kinglets and Swainson's and Varied thrushes. Soaring Turkey Vultures can usually be found overhead, as well as eagles, Cooper's, Red-tailed, and Rough-legged hawks, and American Kestrels. And, on spring evenings, the deep hooting calls of Great Horned Owls and the repetitive whistles of Northern Saw-whet Owls can be heard here.

On your return to Kalispell, stop at a marshy area a mile south of Tally Lake on FS 913 to listen for the wonderful song of Hermit Thrush, the rapid, melodious song of Winter Wren, and the musical whistle-notes of Northern Oriole.

Jewel Basin Route. This route offers trail access to Mt. Aeneas, at 10,000 feet the highest point in the Forest, miles of backcountry trails, and more than thirty pristine, high-mountain lakes. Jewel Basin is 15 miles east of Kalispell, and the scenic loop-hiking route is recommended. This is a designated hiking area—no horses or bicycles. From Kalispell, take U.S. 93 south for 6.8 miles to the

and Cedar Waxwing. A 40-acre riparian zone borders the mouth of swift-flowing Logan Creek, containing a network of wildlife trails that provide access into good birding habitat.

Follow the gravel path north to a footbridge across Logan Creek. Red-naped Sapsucker and Tree and Violet-green swallows nest in cottonwoods and aspens along the creek. American Dippers can often be found feeding along the rocky stream. Take time to watch these fascinating creatures searching for food among the rapids.

From the bridge, walk east through the willows toward the lake, watching for hummingbirds (Calliope, Rufous, and Black-chinned), Willow Flycatcher, Gray Catbird, Cedar Waxwing, Common Yellowthroat, American Redstart, MacGillivray's Warbler, and Fox Sparrow. Beyond, where the trail passes the

lake inlet, scan the lake for Blue-winged Teal, Ring-necked Duck, Barrow's Goldeneye, Bufflehead, Common Merganser, and American Coot. Check the far lakeshore for Bald Eagles; a nest is visible on the hillside.

From the creek mouth, you can follow the narrow shoreline north to the upland forest, watching for Great Blue Herons along the way, or brave the wildlife trails northwest through the drier shrubs to a wetland where a great variety of birds, including Warbling Vireos, can be found. Watch, too, for ungulate antler-rubs on the shrubs and small trees, poisonous prairie rattlesnakes (rare), and harmless garter snakes.

The northwest corner of the area, across FS 2895, contains black cottonwoods and south-facing upland-forest habitats. Four species of woodpecker reside here in spring and summer: Red-naped Sapsucker,

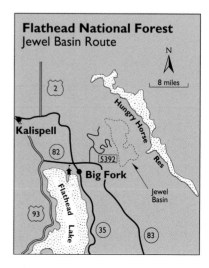

Flathead National Forest
Jewel Basin Route

Birdfinding in Forty National Forests and Grasslands

Montana Route 82 junction, just before the town of Somers. Watch for Yellow-headed Blackbirds and Western Meadowlarks along U.S. 93. Soon after turning left onto Rte. 82, look for water birds in the adjacent wetlands: Horned Grebe, Common Merganser, Barrow's Goldeneye, Bufflehead, Ruddy Duck, Virginia and Sora rails, American Coot, Killdeer, and Black Tern. You may find Downy Woodpecker among the willows, as well as Yellow and MacGillivray's warblers and Willow Flycatchers.

Continue east on Rte. 82 for 7 miles across the Flathead River to Montana Route 35. Rte. 82 passes through an incredible diversity of biotic communities from agricultural lands to wetland forests. This area is included in the annual Bigfork Christmas Bird Count; eighty-four species were recorded in 1991, easily the highest total in Montana. Ospreys nest on telephone poles. Loggerhead Shrikes sit on telephone wires. Great Horned Owls doze on fence posts. Bald Eagle, Northern Harrier, and Common Raven fly overhead. Keep a lookout for Rough-legged Hawk, American Kestrel, Ring-necked Pheasant, Sandhill Crane (occasional), Belted Kingfisher, Bohemian Waxwing, and Red-winged and Yellow-headed blackbirds, as well.

At the junction of Rtes. 35 and 82, turn south toward Bigfork, and in 0.25 mile turn left (east) on Montana Route 83 toward Swan Lake. Follow Rte. 83 for about 2.8 miles to the Echo Lake Road. Then follow the Echo Lake Road for 2.3 miles to a fork, where you should turn right (sign for Jewel Basin) onto a road that leads to a junction with the gravel Jewel Basin Road (FS 5392) in 1.1 miles. Follow FS 5392 for 6.6 miles to the Jewel Basin parking area and trailhead. The final 5 miles are steep, narrow, and contain drainage dips. Be careful, especially if you are driving a low-clearance vehicle; trailers are not recommended.

RING-NECKED DUCK

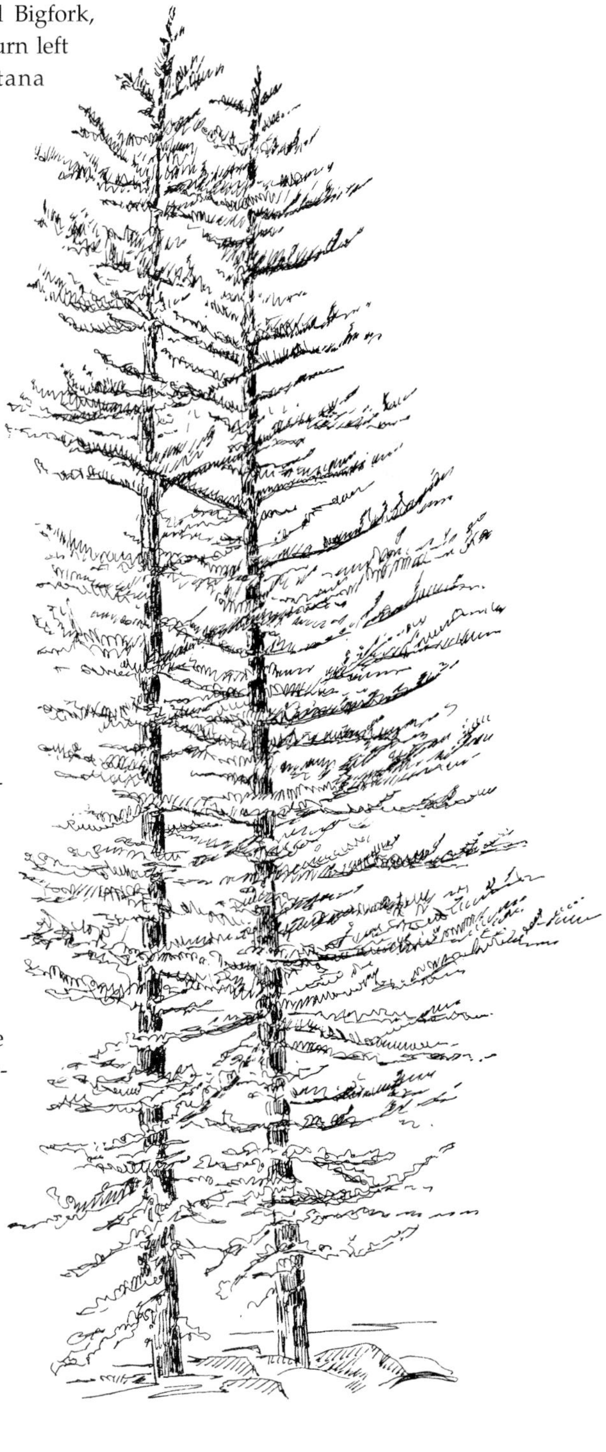

WESTERN LARCHES

The mixed montane forest along the route supports a variety of breeding birds, including Hairy and Pileated woodpeckers, Steller's Jay, Chestnut-backed Chickadee, Hermit Thrush, Western Tanager, and Dark-eyed Junco. At the trailhead and on the hike, expect a number of higher-elevation species, including three species of grouse (Ruffed, Spruce, and Blue), Gray Jay, Clark's Nutcracker, Ruby-crowned and Golden-crowned kinglets, Mountain Chickadee, Gray-crowned Rosy-Finch (alpine tundra), and Pine Siskin.

In fall, numerous raptors pass through the Jewel Basin: Sharp-shinned and Red-tailed hawks, Golden Eagle, American Kestrel, and Merlin.

HERMIT THRUSH

DAVID A. SIBLEY, DRAWING

ACCOMMODATIONS ◆ WEATHER ◆ OTHER ATTRACTIONS

When to visit. Late spring, summer, and early fall are best. Hunting season runs from October through late November. Of the Montana forests covered, only the Flathead provides any type of winter bird-watching opportunities. (Remember that you are in grizzly country—please contact the local ranger stations for their brochure on the precautions to be taken.)

Where to stay. Five developed fee campgrounds and fourteen primitive campgrounds on the Forest. Tally Lake Campground has thirty-nine fee sites, including a picnic area, swimming beach, and group-use facility. Dispersed camping throughout much of the Forest, and commercial campgrounds in the Flathead Valley and adjacent Glacier National Park. Motels, bed-and-breakfast facilities, lodges, and cabins are located in the Flathead Valley.

Weather and attire. Weather can change rapidly. Summer days normally are warm and dry with occasional afternoon thunder storms, but summer nights are cool. Winters are generally cloudy, cold, and wet with abundant snow. Be prepared with warm clothes and rain-gear any time of year.

What else to do. More than 2000 miles of hiking-trails, which range from easy day-hikes to challenging backpacking trips. Sightseeing 110 miles of roadways; fly-fishing; cross-country skiing in winter. River-running in summer; more than 200 miles of the North, Middle, and South Forks of the Flathead River are designated as Wild and Scenic Rivers; caution necessary during high water when dangerous rapids and log jams occur.

Glacier National Park is adjacent to the northeast Forest boundary. The Swan River and Ninepipes National Wildlife Refuges (both good places to observe migrating and breeding waterfowl), and the National Bison Range are located nearby to the south. The Big Mountain near Whitefish is a popular alpine skiing resort. Visit Flathead Lake in summer for sailing, windsurfing, and water-skiing.

For more information. General information, District Office addresses, maps, bird list: Flathead National Forest, 1935 Third Avenue East, Kalispell, Montana 59901; telephone 406/755-5401.

BISON

INDIAN PAINTBRUSH

CARL JAMESFREEMAN, DRAWING

LOLO FOREST
Montana

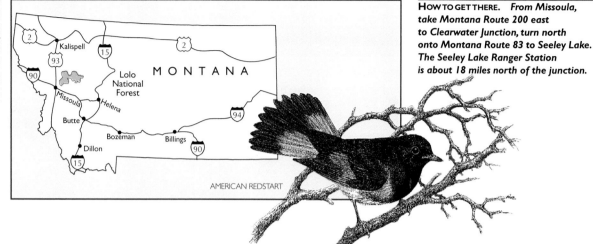

HOW TO GET THERE. *From Missoula, take Montana Route 200 east to Clearwater Junction, turn north onto Montana Route 83 to Seeley Lake. The Seeley Lake Ranger Station is about 18 miles north of the junction.*

AMERICAN REDSTART

ALONG THE BLACKFOOT RIVER, LOLO NATIONAL FOREST

CROWNED BY RUGGED MOUNTAINS and carved by crystalline rivers, Montana's 2-million-acre Lolo National Forest offers sensational scenery and one of the most varied assemblages of birds and mammals to be found anywhere in the Rocky Mountains. Black bear, elk, mule deer, coyote, and badger wander the Forest floor. The endangered grizzly bear and gray wolf find a home here. In summer, verdant high mountain meadows carpeted with wildflowers become a mecca for brilliant butterflies.

Bird Life

All told, more than two hundred species of birds have been recorded on the Forest. Stands of craggy whitebark pines along the ridges provide habitat for Clark's Nutcracker, Mountain Bluebird, Pine Grosbeak, and an occasional Cooper's Hawk.

Subalpine meadows and the surrounding forest are home to Great Gray and Boreal owls, both rare. The Boreal is best seen and heard in February and March at Lolo Pass on U.S. Route 12, about 45 minutes west of Missoula; a parking area

VEERY

wood-habitat attracts Ruffed Grouse, Willow, Least, and Cordilleran flycatchers, Veery, Gray Catbird, Red-eyed Vireo, American Redstart, MacGillivray's Warbler, Northern Waterthrush, and Fox Sparrow.

Birding Route

Clearwater Lakes. This area offers the best birding route on the Lolo Forest. It begins at the Seeley Lake Ranger Station along Montana Route 83, a 1.5-hour drive northeast from Missoula. The area runs along the Clearwater River, which contains rich wetlands of spruce, larch, alder, willow, and reed.

Check the wetlands near the ranger station first. Look for American Bittern, Bald Eagle, and more than two dozen songbirds, such as Willow Flycatcher, Warbling Vireo, and Yellow, Yellow-rumped, and MacGillivray's warblers. The lake also supports nesting Common Loons. From May through September, this magnificent bird can usually be found here with little effort; its wild call is pure delight. During the breeding season from April 15 to July 15, remember to stay at least 300 yards away from nesting birds.

One mile north of the ranger station, on Rte. 83, is a wildlife-viewing sign that directs visitors to the put-in point for the Clearwater River Canoe Trail. This easy 3.5-mile canoe-route along the willow-lined river provides excellent opportunities to see nesting Great Blue Heron, Osprey, Rufous Hummingbird, Red-naped Sapsucker, Willow Flycatcher, Gray Cat-

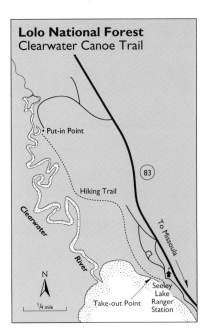

Lolo National Forest
Clearwater Canoe Trail

Put-in Point

83

Hiking Trail

Clearwater River

To Missoula

N

Take-out Point

Seeley Lake Ranger Station

1/4 mile

andinformation station, open during the day, is located at the top of the pass.

In breeding season, the lower mountain slopes ring with the songs of Townsend's and Yellow-rumped warblers and Western Tanager. The (return) Canoe Hiking Trail north of Seeley Lake Ranger Station may include Northern Goshawk, Barred Owl, Pileated Woodpecker, Red-naped and Williamson's sapsuckers, and North America's smallest bird—Calliope Hummingbird. Numerous woodpeckers frequent recently burned areas; Downy, Hairy, and Pileated woodpeckers and Northern Flickers feast on the wood- and bark-boring beetles that invade dead and dying trees. The uncommon Black-backed and Three-toed woodpeckers appear almost before the flames die down. Look for them on the Blackfoot/Clearwater Game Range or North Fork Blackfoot River Trailhead (28 miles east on Montana Route 200) and North Fork Blackfoot Road. Harlequin Duck and American Dipper inhabit rocky, fast-moving mountain rivers. Riparian willow-and-cotton-

bird, Yellow and MacGillivray's warblers, American Redstart, and Northern Waterthrush. Watch also for the abundant western painted turtle, muskrat, and white-tailed deer, and an occasional moose. You can also find Barrow's Goldeneye on the lake and Red-naped Sapsucker on the shores of the lake and on the hiking-trail.

The canoe trail take-out point is at the north end of Seeley Lake at the ranger station. You can leave your canoe here and hike back along the 1.5-mile trail to the put-in point, where you parked your vehicle.

If you prefer, you can make it a hiking-excursion only by walking the trail up and back from the Ranger Station. The route offers excellent birding. The first half-mile of the trail winds through an old-growth spruce-and-larch forest where you may find Northern Goshawk (rare), Pileated Woodpecker, Brown Creeper, Solitary Vireo, and Red Crossbill.

Stop at the wildlife-viewing-blind near the ranger station to scope the marsh. Here, in spring and summer, can be found Common Loon, Red-necked Grebe, American Bittern, Great Blue Heron, Tundra Swan

BARROW'S GOLDENEYE

MIMI HOPPE WOLF, DRAWINGS

(spring and fall), Cinnamon Teal, Sandhill Crane, and Yellow-headed Blackbird. Bald Eagles sometimes frequent the mouth of the marsh. And at the north end of the marsh, not far from the viewing-blind, the trail runs along a small gravel dike. Look here for marsh and other birds, including Great Blue Heron, Virginia Rail, Sora, Red-naped Sapsucker, Willow Flycatcher, Gray Catbird, Warbling Vireo, and Yellow and MacGillivray's warblers.

TUNDRA SWAN

ACCOMMODATIONS ◆ WEATHER ◆ OTHER ATTRACTIONS

When to visit.   The best months are late April through September, and the best birding is from May through mid-July.

Where to stay.   Several Forest campgrounds and nearby state and private locations. Motels in Seeley Lake and Clearwater Junction. Advance reservations necessary on summer weekends.

Weather and attire.   Spring and fall are unpredictable; it can snow anytime. Winters are stormy with temperatures in the teens. Summer runs from late June to August, when temperatures can be warm in the daytime and cool at night. Always be prepared for sudden changes in the weather; bring a jacket and a raincoat. Expect mosquitoes in spring and early summer.

What else to do.   Scenic drives along the Clearwater River complex; hikes to waterfalls, avalanche chutes, fire lookouts, and the 74,000-acre Scrapegoat Wilderness Area; canoeing, boating, and sailing; cross-country skiing and snowmobiling on the Forest. To canoe, either bring your own canoe, life-jackets, and paddles, or rent them locally. Ask at the Ranger Station for rental sources. Glacier National Park, Blackfoot/Clearwater Game Range at Clearwater Junction, National Bison Range, and Ninepipe National Wildlife Refuge are all within easy driving distance of Missoula.

For more information.   General and campground information, District Office addresses, maps, Wildlife Viewing Fact Sheets, bird list: Lolo National Forest, Building 24, Fort Missoula, Missoula, Montana 59801; telephone 406/329-3750.

COMMON LOONS

BITTERROOT FOREST
Montana and Idaho

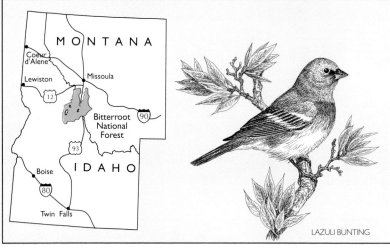

MIMI HOPPE WOLF, DRAWING

HOW TO GET THERE. *From Missoula take U.S. Route 93 south 25 miles to Stevensville. Turn right on the Indian Prairie Loop Road, three miles south of the Stevensville turnoff on U.S. 93 between markers 63 and 64. After 1.3 miles, turn right on St. Mary's Road and after 0.5 mile turn left onto St. Mary's Lookout Road.*

LAZULI BUNTING

BASS CREEK TRAIL IN BITTERROOT NATIONAL FOREST WITH THE BITTERROOT MOUNTAINS IN THE BACKGROUND

LEE F. SNYDER, PHOTOGRAPH

ESTABLISHED IN 1897, the Bitterroot National Forest was one of the earliest of our national Forest preserves and holds the double distinction of being the first to have a permanent ranger station for resource management. Like so many parts of the West, the 1.6 million-acre Forest and its environs offer a study in ecological contrasts. At a 3500-foot elevation, the Bitterroot River valley, with its private lands of river-bottom and foothills, is one of the lowest in western Montana, while the surrounding National Forest rises to more than 10,000 feet. Annual precipitation ranges from a semi-arid 10 to 12 inches in the valley, to 90 inches or more in the Bitterroot Mountains to the west.

This diversity of altitude and climate produces habitats that range from sage-brush grasslands on the warmest and driest areas to mesic spruce forests in cooler, wetter places. Cottonwood and aspen occupy riparian locales, while conifer forests dominate the upland sites. Wildflowers abound in the valley and on the alpine tundra. In fact,

GOLDEN EAGLE

JULIE ZICKEFOOSE, DRAWING

the forest is named for the unique bitterroot flower, whose tuberous root served as a dietary staple for the local Kootenai/Salish Indians. In spring, showy yellow balsamroot mixed with purple lupine and pastel red paintbrush creates a spectacular mosaic on south-facing slopes. The large flowers of low elevations contrast with the minute blossoms of alpine phlox and heath. Flowering shrubs like chokecherry, ninebark, mock orange, and dogwood add to the display in late April, May, and June.

The Bitterroot has its full share of sought-after megafauna. Rocky Mountain elk inhabit the entire Forest and are readily visible in early spring. Mule and white-tailed deer, moose, Rocky Mountain bighorn sheep, and mountain goats can easily be found in select environments. Other large mammals, such as black bear, mountain lion, bobcat, pine marten, and wolverine, also occur on the Forest, but population densities are low, and it would be a real treat to run across any of these species. Smaller mammals, like yellow-pine chipmunk, golden-mantled ground-squirrel, yellow-bellied marmot, and pika are never more than a few steps away at higher elevations. And swallowtail and painted lady butterflies are everywhere during some years.

Bird Life

At least 170 species of birds occur in the Bitterroot Valley and surrounding National Forest. Migratory waterfowl and shorebirds visit the valley bottom. The Forest provides a wide range of upland species, including Northern Goshawk, Golden Eagle, Ruffed Grouse, the hard-to-find Spruce Grouse, Wild (Merriam's) Turkey, Western Screech-Owl, Flammulated, Great Horned, Barred, Boreal, and Northern Saw-whet owls, Northern Pygmy-Owl, and Vaux's Swift. Also look for Lewis's, Black-backed, and Pileated woodpeckers, Violet-green and Cliff swallows, White-breasted and Pygmy nuthatches, American Dipper, Western and Mountain bluebirds, Swainson's, Hermit, and Varied thrushes, Townsend's Solitaire, MacGillivray's Warbler, Western Tanager, Lazuli Bunting, Black-headed, Pine, and Evening grosbeaks, Red and White-winged (rare) crossbills, and Pine Siskin.

A few birds occur here only in the cold months and move north to breed. Up to thirty Bald Eagles winter on the forest, along with Rough-legged Hawk, Bohemian Waxwing, Northern Shrike, and Common and Hoary (difficult in this part of the state) redpolls.

Birding Routes

For the hiking birder, U.S. Route 93 south of the Missoula provides access to four prime birding spots. Two areas, St. Mary's Peak Trail and St. Mary's Lookout Road, provide good birding for a one-day excursion in late spring and summer. Two other nearby places worthy of a visit are the Charles Waters campground for low-elevation forest and riparian species, and the Willoughby Tract for sage-brush and grassland species. For the hardy winter visitor and owl lover, Lost Trail Pass, 45 miles south of Hamilton on U.S. 93, is accessible in the winter months of the owl breeding season.

St. Mary's Peak Trail is reached by St. Mary's Lookout Road (FS 739). This road is single-lane with numerous turnouts suitable for all passenger vehicles, but not for cars with trailers or for large recreation vehicles. The 13-mile St. Mary's Lookout Road passes through a low-elevation ponderosa pine and Douglas-fir forest that, with increasing elevation, gradually changes to a subalpine forest dominated by lodgepole pine and subalpine fir. At mid-elevation, notice the old stands of western larch trees as you proceed up the road.

BOREAL OWL FAMILY

Road passes through a young ponderosa pine forest with a shrubby understory. Watch here for Ruffed Grouse in the small draws, Rufous-sided Towhee in the understory, and White-breasted and Pygmy nuthatches, Brown Creeper, and Western Tanager in the forest.

At about mile 10, where the road ascends into a rather wet forest dominated by western larch trees, stop and bird along the roadway. Here you are likely to find Hairy and Pileated woodpeckers, Red-breasted, White-breasted, and Pygmy nuthatches, Hammond's and Cordilleran flycatchers, and Red and White-winged crossbills. Four of the small owls occur here on occasion, as well, although three of these are active only at night—Western Screech-Owl, Flammulated Owl, and Northern Saw-whet Owl. Northern Pygmy-Owl is often about during the daylight hours; its *too too too* call can help to locate this little raptor.

From the end of the St. Mary's Lookout Road, a well-marked trail, rated moderately-strenuous, climbs gradually for 4.5 miles through subalpine forest to alpine meadows at 9300 feet. The bird life includes Hairy Woodpecker, Hammond's and Cordilleran flycatchers, Black-capped and Mountain chickadees, Ruby-crowned Kinglet, Mountain Bluebird, and Yellow-rumped Warbler. The fortunate birder may also find Three-toed and Black-backed woodpeckers. Calliope and Broad-tailed (rare) hummingbirds may be seen feeding among the abundant alpine flowers, especially in fall. And in the highest meadows, watch for Gray-crowned Rosy-Finch along the edges of melting snowbanks.

Look carefully at the raptors soaring on the summer thermals. Golden Eagle and Prairie Falcon might be found among the more common Red-tailed Hawks and American Kestrels. Black Swifts have also been seen feeding on airborne insects, although there are no breeding records in the area. In addition, yellow-pine chipmunks and golden-mantled ground-squirrels and mountain goats are occasionally seen on the rocky crags.

The views from St. Mary's Lookout are magnificent. In the foreground, alpine vegetation abounds. Glacial tarns (small mountain lakes) are visible to the left and right. Subalpine larches are abundant in the glacial basins; their feathery green spring and summer dress changes to spectacular yellow colors in late fall. And the Bitterroot Valley, from Darby to Stevensville, lies in full view.

The Lee Metcalf National Wildlife Refuge, located on the Bitterroot Valley floor, shimmers in the summer sun, and beyond are the rolling hills of the Sapphire Range. Look south along the Bitterroot Range where Trapper Peak (highest peak in the range at 10,157 feet) dominates the skyline. To the southwest is extensive wilderness: Selway–Bitterroot and Frank Church River-of-No-Return

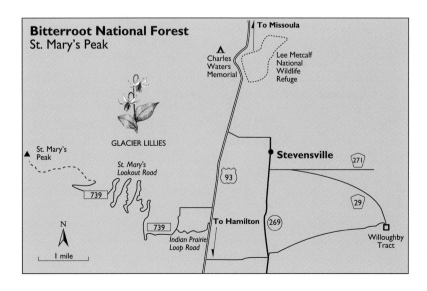

Bitterroot National Forest
St. Mary's Peak

To Missoula

Charles Waters Memorial

Lee Metcalf National Wildlife Refuge

GLACIER LILLIES

St. Mary's Peak

St. Mary's Lookout Road

Stevensville

271

93

29

739

739

To Hamilton   269

Indian Prairie Loop Road

Willoughby Tract

N

1 mile

wilderness areas comprise the largest contiguous wilderness area in the Lower Forty-Eight states.

The Charles Waters Campground is 3.5 miles north of the Stevensville turnoff and 2 miles west of Route 93 on County Road 22. The campground, surrounded by ponderosa pine, Douglas-fir, and lodgepole pine, offers opportunities to view forest and riparian birds by walking the road and Bass Creek Trail. Black-capped and Mountain chickadees are permanent residents, as are Red-breasted, White-breasted, and the less common Pygmy nuthatches and the Brown Creeper. Winter Wrens nest along Bass Creek, and American Dippers commonly inhabit the rushing stream. Red-eyed and Solitary vireos' songs are heard along with the flute-like songs of the Hermit and

CALLIOPE HUMMINGBIRD

Varied thrushes. Vagrant flocks of Red Crossbills and Evening Grosbeaks occasionally move noisily through the Forest.

Willoughby Tract. Take Montana Route 269 south of Stevensville to Montana Route 271. Go east 2 miles to Montana Route 29 (South Burnt Fork Road) on the right. Follow Route 29 in a southeasterly direction for approximately 4 miles, then head one mile due south off Rte. 29. The 40-acre tract of National Forest land

isolated by private surroundings offers a one-mile loop hiking-trail through sage-brush and grasslands, where you will find Western Meadowlark and Vesper Sparrow. Tree Swallow, Black-capped Chickadee, Mountain Bluebird, and Western Tanager are common.

Lost Trail Pass. The most sought-after of the owls that nest in the Bitterroot National Forest is the elusive Boreal Owl, which nests in conifer forests above 6000 feet and calls in February and March. The Lost Trail Pass Ski Area parking lot, 75 miles south of Stevensville on U.S. 93 near the Idaho border, provides an outstanding location to hear this diminutive species. It also has been heard near mile marker 3 along U.S. 93, three miles north of the state line.

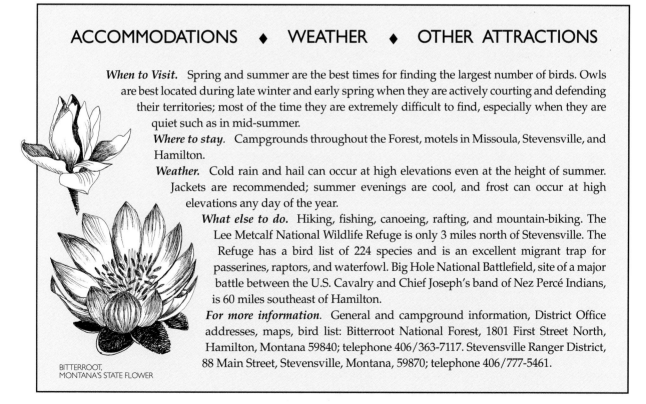

ACCOMMODATIONS ◆ WEATHER ◆ OTHER ATTRACTIONS

When to Visit. Spring and summer are the best times for finding the largest number of birds. Owls are best located during late winter and early spring when they are actively courting and defending their territories; most of the time they are extremely difficult to find, especially when they are quiet such as in mid-summer.

Where to stay. Campgrounds throughout the Forest, motels in Missoula, Stevensville, and Hamilton.

Weather. Cold rain and hail can occur at high elevations even at the height of summer. Jackets are recommended; summer evenings are cool, and frost can occur at high elevations any day of the year.

What else to do. Hiking, fishing, canoeing, rafting, and mountain-biking. The Lee Metcalf National Wildlife Refuge is only 3 miles north of Stevensville. The Refuge has a bird list of 224 species and is an excellent migrant trap for passerines, raptors, and waterfowl. Big Hole National Battlefield, site of a major battle between the U.S. Cavalry and Chief Joseph's band of Nez Percé Indians, is 60 miles southeast of Hamilton.

For more information. General and campground information, District Office addresses, maps, bird list: Bitterroot National Forest, 1801 First Street North, Hamilton, Montana 59840; telephone 406/363-7117. Stevensville Ranger District, 88 Main Street, Stevensville, Montana, 59870; telephone 406/777-5461.

BITTERROOT, MONTANA'S STATE FLOWER

DEERLODGE FOREST
Montana

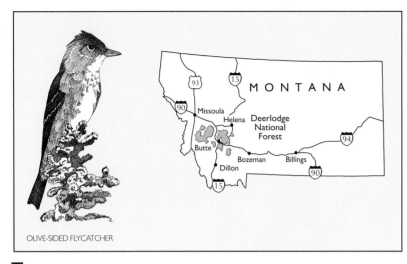

OLIVE-SIDED FLYCATCHER

HOW TO GET THERE. *From Butte take Interstate 90 west for 15 miles to the Montana 1 exit. Follow this highway (also known as the Pintler Scenic Route) west for 6 miles through Anaconda and then 17 miles to Georgetown Lake. The Lake can also be reached by taking the Drummond Exit on I-90, which is 50 miles east of Missoula, and going south on Rte. 1 through Philipsburg for 40 miles.*

THE SHOSHONE INDIANS named the Deerlodge area for a geyser-like calcite mound near a warm springs where white-tailed deer would come to feed in winter. Legend holds that this site is where deer were created and born on the earth. It was the deer's lodge.

The Deerlodge National Forest (1.2 million acres) straddles the Continental Divide for 150 miles and includes sections of eight separate mountain ranges that vary in elevation from 4075 to 10,950 feet. Location, landform, climate, and the Forest's broad range of habitat combine to give Deerlodge yet another of the West's rich biological mixes. Habitats include rivers and lakes, willow riparian areas, dry grasslands, sagebrush parks, wet meadows, aspen stands, extensive mature and old-growth forests, and alpine tundra.

Lodgepole and whitebark pines, Douglas-fir, subalpine fir, and Engelmann spruce are the major tree species on the Forest. A few locations have alpine larch and ponderosa pine. Among the more common wildflowers are pasqueflower, glacier lily, cinquefoil, Indian paintbrush, bitterroot, and lupine.

Large mammals include elk, moose, mule deer, bighorn sheep, and mountain goats. Major large predators, such as mountain lion, lynx, and black bear, are found reliably on the Forest.

Bird Life

About 260 species of birds have been reported from Deerlodge. Although many birds go south for the winter, some remain year-round, and others arrive as visitors from

RED-NECKED GREBE

GAIL DIANE LUCKNER, DRAWING

DAVID A. SIBLEY, DRAWING

more northern areas. Rivers that remain partially open support Bald Eagle, Canada Goose, Mallard, Common Goldeneye, and American Dipper. Interesting winter birds are Bohemian Waxwing, Red and White-winged (rare) crossbills, and Common Redpoll.

April and May bring Sandhill Crane, Cinnamon Teal, Northern Pintail, Ring-necked Duck, and Barrow's Goldeneye. In May, willow riparian areas greet Willow Flycatcher, Ruby-crowned Kinglet, Warbling Vireo, Yellow, MacGillivray's, and Wilson's warblers, Common Yellowthroat, Northern Waterthrush, Rufous-sided Towhee, Lazuli Bunting, Northern Oriole, and Song and White-crowned sparrows.

On the forest, Hermit and Swainson's thrushes, Yellow-rumped Warbler, Western Tanager, Chipping Sparrow, Dark-eyed (Oregon) Junco, Red Crossbill, Pine Siskin, and Evening Grosbeak can be seen; also there are Northern Flicker, Black-capped and Mountain chickadees, Red-breasted Nuthatch, Golden-crowned and Ruby-

GRASS AND PINES, DEERLODGE NATIONAL FOREST

crowned kinglets, and Townsend's Solitaire. In aspen groves, Ruffed Grouse and Red-naped Sapsucker can be found. Gray Jay and Clark's Nutcracker appear at higher elevations, and as snow recedes above treeline, American Pipit and Gray-crowned Rosy-Finch arrive.

Close to 160 species nest on the Forest. Most interesting of these are Red-necked Grebe, Osprey, Northern Goshawk, Swainson's Hawk, Golden Eagle, Prairie Falcon, Blue and Spruce grouse, Calliope and Rufous hummingbirds, Northern Three-toed and Black-backed woodpeckers, Western Wood-Pewee, Olive-sided, Hammond's, and Least flycatchers, Tree and Violet-green swallows, Mountain Bluebird, Yellow-rumped, MacGillivray's, and Wilson's warblers, Western Tanager, and Green-tailed Towhee. Although they are dif-

ficult to find, Great Gray, Northern Saw-whet, and Boreal owls also nest on the Forest.

Fall migrants pass through in September and October, and include a wide variety of raptors, some of which also nest on the forest: Osprey, Bald Eagle, Northern Harrier, Northern Goshawk, and Sharp-shinned, and Cooper's hawks. American Kestrel and Prairie Falcon are relatively common. Be on the lookout for Swainson's and Ferruginous hawks and Peregrine Falcon, which are uncommon to rare.

Birding Route

Georgetown Lake Area. This is one of the best birding spots on the Forest. In summer, the lake is home to more than 350 Red-necked Grebes and lesser numbers of Pied-billed, Eared, and Western grebes. Nestled

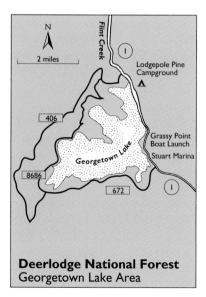

Deerlodge National Forest
Georgetown Lake Area

GREAT GRAY OWL

in a mixed forest–grassland basin at about a 6400-foot elevation, the lake is best reached by driving Interstate 90 west from Butte for 15 miles to the Montana Route 1 exit. Then follow Rte. 1 west for 23 miles through Anaconda to Georgetown Lake. At the lake, take the 12-mile Georgetown Lake Loop-Road that begins at Stuart Marina.

First, park at the marina and scan the lake. Immediately following winter thaw (usually early May), many waterfowl can be observed here, including Mallard, Blue-winged and Cinnamon teals, Gadwall, American Wigeon, Ring-necked Duck, Lesser Scaup, Bufflehead, and Common Merganser. Ospreys arrive in early spring and stay all summer. In late summer and early fall, several hundred American Coots and Common Mergansers frequent the lake. Bald Eagles can be numerous in October and November before the lake freezes for the winter.

Then continue north on Rte. 1 for 0.25 mile to the parking lot for the Grassy Point Boat Launch on the left. In May, you can see rainbow trout spawning in Emily Spring, a small tributary to Georgetown Lake. Here, too, is a Watchable Wildlife interpretive sign with information about the lake and its Red-necked Grebe population.

Continue north on Rte. 1 for 0.7 mile and park on the right, just past the Seven Gables Motel. A small adjacent pond often harbors Mallards, Cinnamon Teal, and (occasionally) Ruddy Ducks. On the lake side of the road, check for Killdeer, Spotted Sandpiper, and Sora along the lakeshore and adjacent wetlands.

Courting and nesting Red-necked Grebes can be ob-

served close at hand. Osprey and Belted Kingfisher are commonly sighted as well.

Now go north 1.4 miles on Rte. 1 to the Lodgepole Pine Campground and Trailhead at the Echo

SWAINSON'S THRUSH

Lake Road turnoff. Walk the half-mile loop-trail that traverses lodgepole pine and subalpine fir communities; you are likely to find Downy and Hairy woodpeckers, Gray Jay, Clark's Nutcracker, Mountain Chickadee, Golden and Ruby-crowned kinglets, Yellow-rumped Warbler, Western Tanager, Dark-eyed Junco, Chipping Sparrow, Red Crossbill, and Cassin's Finch.

After birding the campground area, return to Rte. 1, drive a short distance, and turn left onto Georgetown Lake Road [Forest Service Road (FS) 406] and cross the dam. In about 3 miles you will come to the intersection with FS 8686; you have the choice to continue on FS 406 along the ridge through fields of wildflowers or to turn onto FS 8686, which follows the lake shore. On either of

YELLOW-RUMPED WARBLER

these routes in summer look for Osprey, Red-tailed Hawk, American Kestrel, Common Nighthawk, Mountain Bluebird, and Vesper and Savannah sparrows. Gray and Steller's jays, Clark's Nutcracker, and Black-capped and Mountain chickadees are year-round residents. Although Great Gray Owl is considered uncommon on the Forest, the likelihood of a sighting is greatest while following one of these routes. Early or late in the day they may be found hunting from perches near meadow edges. Both FS 406 and FS 8686 intersect FS 672 near the southern end of Georgetown Lake. A right turn onto FS 672 leads to East Fork Reservoir and the gateway to trailheads in the Anaconda–Pintlar Wilderness Area.

A left turn onto FS 672 continues to follow the lake shore. Stop at Stuart Mill Bay, just past the Georgetown Lake Lodge. The bay is surrounded by willow thickets, much favored by moose. This is another good place to watch Red-necked Grebes as they construct their nesting-platforms, incubate eggs, and care for their young. Also, the exposed mud-flats make this sheltered bay particularly good for migrating shorebirds. In spring and fall, watch for American Avocet,

ACCOMMODATIONS ◆ WEATHER ◆ OTHER ATTRACTIONS

When to visit. Late spring, summer, and early fall are best for birding. Georgetown Lake is usually frozen until mid-May, although Stuart Mill Bay opens slightly earlier.

Where to stay. Both full-service and primitive campgrounds around the lake. Motels in Anaconda and Philipsburg.

Weather and attire. Summers are pleasant, but winters are extremely cold.

What else to do. On the Forest in summer: fishing, boating, canoeing, hiking, and mountain-biking. Rock Creek is an internationally known "blue ribbon" trout stream; nearby is the Anaconda–Pintler Wilderness Area; visit Lost Creek State Park to view mountain goats, bighorn sheep, and pikas. The Warm Springs Wildlife Management Area is excellent for waterfowl and Sandhill Cranes. In Butte, try birding around Homestake and Delmoe lakes, southeast of town.

For more information. General and campground information, District Office addresses, maps, bird list: Deerlodge National Forest, P.O. Box 400, Federal Building, 400 North Main, Butte, Montana 59703; telephone 406/496-3400.

Semipalmated Plover, Greater and Lesser yellowlegs, Willet, Long-billed Dowitcher, and Common Snipe.

Continue another mile down the road to complete the loop route and arrive at the junction with Rte. 1, just south of the Stuart Marina.

MIMI HOPPE WOLF, DRAWING

BIGHORN SHEEP

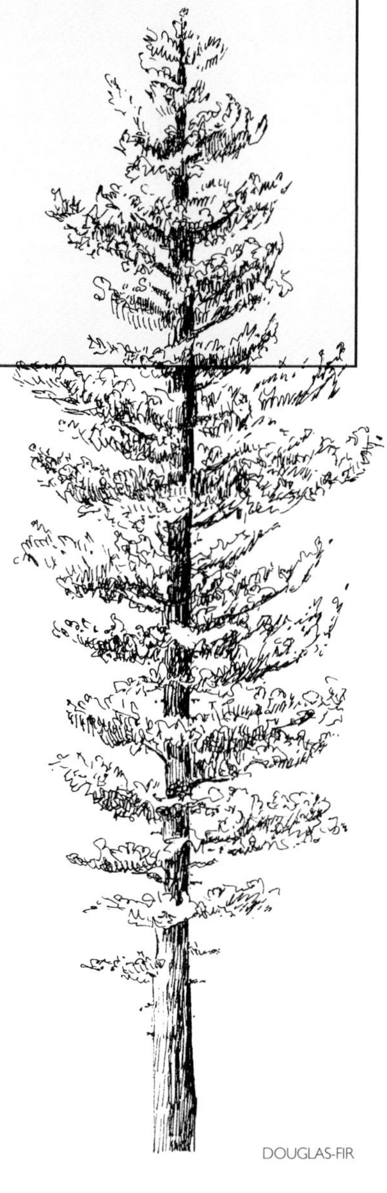

DOUGLAS-FIR

CUSTER FOREST
Montana and the Dakotas

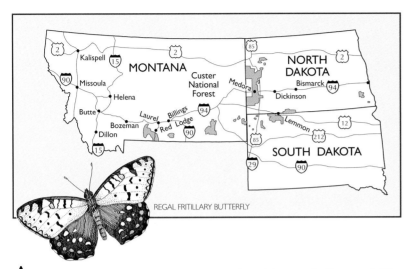

REGAL FRITILLARY BUTTERFLY

HOW TO GET THERE. *Beartooth District—From Billings, Montana, go 17 miles west on Interstate 90 to Laurel then south on U.S. Route 212 to Red Lodge. Little Missouri Grasslands— Medora, North Dakota, is located approximately 50 miles west of Dickinson, North Dakota, on I-94.*

AT JUST OVER 2,450,000 ACRES, Custer National Forest is not the biggest of the holdings, but it spreads across more territory than any other, stretching in patches from Montana's Yellowstone Park nearly 650 miles eastward into the Dakotas. There are mountains, plateaus, badlands, grasslands, and finally the flat, lazy braid of hardwoods along the Sheyenne River in eastern North Dakota.

As might be expected, rarities abound in this vast domain named after George Armstrong Custer, the reckless Indian fighter who went to his doom against the Sioux and Northern Cheyenne at the Little Bighorn in 1876. No fewer than twenty-one threatened, endangered, or sensitive wildlife species are found on or adjacent to the Forest. Included are three bats (pallid, Townsend's big-eared, and spotted) and a number of birds: Ferruginous Hawk, Harlequin Duck, Greater Prairie-Chicken, Boreal Owl, and Black-backed Woodpecker. Custer National Forest also is noted for several unique or rare butterflies, among them Hayden's ringlet, Weidemeyer's admiral, and

northern blue on the Beartooth District, and the Dakota skipper, regal fritillary, and tawny crescent in the Dakotas.

The Forest supports an abundance of ungulates, including elk, mule and white-tailed deer, moose, pronghorn, bighorn sheep, and mountain goat. Grizzly and black bear, mountain lion, lynx, bobcat, and red fox can all be found in appropriate habitat. The Beartooth District is also part of the gray wolf recovery effort in the Greater Yellowstone Ecosystem.

Bird Life

Because of the extreme distances and diversity of habitats, the Forest list is impressive—more than 350 species, ranging

from those that occur only in boreal zones to typical prairie birds. Boreal specialties include—besides Boreal Owl, Harlequin Duck, Blue Grouse, Three-toed and Black-backed woodpeckers—Gray Jay, Red-breasted Nuthatch, Pine Grosbeak, Cassin's Finch, Red Crossbill, and Pine Siskin. The prairies, on the other hand, are home to Greater Prairie-Chicken, Sharp-tailed Grouse, Upland Sandpiper, Long-billed Curlew, Sprague's Pipit, Clay-colored and Baird's sparrows, Lark Bunting, Chestnut-collared Longspur, and Bobolink.

KENN KAUFMANN, DRAWING

BLUE GROUSE

RUDOLF KOES, DRAWING

Birding Routes

With seven ranger districts and four national grasslands, a visiting birder is faced with innumerable choices. Two readily accessible areas, however, will give you an excellent sampling of what the Custer National Forest has to offer. These are the Beartooth Scenic Highway on the western edge of the Forest and the Little Missouri National Grassland in the east.

Beartooth Scenic Highway. Montana's magnificent Beartooth Plateau includes about 80,000 acres of rolling alpine terrain, much of it more than 6000 feet above the lower plains. The land is bejeweled with wildflowers and sparkling lakes, and from some rises you can see almost forever in the crystalline air. Few people who cross this vast stretch of unbroken high-country ever forget it.

Your tour of the Scenic Highway (U.S. Route 212) offers excellent birding along a 60-mile route that follows Rock Creek and ascends the Beartooth Plateau. The trip begins in Red Lodge, Montana, at the Forest Service Ranger Station, one mile south of town on U.S. 212. Travel south on U.S. 212 for 4 miles and turn left at the Forest Service Campground sign onto Forest Service Road (FS) 379. This road follows Rock Creek for approximately 4 miles and eventually rejoins U.S. 212. In the meantime, you will pass through a varied mix of riparian, conifer, and sage-brush habitats. Two campgrounds, Sheridan (1.7 miles) and Ratine (3.2 miles), are located along FS 379 and are good places to camp and to bird.

Work the riparian habitat along Rock Creek for migrant and nesting warblers from late May to mid-July. Orange-crowned, Yellow, Yellow-rumped, Townsend's, MacGil-

livray's, and Wilson's warblers and Ovenbird are common here, along with American Redstart, Common Yellowthroat, and Yellow-breasted Chat. Look for Red-naped Sapsucker, House Wren, and Solitary, Warbling, and Red-eyed vireos, as well as Lazuli Bunting, Rufous-sided Towhee, and Song Sparrow. During April and May, listen for the drumming of Ruffed Grouse.

The adjacent forest is good for Lewis's, Downy, Hairy, and Three-toed woodpeckers, Dusky, Hammond, and Least flycatchers, Black-capped and Mountain chickadees, Brown Creeper, Red-breasted and White-breasted nuthatches, Ruby-crowned Kinglet, Townsend's Solitaire, Veery, Swainson's and Hermit thrushes, Western Tanager, Black-headed Grosbeak, Chipping Sparrow, and Pine Siskin. Blue Grouse can be heard booming in the conifer stands from March to mid-May.

In the open sage-brush areas, you should find Eastern and Western kingbirds, Green-tailed and Rufous-sided towhees, and Brewer's, Vesper,

SHERIDAN CAMPGROUND

Lark, and Savannah sparrows.

A spur road (FS 346), 2.4 miles south of the point where FS 379 rejoins U.S. 212, will take you to the Lake Fork of Rock Creek. This road follows the creek for 1.8 miles and terminates at a trailhead into the Absaroka-Beartooth Wilderness. Lake Fork is a clear, cascading creek and prime habitat for American Dipper. Keep an eye out for Harlequin Duck along the quieter sections of the creek. In the lodgepole pine stands, watch for Three-toed Woodpecker, Dark-eyed Junco, Red Crossbill, and Cassin's Finch. You may even find Black-backed Woodpecker here. In pockets of aspens you are likely to encounter Ruffed Grouse, Red-naped Sapsucker, Downy Woodpecker, and Red-breasted and White-breasted nuthatches.

Return to the junction of U.S. 212 and FS 346, and continue south on U.S. 212 for 1.7 miles, then turn right onto FS 421. This road passes several campgrounds along Rock Creek: Limber Pine, Greenough Lake, Parkside, and M–K. The paved road ends in 0.9 mile at the Limber Pine Campground. At this point the road becomes dirt and rough, and is not suitable for passenger cars. With a high-clearance vehicle, however, you can continue for about 7 miles into Wyoming.

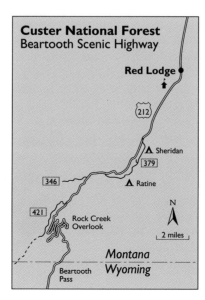

Custer National Forest
Beartooth Scenic Highway

Red Lodge ●

(212)

▲ Sheridan
379

346
▲ Ratine

N

421
Rock Creek
Overlook

2 miles

Montana
Wyoming

Beartooth
Pass

LINCOLN'S SPARROW

Look in open areas along the creek for Spotted Sandpiper, Common Snipe, and American Dipper. Watch also for Willow Flycatchers and Lincoln's Sparrows in willow and aspen stands bordering the meadows. The adjacent forest should produce Ruffed and Blue grouse and four species of flycatchers: Western Wood-Pewee and Least, Hammond's, and Dusky.

In early spring (primarily in March), seven species of owls are possible when they are calling: Eastern Screech-Owl (local) and Great Horned, Great Gray, Long-eared, Boreal, and Northern Saw-whet after dark; and Northern Pygmy-Owl during the daylight hours. Cooper's and Sharp-shinned hawks and Northern Goshawk can be seen here throughout the summer.

Return to U.S. 212 and turn right. South of FS 421, the Beartooth Highway begins to climb steeply for 5000 feet and to switchback across the face of Line Creek Plateau. After 8 miles, stop at the Rock Creek Overlook pull-off on the left and walk 100 yards to the overlook. From here you can look down into Rock Creek, almost 2000 feet below. A short hike west along the overlook trail offers breathtaking views of Upper Rock Creek Canyon and Hell Roaring Plateau. The stand of Engelmann spruce and subalpine fir along the overlook trail is good for Three-toed Woodpecker, Gray Jay, Clark's Nutcracker, Mountain Chickadee, Pine Grosbeak, and Red Crossbill. Scan overhead for Golden Eagle, Prairie Falcon, White-throated Swift, and Cliff Swallow. Listen for the descending songs of Canyon Wrens among the cliffs below the overlook.

The Wyoming state line is approximately 5 miles to the south. As you approach the boundary, U.S. 212 levels out at nearly 10,000-feet elevation, and the high plateau presents an Arctic–alpine wonderland. Here you may find American Pipit and Black Rosy-Finch. In late summer, Golden Eagle, Prairie Falcon, and even Peregrine Falcon frequent this high-country area.

From the state line you can continue across Beartooth Pass (10,947 feet) to the village of Cooke City and Yellowstone National Park, a distance of about 44 miles, or you can return to Billings and head 300 miles east on U.S. 94 for exploration of another part of Custer National Forest.

Little Missouri Grassland. This 1,000,000-acre National Grassland lies in western North Dakota and is a land of wild rivers, prairies, canyons, and buttes. Large cottonwood groves along the Little Missouri River, juniper groves on the hillsides, short-grass prairie on the plateaus, and ash woodland in the canyons provide a rich mosaic of habitats. You can sample the area by taking the 58-mile, self-guided Wildlife and Scenic Tour. The road is well marked; points of interest are identified by numbered posts, and directions to various locations are indicated by arrows on the posts. The tour starts at the visitor center of the south unit of Theodore Roosevelt National Park in Medora.

The first stop, 8.8 miles from the visitor center, offers a view of the cottonwood bottoms lining the Little Missouri River. There are no trails, but stands of cottonwoods along the Little Missouri are accessible by foot. In spring and summer, look for Swainson's Hawk, Golden Eagle, American Kestrel, Black-billed Cuckoo, Common Nighthawk, Red-headed, Downy, and Hairy woodpeckers, Northern Flicker, Western Wood-Pewee, Willow and Least flycatchers, Western and Eastern kingbirds, Tree Swallow, Blue Jay, Black-billed Magpie, White-breasted Nuthatch, Brown Creeper, House Wren, Eastern Bluebird, Gray Catbird, Black-and-white Warbler, American Redstart, Ovenbird, Yellow-breasted Chat, Black-headed Grosbeak, Rufous-sided Towhee, Chipping Sparrow, and Northern Oriole. After dark, listen for owls. Eastern Screech-Owls and Great Horned and Long-eared owls frequent the river bottoms.

Continue another 5.9 miles to Site 2, an area of green ash draws and juniper-dominated hillsides. From mid-May through early June, you can expect such migrating warblers as Tennessee,

CHESTNUT-COLLARED LONGSPUR

Orange-crowned, Blackpoll, and Northern Waterthrush. Nesting warblers include Yellow and Black-and-white, American Redstart, Ovenbird, and Common Yellowthroat. Warbling and Red-eyed vireos are commonly seen. Other species to expect: House Wren, Swainson's and Hermit thrushes, Brown Thrasher, Cedar Waxing, Lazuli Bunting, Chipping, Clay-colored, Field, Lark, and Song sparrows, and American Goldfinch. Watch for Wild (Merriam's) Turkeys. If you visit in late fall, winter, or early spring, you may find Bohemian Waxwing, Northern Shrike, American Tree Sparrow, and Common Redpoll.

At Site 3, another 2.9 miles along the tour, check the east side of the road for Sharp-tailed Grouse. Males utilize this as a dancing-ground from late March through early May, performing their courtship displays at dusk and dawn with the greatest activity from daybreak to sunrise. Observers should stay in their vehicles and remain as quiet as possible.

To continue the tour, return to the Moody Plateau intersection near Site

2, and turn right. Site 4 is 3.7 miles from Site 3 and normally offers a wide variety of wildlife. One specialty is bighorn sheep. The "Audubon" bighorn historically was a common sub-species in the badlands of North Dakota, but unregulated hunting wiped out the population by 1905. California bighorn, considered biologically and ecologically similar to Audubon, were successfully introduced, beginning in 1956; the herd today numbers 250 to 300 animals. Also watch for elk, mule deer, and pronghorn.

Moody Plateau is excellent for birds of the short-grass prairie. Look for Sharp-tailed Grouse, Upland Sandpiper, Long-billed Curlew, Eastern and Western kingbirds, Horned Lark, Eastern and Mountain bluebirds, and Sprague's Pipit. Also present may be Loggerhead Shrike, Dickcissel, Vesper, Lark, Savannah, and Baird's sparrows, Lark Bunting, Chestnut-collared Longspur, Bobolink, and Western Meadowlark. Keep an eye out for such raptors as Northern Harrier, Swainson's, Red-tailed, and Ferruginous hawks, Golden Eagle, Merlin, and Prairie Falcon. The hawk-watching is best during fall migration from mid-September to mid-October. In winter, the open prairie supports big flocks of Lapland Longspurs and Snow Buntings, as well as Horned Larks, the most common bird in North Dakota (year-round).

The large butte visible to the southwest is Bullion Butte. These sheer escarpments provide cliff nesting sites for Red-tailed Hawk, American Kestrel, Golden Eagle, Prairie Falcon, Great Horned Owl, and other species.

As you continue the tour, the next

FERRUGINOUS HAWK (IMMATURE)

6 miles pass through private cattle ranches; remain on the road. In 9.7 miles, turn off the main road down Davis Creek toward Initial Rock; Site 5, 1.7 miles down this side road, provides a view of a Golden Eagle nest in a cottonwood tree. The eagles usually have two or more nest sites up to three miles apart that they utilize in alternate years, so any given nest may be inactive at the time of your visit.

To reach Site 6, continue 0.6 mile beyond Site 5 to Initial Rock. This place gets its name from Privates W. C. Williams (Company H) and F. Neely (Company M) of Custer's ill-fated 7th Cavalry, who carved their initials into a sandstone boulder on their way to the Little Big Horn.

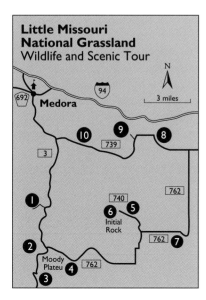

Little Missouri National Grassland
Wildlife and Scenic Tour

To continue the tour, return to the main road and turn left. Site 7 is 4.9 miles from Site 6 and contains a number of reddish knobs, much favored by rattlesnakes. Watch out! This rugged terrain provides nesting sites for raptors, such as Prairie Falcon, American Kestrel, and Red-tailed Hawk, as well as White-throated Swift, Say's Phoebe, Cliff Swallow, and Rock Wren.

Site 8 is 8.3 miles farther on. Most of the adjacent land is privately owned, so please do not trespass. Crops include wheat and alfalfa hay that together with the native prairie habitat give food and cover to Gray Partridge, Ring-necked Pheasant, and Sharp-tailed Grouse. Watch for Northern Harrier, Swainson's and Ferruginous hawks, Golden Eagle, Horned Lark, Lark Bunting, Western Meadowlark, and Brown-headed Cowbird.

Drive another 1.9 miles to Site 9. You will find a colony of black-tailed prairie-dogs. Look here for Burrowing Owl, Horned Lark, Mountain Bluebird, McCown's and Chestnut-collared longspurs, and (in winter) Snow Bunting. Prairie-dog colonies also provide habitat for the endangered black-footed ferret, as well as swift fox, coyote, badger, long-tailed weasel, prairie rattlesnake, and black-widow spider.

As you drive toward Site 10, 4.8 miles beyond Site 9, notice the petrified wood stumps along the road. These stumps are remnants of a prehistoric time when North Dakota possessed an extensive forest of Sequoia trees.

At Site 10, look for a Golden Eagle nest beneath the over-hanging slab of sandstone on the cliffs to the north of the road. With binoculars or a spotting scope you can see adults or nestlings when the nest is occupied.

This is the final stop; Medora is 6.3 miles ahead on the tour route. If time permits, you may wish to explore the Little Missouri River near Medora. There are plenty of places to stop and scan the river. You are likely to find American White Pelican, Great Blue Heron, American Avocet, Killdeer, Willet, Spotted Sandpiper, Marbled Godwit, Wilson's Phalarope, rarely Forster's and Black terns, and Belted Kingfisher. In migration, you should also find Greater and Lesser yellowlegs and Solitary and Least sandpipers. Bald Eagles are observed regularly in late fall and occasionally during the winter months.

ACCOMMODATIONS ◆ WEATHER ◆ OTHER ATTRACTIONS

When to visit. Late spring, summer, and early fall are best. Mid-September to late October is good for migrating raptors. The Beartooth Highway is generally open from Memorial Day through September (temporary summer closings due to snow are possible).

Where to stay. Campgrounds throughout the Forest and adjacent federal and state areas. For the grasslands, motels in Medora, Dickinson, Beach, Bowman, Belfield, and Watford City. For the Beartooth, accommodations plentiful in Red Lodge, but reservations advisable for summer weekends.

Weather and attire. It is extremely cold in winter and very hot in summer. Inclement weather can occur anytime. Always carry a jacket and drinking water. In wet weather, dirt roads can be very slippery and impassable.

What else to do. Hiking, fishing, white-water rafting, float trips, rock collecting, spelunking, horseback riding, hunting, mountain-biking, looking for fossils, photography, and canoeing on the Little Missouri River are all possible on the Forest. Visit Theodore Roosevelt National Park, including Theodore Roosevelt's Ranch, as well as the historic area of Medora. Lake Sakakawea to the north is a huge impoundment that attracts many shorebirds and waterfowl, including the endangered Piping Plover and Least Tern. In the Beartooth area, Little Bighorn Battlefield National Monument and Yellowstone National Park, are within easy driving distance. Not to be missed is Jimmy Joe Campground near East Rosebud Lake, Roscoe, Montana, for spring and summer wildflowers that attract about twenty species of butterflies and skippers.

For more information. General and campground information, District Office addresses, maps, bird list: Beartooth Ranger District, Route 2, Box 3420, Red Lodge, Montana 59068, 406/446-2103; and Medora Ranger District, Route 3, Box 131-B, Dickinson, North Dakota 58601, 701/225-5151.

BEARGRASS

BRIDGER–TETON FOREST
Wyoming

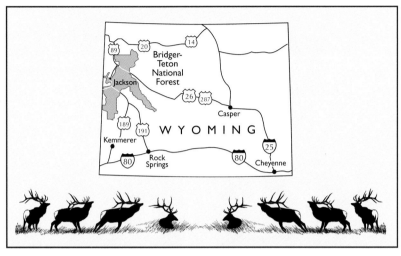

HOW TO GET THERE. *In Wyoming head north off Interstate 80 on U.S. Route 189 at Evanston and U.S. Route 191 at Rock Springs or west off Interstate 25 at Casper on U.S. Route 26 to Jackson; from Idaho take Rte. 26 off Interstate 15 at Idaho Falls; and from Montana take U.S. Route 89 south off Interstate 90 at Livingston or at U.S. Route 212 to Rte. 89 at Laurel. Parts of U.S. 26, U.S. 189, U.S. 191, and U.S. 212 are included in the Wyoming Scenic Byway system.*

THE TETONS TOWER OVER A PIONEER SETTLEMENT ON THE ROAD TO THE BRIDGER–TETON

RENOWNED FOR ITS MAGNIFICENT scenery, the 3,400,000-acre Bridger–Teton National Forest is the second largest such holding outside Alaska. Only the four-million-acre Toiyabe National Forest in Nevada surpasses it in size. Its domain includes 1,200,000 acres of the Teton, Gros Ventre, and Bridger wilderness areas. The Teton, Gros Ventre, Wind River, and Wyoming ranges rise from 5900 to 13,785 feet above sea level. Within the ranges are the headwaters of three major rivers: the Green, Snake, and Yellowstone. In addition, the Forest is part of the Greater Yellowstone Ecosystem, the largest remaining area of undeveloped lands in the Lower Forty-Eight.

There are three major vegetation areas. The drier Great Basin zone of the southern and southwestern portion of the Forest is dominated by mountain mahogany, big sage-brush, saltbush, bitterbrush, and aspen. Blue spruce, limber pine, big sage-brush, and rabbitbrush characterize the wetter Southern Rocky Mountain zone in the center of the Forest, while the Northern Rocky Mountain zone is primarily cloaked in whitebark

Bridger–Teton Area
Fall Creek and
Gros Ventre Roads

N

5 Miles

To Moran
Junction

Road

Gros Ventre

Kelly

Lower
Slide
Lake

Upper
Slide
Lake

30400

26
189
191

National
Elk Refuge

Wilson

22

Jackson

Snake River

Fall
Creek
Road

Butler
Creek
Ranch

31000

26
189
191

Hoback
Junction

189
191

To
Pinedale

Hoback River

Astoria
Hot Springs

26

WESTERN TANAGER

Bird Life

A total of 355 species of birds have been reported on the Bridger–Teton. Of these, 81 are year-round residents, 157 are summer inhabitants, 68 are there during migration, and 14 visit only in winter. The remaining 35 species are regarded as accidental.

Bald Eagle and Peregrine Falcon—both still listed as endangered—grace the Forest. Northern Goshawk, Great Gray and Boreal owls, and Three-toed Woodpecker are Forest Service "sensitive species," with concentrations on the Greys River drainage. Other sensitive species are Trumpeter Swan (permanent resident) and Harlequin Duck (irregular from spring to fall). Hammond's Flycatcher, which is less common than its close relative Dusky Flycatcher over most of the Forest, can also be found on the Greys River drainage.

Trumpeter Swans usually can be viewed at several of the larger undeveloped lakes that are accessible by road, such as Upper Slide Lake in the Gros Ventre drainage, Mosquito Lake on Union Pass Road, and Lily Lake on Forest Service Road (FS) 024.

Sandhill Crane and Ruffed, Blue, and Sage grouse are common on the Forest. Blue Grouse is found within the forest itself, while Ruffed inhabits the deciduous edges.

pine and common juniper. Douglas-fir, subalpine fir, and Engelmann spruce are widespread in the montane sections, with cottonwood, willow, alder, and dogwood found in riparian areas.

Primary wildflower months are June and July in the Jackson area and one to two months earlier on the Forest's southern portion. The land is then alive with a palette of yellows, blues, reds, and whites. Lupines, locoweed, buckwheat, Indian paintbrush, scarlet gilia, evening primrose, asters, and goldenrod are commonly found in the grasslands and sage-brush flats. In the conifer forests are columbine, pinedrop, lilies, heart-leafed arnica, spring beauty, and fairy-slipper orchid. Wet meadows and marshes produce elephant-head, glacier lily, marsh marigold, and various species of monkey flowers. Mountain meadows offer shooting-star, figwort, fireweed, wild sweet William, wild geranium, bitterroot, mule's ear, and mountain blue bell.

The multitude of habitats supports all of the big game species found in the Intermontaine West, such as elk, mule deer, pronghorn, Rocky Mountain bighorn sheep, mountain goat, and black bear. The Bridger–Teton is home to the threatened grizzly bear. Mountain lion, lynx, wolverine, fisher, pine marten, ground-squirrels and chipmunks, and a veritable ark of other animals help complete the picture. The lakes, ponds, and streams hold Colorado River and Snake River fine-spotted trout and Bonneville cutthroat trout. The Kendall Springs dace, a 1½-inch-long relative of the minnow on the Federal Endangered Species List, is found in no other place in the world.

SAGE GROUSE

DAVID A. SIBLEY: DRAWING

Sage Grouse are best observed north of Jackson in the sage-covered valley bottoms adjacent to Grand Teton National Park and Jackson Airport, which are also good for Sage Thrasher and Brewer's Sparrow. The highest concentration of leks can be seen on a tour run by the National Park Service during mid-April, usually just one weekend, so call the Park Service ahead of time.

Birding Routes

Fall Creek Road. If you have only a few hours, this is the way to go. The road, officially known as FS 31000, passes through a multitude of habitats from river bottom to montane forest, and it is not unusual to find sixty species here during the nesting season (June and July)

The tour begins 12 miles south of Jackson (Jackson Hole is the old name) at the Fall Creek Exit on U.S. Route 26 just before the Fall Creek/Wilson road sign. The route is approximately 18 miles in length and ends at Highway 22 at Wilson, which is 8 miles west of Jackson. Fall Creek Road (FS 31000) is dirt most of the way, not heavily traveled, and has numerous pull-offs.

The first stop is 0.4 mile beyond the Fall Creek/Wilson road sign. Check the marshy area here for Common Snipe, Sora, Yellow, Wilson's, and MacGillivray's warblers, and Common Yellowthroat. Watch also for Red-tailed Hawk, Calliope and Broad-tailed hummingbirds, Ruby-crowned Kinglet, Warbling Vireo, and White-crowned Sparrow.

As the road climbs into more open areas, it passes marshes with extensive willows. Look for Spotted Sandpiper, more snipe, Dusky Flycatcher (the most common *Empidonax)*, Marsh Wren, Black-headed Grosbeak, Western Tanager, and Fox, Song, and Lincoln's sparrows. All three accipiters are possible here, and Northern Harrier is occasionally seen, as well.

At Prichard Pass (mile 2.2, elevation 6600 feet), check the forested area for Sharp-shinned and Cooper's hawks, Red-naped and Williamson's sapsuckers, Dusky Flycatcher, House Wren, and Chipping Sparrow. In another mile, stop at a bridge across a small stream. The willow flats here are good for Yellow and McGillivray's warblers, Common Yellowthroat, and White-crowned Sparrow. The sage-brush hills are home to Lazuli Bunting, Green-tailed Towhee, and Brewer's Sparrow. Shortly after you cross the stream, a dirt road on the right leads to the trailhead for Munger Mountain. Walk up the trail for a half-mile or so; the place is a hotspot for Blue and Ruffed grouse. Goshawks have been seen in this area.

The flood-plains at mile 7, just before you reach Red Top Meadows, are great for Calliope, Broad-tailed, and Rufous hummingbirds, Willow Flycatcher, Tree, Violet-green, Bank, and Barn swallows, and Brewer's Blackbird. In the rocks to the south, look for Clark's Nutcracker and Rock Wren.

The rest of the route is through state and private lands, but two stops are worth mentioning. At mile 8.5, the sage-brush on the right is excellent for Green-tailed Towhee. After cresting a small rise at mile 13.2, you will have a panoramic view of the Snake River and Gros Ventre and Teton mountains; keep a lookout for Osprey, Bald Eagle, Swainson's and Red-tailed hawks, and American White Pelican while enjoying the scenery. At the junction with Wyoming Route 22 in Wilson, turn right and drive 8 miles back to Jackson.

BLACK-HEADED GROSBEAK

Gros Ventre Road. Pronounced *growvont* locally, this road takes you northeast of Jackson through extensive sage-brush flats to the site of a massive 1925 landslide that created Lower Slide Lake. The most sought-after birds on this route are Trumpeter Swan, Prairie Falcon, Sage Grouse, and Sage Thrasher.

Gros Ventre Road begins north of Jackson off U.S. 26, just past the Kelly sign. Shortly after the settlement of Kelly, turn right (east) at the sign for Forest Service Campgrounds. This route is rarely traveled by the hordes of tourists in the "Hole" and provides excellent birding opportunities and possible sightings of moose, bighorn sheep, and pronghorn.

Stop anyplace on the sage-brush flats to find Sage Grouse (easiest in early spring), Sandhill Crane, American Kestrel, Northern Harrier, Prairie Falcon, Sage Thrasher (rare), and Brewer's, Vesper, and Savannah sparrows. Fence posts are convenient perches for Western Meadowlark, Mountain Bluebird, and Eastern Kingbird. Keep your eyes peeled for Golden Eagle, Red-tailed and Swainson's hawks, and Short-eared Owl. Along the first hundred yards of the road, a ridge on the left provides an excellent vantage point for various raptors preying on the ground-squirrels infesting the right side of the road. There is a sizable area of aspen here that attracts nesting Orange-crowned Warblers.

The sage-brush flats offer nesting Tree Swallows, American Robins, Yellow Warblers, and White-crowned Sparrows. Smaller numbers of Northern Flicker, House Wren, Mountain Bluebird, Warbling Vireo, MacGillivray's Warbler, and Green-tailed Towhee can be found here also. Lower Slide Lake supports Rock Wren, Barrow's Goldeneye, Ring-necked Duck, and American Wigeon. After you pass Lower Slide Lake, the road is high up the bank. Violet-green Sparrows nest along the cliffs.

Gros Ventre Road crosses two bridges, at 8.3 and 11.8 miles, both of which have nesting Cliff Swallows beneath the spans. American Dipper is sometimes seen bobbing about the rocks of these streams. Look toward the cliffs between Lower Slide Lake and Crystal Creek for nesting Bald Eagles and Peregrine Falcons.

A Trumpeter Swan area is located at Upper Slide Lake about 20 miles along the road. Just before reaching the swan overlook, which is on the left, watch for a round pond on the right below a small hill. You may get a much closer view of ducks and swans here than at the overlook. Barrow's Goldeneye and Ring-necked Duck as well as Cinnamon and Green-winged teals, are found on many of the small ponds on this area near Jackson. River otters may also be seen playing in the water.

Gros Ventre Road is unpaved beyond the east side of Lower Slide Lake,

and travel on this segment of the route is not advised after heavy rain. From December to April, the road is not plowed beyond Lower Slide Lake and is open only to snowmobiles.

Teton Wilderness. The Wyoming Centennial Scenic Byway (U.S. Routes 287 and 26 from Moran Junction), 31 miles north of Jackson, provides opportunities for Osprey, Red-tailed Hawk, and Northern Harrier as well as Trumpeter Swan, Sandhill Crane, and other water birds. A good loop on FS 30100 begins south of the highway approximately 7.5 miles east of Moran Junction at the Forest Service Hatchet Campground. FS 30100 climbs 6 miles to Lily Lake, home to a pair of swans, or "Trumps" in the local parlance, and travels down to join the main road approximately 8.5 miles east of the starting point. Now turn left, back toward the Junction, and drive 4.25 miles to Four-mile Meadow Picnic Area. Then go left (north) on FS 30050, or Buffalo Valley Road, through Turpin Meadows. This 12-mile road is one of the best routes in the forest for Common Raven, Red-tailed and Swainson's hawks, Orange-crowned and Yellow-rumped Warblers, Black-headed Grosbeak, Green-tailed Towhee, and Chipping and Brewer's sparrows. FS 30050 rejoins the main road 3.5 miles east of Moran Junction.

Green River Road. This route, southeast of Jackson near Pinedale, terminates at Green River Lakes in the Wind River Range. A short walk along the lakeshore will provide fine birding and what many people believe is the most beautiful and spectacular view in Wyoming.

Start your tour by taking the Wyoming Centennial Scenic Byway, U.S. Route 191, south from its intersection in Jackson with Rte. 22. Turn left at Hoback Junction (14 miles) toward Pinedale. At 58.8 miles from

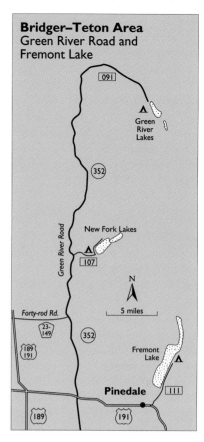

Bridger–Teton Area
Green River Road and Fremont Lake

Jackson, turn left (east) onto County Road (CR) 23-149, a gravel road also known as Forty-rod Road. This 5-mile-long shortcut to the Green River Road will take 19 miles off your trip. Turn left when you reach the Green River Road, Wyoming Route 352, which follows the scenic Green River Valley for more than 40 miles, just over half of which is paved. Drive 6.4 miles to the New Fork Lakes turnoff, FS 107, turn right, and go 3.4 miles to the lakes. When you get there, bear left and go up the north side to the Forest Service Narrows Campground at the end. Western Screech-Owls have been heard in July here at night for a number of years; at dusk you have a good chance of seeing the birds as well. The best place to watch for the screech-owl is just as you approach the campground. Great Horned Owl may appear at the lower end. Other birds in the area include Ruffed Grouse, Broad-tailed Hummingbird, Red-naped and Williamson's sapsuckers, Dusky Flycatcher,

TRUMPETER SWAN

Steller's Jay, Hermit Thrush, Warbling Vireo, Yellow-rumped Warbler, Black-headed Grosbeak, Lincoln's Sparrow, and Red Crossbill.

Return to Rte. 352 and turn right (north). In 11.2 miles the pavement ends as you enter the Forest, leaving 19.8 more miles on a dirt road to the Green River Lakes Campground. An easy walk to Clear Creek Falls on the east side of the lake will give you a good shot at Three-toed Woodpecker, Osprey, Dusky and Olive-sided flycatchers, and Gray Jay. Other birds to expect are Red-naped Sapsucker, Steller's Jay, Clark's Nutcracker, Fox Sparrow, Pine Siskin, and Cassin's Finch. Northern Goshawk may be seen here as well.

The home of the endangered Kendall Warm Springs Dace is along this route. The springs are approximately 4 miles north of the Forest boundary and have a constant temperature of 84.4° F year-round, which is the requirement of these tiny fish. At breeding time, the males are purple and the females are green.

Fremont Lake is a worthwhile side trip if you have time. The lake, roadside, and campground at the end of the road offer good birding for waterfowl and a variety of sage-brush and montane species. From the Green River tour you can take the road through Cora to Pinedale. Or, from Jackson, take U.S. Route 189 south for 14 miles to the junction with U.S. Routes 26, 89, and 191. Go southeast on U.S. 189/191 for 53 miles until the two routes divide, then follow U.S. 191 east 11 miles to Pinedale. Just east of Pinedale on U.S. 191, turn left onto Fremont Lake Road, to Fremont Lake and the White Pine Ski Area; the road ends at a campground after about 11 miles.

Look for waterfowl and Osprey from the lakeside at the campground. Harlequin Ducks and (probably Western) screech-owls have been reported here. Check the surrounding forest and nearby sage-brush meadows for Red-naped Sapsucker, Dusky Flycatcher, Red-breasted Nuthatch, MacGillivray's, Yellow-rumped, and Yellow warblers, Green-tailed Towhee, and Chipping Sparrow. Watch also for snowshoe hare in the forest and for beaver along the lakeshore.

ACCOMMODATIONS ◆ WEATHER ◆ OTHER ATTRACTIONS

When to visit. Although the Forest is open all year, the period between Memorial Day and Labor Day receives the heaviest traffic. To avoid crowds and find migrants, visit in May and September to early October. But be careful; hunting season is underway in fall, and birding is best confined to the roads and campgrounds. Another note of caution: the Teton Wilderness and the Buffalo and Spread Creek drainages are grizzly bear territory; before visiting, stop in at a District Ranger Office for the latest information and a review of standard precautions.

Where to stay. Campgrounds scattered throughout the Forest. Numerous motels in Jackson, Pinedale, and Alpine. Reservations recommended in summer and fall and also for Jackson in winter.

Weather and attire. Summers are usually mild with daytime temperatures in the 60s to 80s, and lows below freezing at elevations of 7000 feet and higher. Spring and fall generally have temperatures about 20° F below the summer highs and 10° F below the summer lows. Winters are severe with low temperatures normally in the 10-to-30° F range with occasional plunges to minus 50° F. Snowfall accounts for two-thirds or more of the annual precipitation with much of the remainder falling as summer afternoon thundershowers. A jacket or rain-gear is recommended at all times in summer. Dress for extreme cold in winter.

What else to do. Hiking (about 3000 miles of backcountry trails), skiing (two alpine areas, helicopter, two nordic centers, and 41 miles of marked cross-country trails), snowmobiling (220 miles of groomed trails), canoeing, rafting, motor-boating, wind-surfing, mountain-biking, horseback riding, fishing, and mountaineering. The Jackson aerial tram provides easy access to alpine habitat, where a short walk to the edge of the snow-fields offers a good chance to find Black Rosy-Finches. FS 30500 to Granite Hot Springs (a good spot for Three-toed Woodpeckers), approximately 11 miles south of Hoback Junction on U.S. 191, is considered one of the most attractive side-roads in the Forest.

Grand Teton and Yellowstone National Parks are close by. So is the National Elk Refuge, where thousands of elk can be seen in winter. Periodic Spring, east of Afton, is renowned as the largest of only three natural cold-water geysers in the world.

For more information. General and campground information, District Office addresses, maps, bird lists: Bridger–Teton National Forest Visitor Center, 340 N. Cache Street in Jackson or P.O. Box 1888, Jackson, Wyoming 83001; telephone 307/733-2752 or 739-5500. There is also a Ranger office in Pinedale, 210 West Pine Street, P.O. Box 220, Pinedale, Wyoming 82941; telephone 307/367-4326.

WASATCH–CACHE FOREST
Utah and Wyoming

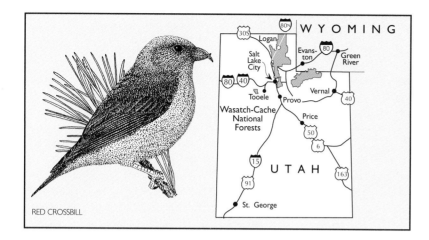

RED CROSSBILL

HOW TO GET THERE. *Take Interstate 80 east from Salt Lake City. For Mirror Lake, go to Silver Creek Junction, turn right on U.S. Route 40 toward Heber City, exit at the Kamas Exit, Utah Route 248, and continue east to Kamas (40 miles from Salt Lake City). From Kamas, take U.S. 150 for 33 more miles.*
For Henry's Fork Drainage, continue east on I-80 for 38 miles through Fort Bridger. Turn right (south) on Wyoming Route 414 toward Mountain View. After 3.3 miles, turn right onto Wyoming Route 410 in Mountain View (see page 75 for further directions).

DEVIL'S CASTLE AND GOLDEN ASPENS, WASATCH–CACHE NATIONAL FOREST

THIS FOREST WAS THE LAND of the trailblazers and mountainmen. Among the first to lay claim in the early 1800s were Jim Bridger and Kit Carson and their rough, tough, beaver-trapping cohorts from the Rocky Mountain Fur Company. By 1846, wagon trains were rattling through Utah on the way to California. But the country was so rich that many would-be Californians stopped right where they were and inevitably over-logged and over-timbered much of the area. At last, in 1906, President Theodore Roosevelt proclaimed the Wasatch National Forest to protect our natural heritage. Two years later, T. R. added the Cache National Forest, named for the Cache Valley, where the trappers once cached their furs.

Today's 1,219,748-acre Wasatch–Cache National Forest extends in a huge L-shape south from the Idaho border to Salt Lake City and east along the Wyoming line. The region's best-known feature is the Uinta Range, which rises to 13,528 feet at the summit of King's Peak and is the continent's greatest East–West massif outside of Alaska. Yet the whole Forest is grandly mountainous with high ridges and glacial moraines separating vast, verdant basins. The Forest Service maintains a good bit of it in a pristine state, including the 456,704-acre High Uintas Wilderness Area.

About half the Wasatch–Cache is forested. Lower elevations are dominated by Gambel oak, bigtooth maple, arrowhead, balsamroot, Indian paintbrush, and scarlet gilia. Willows, birch, and sedge are most prominent in riparian areas. Mid-elevations contain extensive conifer forests with lodgepole pine, Douglas-fir, and juniper interspersed with sagebrush and grassy openings. Engelmann spruce and subalpine fir prevail near the treeline. Scattered patches of aspen occur throughout. Variety is added by isolated meadows and willow fields. The remaining landscape is composed of talus slopes, boulder fields, and water. Nearly five hundred glacially-formed lakes and four hundred miles of streams grace the High Uintas. Many of the lakes and streams are stocked with fish. Cutthroat and eastern brook trout are most common, but rainbow and California golden trout, as well as Arctic grayling, are found in a few lakes.

The Forest furnishes habitat for elk, mule deer, moose, Rocky Mountain bighorn sheep, mountain goat, black bear, mountain lion, bobcat, coyote, fox, badger, pine marten, mink, and long-tailed weasel. Other small mammals include a variety of squirrels, yellow-bellied marmot, porcupine, beaver, and pika. Among the reptiles and amphibians are tree and side-blotched lizards, tiger salamander, and boreal chorus, northern leopard, and spotted frogs.

Bird Life

A total of over two hundred species has been recorded within the Wasatch–Cache National Forest. Birds of special interest are Northern Goshawk, Golden Eagle, Blue Grouse, White-tailed Ptarmigan, Three-toed Woodpecker, Northern Saw-whet Owl, Black Rosy-Finch, and Red Crossbill. Additional breeding birds of the Forest likely to be encountered are Western Wood-Pewee, Olive-sided, Dusky, and Hammond's flycatchers, Violet-green Swallow, Gray Jay, Clark's Nutcracker, Mountain Chickadee, Rock Wren, Ruby-crowned Kinglet, Townsend's Solitaire, MacGillivray's Warbler, Western Tanager, Black-headed Grosbeak, Lazuli Bunting, Lincoln's

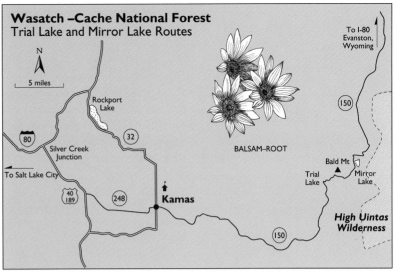

and White-crowned sparrows, Cassin's Finch, and Pine Siskin.

Birding Routes

Four excellent birding areas are Trial Lake, Bald Mountain, Mirror Lake, and Henry's Fork Drainage. Note that Trial Lake and Bald Mountain are but two possible stops along the route to Mirror Lake. Also, be aware that only the ptarmigan is unique at Henry's Fork. All other birds can be found more easily in other places.

Trial Lake. From Kamas, take Utah Route 150 east toward Mirror Lake (33 miles). This route leads through spectacular mountain scenery. Watch for the sign for Trial Lake at 26.2 miles from Kamas. Turn left and follow the signs into the campground. The trails in and around the campground are often good for Willaimson's Sapsucker, Three-toed Woodpecker, Gray Jay, Pine Grosbeak, Cassin's Finch and Red Crossbill. The lake is usually totally birdless, as are most in the Uintas.

Bald Mountain. Just before reaching Mirror Lake, Rte. 150 crosses Bald Mountain Pass (11,000

MACGILLIVRAY'S WARBLER

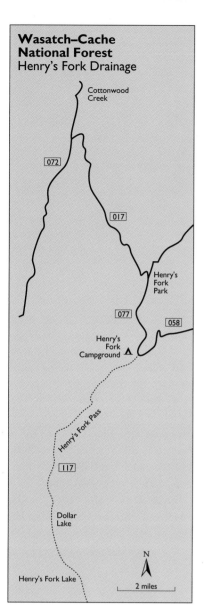

Wasatch–Cache National Forest
Henry's Fork Drainage

Cottonwood Creek

072

017

Henry's Fork Park

077

058

Henry's Fork Campground

Henry's Fork Pass

117

Dollar Lake

Henry's Fork Lake

N

2 miles

feet). Look for the Bald Mountain picnic-area sign and turn left into the parking lot at the Bald Mountain Trailhead. From here a trail goes to the top of Bald Mountain (11,947 feet). In summer you may see Rock Wren, Mountain Bluebird, Townsend's Solitaire, Hermit Thrush, American Pipit, Chipping and White-crowned sparrows, and Cassin's Finch near the trailhead. The talus slopes of this 11,947-foot peak are ideal breeding habitat for Black Rosy-Finch, and, on rare occasions, they have been observed at the main parking lot. The easiest birding route is to walk toward the restrooms near

the trailhead, climb the small rise to the right, descend toward the basin, and walk along the base of the talus slope that forms the side-face of Bald Mountain. Scan the rocks, especially those near snow banks, for the rosy-finches. If this short hike is not successful, the fairly strenuous two-mile hike to the top of Bald Mountain may be in order. The latter hike is often required later in the summer when the snow has melted off the lower slopes. The top of Bald Mountain gives a spectacular view of some fifty glacially-formed lakes, but there are few species other than the Black Rosy-Finch and American Pipit.

Mirror Lake. From Bald Mountain Pass, the road drops into the basin that holds Mirror Lake, at 10,050-foot elevation and one of the most popular lakes in the area. Watch for the sign to the lake (fee required) 2.4 miles from Bald Mountain Pass. Turn right, and proceed to the parking lot. The campground and surrounding spruce–fir forest is a good area in which to find Three-toed Woodpecker, Gray Jay, Clark's Nutcracker, Mountain Chickadee, Red-breasted Nuthatch, Golden-crowned and Ruby-crowned kinglets, Yellow-rumped Warbler, Lincoln's Sparrow, Dark-eyed Junco, Pine Grosbeak, Cassin's Finch, and Red Crossbill. At the parking area you will find a trailhead for the High Line Trail, which leads into the High Uintas Wilderness Area and to the trails around the lake. It is an easy walk through old-growth forest, lush green meadows, and wetlands of the Duchesne River headwaters. Look for Northern Goshawk, Golden

Eagle, Blue Grouse, Calliope and Broad-tailed hummingbirds, Three-toed Woodpecker, Olive-sided and Hammond's flycatchers, Violet-green Swallow, Gray Jay, Clark's Nutcracker, Mountain Chickadee, Brown Creeper, MacGillivray's Warbler, Vesper and Lincoln's sparrows, Dark-eyed (Gray-headed) Junco, Pine Grosbeak, Cassin's Finch, and Red Crossbill.

Henry's Fork Drainage. To get to this area, take Interstate 80 east from Salt Lake City into southwest Wyoming. Take Exit 34 (set your trip odometer to 0.0) and continue through Fort Bridger to a stop-sign (5.2). Turn right (south) onto Wyoming Route 414 heading toward Mountain View. After 3.3 miles (8.5), turn right onto Wyoming Route 410 in Mountain View. The road bends toward the west, and a graveled road (Uinta County Road 246)—marked Wasatch National Forest—heads south. At a fork at 22.5 miles, stay left. Continue and cross the Forest Boundary at 24.0 miles. Here, Uinta County Road becomes FS 072. At mile 27.7, FS 072 junctions with FS 017. Bear left. At mile 34.7, turn right on FS 077 toward Henry's Fork Campground and the trailhead.

The trail (FS 117) starts at 10,500 feet and goes above the timberline, where it hooks into a network of trails through the High Uintas Wilderness. While exploring this area can be a marvelous adventure, it should not be attempted

BLACK ROSY-FINCH

SHAWNEEN FINNEGAN, DRAWING

by the inexperienced. The hiking is strenuous and at high elevation with unpredictable weather. If you do decide to give it a try, a detailed map of the trails is essential and can be obtained from the Forest Service. Most birders and hikers backpack in, set up a base camp somewhere in the basin about five miles up the main trail (FS 117), and day-hike after the ptarmigan. Water is difficult to boil at this altitude; most people carry it in or equip themselves with chemical purifiers. Golden Eagle, Williamson's Sapsucker, Gray Jay, Mountain Chickadee, American Pipit, Dark-eyed Junco, Black Rosy-Finch, Cassin's Finch, and Red Crossbill all may be found here as well as elsewhere. But the prize, of course, is the White-tailed Ptarmigan.

The much sought-after ptarmigan can be found about 9 miles up the drainage at the headwaters of Henry's Fork. Many birders have had success by continuing over Gunsight Pass and into Painter Basin. For this treasure hunt, late August is preferred by local birders.

VESPER SPARROW

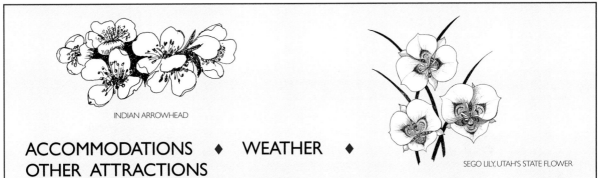

INDIAN ARROWHEAD

SEGO LILY, UTAH'S STATE FLOWER

ACCOMMODATIONS ◆ WEATHER ◆ OTHER ATTRACTIONS

When to visit. Because of the unpredictable weather, the best times to see the birds and other wildlife species of this high country are from June to mid-October. Winters are severe at high elevations, and in some winters the roads are inaccessible until mid- to late June. Ptarmigan are best searched for in late August or early September.

Where to stay. Camping facilities at all the trailheads and elsewhere in the Forest. Motels in Salt Lake City and in Evanston and Lyman, Wyoming.

Weather and attire. Snow has been recorded every month of the year but really starts after mid-September. Temperature extremes can be expected anytime. Afternoon thunderstorms are frequent in summer. Dress in layers for extreme temperatures, and naturally, good hiking footwear is important.

What else to do. Nearby are Flaming Gorge National Recreation Area, famous for its fishing and other water sports; Fossil Butte National Monument, with fossilized plant- and animal-life fifty million years old; and Dinosaur National Monument, renowned for its assemblage of dinosaur fossils. Great Salt Lake is so important to shorebird migration that it was given hemispheric status in the Western Hemisphere Shorebird Reserve Network. Bear River Migratory Bird Refuge, 15 miles west of Brigham City, is considered one of the nation's hot spots for birding. Salt Lake City offers Hogle Zoo, Tracy Aviary, and Pioneer Trails State Park.

For more information. General and campground information, District Office addresses, maps, bird list: Wasatch–Cache National Forest, 8230 Federal Building, 125 South State Street, Salt Lake City, Utah 84138; telephone 801/524-5030.

ROUTT FOREST
Colorado

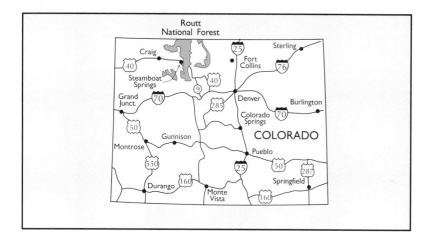

Routt National Forest

Craig · Sterling
Fort Collins
Steamboat Springs
Grand Junct. · Denver · Burlington
Colorado Springs
COLORADO
Gunnison
Montrose · Pueblo
Durango · Springfield
Monte Vista

HOW TO GET THERE. *From Denver, take Interstate 70 west for about 40 miles to exit 232 (Granby, Winter Park, U.S. Route 40), then follow scenic U.S. 40 northwest for about 124 miles to Steamboat Springs. Or, continue west on I-70 for an additional 28 miles to Exit 205 (Colorado Route 9, U.S. Route 6), then take Colorado Route 9 north 38 miles to Kremmling and turn left onto U.S. 40. Steamboat Springs is 55 miles northwest of Kremmling.*

WESTERN "QUAKERS" (ASPEN)

THE ROUTT NATIONAL FOREST was established in 1905 as the Park Range Reserve by Theodore Roosevelt, who knew the area well. He hunted the California Park country in the 1890s when the area was known for its large populations of elk, deer, and pronghorn. In 1908, Roosevelt changed the name of the forest to honor Colonel John N. Routt, the last territorial and first state governor of Colorado.

Centered on the Continental Divide of the central Rocky Mountains, the Routt Forest encompasses more than 1,000,000 acres of gorgeous scenery and highly diversified habitat. The Routt extends from 6750 feet to 13,533 feet in elevation and offers the visitor everything from alpine tundra to high mountain lakes, boreal forests, sage-brush flats, and extensive groves of aspen.

This is the domain of elk, moose (look for them in willow habitats, especially in the North Park area south of Walden), mule deer, and pronghorn (occasionally, in open sage-brush areas). Here, too, you may spot one of the large carnivores—black bear, mountain lion, and bobcat.

Conspicuous smaller mammals include yellow-bellied marmot, Richardson's ground-squirrel, Fremont's red squirrel, and Colorado and least chipmunks. Beavers inhabit lakes and ponds throughout the Forest.

Reptiles are relatively rare, but an occasional western terrestrial garter snake or rattlesnake is found. Amphibians are frequently overlooked, but there are opportunities to view the strikingly-marked tiger salamander in high-mountain pot-holes and lakes, hear the songs of chorus frogs near wet meadows and shallow lakes, or stumble upon a boreal western toad. Numerous butterflies, including fritillary, mourning cloak, and zebra swallowtail, are about during the warmer months.

Bird Life

More than 220 species have been found on the Forest. The lakes, potholes, and beaver ponds of the Big Creek Lakes area in the northeast portion of the Forest are excellent for water birds. Pied-billed and Eared grebes, which breed in nearby North Park, may be found, as well as a variety of ducks, Osprey, Wilson's Phala-

LEE F. SNYDER, PHOTOGRAPH

rope, Black and Forster's terns, and possibly Franklin's Gull. Of particular local interest is Bufflehead, which was recently confirmed as nesting around the kettle lakes south of the Big Creek Lakes.

The lakes are reached from Walden. Take State Route 125 north to Cowdrey, turn left (west) onto Road 6 to its intersection with Road 6A, then left again to the lakes.

Birding Routes

Of the many fine birding locations on the Forest, two stand out. The Red Dirt Road Loop offers a remarkable range of habitats; there is no better introduction to the Forest's bird life. California Park, northwest of Steamboat Springs, is known for the largest Sandhill Crane population in Colorado.

Red Dirt Road Loop, an approximately 110-mile trip, covers the area between Steamboat Springs on the west and Kremmling on the east. Take U.S. Route 40 east from Steamboat Springs. Soon the highway begins to climb to Rabbit Ears Pass on

the Continental Divide; you will enter the Forest 10 miles from downtown Steamboat Springs. Pull-outs provide spectacular views of Lake Catamount and the Flattop Mountains, 30 to 50 miles to the southwest, but the traffic is too heavy for serious birding.

The ascent to Rabbit Ears Pass (9426 feet) takes you over two lower passes with mountain meadows between them. Beautiful picnic sites are located at Ferndale and Harrison Creek, about 1 mile and 2 miles, respectively, after you enter the Forest; several campgrounds are available in this highland setting. In spring and summer, stop and bird each area for Gray Jay, Mountain Chickadee, Redbreasted Nuthatch, Golden-crowned and Ruby-crowned kinglets, Yellow-rumped (Audubon's) Warbler, Pine Grosbeak, Cassin's Finch, Red Crossbill, and Pine Siskin.

After crossing the west pass, the highway descends through a series of open meadows and extensive willow-dominated riparian areas. Watch these habitats for moose. The willow bottoms are utilized by White-tailed Ptarmigans in winter, but they move onto the higher slopes in spring and summer.

Walton Creek Campground is located 3.2 miles past the west summit. Continue 4

RED-NAPED SAPSUCKER

miles beyond the campground and turn right onto Forest Service Road (FS) 100, shown as Red Dirt Road or Buffalo Park Road on various road-maps. Drive slowly for logging trucks occasionally utilize this narrow dirt road. In less than 0.2 mile you will see a small pond on the left. Check it out for Mallard and Spotted Sandpiper, and look for Tree, Violet-green, and Cliff swallows overhead.

The first 10 miles of FS 100 pass through a conifer forest interspersed with open meadows. At 3.5 miles beyond the pond, stop to scan the forested area on the left for Northern Goshawk. Blue Grouse may also be found in this area, as well as Hairy Woodpecker, Williamson's Sapsucker, Gray Jay, Clark's Nutcracker, Mountain Chickadee, Dark-eyed (Gray-headed) Junco, and Pine Grosbeak. Snowmobilers have reported hearing and seeing Boreal Owls along several portions of this road. Continuing south, you will pass through a series of older clearcuts that are now a mix of meadows with young trees. These areas are ideal for Sharp-shinned and Cooper's hawks, Northern Goshawk, Red-tailed Hawk, Common Raven, and Dark-eyed Junco. Watch for soaring Golden Eagles as well.

In about 12 miles, after crossing a cattle-guard, you will enter the area known as Buffalo Park, a large

ELK

77

meadow complex. This area is utilized by several nesting pairs of (Greater) Sandhill Cranes, listed as "sensitive" by the Forest. Several of the pull-outs along the edge of the meadow provide excellent viewing. Look for Song and Lincoln's sparrows in the low shrubbery along the meadow edges and for Willow Flycatcher and MacGillivray's Warbler in the willow thickets.

Just beyond the meadow, a short unmarked spur-road leads off to the right to one of several unimproved campsites. Walk into the forest past the spur-road and along a small creek. Watch for Hairy Woodpecker, Red-naped Sapsucker, Mountain Chickadee, Ruby-crowned Kinglet, and Red-breasted Nuthatch. Listen for the beautiful song of Hermit Thrush. Fremont's red squirrels will probably scold you from the lower branches. In about 0.25 mile the stream enters a meadow. As you walk along the meandering stream, small trout can be seen darting for shelter. Elk and mule deer frequent the area at dusk and dawn. If you are here in July, the wet meadows contain a

wide assortment of blooming wild-flowers. The more common bird species here may include Gray Jay, Ruby-crowned Kinglet, White-crowned and Lincoln's sparrows, and Dark-eyed Junco.

Return to Red Dirt Road and continue on for 1.5 miles to a spur-road on the left at the south end of Buffalo Park meadow. This side road runs in and out of the forest, providing different views of the meadow and terminates at a closed gate after about one mile. Look in spring and summer for Broad-tailed hummingbird (Calliope is a rare August migrant), Gray Jay, Mountain Bluebird, Townsend's Solitaire, Warbling Vireo, Yellow-rumped Warbler, and Pine Siskin. Also check the numerous snags for Hairy and Three-toed woodpeckers, Black-capped and Mountain chickadees, House Wren, and Mountain Bluebird.

Back on the main route, you will soon (just beyond a cattle-guard) pass through stands of lodgepole pines. The large numbers of old snags are remnants of a massive insect kill in the 1950s. This en-

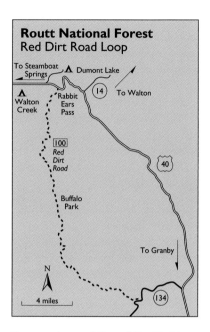

Routt National Forest
Red Dirt Road Loop

To Steamboat Springs · Dumont Lake · To Walton · 14 · Walton Creek · Rabbit Ears Pass · 100 Red Dirt Road · 40 · Buffalo Park · To Granby · N · 134 · 4 miles

tire area is good Boreal Owl habitat; they have been found for the next 5 miles beyond the cattle-guard. Here, too, is a good place to look for Blue Grouse.

In another 1.6 miles, the road bends sharply around a large meadow with willows. In summer, check this area for Willow and Cordilleran flycatchers, Warbling Vireo, and Yellow-rumped, MacGillivray's, and Wilson's warblers.

In another 5.7 miles, Red Dirt Road again crosses a cattle-guard. Stop at the pull-out with a bulletin-board on the left and bird the adjacent area. The mix of aspen, meadow, sage-brush, and coniferous-forest habitats attracts a wide variety of birds. Red-breasted Nuthatches can be heard in the spruce trees, while Warbling Vireos sing their rambling song in the aspens. Look here, also, for Red-naped Sapsucker, Tree Swallow, and House Wren. Green-tailed Towhees and White-crowned Sparrows frequent the sage-brush and meadows, Western Wood-Pewees

BUFFLEHEAD

Birdfinding in Forty National Forests and Grasslands

work the meadow edges, and Red-tailed Hawks circle overhead. Mountain Bluebirds and American Robins are everywhere.

In a few more miles Red Dirt Road leaves the National Forest and enters private property. You will find a dramatic change from forest to sagebrush and aspen. For the next 4 miles watch for Vesper and White-crowned sparrows along the roadside and Mountain Bluebird on the wires overhead. Other species to expect include Northern Harrier, Red-tailed Hawk, Golden Eagle, American Kestrel, Sage Grouse, and Townsend's Solitaire.

Red Dirt Road ends at the intersection with Colorado Route 134. A right turn at Rte. 134 will take you back west to Steamboat Springs over a long (62 mile) but scenic route through Gore Pass to Colorado Route 131. To continue the Loop, however, turn left onto Rte. 134 and drive east toward U.S. Route 40. In about 3.5 miles Rte. 134 comes out of the valley and enters a flat at a ranch. Watch the fences here for Red-tailed Hawk, Western Kingbird, Western Meadowlark, and Red-winged, Brewer's, and (occasionally) Yellow-headed blackbirds. Also watch out for dogs along this road; they love to hide in the ditch and suddenly dart out at passing cars.

Rt. 134 ends in another mile at U.S. 40. A dam is planned for Muddy Creek near here, and a new reservoir will result in some major changes in the habitat and bird life of the area. For now, the area is dominated by big sage-brush and Black-billed Magpies.

Turn left onto U.S. 40 to return to Steamboat Springs. Traffic along U.S. 40 can be heavy, so sudden stops are

not recommended. Along the 20-mile stretch from the intersection of Rte. 134 and U.S. 40 to Colorado Route 14, check the fields for pronghorn. In winter, thousands of elk move out of the surrounding mountains to overwinter in this area.

Just 1.6 miles north from the intersection of Rte. 134 and U.S. 40, the road makes a bend to the left before dropping down into a series of draws. Pull off to the right and look down the creek. A series of oxbows are usually occupied by waterfowl, especially Mallard, Blue-winged Teal, and Northern Shoveler.

The next 15 miles are dominated by hayfields. Watch the fences for Mountain Bluebird and Loggerhead Shrike. About 18 miles from Rte. 134 the highway climbs back into the mountains. On the left side is a series of beaver ponds that should be checked carefully. Mallard, Blue-winged and Cinnamon teals, Lesser Scaup, and Vesper and Lincoln's sparrows are all possible. Cliff Swallows feed over the ponds and nest across the road under the eaves of the houses. Tree, Violet-green, Northern Rough-winged, and Barn swallows may be found, as well.

At the intersection with Rte. 14, the highway crosses the Continental Divide at Muddy Pass from the Colorado River drainage to the North Platte drainage, reenters the Forest, and crosses the Divide again on Rabbit Ears Pass. A pond shortly beyond the intersection with Colorado 14 usually has Ring-necked Ducks. At 1.8 miles past the intersection, the road makes a wide hairpin curve around a series of beaver ponds and

forest stands. Park in the pull-off on the right and walk around in the area. Western Wood-Pewee, Mountain Chickadee, Ruby-crowned Kinglet, and Pine Grosbeak are common, and Yellow and Wilson's warblers frequent the brushy edges of the ponds. Yellow-rumped and MacGillivray's

LOGGERHEAD SHRIKE

warblers are possible, and yellow-bellied marmots can usually be heard whistling from across the highway.

U.S. 40 west will take you back to Steamboat Springs, passing the north end of Red Dirt Road (FS 100) 0.5 mile beyond the east summit of Rabbit Ears Pass. Near here on the right (north) is Dumont Lake, which offers good birding in the campground and recreation area. You should look for Mallard, Spotted Sandpiper, Killdeer, Common Snipe, Gray Jay, Olive-sided Flycatcher, Ruby-crowned Kinglet, Yellow-rumped Warbler, Lincoln's and White-crowned sparrows,

Cassin's Finch, Pine Grosbeak, and Pine Siskin.

California Park is reached by driving west from Steamboat Springs on U.S. 40 for 22 miles to Hayden and then turning north onto Routt County Road (CR) 80 (gravel) for about 16 miles until you enter the National Forest and come to FS 150. The Forest Service road passes through open park land with surrounding aspen groves, a major nesting area for Sandhill Cranes. More than fifty pairs of these marvelous creatures nest here during summer. Although the area is closed during nesting in May and June, the cranes are easily viewed from the road for the remainder of the summer. Both resident and non-resident flocks of Sandhill Cranes stage near Hayden in the spring (15 March to 15 April) and in the fall (15 August to 15 October).

California Park also is an excellent place to view Northern Harrier, Prairie Falcon, and Sage and Sharp-tailed grouse, as well as the common birds listed elsewhere for aspen, sage, and meadow habitats.

MIMI HOPPE WOLF, DRAWING

MOUNTAIN CHICKADEE

ACCOMMODATIONS ♦ WEATHER ♦ OTHER ATTRACTIONS

When to visit. June through early October is generally snow-free, and most major roads are open and passable, although many of the higher-elevation roads may not be open until mid-July. Check with the local Forest District Offices to determine seasonal road-closures.

Where to Stay. Numerous developed and undeveloped camping areas on the Forest. Motels can be found in Steamboat Springs and Kremmling, as well as in Walden, Craig, Oak Creek, Phippsburg, Hahns Peak, Hayden, and Clark.

Weather and attire. Summer offers mostly warm days (60s to 80s) with cool nights (30s to 50s), but these conditions can deteriorate rapidly. Winters are severe with heavy snows. Always bring warm clothing and rain-gear at any time of the year. Beware of sudden thunderstorms and lightning in the warmer months. Sunscreen and insect repellents are suggested in spring and summer, and be sure to pack sunscreen for winter ski trips.

What else to do. On the Forest: Hiking, backpacking, pack-horse trips, boating, whitewater rafting, kayaking, fishing, alpine and cross-country skiing, and snowmobiling (Red Dirt Road is excellent in winter). Adjacent to the Forest, the Arapaho National Wildlife Refuge provides self-guided auto tours, primarily for waterfowl, and the Colorado Division of Wildlife maintains several viewing areas in North Park south of Walden to observe courting Sage Grouse in March. Other points of interest: Mount Zirkel and Flat Tops Wilderness, Flat Tops Trail (National Scenic Byway), Dinosaur National Monument (100 miles west), and Steamboat Ski Area.

For more information. General and campground information, District Office addresses, maps, bird list: visitors centers in Steamboat Springs and Kremmling, and Routt National Forest, 29587 W. U.S. Highway 40, Suite 20, Steamboat Springs, Colorado 80487; telephone 303/879-1722.

BLUE COLUMBINE, COLORADO'S STATE FLOWER

ARAPAHO FOREST
Colorado

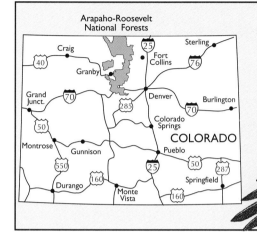

Arapaho-Roosevelt
National Forests

COLORADO

HOW TO GET THERE. *For Guanella Pass, take Interstate 70 west from Denver for 42 miles to the historic mining settlement of Georgetown (Exit 228). To reach Granby from Denver, take I-70 west for about 40 miles to Exit 232 (Granby, Winter Park, U.S. Route 40), then follow U.S. 40 northwest over Berthoud Pass, through Winter Park and Fraser, for about 45 miles.*

OSPREY

MIMI HOPPE WOLF, DRAWING

WHITE-TAILED PTARMIGAN, Red-naped and Williamson's sapsuckers, Three-toed Woodpecker, Hammond's, Dusky, Cordilleran, and Willow flycatchers, and Brown-capped, Black, and Gray-crowned rosy-finches are Colorado specialties that birders can seek with success on the Arapaho National Forest. After roads to the high country open in May or June, summer and fall birding offer long daylight hours, spectacular mountain scenery, and a variety of subalpine and alpine breeders. The summer-resort facilities at Grand Lake, as well as the proximity of Rocky Mountain National Park, offer the entire family a wide choice of vacation activities and lodging. During winter, a day-trip from Denver will take you to 11,669-foot-high Guanella Pass, wintering-ground for snowy-plumaged White-tailed Ptarmigan.

The Arapaho National Forest—established in 1908 by Theodore Roosevelt—is named after the plains Indian tribe that frequented the region for summer hunting. That portion of the Arapaho administered as part of the Arapaho and Roosevelt National Forests encompasses 475,000 acres along the Continental Divide at altitudes ranging up to 14,260 feet.

Approximately 11 percent of the Forest is alpine tundra. Below treeline Engelmann spruce, subalpine fir, and limber pine predominate at higher elevations, while lodgepole pine, Douglas-fir, and quaking aspen carpet the lower slopes. Blue spruce, alder, birch, narrow-leaf cottonwood, and a variety of willows line the streams. In summer, a riot of wildflowers—from Indian paintbrush to alpine forget-me-not, calypso orchid, lupine, and columbine—brightens tundra, forest, and meadows. Mammals—ranging in size from stately elk and nimble Rocky Mountain goats to yellow-bellied marmots and pikas—abound. Scores of different species of butterflies find their preferred habitats on the Forest.

Bird Life
Well over two hundred resident and migratory species have been recorded within the Forest's diverse ecosystems. While few waterfowl remain to breed, the larger lakes and ponds attract a variety of migrants. The breeders include Green-winged Teal, Mallard, Ring-necked Duck, and American Coot. Northern Pintail, Blue-winged Teal, Northern Shoveler, American Wigeon, and Ruddy Duck are regular migrants; lesser numbers of Eared Grebe, Cinnamon Teal, and Redhead are found. Pied-billed and Western grebes (look carefully for Clark's; they occur, too) are non-breeding summer visitors, and Common and Barrow's goldeneyes can often be found in winter.

Up to fifteen species of migrant shorebirds frequent the Forest's wetlands and shorelines, including: American Avocet, Solitary Sandpiper, Willet, Western, Least, and Baird's sandpipers, Long-billed

VIEW FROM MOUNT EVANS, ARAPAHO NATIONAL FOREST

Birding Routes

Two very different locations, Guanella Pass–Mount Evans and the Arapaho National Recreation Area, offer an excellent sampling of the birds to be found on the Arapaho at all seasons.

Guanella Pass–Mount Evans. White-tailed Ptarmigan tops the wish-list of most birders visiting Colorado's high-altitude country. During suitable winter weather, it can be found with relative ease on Guanella Pass—if you're sharp enough to spot its coal-black eye against the grouse's immaculate snow-colored plumage as it quietly feeds on willows. Late October through mid-April are the best months to make the trip. Hordes of cross-country skiers and day-trippers visit the pass on sunny winter weekends, so plan to arrive early. Sunny days with no wind or light southerly breezes may be most favorable for finding ptarmigan close to

Dowitcher, and Wilson's and Red-necked phalaropes. Killdeer, Spotted Sandpiper, and Common Snipe remain to nest.

The Arapaho's forests are home, especially in summer, to a varied assortment of western species: Northern Goshawk, Blue Grouse, Northern

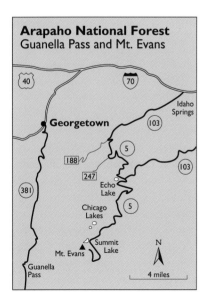

Arapaho National Forest
Guanella Pass and Mt. Evans

40 • 70 • Idaho Springs • 103 • Georgetown • 5 • 188 • 247 • 103 • 381 • Echo Lake • Chicago Lakes • 5 • Mt. Evans • Summit Lake • Guanella Pass • N • 4 miles

Pygmy-Owl, Boreal Owl, Broad-tailed Hummingbird, Red-naped and Williamson's sapsuckers, Three-toed Woodpecker, Western Wood-Pewee, and Olive-sided Flycatcher.

Four *Empidonax* flycatchers divide different habitats: look for Hammond's in conifers, Dusky in brush, aspen, and willows, Willow in willow tracts, and Cordilleran in ravines and around mountain cabins. The Forest also holds Tree and Violet-green swallows, Gray and Steller's jays, Clark's Nutcracker, Mountain Chickadee, American Dipper, Western Bluebird, Townsend's Solitaire, Swainson's and Hermit thrushes, Solitary Vireo, Western Tanager, Black-headed Grosbeak, Green-tailed Towhee, Pine Grosbeak, Cassin's Finch, and Pine Siskin. MacGillivray's and Wilson's warblers and Fox, Song, and Lincoln's sparrows prefer the wetlands, while Great Horned Owl, Black-billed Magpie, and Mountain Bluebird are found in the more sparsely forested open country.

WHITE-TAILED PTARMIGAN

the road. Away from the road the snow can be deceptively deep, requiring snowshoes or cross-country skiis.

After exiting Interstate 70 at Georgetown (exit 228), drive through town to Rose Street (County Road (CR) 381), checking feeders along the way for all three species of rosy-finches. Turn south on CR 381, which climbs about 9.3 miles to Guanella's summit. Stop along the way to check for Pine Grosbeak, Red Crossbill, and Pine Siskin.

At the pass you will see a sign to a trail leading southwest toward a low hill. Small flocks of ptarmigan are often found feeding on tips of willows sticking through the snow at the base of the hill on either side of the trail. Continue up the trail to and past the hill's summit if need be. If you stray off the trail, take great care not to walk on the willows. They are the birds' sole winter food source and grow slowly at high altitude.

In April, most of the Guanella Pass ptarmigan move about 10 miles east to their breeding-grounds on Mount Evans, also on the Arapaho National Forest. By about Memorial Day, when the road to the 14,200-foot summit opens, nesting is well underway. The mottled-plumaged hens

will introduce their chicks to the rigors of alpine life between mid-June and mid-August.

To reach Mount Evans, leave Interstate 70 at Idaho Springs (exit 240, Colorado Route 103), about 30 miles west of Denver. Follow winding Rte. 103 for about 14 miles to just beyond Echo Lake (elevation 10,600 feet), where you should turn right onto Colorado Route 5, the highest paved road in the U.S. After turning onto Rte. 5, you will climb through subal-

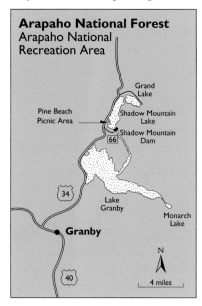

PINE GROSBEAK

pine forest for the first few miles. As you approach timberline (11,500 feet), the trees become fewer, and dense groves of Engelmann spruce give way to open forests. Watch for Wilson's Warblers in the open areas of willows and White-crowned Sparrows in both willows and spruce forests.

The road soon tops out onto the tundra, which is a blaze of color in the summer. Brown-capped Rosy-Finches nest only on the rugged cliff-faces, but often feed about the edges of Summit Lake (12,830 feet). If you do not see them near the parking lot, walk to the right a short distance until you can look over the rim to the Chicago Lakes far below. The rosy-finches often fly about the face of the cliffs and commonly feed on insects trapped on remnant snowbanks. Prairie Falcon, Common Raven, Horned Lark, and American Pipit are also found around the lake. Spotted

Sandpipers nest here, and Baird's Sandpiper is a regular fall migrant.

One area where White-tailed Ptarmigans have been found regularly is just above Summit Lake. Go up the road for 0.25 mile beyond the chain and then climb the hill on the right. Again, early morning is best before other hikers disturb the birds.

On your way back to I-70 via Rte. 103, take the turnoff for West Chicago Creek Campground, about 6 miles from Echo Lake. This road leads through stands of quaking aspen, where you can find nesting Red-naped Sapsucker, Tree and Violet-green swallows, Black-capped and Mountain chickadees, Red-breasted Nuthatch, and Warbling Vireo.

Arapaho National Recreation Area. To experience another facet of the Arapaho's diversity in summertime, you should visit the 36,000-acre Arapaho National Recreation Area located a few miles west of the Continental Divide near Granby. From Granby take U.S. Route 34, north toward Grand Lake and the west entrance to Rocky Mountain National Park. After 12.5 miles, turn right at the Pine Beach Picnic Area sign. Park at the picnic parking area and walk east along the shore of Shadow Mountain Lake to scan for ducks and geese in the wetland areas and about the islands. Ospreys nest on the islands here, Common Snipe may be heard winnowing overhead or seen feeding in the sedges, and Tree and Violet-green swallows course over the lake. California and Ring-billed gulls may be numerous on the lake. River otters are seen occasionally; you may find their fish-scale-filled scat along the lakeshore.

Arapaho National Forest
Arapaho National Recreation Area

Grand Lake

Pine Beach Picnic Area

Shadow Mountain Lake

Shadow Mountain Dam

66

34

Lake Granby

Monarch Lake

Granby

34

40

N

4 miles

In the trees and open areas around Pine Beach look for Great Horned Owl, Broad-tailed Hummingbird, Williamson's Sapsucker, Steller's Jay, Red-breasted Nuthatch, Brown Creeper, Ruby-crowned Kinglet, Mountain Bluebird, and Pine Grosbeak.

Return to Route 34, turn left for 100 yards, and left again onto paved County Road 66. Drive two miles to Shadow Mountain Dam, from which you may study waterfowl and shorebirds in the open channel to the west as well as downstream on the Colorado River. The building below the dam is used by the Colorado Division of Wildlife to collect and milk spawning Kokanee salmon in November and December. As many as twenty wintering Bald Eagles congregate at the dam to take advantage of the salmon run, and river otters make sure to get their share. You may see them slide down the snow on the dam spillways into the pool below.

The abundance of relatively undisturbed forested shoreline habitat and fishable open water create excellent Osprey habitat. The Osprey population within the Arapaho National Recreation Area has increased from four pairs in the early 1970s to 22 pairs in 1992 (12 pairs fledged young). The Ospreys, which arrive in late April, have fledglings active about their nests until late August, and they leave for their southern wintering-grounds in late September. Nesting Ospreys may be viewed on all five lakes within the Arapaho National Recreation Area, but are extremely sensitive to human disturbance when nesting. Birders are asked to heed all posted closures. Observers should always leave at least a 500-foot buffer between themselves and nesting Ospreys.

CARL JAMES FREEMAN, DRAWING

RIVER OTTERS

ACCOMMODATIONS ◆ WEATHER ◆ OTHER ATTRACTIONS

When to visit. Waterfowl as well as many forest and alpine residents can be found year-round, but the greatest avian diversity occurs in May and September during migrations. Rocky Mountain specialties such as Red-naped and Williamson's sapsuckers, Olive-sided, Hammond's, and Dusky flycatchers, Tree and Violet-green swallows, Ruby-crowned Kinglet, Swainson's and Hermit thrushes, and Wilson's Warbler are best seen and heard in June and July. Come to Shadow Mountain Dam for Bald Eagles from November through February; December through February are the best months for ptarmigan at Guanella Pass.

Where to stay. Campgrounds throughout the Forest and in adjacent towns as well as in Rocky Mountain National Park. This popular summer resort area has many motels; early reservations are recommended, particularly on weekends.

Weather and attire. Summer days are generally warm and sunny—often with afternoon thunderstorms—but because of the altitude, be prepared for chilly or genuinely frigid nights. Insect repellent is recommended during the summer, and sunscreen is a necessity at high altitude. In winter, storms frequently cause pass and road closures and hazardous driving conditions. Do not venture into the Rockies unprepared. On Guanella Pass, in particular, you must take the responsibility for your own survival. Be informed about the symptoms of hypothermia and altitude sickness and be mentally prepared to retreat if either occurs.

What else to do. On the Forest: hiking, fishing, hunting, boating, canoeing, horseback-riding, mountain-biking, ranger-led nature walks, scenic drives. Cross-country skiing and snowmobiling are popular winter activities, with equipment rentals in Winter Park, Granby, and Grand Lake. Rocky Mountain National Park with its unparalleled Trail Ridge Road (and more possibilities for summer ptarmigan and Brown-capped Rosy-Finches) is a few miles north of Shadow Mountain Lake on U.S. 34; Indian Peaks Wilderness Area straddles the Continental Divide immediately to the east; Never Summer Wilderness Area is 10 miles to the north. About 20 miles west of Georgetown off Interstate 70, a spectacular section of U.S. 6 winds over 11,992-foot Loveland Pass. Hiking-trails lead in both directions from the top of the pass, offering opportunities to see pikas, American Pipits, and possibly ptarmigan.

For more information. General and camping information, District Office addresses, maps, bird list: Sulphur Ranger District Office, Arapaho National Forest, 62429 Highway 40, P.O. Box 10, Granby, Colorado 80446; telephone 303/887-3331.

HAREBELL

COCONINO FOREST
Arizona

JEREMY PEARSE, DRAWING

DAPHNE GEMMILL, PHOTOGRAPH

COMMON BLACK-HAWK

HOW TO GET THERE. *Flagstaff is conveniently located in north–central Arizona at the junction of Interstates 40 and 17, about 140 miles north of Phoenix and 250 miles southeast of Las Vegas. Both the Page Springs–Oak Creek and Verde areas are accessible from Cottonwood, which is about 50 miles southwest of Flagstaff via U.S. Route 89A, or 64 miles via I-17 south and Arizona Route 260 north. From Phoenix, take I-17 north for 85 miles to Exit 285, Rte. 260, then go north on Rte. 260 for 14 miles.*

ARIZONA IS TYPICALLY PICTURED as deserts, not alpine tundra. Yet dominating the north–central part of the state is the extremely diverse Coconino National Forest that features a variety of ecosystems, from desert to montane forest to alpine tundra. This 1.8-million-acre Forest ranges in elevation from 2600 feet in the arid lowlands to 12,648 feet at the top of Humphrey's Peak, Arizona's highest. It was here that Dr. C. Hart Merriam and Vernon Bailey hit upon the concept of "life zones," while exploring the region in the late 1800s. Although no longer widely used, this theory provided the foundation for our modern understanding of the ecology of the western U.S.

A climb through the Coconino will put it all together in one splendid natural-history adventure. You will begin your tour in the classic desert environment of grasses and shrubs, which include prickly-pear cactus, mesquite, and cat's claw acacia. Black-tailed jackrabbits, Ord's kangaroo rat, and collared peccary can be found in this arid habitat, along with such butterflies as goatweed and paintbrush checkerspot. As you

CURVE-BILLED THRASHER AND CHOLLA CACTUS

PAINTED REDSTART

move higher, riparian habitats below 5000 feet are cloaked in dense forests of Arizona sycamore, Fremont and narrowleaf cottonwoods, Arizona alder, Arizona walnut, velvet ash, and several species of willow, with an understory of wild rose, coffeeberry, and wild grape. Watercress, monkeyflower, sedges, and grasses grow along the stream banks. Here you will find desert shrew, cave bat, white-tailed antelope ground-squirrel, desert cottontail, silky pocket mouse, and cactus mouse. Kit fox and hooded skunk are rare. The warm and dry areas of the Forest support a number of reptiles, such as mountain kingsnake, western garter snake, collared lizard, and short-horned lizard. Butterflies include goggle-eye, live-oak hairstreak, and russet skipperwing.

Above 5000 feet, a major portion of the Coconino is dry woodland habitat of pinyon pine–juniper and widely spaced ponderosa pine, representing the southern end of the Colorado Plateau, which contains the largest concentration of these majestic trees in the U.S. The mid-elevation forest is interspersed with Douglas-

fir and Gambel oak and has an understory mainly of grasses and wildflowers. This is where you may encounter Abert's tree-squirrel and golden-mantled ground-squirrel, brush and pinyon mice, gray-collared chipmunk, and white-tailed deer. Eastern fence, tree, and side-blotched lizards are among the most conspicuous reptiles, while Arizona sister, grasshopper satyr, and coppermark are some of the butterflies present in this zone.

The mixed forest above 9000 feet is characterized by corkbark fir and Engelmann spruce, with willows and alders in riparian areas. It is home to the red squirrel, mule deer, and elk. Western white, western tiger swallowtail, prairie arctic, and western admiral are some of the butterflies found in the mixed-conifer forests.

Between 10,000 and 11,500 feet, you will see more Engelmann spruce and bristlecone pine (found nowhere else in Arizona) above masses of vari-hued columbine, creeping juniper, and gooseberry bushes.

At the top of your climb you reach the Alpine tundra with moss campion, Alpine avens, and Alpine sunflowers.

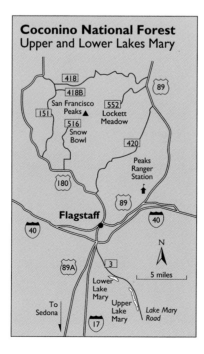

Coconino National Forest
Upper and Lower Lakes Mary

Bird Life

More than three hundred species of birds have been found on the Coconino National Forest. Your birding begins with such desert-dwellers as Greater Roadrunner, Lesser Nighthawk, Verdin, Crissal Thrasher, Abert's Towhee, and Black-throated Sparrow. Lowland forests and riparian areas hold Common Black-Hawk, Yellow-billed Cuckoo, Belted Kingfisher, Black Phoebe, Bridled Titmouse, Yellow Warbler, and Abert's Towhee. The ponderosa pine forest is habitat for Wild Turkey, Acorn Woodpecker, Violet-green Swallow, Steller's Jay, Common Raven, Mountain Chickadee, White-breasted and Pygmy nuthatches, Western Bluebird, Solitary Vireo, and Virginia's and Grace's warblers.

The higher mixed and montane forests and riparian communities are havens for Cooper's Hawk, Williamson's and Red-naped sapsuckers, Three-toed Woodpecker, Clark's Nutcracker, Mountain Chickadee, American Dipper, Townsend's Solitaire, Warbling Vireo, Western Tanager, Evening Grosbeak, and Red Crossbill. At the very top of the Coconino, American Pipit nests on the treeless alpine tundra.

Birding Routes

The forest contains a number of good birding areas, but five are exceptional: the Lower and Upper Lakes Mary; Oak Creek Canyon; Page Springs and Lower Oak Creek; Verde Valley; and the Snow Bowl Ski Area and Hart Prairie Road.

Lower and Upper Lakes Mary are two man-made reservoirs a few miles southeast of Flagstaff. Take a right turn at the light prior to I-40 onto U.S. Route 89A south; go to the first traffic light by the EconoLodge and take a left on Beulah; go under the underpass; and take the first left on FS 3 (not signed), Lake Mary Road. Drive southeast for just over 7 miles to Lower Lake Mary; a good place to stop is the Lake Mary Monument, 0.2

mile beyond the dam that creates the lake. This is a vantage point for observing migratory waterfowl. Pied-billed and Eared grebes, Canada Goose, Mallard, Northern Pintail, Cinnamon Teal, Northern Shoveler, American Wigeon, Canvasback, Red-head, Ring-necked and Ruddy ducks, and Bufflehead can often be found here in spring and fall. Other birds to watch for include White-faced Ibis, Golden Eagle, Townsend's Solitaire, Yellow-headed Blackbird, and various sparrows, including Chipping, Vesper, Lark, and White-crowned. In late fall and winter, Bald Eagles frequent the tall pine snags near the lake. Sightings of ten to twenty of these majestic birds are not uncommon. Continue southeast on Lake Mary Road for another 3.3 miles to Upper Lake Mary. This larger and deeper lake is more likely to have concentrations of diving ducks, Common Loon, Western Grebe, and rarities, which have included Pacific Loon, Tundra Swan, Ross's Goose, Oldsquaw, all three scoters, and Hooded Merganser. The parking lot at the boat ramp is a good place to observe Osprey hunting for fish. In spring and fall, shorebirds including Killdeer, Black-necked Stilt, American Avocet, Greater and Lesser yellowlegs, Willet, Western and Least sandpipers, Long-billed Dowitcher, and Wilson's Phalarope visit the lakes.

The ponderosa pine forest dominates the surrounding area, situated at about 7000 feet, and a spring or summer walk through the woods or along any Forest Service Road off Lake Mary Road will likely produce Wild Turkey, Lewis's and Acorn woodpeckers (both near oaks), Western Wood-Pewee, Steller's Jay, Mountain Chickadee, White-breasted and Pygmy nuthatches, Virginia's and Grace's warblers, and Western and Hepatic tanagers.

Oak Creek Canyon. This site combines good birding with spectacular scenery. Located between

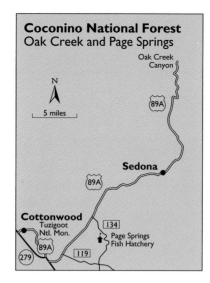

Flagstaff and Sedona, the rather narrow canyon supports a permanent stream that extends from mixed-coniferous forest at the head to pinyon pine and juniper chaparral habitat at the mouth. From Flagstaff go south on U.S. 89A 11 miles. Here the road switchbacks down 1.5 miles to the creek. The canyon continues for about 14 miles to the town of Sedona. There are numerous campgrounds, picnic areas, and pullouts in the canyon bottom that give access to the creek and adjacent forest. Band-tailed Pigeon, Northern Pygmy-Owl, Steller's Jay, Brown Creeper, Canyon Wren, Hutton's Vireo, Virginia's and Red-faced warblers, and Painted Redstart can be found in the cooler, upper half of the canyon, while White-throated Swift, Gray Flycatcher, Cassin's Kingbird, Scrub Jay, Plain Titmouse, Bushtit, Gray Vireo, Black-throated Gray Warbler, Rufous-crowned and Black-chinned sparrows, and three orioles—Hooded, Northern and Scott's—occupy the slopes and riparian vegetation of the warmer, lower portion.

Page Springs and Lower Oak Creek. The best birding area on Lower Oak Creek is the Page Springs Fish Hatchery, located between Sedona and Cottonwood. Continuing south on U.S. 89A from Sedona about 9 miles, turn left onto Forest Service Road (FS) 134 at the Page Springs

sign. Go 2.8 miles to the Oak Creek bridge and continue another 0.4 mile to the fish hatchery. There is a parking area and visitors center with access to riparian vegetation and dense undergrowth. Much of the best habitat was destroyed when the trout hatchery was modernized, but it is a good place in spring and summer for several sought-after species: Black-crowned Night-Heron, Common Merganser (in the creek), Common Black-Hawk, Yellow-billed Cuckoo, Black-chinned Hummingbird, Gila Woodpecker, Brown-crested Flycatcher, Bridled Titmouse, Bell's Vireo, Lucy's Warbler, Yellow-breasted Chat, Summer Tanager, Blue Grosbeak, and Abert's Towhee. The hatchery has ten open ponds situated on the west side of Oak Creek, across from the restaurant, 0.5 mile back toward U.S. 89A. Other birds to be expected here are Great Blue and Green herons, a scattering of ducks from September to April, American Kestrel, Gambel's Quail, Belted Kingfisher, Phainopepla, and occasionally a few migrant shorebirds.

The Verde Valley sites include Peck's Lake, Dead Horse Ranch State Park, and Tavasci Marsh, all within a

GRAY VIREO

belt of riparian and desert upland habitat, situated at about 3500 feet along the river from Clarkdale southeast for a few miles to Cottonwood. From U.S. 89A in Cottonwood take Arizona Route 260 (Main Street), and follow the signs to Dead Horse Ranch State Park. The park supports many of the desert and riparian birds listed below. After crossing the Verde River, continue past the park entrance. In a few miles the dirt road slopes downhill into a broad drainage. The ancient Native American ruins of Tuzigoot National Monument are visible on the opposite slope. Stop at the bottom near the fence stile allowing entrance to Tavasci Marsh. This site is a small spring-fed marsh, uncommon habitat in the desert. The marsh, formerly privately owned, is now the property of the Arizona Game and Fish Department and is scheduled for rehabilitation after years of overgrazing by cattle. Continue on the dirt road past the entrance to Tuzigoot National Monument, where the now-paved road proceeds on to U.S. 89A. Just before crossing the Verde River bridge, turn right on the dirt road toward Peck's Lake. Turn right again at the large out-of-place-looking house. This road circles Peck's Lake, an ox-

BRIDLED TITMOUSE

bow of the Verde River, and rejoins the main road near the house.

These areas contain classic desert riparian habitats associated with perennial streams that support diverse avian communities. A variety of herons and egrets, waterfowl, and rails use the Tavasci Marsh and Peck's Lake for feeding and nesting, along with Anna's Hummingbird, Black Phoebe, Vermilion and Ash-throated flycatchers, Western Kingbird, Violet-green, Northern Rough-winged, and Cliff swallows, Bridled Titmouse, Marsh Wren, and Northern Cardinal.

The desert and desert-grasslands along the road from Dead Horse Ranch State Park and surrounding Peck's Lake support a further group of birds. Look for Red-tailed and Ferruginous (in winter) hawks, Greater Roadrunner, Lesser and Common nighthawks, Ladder-backed Woodpecker, Say's Phoebe, Cassin's Kingbird, Common Raven, Verdin, Canyon and Rock wrens, Crissal Thrasher, Canyon and Abert's towhees, and in fall and winter Sage Thrasher, Brewer's, Vesper, Lark, and Sage sparrows, and Western Meadowlark.

Snow Bowl Ski Area and Hart Prairie Road lie between 7000 and 12,600 feet elevation northwest of Flagstaff. From the junction of U.S. Routes 89 and 180 in downtown Flagstaff, take U.S. 180 north for 7 miles to the Snow Bowl at 9500 feet intersection and turn right onto FS 516; the Snow Bowl is 7 miles ahead. This route passes through ponderosa pine forest, high meadows, and mixed coniferous forest as it climbs the San Francisco Peaks. Typical ponderosa pine community birds occur along the lower road, and boreal species such as Three-toed Woodpecker, Clark's Nutcracker, Red-breasted Nuthatch, Golden-crowned Kinglet, Hermit Thrush, Yellow-rumped Warbler, and Dark-eyed Junco can be found at higher elevations. Good areas in the boreal forest are found around the upper ski-lodge and

along the Humphrey's Peak Trail starting at the upper ski-lodge. This trail winds to the top of Humphrey's Peak, the highest point in Arizona at 12,643 feet and home to nesting American Pipits, after passing through excellent Three-toed Woodpecker habitat. Spotted and Northern Saw-whet owls have been found along FS 516 below the Snow Bowl. For the less energetic, the first 1.5 miles of the Humphrey's Peak Trail plus the chair-lift to the top of Agassiz Peak at 11,500 feet will provide excellent birding opportunities. The ski-lift and operates from 10 AM to 4 PM during the summer. Opening dates vary from year to year; visitors should check with the lodge.

Afterwards, return to U.S. 180, turn right (northwest), and drive 2.5 miles to the Hart Prairie Road (FS 151) on the right. This route passes through ponderosa pine forest, grassland meadows, and aspen groves. Forest species are similar to those near Lake Mary, but in the vicinity of Fern Mountain about 5 miles along FS 151 a few additions include: Northern Goshawk, Sharp-shinned and Cooper's hawks, Golden Eagle, Red-naped and Williamson's sapsuckers, Olive-sided, Dusky, and Cordilleran flycatchers, Purple Martin, Brown Creeper, House Wren, MacGillivray's Warbler, Black-headed Grosbeak, Green-tailed Towhee, and Lincoln's Sparrow.

Continue on FS 151 for 7 miles to FS 418B and turn right; it is about one mile to Little Spring. Park on FS151 and walk the road. This is an excellent place to find high-country birds, such as Broad-tailed Hummingbird, Williamson's Sapsucker, Clark's Nutcracker, Evening Grosbeak, and Red Crossbill. After dark, Northern Saw-whet Owl is sometimes found here.

Return to FS 151 and turn right. In one mile, FS 151 intersects FS 418, which you can take to the right (east) for about 10 miles to U.S. 89, making a loop around the San Francisco Peaks (total distance is 50 miles, Flag-

F.P. BENNETT, DRAWING

staff to Flagstaff). Pinyon Jays can often be seen along U.S. 89 from FS 418 to a few miles north of Flagstaff. Or you may wish to continue north on FS 151 for 1.5 miles to where it intersects U.S. 180, a key route between Flagstaff and Grand Canyon National Park.

If you want to keep birding, go south on U.S. 89, 0.7 mile to FS 552 to Lockett Meadow. The road is a narrow washboard track with panoramic views to the north and east. The meadow is inside a quiet caldera. This island of emerald green is ringed with aspens coloring the steep volcanic slopes with gold in early fall. In spring and summer, the penstemon, lupine, and sunflowers add sparkling reds, blues, and yellows. The 2-mile moderate Inner Basin Trail into the heart of the ancient volcano begins in the day area parking spot halfway around the campground road. The permanent residents are Sharp-shinned Hawk, Northern Goshawk, Blue Grouse, "Mexican" Spotted Owl, Three-toed Woodpecker, Steller's Jay, Clark's Nutcracker, and Mountain Chickadee. These birds are joined in the summer by Band-tailed Pigeon, Flammulated Owl, Williamson's Sapsucker, Greater Pewee, Dusky and Cordilleran flycatchers, Hermit Thrush, Solitary and Warbling vireos, and Western Tanager. Adding to the color of fall foliage are neotropical migrants. Watch for Nashville, Yellow-rumped, Townsend's, and Hermit warblers. Porcupine, elk, and black bear frequent the basin.

FLAMMULATED OWL

ACCOMMODATIONS ♦ WEATHER ♦ OTHER ATTRACTIONS

When to visit. The Forest is open all year, but the best time to visit is late spring or early fall.

Where to stay. Forest Service and state campgrounds; numerous motels in Flagstaff and Sedona.

Weather. The slopes of the San Francisco Peaks can be extremely cold in winter but sunny and warm in summer. The Lake Mary area, at about 7000 feet, has cold winters that are rarely severe although there can be deep snow. Spring, normally windy and cool; summer, frequent afternoon thunderstorms; fall months, warm and dry. Nights are cool at all seasons. The lower Oak Creek and Verde Valley areas, at about 3500 feet, have mild winters. Spring, normally warm and pleasant; summer can be very hot; fall months, warm and dry.

Be prepared for variable weather conditions. Jackets and rain-gear are always appropriate. Wear sunscreen when it is sunny at any season; high-elevation sunburns can be severe.

What else to do. Driving, hiking, fishing, boating (in Upper Lake Mary), swimming and other water-related activities. Grand Canyon National Park, with its awesome vistas, is 70 miles north of Flagstaff. Walnut Canyon, Sunset Crater, and Wupatki National Monuments, Kachina Peaks Wilderness, and Sycamore Canyon Wilderness are all near Flagstaff. Other areas of interest at Flagstaff include the Museum of Northern Arizona, featuring Native American cultures, and the Lowell Observatory, where the planet Pluto was first discovered. Tuzigoot and Montezuma Castle National Monuments, south of Sedona, contain prehistoric cliff dwellings and other ruins from about A.D. 1300.

For more information. General and campground information, District Office addresses, maps, bird list: Coconino National Forest, 2323 E. Greenlaw Lane, Flagstaff, Arizona 86004; telephone 602/527-3600.

PRICKLY PEAR

CORONADO FOREST
Arizona

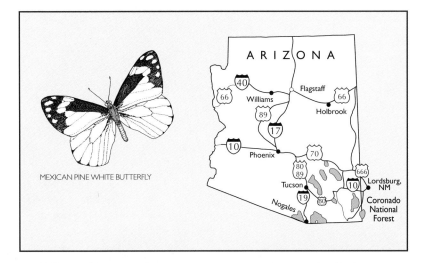

MEXICAN PINE WHITE BUTTERFLY

A R I Z O N A

Flagstaff
Williams
Holbrook
Phoenix
Tucson
Nogales
Lordsburg, NM
Coronado National Forest

KENN KAUFMAN, DRAWING

HOW TO GET THERE. *For Madera Canyon, go south from the junction of Interstates 10 and 19 in Tucson on Interstate 19 for 23 miles to Continental (Exit 63, sign for Madera Canyon). Go east under I-19 for 1.1 mile to White House Canyon Road, FS 62. For Cave Creek Canyon, go east from Tucson on I-10 for 120 miles to the San Simon-Portal Road (Exit 382). Take this good, gravel road south for 25 miles to Portal. If there have been recent heavy rains, continue on I-10 another 14 miles to the exit for U.S. Route 80 in New Mexico. Take Rte. 80 south for 28 miles to New Mexico Route 533, Portal Road, and turn right. The road soon crosses back into Arizona and continues 7 miles to Portal.*

CAVE CREEK CANYON, CORONADO NATIONAL FOREST

DAPHNE GEMMILL, PHOTOGRAPH

"**B**IRDWATCHERS ARE DRAWN to southeastern Arizona as golfers are to St. Andrew's in Scotland or baseball fans to the Cooperstown Hall of Fame: it's a pilgrimage." So wrote Joan Easton Lentz in *Great Birding Trips of the West*, and she continues, "Almost from the onset of our birding careers, we've heard stories about the exotic species inhabiting the 'Mexican mountains' of southeastern Arizona, and this trip is one of the tops for bird-finding, not only in the West but in all of North America."

What makes southeastern Arizona unique is a series of mountain ranges, which have been described as "sky islands" rising out of a sea of desert scrub. Ranging from 2000 to nearly 11,000 feet in elevation, these isolated prominences feature some of the greatest diversity of plant- and animal-life in the U.S. Plant communities vary from Sonoran and Chihuahuan desert scrub at drier, lower altitudes, through grasslands, oak woodlands, ponderosa pine, mixed conifer, to spruce–fir forests on the high mountain peaks.

Many of these mountain ranges, such as the Santa Rita, Huachuca, Chiricahua, and Pinaleño mountains, are part of the 1.7-million-acre Coronado National Forest. Superb birding spots abound. A few of the meccas include Mt. Lemmon; Mt. Graham; Carr, Ramsey, and Miller canyons in the Huachucas; Madera Canyon in the Santa Ritas; and Cave Creek Canyon in the Chiricahuas.

The best seasons are from early May through September. In spring, cacti, yucca, century-plants, and myriad perennials and annuals, such as poppies, verbenas, and mustards, produce contrasting arrays of wildflowers, although spring bloom is variable. The best blooming season is late summer, after the start of the rainy season, when many other varieties of flowers, such as amaranths, morning-glories, lupines, and mints, add their brilliant colors to the landscape. This is also the best time to look for butterflies, including the great blue hairstreak, mourning cloak, red-spotted purple, and silver-spotted skipper. In late summer, southeastern Arizona is one of the best places in the U.S. to find a wide variety of butterfly species.

The warmer months bring out tiger salamander (the only salamander seen in Arizona); Mexican garter, western hog-nosed, and gopher snakes; canyon tree-frog; and Clark's spiny lizard. Lucky observers may find the beautiful Sonoran mountain kingsnake; this harmless red, black, and yellow snake is often mistaken for the venomous Arizona coral snake which, along with at least eight species of rattlesnake, occur on the Forest. Watch where you put your hands and feet.

The Coronado is home to the Mount Graham red squirrel, a small, reddish tree-squirrel that is federally listed as endangered since it is found only on Mount Graham. Other tree-squirrel species on the Coronado include the Mexican fox squirrel, a large, reddish tree-squirrel with a bushy tail, living in pine–oak and riparian forests, and the Arizona gray squirrel with its white belly; the coati, a raccoon-like animal with a long snout and ringed tail that usually travels in bands; and the rather common hog-nosed skunk, easily identified by its all-white tail. Other mammals to be encountered include cliff chipmunk, raccoon, spotted, striped, and hooded skunks, porcupine, collared peccary (javelina), coyote, gray fox, and white-tailed deer. If you are extremely fortunate, you may see a bobcat.

Bird Life

More than four hundred bird species have been recorded for southeastern Arizona, and a single visit to the Coronado National Forest will often produce 150 species or more. The area's biggest drawing-cards are the Mexican birds that reach the northern edge of their breeding-range here: Zone-tailed and Gray hawks, Montezuma Quail, Buff-collared Nightjar, Elegant Trogon, Strickland's Woodpecker, Greater Pewee, Sulphur-bellied and Dusky-capped flycatchers, Thick-billed Kingbird, Mexican Chickadee, Rose-throated Becard, Red-faced Warbler, Varied Bunting, and Botteri's, Five-striped, and Rufous-winged sparrows. Occasional Mexican summer vagrants, such as Eared Trogon, Aztec Thrush, Flame-colored Tanager, Rufous-capped Warbler, Slate-throated Redstart, and Yellow Grosbeak also turn

LUCIFER HUMMINGBIRD

up on the Coronado. In winter look for Ruddy Ground-Dove and Rufous-backed Robin.

Vying for your attention with the Mexican specialties are the night birds, including nine species of owls that can be heard calling from May to early July. Then there are the hummingbirds. It is not unusual to see ten of the possible sixteen species for southeastern Arizona; in some years fourteen are seen. Hummingbird activity peaks from July to September when migrants join the summer residents. Regularly seen are Broadbilled, Blue-throated, Magnificent, Black-chinned, Anna's, Costa's, Calliope, Broad-tailed, Rufous, and Allen's hummingbirds. The rare hummers are White-eared, Plain-capped Starthroat, Bery:lline, Lucifer, and Violet-crowned.

Birding Routes

Of the many choice birding sites within Coronado National Forest, Madera and Cave Creek canyons offer the greatest diversity. Although two days or more should be planned for exploring Madera Canyon, its proximity to Tucson permits shorter visits; even half-a-day will bring a smile to a birder's face. Cave Creek Canyon requires a longer stay but promises a longer list of species.

Madera Canyon can be reached by taking Forest Service Road (FS) 62 in Continental, crossing over the railroad tracks, and driving 7 miles through a Forest Service Experimental Range. Desert-grassland birds along this route include Gambel's Quail, Greater Roadrunner, Say's Phoebe, Cactus Wren, Curve-billed Thrasher, Black-tailed Gnatcatcher, and House Finch. After the summer rains begin, Cassin's and Botteri's sparrows can be heard singing. In winter, Lark Bunting and numerous sparrows are also abundant. This area is where the first Five-striped

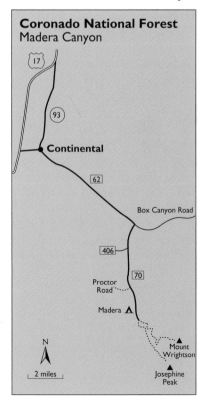

Coronado National Forest
Madera Canyon

Continental

Box Canyon Road

Proctor Road

Madera

Mount Wrightson

Josephine Peak

N

2 miles

Sparrow was discovered in the U.S., although it has seldom been seen here since.

The rare antelope jackrabbit, whose range barely extends into the U.S., can sometimes be found here. It is larger and whiter than the more common black-tailed jackrabbit and has a habit of showing the white of its belly as it runs. In addition to the rabbits, you should see an antelope squirrel. It looks like a chipmunk with a white flag for a tail.

At the junction of Box Canyon Road (FS 62) and FS 70 (7 miles), turn right (south) onto FS 70 toward the mountains. You will soon cross two small bridges. The second bridge (0.8 mile beyond the junction) crosses Florida Wash. A walk down the shallow wash should produce Verdin, Crissal Thrasher, Phainopepla, Northern Cardinal, Pyrrhuloxia, Varied Bunting, Canyon Towhee, and Black-throated Sparrow. In spring and summer, look for Black-chinned and Costa's hummingbirds, Ash-throated Flycatcher, Bell's Vireo, and Lucy's Warbler. Birders come here in the evening to look and listen for the rare Buff-collared Nightjar. Please do not use tapes.

Aside from the nightjar, the rarest bird found in the wash is Rufous-winged Sparrow. In winter, there are a number of other sparrows; Brewer's and Chipping sparrows are the ones most likely to be confused with the Rufous-winged.

Hummingbirds are best seen on the hillside above the wash, where there is a stand of ocotillo whose bright red flowers appear in May and June. The blossoms attract numerous Black-chinned and a few Costa's, although the latter is more reliable in March and April.

Botteri's Sparrow is easily found in July and August in the brushy grasslands along FS 406, which is 0.7 mile above Florida Canyon. Cassin's Sparrow is here also, and it is difficult to separate the two except by song.

About 3 miles above Florida Wash shortly before the road reaches the edge of the oak woodland, a well-marked turnoff to the right leads to the parking area for Proctor Road. From here, a blacktop path offers easy hiking and even wheelchair access upstream along Madera Creek. This is an excellent birding area at all seasons. In summer, watch for Northern Beardless-Tyrannulet, Bell's Vireo, Summer Tanager, Blue Grosbeak, and Varied Bunting. Check the stream in fall and winter for the locally rare Louisiana Waterthrush.

Above Proctor Road, FS 70 enters the oak woodlands. Year-round species include Montezuma Quail, Northern (Red-shafted) Flicker, Acorn, Ladder-backed, and Strickland's woodpeckers, Say's Phoebe, Gray-breasted Jay, Bridled Titmouse, Bushtit, White-breasted Nuthatch, Bewick's, Canyon, and Rock wrens, Blue-gray Gnatcatcher, Hutton's Vireo, Rufous-crowned and Chipping sparrows, Yellow-eyed Junco, and House Finch. Watch overhead for the ubiquitous Turkey Vulture, the occasional Golden Eagle, Northern Raven, and the handsome White-throated Swift.

At night from May through early July listen for Flammulated, Great Horned, Elf, and Spotted owls, Western and Whiskered screech-owls, Lesser Nighthawk, Common Poorwill, and Whip-poor-will. For years, an Elf Owl has nested in a utility pole in front of the Santa Rita

Lodge, where owl-watching is a nightly ritual.

The Madera Picnic Grounds (on the right, a mile past Proctor Road) are a nice place for a snack, although you may have to share your meal with Acorn and Strickland's woodpeckers, Gray-breasted Jays, and Bridled Titmice. In summer, you should also see Western Wood-Pewee, Dusky-capped Flycatcher, Cassin's Kingbird, and Black-headed Grosbeak. The huge sycamore over the lower tables often hosts a pair of nesting Sulphur-bellied Flycatchers, which can easily be located by their high-pitched, squeaky calls. At night, Whip-poor-wills call from the shadows of the oaks, and Common Poorwills from the hillside. Elf Owls yip and chatter away from their nesting holes in the snag atop a sycamore at the upper end of the picnic area, and Whiskered Screech-Owl can be heard in the oaks.

A walk downstream from the picnic area is productive in early morning. The stillness is broken by the calling of Cassin's Kingbirds and the singing of canyon tree-frogs. A pair of Black Phoebes often scolds from their nest under the bridge. Watch for hummingbirds feeding on the bright-red *Bouvardia* flowers.

The west bank of the stream can also be very birdy. Look for Rock and Canyon wrens among the rocks and for Bewick's Wren and Bushtit in the live oaks. Ash-throated and Brown-crested flycatchers are usually present. An excellent blacktopped trail leads downstream to connect with the trail system at Proctor Road, and upstream to the vicinity of Santa Rita Lodge.

About 0.5 mile below the picnic area is the ranger's cabin. It is time to turn back. It is best to return by the road so that you can search the sky for hawks and Golden Eagles.

Santa Rita Lodge, where you should stop to check the humming-bird feeders, is 0.25 mile above the picnic area. Species likely to be seen are Broad-billed (the most common hummingbird here), Violet-crowned (rare in late summer), Magnificent, Blue-throated, Black-chinned, Anna's, and Broad-tailed (the cricket-like trill made by the wings of the male is heard more often than the bird is seen). About 0.2 mile above the lodge is a nature trail with labeled plants along the first 200 yards. The trail climbs the dry hillside and follows the stream for about a mile to the road—which is a pleasant return route. Although birding it is not particularly good along the trail, you do get a fine view of the valley; birding is better along the road.

The road continues a mile beyond the lodge, ending in a confusing series of little circles. You can drive around all of them, however, in about two minutes and learn that there are two parking areas and the Roundup Picnic Ground.

At the lower end of the upper parking area, a good place at night for Whisk-ered Screech-Owl, you will find the trailhead for Mount Wrightson. This 7-mile trail requires plenty of stamina but offers choice scenery and good birds. At first the trail passes through oak woodlands, and the birds are about the same as those you have been seeing. Elegant Trogons have nested along the stream. Beyond this area, the trail climbs the dry hillside. Here you can find Hutton's Vireo, Greater Pewee, Black-throated Gray Warbler, and, sometimes, Red-faced Warbler. This is about as low as the Red-faced gets during the breeding season.

If you make it all the way to the conifers, you should find Steller's Jay, Pygmy Nuthatch, Brown Creeper, Western Bluebird, Yellow-rumped, Grace's, Red-faced, and Olive warblers, Hepatic and Western tanagers, Red Crossbill, and Pine Siskin.

The Josephine Saddle Trail, which also begins in the upper parking area, is another good birding route, although it is not so well marked nor maintained. Yet neither is it likely to be crowded. To reach this trail, go

MONTEZUMA QUAIL

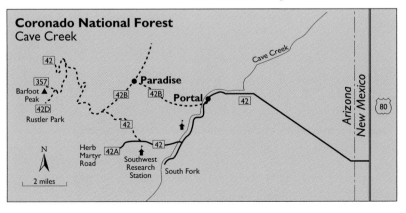

ELEGANT TROGON

hua Mountains offers spectacular scenery as well as sensational birding. Many birders consider these mountains the best birding spot in the U.S.

Above the creek are soaring cliffs and rock outcrops, dotted here and there with shallow cave-like formations (hence the name Cave Creek). These caves were used by early Indians, who farmed the area before being displaced by the more aggressive Apaches in the 1600s. One can still find bits of broken pottery and the tiny cobs of dwarf corn cultivated by the cave-dwellers; it is illegal to collect these artifacts, so please leave them where you find them.

Although rather short and narrow, Cave Creek Canyon contains a broad spectrum of habitats, all accessible by road. The grasslands of the plains give way to a narrow band of honey mesquite and Arizona sycamore along the stream and to thickets of scrub oak, mountain mahogany, and other bushes on the dry slopes. As the terrain climbs slowly, the mesquite disappears, and trees become more numerous. The entrance to the canyon proper is framed by towering, rose-colored cliffs and spires, which are made even more beautiful

by a bright green lichen. Within the canyon, the broad valley floor is canopied by white-trunked sycamores, Arizona black walnut, Apache pine, Arizona cypress, and a variety of live oaks. In places, the thick woodland opens to reveal the magnificent cliffs rising hundreds of feet almost directly overhead. This wonderful scene is further enhanced by a lovely creek of clear, cold water.

Start your birding tour at the town of Portal. (A side trip on the road from Portal to Paradise is worth taking for Montezuma Quail (rare), Scrub Jay, Plain Titmouse, and Black-chinned Sparrow.) In about 0.5 mile, the Cave Creek Canyon road forks. Take the left fork (FS 42) and drive 1.3 miles to the ranger station, where a sign shows the location of the canyon roads, trails, and campgrounds. Continue beyond the ranger station for 0.3 mile to a side road (first of two) to the left and drive to the end (1.4 miles). This is the famous South Fork of the canyon and the beginning of the 7-mile South Fork Trail. The lower part of the trail is one of the best birding spots in the canyon.

Birds to look for in the lower part of the canyon and along the first 1.5 miles of the trail (the complete list is much too long to print here) include most of the species listed above for

SHAWNEEN FINNEGAN, DRAWING

past the cable at the end of the parking area and follow a dirt road. In 0.25 mile, another trail turns sharply left. Take this trail, which follows the stream bed. Northern Goshawk, Magnificent Hummingbird, Elegant Trogon, and Painted Redstart have nested near a fenced water-intake, in 0.4 mile. About a mile above the road the trail leaves the stream bed and climbs into the oaks on the west side of the canyon. Watch for Wild Turkey, Montezuma Quail, and Red-faced Warbler. The trail continues to the saddle and the pines.

At night, in spring and early summer, the dirt road above the parking area is good for Flammulated Owl, Whiskered Screech-Owl, Common Poorwill, and Whip-poor-will. Flammulated Owls are most common in the oaks near the upper end of the road. This small dark-eyed owl can be missed because it gives only one soft, very low hoot at a time and often perches right next to the tree trunk.

Cave Creek Canyon. For those who can stay longer than a few days, Cave Creek Canyon in the Chirica-

Birdfinding in Forty National Forests and Grasslands

Madera Canyon, plus Peregrine and Prairie falcons. Elegant Trogon is regular here, too. In fact, this spot has probably provided more birders with their life trogon than any other place in the country. Many of the Mexican vagrants, such as Eared Trogon, Rufous-backed Robin, Aztec Thrush, and Flame-colored Tanager have been found here.

A second side road, Herb Martyr Road or FS 42A, starts at the Southwest Research Station and goes to tiny Herb Martyr Lake (2 miles). Purple Martins and Violet-green Swallows can usually be found feeding over the lake. Red Crossbills frequent the surrounding pines. Also, this is a good place to hear coyotes at night. The feeders at the research station are great for studying hummers at close range.

Beyond the research station, the main road climbs out of the canyon into the oak woodlands. The Paradise Road (FS 42B) intersection, in 4 miles, is a good spot for Flammulated Owls after dark.

Birds can be relatively scarce in the dry oak-woodland habitat, but watch for Wild Turkey, Montezuma Quail, Strickland's Woodpecker, Gray-breasted Jay, (Brown-throated) House Wren (uncommon, usually below 7500 feet), and Black-throated Gray Warbler. In spots, where you can take your eyes off the narrow, twisting road, scan the skies for Northern Goshawk and Zone-tailed Hawk.

At Onion Saddle (3.3 miles), turn left on FS 42D toward Rustler Park (8500 feet). The view from this road is spectacular. It seems as if the whole western part of New Mexico is laid out at your feet, and you can see mountains 100 miles away in

Mexico. The dry, oak-brush hillsides in this area are good for Virginia's Warbler.

The road levels out and forks after 2 miles; the left fork goes 1 mile to Rustler Park while the right fork (FS 357) goes 1 mile to Barfoot Park. The area around the junction and along the road toward Rustler Park is one of the best places to find Mexican Chickadee, Red-faced Warbler, and Hepatic Tanager. Other birds to watch for among the ponderosa pines are Northern Goshawk, Band-tailed Pigeon, Flammulated Owl, Northern Pygmy-Owl, Common Nighthawk, Whip-poor-will, White-eared (rare, in summer), Broad-tailed, and Rufous hummingbirds, Hairy Woodpecker, Northern (Red-shafted) Flicker, Cordilleran Flycatcher, and Violet-green Swallow. Also check for Steller's Jay, Northern Raven, White-breasted and Pygmy nuthatches, Brown Creeper, House Wren, Western Bluebird, Hermit Thrush, American Robin, Yellow-rumped, Grace's, Red-faced, and Olive warblers, Western Tanager, Black-headed Grosbeak, Chipping Sparrow, Yellow-eyed Junco, and Red Crossbill.

The Rustler Park road is delightful. Drive 0.25 mile beyond the cattle-guard to a small spring. The trickle of water acts on the birds like a magnet, and just about everything in the area can be seen by sitting right there. Beyond the spring, the road forks; the ranger station is on the left, and the campground is to the right.

BROAD-TAILED HUMMINGBIRD

Below the campground is an enchanting little meadow. In late May, it turns blue with Rocky Mountain iris; then Broad-tailed Hummingbirds hold aerial birdfights to protect their feeding-territories. In August, it again turns blue, but this time from Chiricahua delphiniums that attract hundreds of Rufous Hummingbirds. An unforgettable sight is a flock of Wild Turkeys strutting across the meadow at dawn.

From the campground, a trail leads up the ridge and then forks. The left fork goes through the Chiricahua Wilderness to the top of Chiricahua Peak (9795 feet). This hike—only 5 miles as the raven flies—is an all-day affair, but is most rewarding. Along the way you will pass extensive stands of Engelmann spruce, where Golden-crowned and Ruby-

VIOLET-CROWNED HUMMINGBIRD

crowned kinglets nest. The right fork goes 1.5 miles to Barfoot Peak, a much easier hike and almost as satisfying.

The Barfoot Peak Trail provides tree-top views of the lower slopes, good for spotting warblers, tanagers, and Red Crossbills in the canopy. Watch also for the small, brown bunch-grass lizard, another Mexican species, among fallen logs and bunches of grass.

The view from the lookout at the top of Barfoot Park makes the hike even more enjoyable. You can see the whole of the Chiricahuas, Sulphur Springs Valley, a good part of New Mexico, and those faraway mountains in Mexico. The best way back to Rustler Park is to continue 0.3 mile to the Barfoot Park Road and follow it back—3 miles round-trip.

If you drive to Barfoot Park, take care because the road can be very rough beyond the cattle-guard. The road traverses the north slope with aspens and white fir. In late summer, when many flowers will have disappeared from the rest of the mountain, the still-blooming penstemons will attract the rare White-eared Hummingbird to this area.

_____

Note: Much of this entry is taken from A Birder's Guide to Southeastern Arizona *written in 1965 by James A. Lane, and subsequently amended through seven editions by Lane and Harold Holt, the last revision being in 1989. The* Guide *is now published by the American Birding Association, which undertook a 1992–1993 update for this volume.*

ACCOMMODATIONS ◆ WEATHER ◆ OTHER ATTRACTIONS

When to visit. Birding is best from late spring through late summer.

Where to stay. Numerous campgrounds on the Forest; reservations recommended for holidays and weekends. Lodging in Tucson, Green Valley (below Madera Canyon), or the Santa Rita Lodge. Lodging limited in Cave Creek, but the Cave Creek Ranch in Portal has housekeeping cabins, and the Portal Store has both a café that serves wholesome meals daily and bed-and-breakfast accommodations. The American Museum's Southwestern Research Station is operated as a field station and laboratory for researchers, but cabins with meals, as well as a spring-fed pool, are available to birders and naturalists.

Weather and attire. Late spring and summer, especially May and June, are extremely hot, except in the canyons and in the high mountains. July usually brings afternoon rainstorms that can drop the temperature dramatically. Rain gear and warm clothing are, therefore, recommended in summer; they are essential in the high mountains. The summer monsoon usually causes significant green-up; many birds wait to nest during this rainy season.

What else to do. The Nature Conservancy's "Mile Hi" Reserve in Ramsey Canyon (Huachuca Mountains) is famous for its fifteen species of hummingbirds. The Conservancy's Patagonia–Sonoita Creek Sanctuary, off Arizona Route 82 near the town of Patagonia, is an excellent place to look for Gray Hawk, Vermilion Flycatcher, Thick-billed Kingbird, and Rose-throated Becard. Another good spot for these species is a rest stop on Rte. 82, about a mile south of the Sanctuary and 5 miles south of Patagonia. Saguaro National Monument and the Arizona–Sonoran Desert Museum at Tucson are worth a visit. Historic Bisbee's Lavender Pit Copper Mine is one of the largest open-pit mines in the world. The Geronimo Monument at Apache, just south of the Portal turnoff, testifies to the early American inhabitants of the area.

The Forest is rich in historic sites ranging from prehistoric villages, campsites, and farm fields to pioneer-era homesteads, military camps, and mines. Once the frontier of northern New Spain, the area features outstanding examples of Spanish missions.

For more information. General and campground information, District Office addresses, maps, bird list: Coronado National Forest, 300 W. Congress, Tucson, Arizona 85701; telephone 602/670-4552. Douglas Ranger District (Chiricahuas), 602/354-3468; Sierra Vista Ranger District (Huachucas), 602/378-0311; Nogales Ranger District (Santa Ritas and Atascosas), 602/281-2296; Safford Ranger District, 602/428-4150.

MEXICAN POPPY

The Great Plains,
Great Lakes,
and Northeast

BLACK HILLS FOREST
South Dakota and Wyoming

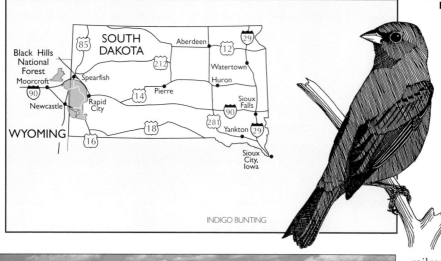

HOW TO GET THERE. *Rapid City is the largest nearby city offering commercial airline service and rental cars. It is located on the northeast boundary of the National Forest. Spearfish is located approximately 45 miles northwest of Rapid City along Interstate 90.*

INDIGO BUNTING

MICHAEL O'BRIEN, DRAWING

THE BLACK HILLS OF BLACK HILLS NATIONAL FOREST

railroaders, loggers and cattlemen, miners and sod-busting farmers.

Today, the 1.2 million acres set aside for the Black Hills Forest are intensively utilized by timber and cattle interests. Yet the Forest Service has taken care to manage the area for wildlife as well. Substantial sections remain in a natural state, and opportunities for study and enjoyment are plentiful.

The primary forest in the Black Hills is ponderosa pine, but areas dominated by spruce, aspen, and oak, as well as large open parks and smaller meadows, also exist. Black Hills (white) spruce is found in cool, moist areas, especially on north-facing slopes at higher elevations. Aspen grows at the edges of mountain meadows and in areas that have been logged or burned. Understory vegetation includes such shrubs as snowberry, serviceberry, wild rose, choke-cherry, and kinnikinnick.

Both white-tailed and mule deer are found in abundance, and small populations of elk, bighorn sheep, and mountain goat have been successfully introduced. Pronghorn and bison herds still roam the plains and

NATHANIEL R. WHITNEY, PHOTOGRAPH

FRONTISPIECE: ROBERT E. MUMFORD, PHOTOGRAPH; HURON NATIONAL FOREST

THE BLACK HILLS do not approach the heights or the life-zone diversity of the Rockies; the highest point, Harney Peak, reaches only 7242 feet. And the region cannot be called unspoiled by any stretch of the imagination. The sacred Sioux hunting-grounds were first defiled by the Gold Rush of 1874. And while Sitting Bull found his revenge against the man responsible, General George Armstrong Custer, at the Little Big-horn two years later, the Europeans just kept coming—bison hunters and edges of the Black Hills in adjacent Custer State Park and Wind Cave National Park. Beaver can be found along many permanent streams, and lucky observers can occasionally catch glimpses of pine martens within the canopy of spruce stands.

Bird Life

The Black Hills are known for their blend of western, northern, and eastern birds. Of the 190 species recorded from the Forest, many are typical western montane birds such as White-throated Swift, Red-naped Sapsucker, Dusky and Cordilleran flycatchers, Canyon Wren, Mountain Bluebird, Townsend's Solitaire, Yellow-rumped (Audubon's) and MacGillivray's warblers, Western Tanager, Cassin's Finch, and the regionally endemic Dark-eyed (White-winged) Junco. Specialties of the northern coniferous forest include Northern Goshawk, Northern Saw-whet Owl, Three-toed and Black-backed woodpeckers, and Brown Creeper. Northern Goshawk is classified by the Forest Service as a "sensitive" species, and therefore information on specific nest locations cannot be publicized. In general, Goshawks prefer dense stands of tall ponderosa pine, where the individual trees are at least 5 to 8 inches in diameter and the canopy is thick enough that understory vegetation is limited. Saw-whet Owls are probably widespread in the Hills, but, being strictly nocturnal, they are hard to find. They frequently nest or roost in old woodpecker holes in pine snags. Wild Turkeys were introduced early in the century and are now common throughout the Forest. At the same time, the Black Hills possess many characteristics of the eastern deciduous forest; these

are most evident in the riparian corridors that cross the plains from the east. Species such as Broad-winged Hawk and Orchard Oriole reach the western edge of their breeding-range here. Some of the closely related species that nest on the Forest include western Black-headed and eastern Rose-breasted grosbeaks and western Lazuli and eastern Indigo buntings.

Although most birders come to the Black Hills in summer, each season has its own rewards. For hardy winter birders, Bald Eagle, Bohemian Waxwing, Common Redpoll, and Gray-crowned Rosy-Finch are possible. The last may appear anywhere in the area, but they are most frequent in the uplands between Hill City and Custer, where they like weedy gravel roadsides and parking lots. Spring and fall migrants include Eared and Western grebes, Gadwall, Redhead, Lesser Scaup, Bufflehead, American Avocet, and numerous other shorebirds on or about the many reservoirs. Water birds are pretty much limited to the larger lakes. During spring and fall migration, they may be found on any or all of the artificial lakes in the region, including Pactola Reservoir, Sheridan Lake, and Deerfield Lake in the Black Hills Forest, and Bear Butte and Angostura Reservoirs in the nearby grasslands. During migration, they appear after strong cold fronts—they migrate through here in numbers, and, in winter, may be found wherever open water is available. This results in a high concentration of ducks, beginning in November and continuing through March, on such open water as Canyon Lake at the southwest corner of Rapid City. Specifically, Gadwall, Redhead, and Bufflehead winter on Canyon Lake, and Lesser Scaup is regular in spring and fall migration. Once the water is open, Bear Butte Reservoir, located in Bear Butte State Park about 5 miles northeast of Sturgis, is a good place to find both grebes and American Avocet, as well as all the ducks mentioned above.

Birding Routes

Prime birding locations on the Forest are found in the canyons where riparian corridors enter the Black Hills. The best of these are Spearfish Canyon and Little Spearfish Trail.

Spearfish Canyon. This canyon may be reached from the town of Spearfish. Follow Business I-90 into Spearfish, then turn south at the junction with U.S. Route 14A. Follow Rte. 14A southwest toward Savoy (15 miles); this road is a designated National Forest Scenic Byway with many numbered (corresponding to mileage) interpretive signs.

AMERICAN DIPPER

SHAWNEEN FINNEGAN, DRAWING

SPEARFISH CANYON, WHERE INDIANS SPEARED FISH LONG BEFORE THE TOWN EXISTED

AILEEN R. LOTZ, PHOTOGRAPH

A brochure describing the natural and cultural history of each stop is available from the Forest Service office in Spearfish or from the Homestake Mining Company in nearby Lead.

Within a mile of the start of the Scenic Byway, you will enter Spearfish Canyon, a spectacular, high-walled limestone corridor carved by Spearfish Creek. Although traffic on Rte. 14A can be considerable, the canyon is usually productive. The best spots are above interpretive Site 4.1, where there is water in the creek. Look for Indigo and Lazuli buntings, which are widespread in the canyon bottoms. They are fairly easy to find, in fact, throughout the Black Hills at all lower canyon levels. From this point north, the creek is diverted to supply water for the town of Spearfish. To avoid creating a traffic hazard, birders should park at the interpretive site and walk a short distance along the creek.

Among year-round residents are Belted Kingfisher, Blue Jay, Black-capped Chickadee, and American Dipper. In summer, look for Western Tanager and Black-headed Grosbeak. Watch for Bald Eagle ranging up and down the canyon in winter.

Wild Turkey, Lewis's Woodpecker, and Blue Jay are good bets in the oaks and other deciduous habitat between interpretive Sites 1.2 and 8.6, as well as at Site 12.8. Adequate pull-offs are available at most of the sites. Look for Northern Flicker, Black-capped Chickadee, and Pine Siskin. In summer, common species include White-throated Swift, Violet-green Swallow, Mountain Bluebird, Veery, Red-eyed and Warbling vireos, and Black-headed Grosbeak.

From Site 8.1 to just north of Site 12.8 conifers are mixed in with the deciduous trees, and coniferous forest dominates the route between the bridge south of Savoy and Site 18.3. Year-round residents include Sharp-shinned Hawk, Red-breasted and White-breasted nuthatches, Dark-eyed Junco, and Pine Siskin. In summer, you will likely find Western Wood-Pewee, Dusky and Cordilleran flycatchers, Ruby-crowned Kinglet, and House Wren. In winter, Bohemian Waxwing and Pine and Evening grosbeaks are occasionally present.

Scattered grassy patches occur along the roadside and stream bank between Savoy and Cheyenne Crossing, 6 miles south of Savoy, and there is a limited amount of grassland at the mouth of Spearfish Canyon at the beginning of the Scenic Byway. American Robin, Dark-eyed (White-winged) Junco, and American Goldfinch can be found here year-round, and Golden Eagles appear from time to time. Turkey Vulture, Red-tailed Hawk, Eastern Kingbird, and

"WHITE-WINGED" DARK-EYED JUNCO

SHAWNEEN FINNEGAN, DRAWING

Western Meadowlark are common in summer. Clay-colored Sparrow is a rare migrant.

Little Spearfish Creek is accessible by Forest Development Road (FDR) 222 traveling west from Savoy. This is a well-maintained gravel road that meanders along Little Spearfish Creek past Roughlock Falls Picnic Area, the location of the winter-camp scenes used in the movie *Dances with Wolves*. Four miles beyond the junction of Rte. 14A and FDR 222 is the Rod and Gun Campground

The shoreline of Little Spearfish Creek provides some of the better riparian, willow-shrub habitat in the Black Hills. Veery, MacGillivray's Warbler, and Song Sparrow are common here. Other species to watch for include Dusky Flycatcher, Common Yellowthroat, Wilson's Warbler, and Black-headed Grosbeak. The nearby canyon walls provide habitat for White-throated Swifts, and the waterfalls found along the creek sometimes are utilized by nesting American Dippers. Except on midsummer weekends when there are many visitors, this species can best be seen at Roughlock Falls Picnic Area.

At the Rod and Gun Campground, which is a good place to bird in its own right, you will find the trailhead for the Rimrock Loop-Trail that leads to the top of the canyon. The well-marked, 7-mile-long route winds through a mixed forest of white spruce, ponderosa pine, aspen, and mixed deciduous undergrowth. Along the stream and cliffs, Belted Kingfisher, White-throated Swift, Cliff Swallow, and Canyon Wren can be expected. As you climb through the aspen groves, you are likely to find Ruffed Grouse, Downy Woodpecker, Red-naped Sapsucker, Cor-

BELTED KINGFISHER

dilleran Flycatcher, Red-eyed and Warbling vireos, and Ovenbird. If you are lucky, you may encounter a Broad-winged Hawk.

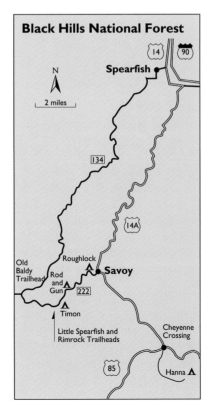

Black Hills National Forest

2 miles

Spearfish

Roughlock

Old Baldy Trailhead

Rod and Gun

Savoy

Timon

Little Spearfish and Rimrock Trailheads

Cheyenne Crossing

Hanna

Once you reach the coniferous forest at higher elevations, watch for Red-breasted and White-breasted nuthatches, Yellow-rumped Warbler, Dark-eyed (White-winged) Junco, and Red Crossbill. At the top of the loop are spectacular views that make the moderately steep climb well worth the effort. You will enjoy the sight of Turkey Vultures soaring below you. For anyone with limited time or endurance, a shortcut loop is available to return to Little Spearfish Creek and Campground halfway through the loop.

Little Spearfish Trail. From the Rod and Gun Campground, you can either return to Savoy or continue driving up FDR 222 to Timon Campground and the Little Spearfish Trailhead. This 5-mile loop follows the creek for a mile before climbing onto the Limestone Plateau. Little Spearfish Trail is the only place where you can walk the creek away from a developed roadway. Eventually, it descends to FDR 222, where it intersects Rimrock Trail and returns to Timon Campground along the roadway. The white spruce habitat near the campground is a good place to find both Ruby-crowned and Golden-crowned kinglets, Gray Jay, Black-capped Chickadee, and Townsend's Solitaire. Along the trail, 0.25-mile above the campground where the stream branches out into a wide marshy flat, are two recently constructed ponds. Check this area for waterfowl and Great Blue Heron.

Two additional birding locations are nearby. Hanna Campground is on East Spearfish Creek along FDR 196, 2.1 miles south of Cheyenne Crossing. The campground is good for birds associated with northern conifers including Three-toed Woodpecker, which can be sought in any spruce forest. Search old burns for Black-backed Woodpeckers and pines at lower elevations for Pinyon Jays. Old Baldy Trail, off FDR 134, is 1.2 miles northwest of Timon Campground and just beyond the junction of FDR 222 with FDR 134. The 6.1-mile-long trail passes through a section of the most extensive aspen and birch forest in the Black Hills. Ruffed Grouse, Red-naped Sapsucker, Red-eyed and Warbling vireos, and Ovenbird are common here, along with Dusky and Cordilleran flycatchers, and Mountain Bluebird.

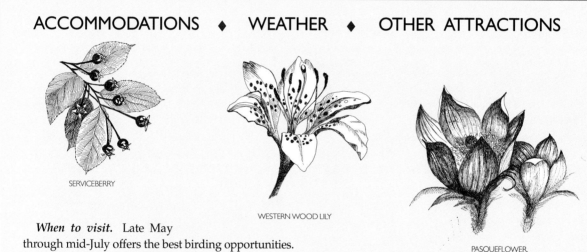

ACCOMMODATIONS ◆ WEATHER ◆ OTHER ATTRACTIONS

SERVICEBERRY

WESTERN WOOD LILY

PASQUEFLOWER, SOUTH DAKOTA'S STATE FLOWER

When to visit. Late May through mid-July offers the best birding opportunities.

Where to stay. Several National Forest and private campgrounds; motels in Spearfish, Sturgis, Lead, and Deadwood.

Weather and attire. Summer visitors should carry a light jacket and rain-gear; thunderstorms with brief, heavy rains are possible anytime during the summer months. Poison ivy grows throughout the Black Hills, so long pants and long-sleeved shirts are recommended for hikers, followed by careful bathing as soon as possible after exposure.

What else to do. Fishing, hiking, horseback riding, mountain-biking in summer, cross-country and down-hill skiing and snowmobiling in winter. Tour the D.C. Booth Historic Fish Hatchery in Spearfish to see brown and rainbow trout; take a guided tour of the famed Homestake Gold Mine in nearby Lead; drive to the summit of 7064-foot Terry Peak near Lead for a panoramic view of the Black Hills; or visit the historic mining town of Deadwood.

Other attractions within a few hours of Spearfish include Wind Cave National Park, Badlands National Park, Jewel Cave National Monument, several privately owned caves that offer guided tours, Devils Tower National Monument, and Mount Rushmore National Memorial.

For more information. General and campground information, District Office addresses, maps, bird list: Black Hills National Forest, RR 2, Box 200, Custer, South Dakota 57730; telephone 605/673-2251.

COMANCHE GRASSLAND
Colorado

CARL JAMES FREEMAN, DRAWING

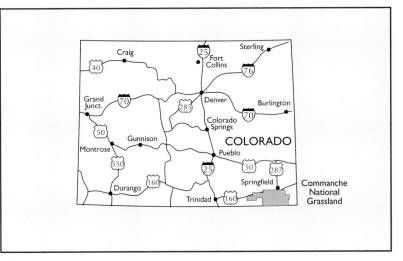

HOW TO GET THERE. *Springfield can be reached from Pueblo, Colorado, by taking U.S. Route 50 east 122 miles to Lamar, then U.S. Routes 287 and 385 south for 49 miles; or, by taking Interstate 25 south for 84 miles to Trinidad and U.S. Route 160 east for 121 miles. Amarillo, Texas, is 165 miles south via U.S. 287.*

COLLARED LIZARD

WITH AN AVERAGE ELEVATION of 5000 feet, the Comanche National Grassland is in an area of the West properly known as the High Plains. Located in extreme southeastern Colorado, this national treasure spreads across 435,707 acres rich in natural and cultural history and recreational opportunities. Spectacular canyons, peaceful prairies, remains of ancient civilizations, and myriad wildlife species await visitors to this untrammeled setting.

Three distinct ecological communities occur on these mile-high plains: mid-grass and short-grass prairies and canyonlands. The mid-grass prairie lies in the eastern portion of the area and contains bluestems, gramas, needle-and-thread, and sand love-grasses; sunflower; wild rose; stick leaf; and wild buckwheat. The short-grass prairie of the northern and western areas, termed "hard lands" because of the high clay content, are known for blue grama, buffalo grass, western wheatgrass, galleta, red three-awn, needlegrass, prairie coneflower, scarlet globemallow, daisy, prickly pear, silky sophora, slender scurf-pea, and vetches. Finally, the canyonlands scattered throughout the area are characterized by sheer sandstone walls, box elder, cottonwoods, juniper, and pinyon pine. They encompass the least acreage but possess the highest biological diversity.

The grassland is home to white-tailed and mule deer, pronghorn, coyote, swift fox, badger, and prairie-dog. Among the reptiles are Eastern short-tailed and yellow-collared lizards, and Western spiny soft-shell and ornate box turtles. The harmless Texas long-nosed, Plains, and bull snakes also inhabit the area.

Bird Life
Like the Black Hills, Comanche National Grassland lies at a natural crossroads. Among the 250 species of birds recorded here are many at the extremes of their normal range. This is where southwestern desert-birds, such as Scaled Quail, Greater Roadrunner, Ladder-backed Woodpecker, Chihuahuan Raven, and Curve-billed Thrasher, near the northern limits of their range, encounter eastern birds, such as Northern Bobwhite, Red-headed Woodpecker,

PATRICIA J. MOORE, DRAWING

LONG-BILLED CURLEW

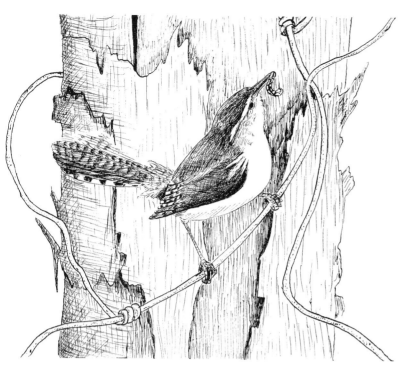

BEWICK'S WREN

CARL JAMES FREEMAN, DRAWING

Eastern Phoebe, Brown Thrasher, and Dickcissel, at the western edge of their breeding-ranges.

The most sought-after bird of the Grassland is the Lesser Prairie-Chicken. This species (listed as threatened in Colorado) resides on the mid-grass portion of the Grassland and is most approachable in early spring during courtship. Other birds of the Grassland include Mississippi Kite (not widespread), Black-chinned Hummingbird, Le-

wis's Woodpecker, Cassin's Kingbird, Scissor-tailed Flycatcher, Plain Titmouse, Bushtit, Bewick's Wren, Rufous-sided and Canyon towhees, and Cassin's and Rufous-crowned sparrows.

Birding Routes

Mid-grass Prairie. To visit the mid-grass prairie and the Lesser Prairie-Chickens, go south from Spring-field on U.S. Route 287 for 20 miles to Campo, then turn left (east) on 4th Avenue, which becomes County Road (CR) J. Follow CR J for 8 miles to CR 36, turn right, and drive 2 miles south to CR G. Turn left on Road G and drive 4 miles east to a gate on the right marked Pasture 1AE.

The Prairie-Chickens display from mid-March into late May with the peak of their courtship rites occurring from mid-April to early May. A viewing-blind has been constructed by the Forest Service near a lek in pasture 1AE so that visitors can watch the fascinating antics with minimum disturbance to the birds. The three-person blind is available by reservation only; anyone wishing to visit the display-grounds should contact the Forest Service's Springfield office. Plan to be in the blind before dawn to have the best chance at watching the performance, though it sometimes continues until 9 AM and is repeated with less conviction in the evening.

SCALED QUAIL

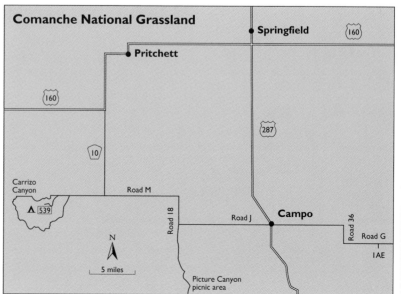

MIMI HOPPE WOLF, DRAWING

Some of the other noteworthy breeding species to watch for in the mid-grass prairie east of Campo are Swainson's and Ferruginous hawks, Prairie Falcon, Scaled Quail, Long-billed Curlew, and Cassin's Sparrow.

Short-grass Prairie. The route through some of the typical short-grass prairie lands passes by several canyons, which can be explored by taking short detours. To start this part of the excursion, retrace your steps to Campo, then continue west on CR J for 10 miles beyond the town to CR 18.

For a detour to Picture Canyon, turn left (south) on CR 18 and drive 4.8 miles to Picture Canyon Road. Turn right and go 2 miles to the parking and picnic area. While viewing the pre-Columbian petroglyphs and pictographs, take time to scan the canyon walls for nest-revealing whitewash and the skies for Prairie Falcon, American Kestrel, Turkey Vulture, and Chihuahuan Raven.

Return to CR 18 and drive north, continuing 3 miles past the intersection with CR J to CR M. Turn left on CR M and go west for 13.3 miles, as the road passes through short-grass prairie. Some of the birds to watch for in these hard lands are Ferrugi-

THE SHEER CLIFFS OF VOGEL CANYON, COMANCHE NATIONAL GRASSLAND

nous Hawk, Golden Eagle, Mountain Plover (scarce), Long-billed Curlew, Burrowing Owl, Chihuahuan Raven, Loggerhead Shrike, and Lark Bunting.

About 5.3 miles west of CR 10 (which is 8 miles west of CR 18 on CR M), watch for a narrow road on the left and follow it for about a mile to the Carrizo Canyon Picnic Area. The place is great for birding—and offers the comfort of the only toilet for miles around. Here you might search for Prairie Falcon, Barn Owl, Wild Turkey (the Merriam subspecies), Greater Roadrunner, Ladder-backed Woodpecker, Pinyon Jay, Chihuahuan Raven, Plain Titmouse, Canyon and Bewick's wrens, and Mountain Bluebird. Curve-billed Thrashers nest in the cholla cactus here.

LESSER PRAIRIE-CHICKENS

SCISSOR-TAILED FLYCATCHER

WALTER MARCISZ, DRAWING

Canyonlands. To explore more of the canyonlands via a loop route through Carrizo and Cottonwood Canyons, return to CR M and turn left (west), following the winding road past Carrizo Canyon for 5.6 miles. Turn left on the road along Cottonwood Canyon, watching on the right for an abandoned cabin a half-mile from the intersection just before the road crosses a small bridge. The trees to your left at this spot are good for Lewis's Woodpeckers, but please respect the rights of private land-owners. Also watch for Cassin's Kingbird, Bewick's and Canyon wrens, Canyon Towhee, and Rufous-crowned Sparrow, in addition to the species mentioned above. Continue on this dirt road for 11.4 miles until you return to the intersection with CR M, completing the loop, 1.3 miles east of the road to the picnic area.

To view more of the short-grass prairie and return to Springfield, go east on CR M for 4 miles to CR 10 and turn left. Take CR 10 north for 9 miles to the junction with U.S. Route 160. Continue straight ahead on U.S. 160, which leads to Pritchett (8.5 miles), then east to Springfield (14 miles from Pritchett).

ACCOMMODATIONS ◆ WEATHER ◆ OTHER ATTRACTIONS

When to visit. The best time to observe the Grassland's bird life is at the beginning of the breeding season, from mid-March to mid-April into early June, when temperatures are still bearable; it can be extremely hot in summer. September through October are also good. Winters can be severe.

Where to stay. No developed campgrounds on the National Grassland, but motels in Springfield and La Junta, where there is another unit of the National Grassland.

Weather and attire. Summertime temperatures can often exceed 100° F. Warm clothing and coats are recommended from March into early May. Later on, light jackets suffice for cool evenings.

What else to do. The Comanche presents a chronicle of history. Picketwire Canyonlands, near La Junta, contain the largest known concentration of dinosaur tracks in the world. Remains of prehistoric Indian cultures can be found in many of the canyons, especially Picture and Vogel canyons. The era of pioneers and hard-won settlement is documented by numerous well-preserved homesteads, and 22 miles of the storied Santa Fe Trail can still be traced through the prairie landscape.

Nearby are Bents Old Fort National Historic Site (near Las Animas east of La Junta), where a large cattail marsh supports Virginia Rail, Red-winged and Yellow-headed blackbirds, Common Yellowthroat, and Song Sparrow. The Two Buttes State Wildlife Area, north of Springfield, is an excellent spot for spring migrants,.

For more information. Travel information, District Office addresses, maps, bird list: Comanche National Grassland, 27162 Highway 287, P.O. Box 127, Springfield, Colorado 81073, telephone 719/523-6591; or the La Junta Office, P.O. Box 817, 3rd St. and East Highway 50, La Junta, Colorado 81050, telephone 719/384-2181.

GLOBE MALLOW
(WILD HOLLYHOCK)

SHASTA DAISY

PRAIRIE CONE-FLOWER
(MEXICAN HAT)

Birdfinding in Forty National Forests and Grasslands

CIMARRON GRASSLAND
Kansas

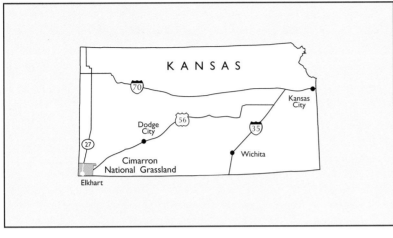

JEREMY PEARSE, DRAWING

HOW TO GET THERE.
Elkhart is situated at the junction of U.S. Route 56 (east–west) and Kansas Route 27 (north–south).

RED-HEADED WOODPECKER

CIMARRON NATIONALGRASSLAND

AILEEN R. LOTZ, PHOTOGRAPH

TUCKED INTO THE SOUTHWEST corner of the state, Cimarron National Grassland is an appealing mix of rolling hills, rocky cliffs, cottonwood groves, yucca, and sage-brush scattered over 108,000 acres of shortgrass and sand-sage prairie. The undulating landscape, characteristic of the southern Great Plains, varies in elevation from 3150 to 3700 feet and is underlain by sandstone, limestone, sand, and gravel.

This part of Kansas originally was the hunting-ground of the Comanche and Kiowa Indians. Later, the Santa Fe Trail cut across the grasslands on its way from Missouri to New Mexico; and because the Cimarron River and surrounding springs held the only water on this stretch of the route, the area became a favorite stopover for parched and weary travelers. Catastrophe overtook the Cimarron in the 1930s when dust storms scoured and devastated the landscape. But the grasslands are coming back, thanks to land-restoration projects by the federal government. Today, the Forest Service is able to manage the rejuvenated Cimarron for wildlife, water conservation, livestock grazing, and recreation.

The display of spring and summer wildflowers is nothing short of dazzling as the prairie literally lights up with brilliant magenta wine-cups, expanses of nodding sunflowers, red and yellow blanket-flowers, and varied cactus blooms. Better still, clouds of butterflies accompany the wildflowers; more than 180 species have been recorded in Kansas.

Wildlife-watchers will be on the lookout for white-tailed and mule deer, red and swift foxes, bobcat, and badger, as well as thirty-one species of salamanders, toads, frogs, lizards, turtles, and snakes. Elk and pronghorn, once native to the prairie, have recently been reintroduced.

Bird Life

No fewer than 333 bird species have been identified on the Grassland. The riparian habitat of the river corridor creates a veritable wooded oasis in the vast sand-sage prairie. That and various man-made wildlife ponds on the Grassland, as well as the water-treatment lagoons for the nearby

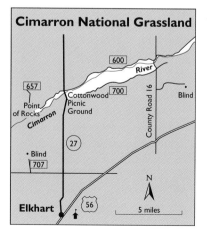

SWAINSON'S HAWK

 is at bottom right with caption LARK BUNTING.

Western Meadowlark and Horned Lark are abundant on the sand-sage prairie; Common Nighthawk, Loggerhead Shrike, and Cassin's, Vesper, and Grasshopper sparrows are common. Lark Bunting is abundant. Curve-billed Thrasher inhabits patches of cholla cactus. Rock Wren frequents rocky outcrops; Chihuahuan Raven can be seen throughout the Grassland; Long-billed Curlew nests in the uplands; and Turkey Vulture, Mississippi Kite, Swainson's and Red-tailed hawks, American Kestrel, and Chimney Swift are often seen flying overhead.

In addition, out-of-range birds occasionally appear on the Grassland. Records include such unusual species as Vermilion and Ash-throated flycatchers, Phainopepla, and Pyrrhuloxia.

Birding Routes
Lesser Prairie-Chicken Site.
The Forest Service has erected blinds on established booming-grounds for observing and photographing the birds during their mating season from March through May with peak activity from mid-April to mid-May. The most accessible blinds are located off County Road (CR) 16, north of Wilburton, on U.S. Route 56. To reach this site from Elkhart, drive east on U.S. 56 for 7 miles to Wilburton and turn left (north) onto CR 16. Drive 3.5 miles to a dirt road on the right that goes 1.25 miles to a parking area. The double blinds are just beyond. Viewers must be in the blinds an hour before sunrise so as not to frighten the displaying birds that boom from before dawn to about 9 AM; occasionally, they boom at dusk, as well.

As many as five to fifteen individuals can be seen displaying at one time. They are only a small part of the approximately one thousand birds that reside on the Grassland—the largest concentration of Lesser Prairie-Chickens on public lands anywhere. Additional grounds with

blinds are scattered throughout the area. A Forest Service brochure, which includes a map and information about the Cimarron's prairie-chickens, can be acquired from the Grassland office in Elkhart.

Cimarron Grasslands Loop.
Begin at Elkhart and drive 8 miles north on Kansas Route 27 to Cottonwood Picnic Ground near the Cimarron River bridge. Stop here and there as the spirit moves you, and you will find many of the prairie birds mentioned above.

In spring and fall, Cottonwood Picnic Ground is a favored stopover spot for migrants. Search among the trees for Eastern and Western wood-pewees, Eastern and Western kingbirds, Eastern Bluebird, Swainson's Thrush, and Orange-crowned, Black-throated Blue, Blackburnian, and Wilson's warblers.

Nesting birds of this oasis include Yellow-billed Cuckoo, Red-headed, Downy, Hairy, and Ladder-backed woodpeckers, Northern (both Yellow-shafted and Red-shafted) Flicker, Western Kingbird, Northern Rough-winged, Cliff, and Barn swallows, Blue Jay, American Robin, Warbling Vireo, Common Grackle, and Orchard and Northern orioles. Look in the adjacent wildlife ponds along the river corridor for Great Blue Heron, Blue-winged Teal, Mallard, Killdeer, and Red-winged Blackbird.

Next, take gravel Forest Service (FS) Road 600, which begins on the left just north of the Cimarron River bridge, and drive one mile west to Point of Rocks Ponds. These lowland areas sometimes flood after spring and

town of Elkhart, encourage all manner of migrants to stop on their journeys north and south.

Lesser Prairie-Chicken is undoubtedly the most sought-after resident bird, but there is much more to enjoy, as well.

Northern Bobwhite and Wild Turkey occur along the river corridors; Scaled Quail can be found around windmills and abandoned homesteads; and Ring-necked Pheasant inhabits areas where grassland meets cropland.

Cimarron National Grassland

(map showing: 600, 657, 700, River, Point of Rocks, Cottonwood Picnic Ground, County Road 16, Blind, Cimarron, 27, Blind, 707, Elkhart, 56, N, 5 miles)

LARK BUNTING

GAIL DIANE LUCKNER, DRAWING

SHAWNEEN FINNEGAN, DRAWING

DAVID A. SIBLEY: DRAWING

early-summer rains. Flood conditions attract Great Egret, Black-bellied Plover, American Avocet, Green-winged Teal, and Northern Shoveler, among other water birds. Continue west a short distance to Point of Rocks (easy to see) and examine the rocky outcrop for Rock Wrens and possibly Rufous-crowned Sparrows and Canyon Towhees. The shrubs on the slopes are worth a check during migration.

Continue along FS 600 for 0.75 mile to the junction with FS 657. Turn right (north) and drive 1.3 miles to an extensive prairie-dog colony. This is an excellent place to find birds typical of the short-grass prairie. Look for Swainson's Hawk, American Kestrel, Scaled Quail, Mourning Dove, Burrowing Owl, Common Nighthawk, Horned Lark, Black-billed Magpie, American Crow, Northern Mockingbird, Loggerhead Shrike, and Cassin's, Vesper, Lark, and Grasshopper sparrows, Lark Bunting, and Western Meadowlark.

Then retrace your steps to Rte. 27, turn right, and go 0.7 mile to Forest Service Road (FS) 700, the first road south of the Cimarron River, and turn left. A series of ponds lines this portion of the route, starting with four Atwood Ponds within an area designated as Cimarron Recreation Area, five miles from Rte. 27. Mallard Pond is another mile, and Wilburton Pond is 1.5 miles beyond Mallard Pond, about 0.25 mile past the intersection with CR 16. Great Blue Heron, Blue-winged Teal, Mallard, Killdeer, Belted Kingfisher, Common Yellowthroat, Red-winged Blackbird, and (occasionally) Yellow-headed Blackbird are found at these ponds. Wild Turkey and Lark Sparrow are frequently seen in the area, as well.

Keep an eye out for raptors along this route. You should see Northern Harrier and Swainson's, Red-tailed, and Ferruginous hawks. Mississippi Kite often can be found along the river corridor. Golden Eagle and Prairie Falcon also occur occasionally on the adjacent prairie, and Sharp-shinned Hawk can be common in spring and fall.

From Wilburton Pond, backtrack 0.25 mile to the junction of FS 700 and CR 16. Park here and walk north a few hundred yards to the Cimarron River, where you will find many of the same species as at the Cottonwood Picnic Ground—and have a chance to pick up the ones you missed earlier. This area is a very good place for owls. Listen and look for Eastern Screech-Owl and Barn, Great Horned, and Long-eared owls.

To return to Elkhart, continue south on CR 16 to U.S. 56 and turn right; Elkhart is 8 miles down the road.

AMERICAN AVOCETS

ACCOMMODATIONS ◆ WEATHER ◆ OTHER ATTRACTIONS

When to visit. The best time to see Lesser Prairie-Chickens is March through May. In spring and fall there are migrants and other resident birds.

Where to stay. Campground at the Cimarron Recreation Area along the south side of the river 4 miles east of Route 27; primitive camping throughout the Grassland. Motels, a small RV park, and bed-and-breakfast facilities in Elkhart.

Weather and attire. Spring and fall weather can change dramatically, so prepare for cool and wet, as well as for warm and dry. Summer daytime temperatures can top 100° F, but evenings generally are cool. Warm clothing is advisable for early-morning visits to the prairie-chicken blinds.

What else to do. A self-guided auto tour of the Grassland (brochure at Forest Service office in Elkhart), hiking, visits to prairie-dog colonies, hunting and fishing in season. If you are interested in history, you can follow along 23 miles of the old Santa Fe Trail, learning about the pioneers' adventures through markers at historic spots.

For more information. General and campground information, District Office addresses, maps, bird list: Cimarron National Grassland, P.O. Box J, 242 E. Highway 56, Elkhart, Kansas 67950; telephone 316/697-4621.

SAGE-BRUSH

NEBRASKA FOREST
Nebraska

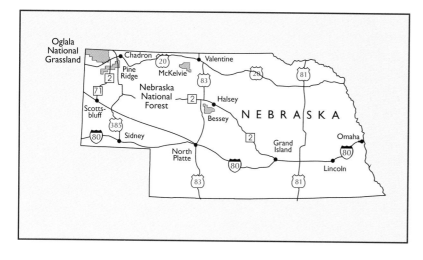

HOW TO GET THERE. *For the Bessey Ranger District, start at the District Office on Nebraska Route 2, just west of Halsey. To reach Halsey, follow Rte. 2 northwest from Grand Island for about 132 miles, or, from North Platte take U.S. Route 83 north for 65 miles to Rte. 2, then go east on Rte. 2 for 18 miles. The McKelvie District is accessible from Valentine, 80 miles north of Halsey via Rte. 2 and U.S. 83. The Pine Ridge District and Oglala National Grassland are accessible from Chadron, at the junction of U.S. 20 and U.S. 385 or Crawford on U.S. 20, Nebraska Routes 71 and 2, in the northwest corner of the state, about 75 miles north of Scottsbluff.*

*O*KLAHOMA! MAY HAVE CAPTURED the imagination of Broadway's songwriters, but Nebraska really *is* where "the corn is as high as a elephant's eye." No one expects the great grain-producer to be renowned for its trees, much less its forests. Yet the Cornhusker State boasts one of the most fascinating forest holdings in the entire USFS system.

The 360,000-acre Nebraska National Forest consists of four widely-separated units, stretching across 250 miles of the central and western parts of the state. Within these four areas, three distinct and contrasting habitat types are represented—the remarkable sandhills of the central section, the ponderosa pine and butte country in the west, and the high plains of the Missouri Plateau grasslands in the extreme northwest. Each is a treasure in its own right.

The 19,000 square miles of Nebraska sandhills represent the largest area of continuous dunes in the Western Hemisphere. They are stabilized by a fragile layer of vegetation that includes a wide collection of grasses, broad-leaved herbaceous plants, and shrubs. And here, tucked away in this sea of ancient, wind-deposited sand, is a man-made forest that offers unusual opportunities for naturalists of every kind.

In the late nineteenth century, Dr. Charles Bessey, a University of Nebraska botanist, demonstrated that various trees could be grown on the dunes. With the aid of pioneer conservationist Gifford Pinchot and others, Dr. Bessey was able to convince President Theodore Roosevelt to create forest reserves in the Nebraska Sandhills. The date was 1902. That legacy, the Bessey Nursery, is the largest man-made forest in the country. The 22,000 acres of planted forest included in the Bessey Ranger District are dominated by ponderosa and jack pines, and pasture juniper interspersed with large expanses of grassland.

Common grasses include sand and little bluestems, switchgrass, sand love-grass, prairie sandreed, and porcupine grass, while some of the more usual wildflowers are prairie coneflower, sunflower, scurf-pea, and spiderwort. Woody vegetation outside the plantations generally occurs in scattered thickets of snowberry, American plum, western chokecherry, hackberry, and green ash. The riparian corridors along the Dismal and Loup Rivers hold cottonwood, box elder, and willows.

Pronghorn are fairly common at Bessey, the eastern edge of their

SAND BLUESTEM ON THE NEBRASKA FOREST

J.G. SCHUMACHER, PHOTOGRAPH

range, as are both mule and white-tailed deer. Porcupine is found here, also near the eastern edge of its (western) range. Coyote is prevalent, and beaver, badger, and various small rodents are found in the Middle Loup valley. Kangaroo rats are numerous in sandy areas but are seldom seen, except along the roads at night. A nighttime drive also will yield great-plains toad, woodhouse toad, bullsnake, and yellow-bellied racer. Prairie rattlesnake can be seen near prairie-dog "towns" in early spring and late fall. Ornate box turtle is frequent in the grassland as are prairie earless lizard and eastern fence lizard.

About 70 miles to the north, the McKelvie District, located in northern Cherry County between the Niobrara River to the north and the Snake River to the south, consists of grassland habitat similar to that found in the Bessey District, although it tends to be somewhat drier. Coniferous plantings are not as extensive as at Bessey, but there is a nice wetland complex of small lakes known as Lord Lakes. Merritt Reservoir State Recreation Area, while not a part of the National Forest, is adjacent to the south edge of the McKelvie Division and is the only lake of any size in or close to the four Nebraska National Forest units. The wildlife of the McKelvie District is similar to that of Bessey.

To the west, about 100 miles away, lies the Nebraska Pine Ridge, a north-facing escarpment stretching from eastern Wyoming across the northwest corner of the state and into South Dakota. The Pine Ridge District is primarily ponderosa pine forest, with typical riparian vegetation in the canyons. Buttes and other erosional elements dominate the landscape.

Finally, in the extreme northwest corner of Nebraska, you will find the Oglala National Grassland, named after the Sioux tribe led by the valiant Crazy Horse and other chiefs; this was part of their sacred bison hunting grounds, and these were the warriors who annihilated General George Armstrong Custer's command in 1876 at the Little Bighorn.

On the Oglala Grasslands, pronghorn is plentiful. In spring the young, usually twins, are often seen. The views of the Pine Ridge escarpment from the grasslands are spectacular, as are the scattered badlands mesas and the formations at Toadstool Park. In the Pine Ridge District, porcupine and coyote are routine.

Bird Life

Situated at the interface of east and west, this widespread Forest has produced on the order of two hundred fifty species over the years. The plantations of the Bessey Nursery serve as a superb migrant-trap in spring and

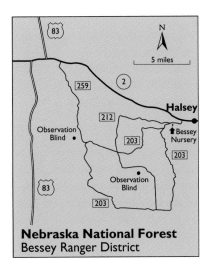

Nebraska National Forest
Bessey Ranger District

fall, and the nearby grasslands of the Ranger District harbor good populations of Greater Prairie-Chicken and Sharp-tailed Grouse. The Lord Lakes in the McKelvie District are good for seeing various grebes. The forested buttes of the Pine Ridge District provide nesting habitat for many western species, such as Lewis's Woodpecker, Pinyon Jay, and Western Tanager, making the area attractive to eastern birders. You can see Prairie Falcon there also. The Oglala Grasslands and the badlands of the Missouri Plateau offer a chance at some typical species of the Great Plains, including Western Meadowlark, Lark Bunting, and Say's Phoebe. For ibises and pelicans, try Kadoka Lake on the Buffalo Gap Grassland in South Dakota. Wete Pond on the same Grassland is a good place to see Trumpeter Swan in spring and summer. (Buffalo Gap Grassland is another section of the Nebraska Forest.)

Birding Routes

Three excursions will give you a taste of the habitats that characterize this diverse and far-flung National Forest.

Bessey Ranger District. The major reason for visiting here is to experience the migrations. Many passerines pass along the Middle Loup River, northwestward in spring (late April through early June) and southeastward in fall (late August through early October); the deciduous vegetation along the river literally teems with birds on good days. The conifers at Bessey are no less birdy. And the grasslands that surround the tree plantations support breeding populations of Swainson's Hawk, Greater Prairie-Chicken, Sharp-tailed Grouse, Upland Sandpiper, Eastern and Western kingbirds, Horned Lark,

Grasshopper Sparrow, Bobolink (rare), and Western Meadowlark.

The best way to bird this relatively compact area is to secure a map from the Forest Service, and then drive and walk the well-marked roads and trails through the coniferous plantations, riparian areas, and open grasslands. The birding is excellent everywhere.

A good day's outing might begin before dawn at the main campground on the Middle Loup River. The entrance is on Nebraska Route 2, 1.5 miles west of the small town of Halsey. After crossing the Middle Loup River bridge just inside the entrance, turn right to Bessey Nursery or go straight to the campground area. Listen for the calls of Common Poorwills and resident Eastern Screech-Owls.

Alternatively, birders in spring might start the day with a visit to one of the grouse and prairie-chicken blinds maintained by the Forest Service. Directions to the blinds can be obtained at the District Ranger's Office. Activity is greatest from the first hint of morning light until about 8 AM, when the birds begin to disperse. You should plan to be in the blind no later than forty-five minutes before sunrise in order not to disturb incoming birds.

Then you should return to the river edges in the vicinity of the main campground and tree nursery for the better part of the morning. This can be followed by working the plantations and prairie by car, using the map provided at the Forest Service office just west of Halsey on Rte. 2.

Birds commonly found in the woody thickets and riparian areas include such permanent residents as Red-tailed Hawk, Hairy and Downy

EASTERN SCREECH-OWL

DAVID A. SIBLEY, DRAWING

woodpeckers, and Northern Flicker, augmented in summer by Brown Thrasher, Rufous-sided Towhee, Chipping Sparrow, and Northern (Baltimore) Oriole. The large conifer plantations provide a permanent home for Great Horned Owl, Black-capped Chickadee, and Red-breasted Nuthatch; the erratic Red Crossbill is present some years. Field Sparrow and Eastern Bluebird frequent the brushy edges of the plantations. Cooper's Hawk nested in 1992 and 1993 and Long-eared Owl in 1993.

Six species of warblers nest on the Forest: Yellow and Black-and-white, American Redstart, Ovenbird, Common Yellowthroat, and Yellow-

breasted Chat. An additional sixteen warbler species occur during migration. Tennessee, Orange-crowned, Chestnut-sided, Yellow-rumped, Black-throated Green, Palm, Bay-breasted, Blackpoll, Mourning, and Wilson's warblers, Northern Parula, and Northern Waterthrush are regular, while Golden-winged, Cape May, Townsend's, and Kentucky warblers are rare. Nesting vireos include Bell's, Red-eyed, and Warbling. Solitary Vireo is a regular transient. Philadelphia and Yellow-throated are rarities. Both Eastern and Western Wood-Pewee may occur in summer, together with other eastern flycatchers, such as Eastern Phoebe and Great Crested Flycatcher. Wood Duck, Mallard, and Blue-winged Teal find prime nesting habitat here.

McKelvie Ranger District. The birds here are similar to those encountered on the Bessey Ranger District, except that it is less of a migrant-trap. On the other hand, the wetlands and the adjacent Merritt Reservoir attract a greater variety of waterbirds, both nesting and migrants. Especially worth checking are the Lord Lakes, a complex of small lakes, and the nearby Steer Creek Campground.

These areas can be reached from the town of Valentine by taking Nebraska Route 97 southwest for about 25 miles to the turnoff for the Merritt Reservoir State Recreation Area, Spur Route S16F. Check the reservoir from the recreation area in spring and fall for migrants such as Eared and Western grebes, American White Pelican, waterfowl, and Franklin's Gull. Western Grebe, although not known to breed here, is a common migrant on the Merritt Reservoir in the McKelvie Division. Eared Grebe occurs on smaller ponds throughout

Nebraska National Forest
Pine Ridge/Oglala

the Forest. The grasslands on the McKelvie District have breeding Upland Sandpipers and a few Eastern Meadowlarks. Try the Lord Lakes for Blue-winged and Cinnamon teals, Wilson's Phalarope (migrant), and a possible White-faced Ibis.

Pine Ridge District. The Black Hills Lookout section of the Nebraska Pine Ridge is a must for visiting birders since it is the only known reliable place in the state for finding Lewis's Woodpecker from mid-May through early September. The birds were attracted to the area by an abundance of dead, standing timber that resulted from the July 1973 Dead Horse Fire.

The area can be reached from Chadron State Park, which is about 8 miles south of Chadron on U.S. Route 385. Turn right into the Park, then at the small, green entrance house, turn left and go straight ahead at the sign that says Scenic Drive. After about a mile, the paved road turns sharply to the right and begins its descent to the main part of the park. At this point watch for Forest Service Road (FS) 714, a gravel road going to the left to the Black Hills Overlook. Turn here and proceed for 0.8 mile, where you will begin to see large, dead snags on rather barren hills on

both sides of the road. Careful searching with both binoculars and spotting scopes, especially on the east side of the road, will usually produce one or more Lewis's Woodpeckers perched on the dead timber. Often the birds fly out in pursuit of flying insects. This is also a good place for raptors and Mountain Bluebird.

The road ends in ponderosa pine forest at the Black Hills Lookout where, on non-hazy days, one can study the landscape as far as the Black Hills of South Dakota, 60 miles away. Some characteristic ponderosa pine forest birds—Pinyon Jay, Yellow-rumped Warbler, Western Tanager—and migrating birds of prey can be seen from this point.

Some of the best land-birding in the Nebraska Pine Ridge is in the canyons formed by the East and West Ash Creeks. If you stop frequently along the road, all

three habitat types noted above can be found here. The area is best reached from Chadron by following U.S. Route 20 west from town. After 8 miles, watch on the left for a sign for FS 706, which goes south. This road will eventually take you into East Ash Creek Canyon. Continue south for approximately 14 miles to a T-junction at the top of the canyon. Turn west on Table Road and then take the first road north (FS 704). This is West Ash Canyon Road; it will take you down the canyon and eventually north to U.S. 20.

Birding is best from mid-May through mid-July, when it is often possible to record seventy to eighty species in a morning. In the pine forests, you can see Northern Saw-whet Owl, Common Poorwill, Pinyon Jay, Pygmy Nuthatch, Mountain Bluebird, Solitary Vireo (plumbeous form), Yellow-

MOURNING WARBLER

DANIEL LANE, DRAWING

rumped (Audubon's) Warbler, Western Tanager, Dark-eyed (White-
winged) Junco, Red Crossbill, and
Pine Siskin. The riparian vegetation
attracts Western Wood-Pewee, Eastern Phoebe (around bridges), Say's
Phoebe (around old buildings),
Black-billed Magpie, Northern (Bullock's) Oriole, Black-headed Grosbeak, and Lazuli Bunting. White-
throated Swift and Violet-green
Swallow nest among the rocky out-
croppings in both canyons, and Rock
Wren is occasional in the same habitat. Other nesting warblers include
Yellow and Black-and-white, American Redstart, Ovenbird, Common
Yellowthroat, and Yellow-breasted
Chat. Golden Eagle is possible overhead or perched on the rocky buttes
at all times of the year, especially in
winter. Also, Townsend's Solitaires
frequent the stands of juniper in
winter.

Oglala National Grassland. For
totally different birding, try the following loop trip
through the
grasslands

TREVOR HERRIOT, DRAWING

LEWIS'S WOODPECKER

and badlands of the Missouri Plateau. From Crawford (20 miles west
of Chadron on U.S. 20) go north on
Nebraska Routes 2 and 71. In about 5
miles, watch for a large sign for Toadstool Park, to the west. From this
sign, continue north on Rtes. 2 and 71
for about 3.2 miles to a sign pointing
to Rock Bass Reservoir toward the
east. Turn right
here and, in a
short dis-

tance, you will see the reservoir.
When not disturbed by fishermen,
this small body of water attracts a
large variety of waterbirds in migration and during the nesting season.
After scanning the reservoir, go back
to Rtes. 2 and 71. Turn south and
backtrack to the large sign for Toadstool Park. Turn right (west) and proceed on FS 904. This road roughly
follows the main line of the
Burlington Northern Railroad on the
west. Typical prairie birds—Western
Meadowlark, Horned Lark, and Lark
Bunting—should be seen on one's
way to Toadstool Park.

In about 12 miles, get ready
for FS 902 that goes west
and ends at Toadstool

FRANKLIN'S GULLS

GAIL DIANE LUCKNER, DRAWING

Birdfinding in Forty National Forests and Grasslands

Park. A walk on the marked Nature Trail through the fossil-rich badlands topography will produce Say's Phoebe and Rock Wren during the nesting season, Golden Eagle and Prairie Falcon at all times of the year, and sometimes roosting Grey-crowned Rosy Finch during the colder months. The lush growth of rabbit-brush along the "wash" to the west and south of the sod house sometimes produces a surprising variety of transient passerine species in late May and early June. A Black-throated Sparrow, only the second record for Nebraska, was observed here in June 1972.

When you have finished birding at Toadstool Park, backtrack eastward to the main gravel road that follows the Burlington Northern Railroad (FS 904). Turn north, pass the "ghost town" of Orella, and watch for FS 900 (Sugarloaf Road) on the right. Turn east and, within the first several miles, watch for Brewer's Sparrow in sage-brush habitat and the occasional Sage Thrasher. Continue eastward past the obvious landmark of Sugarloaf Butte, on the south, scanning for Swainson's and Ferruginous hawks, Long-billed Curlew, and Chestnut-collared Longspur in summer, and Snowy Owl and Snow Bunting in winter. When you reach the paved Rtes. 2 and 71, turn right (south) to return to Crawford.

ACCOMMODATIONS ◆ WEATHER ◆ OTHER ATTRACTIONS

When to visit. Late April through early June and late August to mid-October are the best times to visit at the Bessey Ranger District. From late April to early May you can view the grouse display. From May to July, at the Pine Ridge District, you can see breeding birds in ponderosa pine forest. May through July are best for finding the Oglala Grasslands birds. Although they are limited on Pine Ridge, in April, May, and September you will find woodland migrants throughout the rest of the Forest. Pine Ridge is the part of the Forest to visit in December when you may see Bohemian Waxwing, Harris's Sparrow, and Common Redpoll.

RED ADMIRAL BUTTERFLY

Where to stay. The Bessey District: three developed campgrounds (Cedar, Hardwood, and Organization), one primitive campground (Whitetail). Reservations are required only on major summer holidays. One motel in Thedford and one in Halsey. Dependable eating establishments, Thedford; others in the small towns of Halsey and Dunning. For the northwestern areas, small campgrounds in West Ash Canyon and Toadstool Park, and larger campgrounds at nearby Chadron and Fort Robinson State Parks. Supermarkets, restaurants, and gasoline in Chadron and Crawford.

Weather and attire. The weather in spring and early summer can be unpredictable and highly variable; summer can be uncomfortably hot, while winters can be severe. Fall is the best season of the year. The grouse viewing-blinds can be extremely cold; a warm coat, footwear, and gloves are essential. Wear boots that are cactus resistant, if you plan to hike, and clothing to repel biting insects and ticks. A word of caution: do not attempt to drive unpaved roads during or immediately after a storm, and check for road information before starting out. Prairie rattlesnakes are common, so precautions are advised.

For more information. General and camping information, District Office addresses, maps, bird list: Nebraska National Forest, 125 North Main, Chadron, Nebraska 69337; telephone 308/432-0300.

LITTLE BLUESTEM

JONATHAN ALDERFER, DRAWING

NEBRASKA EXTENSION SERVICE, DRAWING

SUPERIOR FOREST
Minnesota

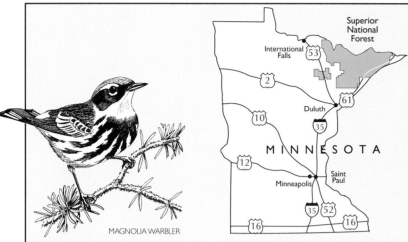

MAGNOLIA WARBLER

DAVID A. SIBLEY, DRAWING

HOW TO GET THERE. *The tour begins in Duluth, which is 150 miles north of Minneapolis–St. Paul via Interstate 35.*

THE 3-MILLION-ACRE SUPERIOR National Forest is situated along a transition zone of two major biomes. The boreal forest with spruce, balsam fir, birch, and aspen reaches its southern limit here; deciduous hardwoods and pines are representative of the more southerly temperate zone.

Minnesota is a land of lakes, and the Forest provides habitat for an abundance of trout, walleye, northern pike, bass, and various panfish. Native wild rice is common in emergent zones. Sphagnum bogs are fragrant and beautiful with their Labrador tea, pitcher-plants, and orchids. A narrow band of maples, remnant of a

warmer climate thousands of years ago, can still be found along the ridge line above Lake Superior. A ground-cover of beaked hazel, alder, bunch-berry, twinflower, ferns, club-mosses, and lichens is common throughout.

Among the Forest's glories are its wolves. Minnesota is home to the largest stable population of eastern timber wolves in the Lower Forty-Eight with around sixteen hundred of these splendid and endangered animals roaming the wild. Moose, black bear, lynx, snowshoe hare, and a wide variety of weasels and rodents also occur here. And eighteen species of reptiles and amphibians reside on the Forest as well.

Bird Life

More than 260 species of birds have been recorded from Superior's varied environments. Of these, 155 species are known to nest. The diversity is such that the Forest hosts the greatest number of breeding birds of any National Forest; 24 of the 50 species of warblers found regularly in North America, for example, discover suitable nesting habitat here.

Late fall can bring a variety of winter finches, sometimes in flocks of

VIEW ON SUPERIOR NATIONAL FOREST

DAVID BARTOL, PHOTOGRAPH

fifty to one hundred birds in good pine and spruce cone or birch catkin years. Species usually include Pine and Evening grosbeaks, Red and White-winged crossbills, Pine Siskin, and Common and (occasionally) Hoary redpolls. In winter, a number of interesting owls may also appear, such as Snowy, Great Gray, Boreal, and Northern Hawk owls.

Birding Route

Grand Marais, Isabella, and Ely Tour.
If you can, give yourself more than one day to bird the Forest. The entire route described below will take three to four days and is well worth the time.

Begin your tour by following U.S. Route 61 north from downtown Duluth for 6.5 miles to the right turn (0.5 mile beyond the Lester River) onto North Shore Scenic Drive, or County Road (CR) 61. The Drive offers splendid views of Lake Superior for the next 20 miles to where it rejoins U.S. 61. Then continue for 84 miles to Grand Marais. You will enter the Superior National Forest near Schroeder, about 75 miles from Duluth and 32 miles southwest of Grand Marais.

In Grand Marais, turn left off U.S. 61 onto Gunflint Trail (CR 12) and drive north for 20 miles to Forest Service Road (FS) 152, again to the left. FS 152, the Lima Mountain Road, is one of the best places in the Forest to find the specialties of the coniferous woods. Hike along the first 2 miles to the junction of FS 315, close to where the first Minnesota nesting-record of Three-toed Woodpecker was documented in 1981. In the black spruce forest along the road in late spring and summer, look for Spruce Grouse, Black-backed Woodpecker, Yellow-bellied, Alder, and Olive-sided flycatchers, Gray Jay, Black-capped and Boreal chickadees, Hermit and Swainson's thrushes, Golden-crowned and Ruby-crowned kinglets, Tennessee, Nashville, Magnolia, Cape May, Yellow-rumped, Black-throated Green, Blackburnian, Palm, Bay-breasted, Mourning, and Canada warblers, Lincoln's and White-throated sparrows, and Rusty Blackbird.

There are no established trails, so you will have to bird from the road or struggle through the dense bogs and forests. It is easy to get lost, however, and the mosquitoes and black flies can be fierce in June and early July.

Birding from the road can be quite satisfactory.

Go north on FS 315 for about 6 miles to where it returns to Gunflint Trail. Stop occasionally to bird the spruce bogs or jack pine woods for the northern breeding species. Boreal Owl is a regular breeding bird along the Gunflint Trail from the junction with FS 325 north to Iron Lake (about 20 miles); the birds are most often heard from dusk to midnight in March and early April and are tame enough to allow close approach—if you can find them.

Return to Grand Marais and head southwest toward Duluth on U.S. 61

NORTHERN HAWK OWL

SPRUCE GROUSE

for 22.5 miles. At FS 336, turn right (north) for 2.2 miles to the Oberg–LeVeaux Trailhead parking area. The 2.2-mile Oberg Trail will reward you with several breathtaking vistas of Lake Superior and the inland maple–hardwood forest. In May, June, and early July, this trail is very good for Black-throated Blue Warbler, an uncommon breeding bird in Minnesota. Also, keep a lookout for Peregrine Falcon. Birds were released from the LeVeaux Cliff site in 1985, 1986, and 1987, and have been seen in the area annually since 1989. From mid-August through mid-November this is also a good place to view migrating raptors: Northern Harrier, Sharp-shinned, Broad-winged, and Red-tailed hawks, and American Kestrel are the most common, but Turkey Vulture, Osprey, Bald Eagle, Northern Goshawk, Cooper's Hawk, and Merlin are regular.

Return to U.S. 61, drive south to Tofte where you will turn north on Sawbill Trail (CR 2), drive 5.6 miles to FS 166, and turn left. Follow FS 166 west for ten miles to CR 7; FS 166 is a beautiful narrow roadway with a canopy of older maples. In the stretches of mixed spruce–deciduous woods, watch for Pileated Woodpecker, Yellow-bellied Sapsucker,

Least Flycatcher, Veery, Red-eyed Vireo, Black-throated Blue and Chestnut-sided warblers, American Redstart, Ovenbird, Scarlet Tanager, and Rose-breasted Grosbeak.

At the junction with CR 7, turn right and drive 5.6 miles to FS 172. As you drive west on FS 172, you will be traveling along the Lauren-

tian Divide. South of the Divide, water flows to Lake Superior and then down the St. Lawrence River to the Atlantic. Water on the north side of the Divide flows north to Hudson Bay.

Continue driving west on FS 172 for 12.2 miles to a sphagnum bog, located .33 mile east of the junction with FS 369. Labrador tea, leather-leaf, cottongrass, pitcher-plants, bog laurel, bog rosemary, bog lily, and (in early summer) dragon's-mouth orchid occur here. The low shrub layer ringing the bog is utilized by Lincoln's and Swamp sparrows. Look for Yellow-bellied Flycatcher, Hermit Thrush, Tennessee Warbler, and Dark-eyed Junco in the scattered trees around the bog. Occasionally, Connecticut Warbler is found here.

Turn north on FS 369 for 1.5 miles to the Trapper's Lake Trailhead and walk the 0.3-mile trail to the lake. You will pass some ancient white-cedars,

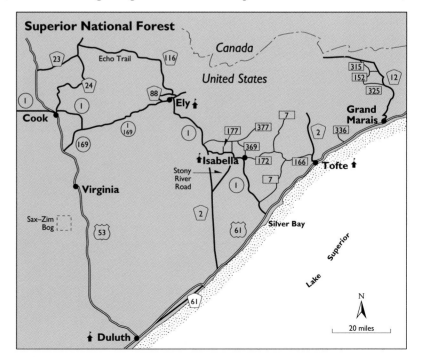

PATRICIA J. MOORE, DRAWING

where you may find Yellow-bellied Flycatcher, Gray Jay, Boreal Chickadee, Winter Wren, Ruby-crowned Kinglet, Swainson's Thrush, Solitary Vireo, Nashville, Magnolia, Yellow-rumped, and Canada warblers, and Northern Waterthrush.

Next, retrace your route to FS 172 and turn right. Drive 1 mile west to the intersection with Minnesota Route 1 in the small community of Isabella; a restaurant and gas station are located here. Continue on to the Forest Service Work Station, a mile west of town on Route 1, where information on road conditions and the like can be obtained. In winter, only a limited number of Forest Service roads are plowed; snow is usually gone from the roads by mid-April, but the gravel roads remain deceptively difficult to travel until mid-May.

Continue west on Rte. 1 for 1.7 miles beyond the Isabella Work Station to the Stony River Forest Road. (If you plan to drive this road in winter, be sure to check the road conditions at the Isabella Work Station first.) At this point, there are two possibilities. If you are visiting from late May through early July and still have not seen a Connecticut Warbler, continue straight ahead on Rte. 1 for 3.4 miles to FS 177 (Mitawan Lake Road), which enters from the right. Take FS 177 north for 0.6 mile to an unmarked paved road to the left, and within 0.2 mile you will enter a large clearing with a paved parking lot and several abandoned building-foundations; this is the former site of an Environmental Learning Center. Park in the first lot on the left and walk about 100 yards to the far southeastern corner of the field. Take the woodland path for about 50 yards to a spruce–

tamarack bog on your right. Walk the wooden boardwalk or along the edge of the bog and look and listen for the Connecticut.

The second possibility—which you can turn to after you've found your Connecticut—is to head south along the Stony River Forest Road. This route, along an abandoned railroad bed, which you can either walk or drive, will take you through one of the area's most productive boreal-

CONNECTICUT WARBLER

forest communities. From late May through early July, you have a chance for Black-backed and Three-toed (rare) woodpeckers, Yellow-bellied and Alder flycatchers, Gray Jay, and Nashville, Cape May, Yellow-rumped, Black-throated Green, Blackburnian, and Wilson's warblers. Stop at any of the black spruce–tamarack bogs and listen for Boreal Chickadee and, yes, there are Connecticut Warblers here, too.

In winter and early spring, especially when conditions are harsh and

food supplies are short farther north, the open areas along Stony River Forest Road provide optimal habitat for Great Gray and Northern Hawk owls. The boreal forest is prime territory for Red and White-winged crossbills, Pine and Evening grosbeaks, and other winter finches.

You have a good chance for Boreal Owl from early March through April, when the birds are calling. The owls hunt through the bogs and nest in cavities in old aspens. Patrol the Stony River Forest Road at night, stopping to listen for their staccato call, which resembles the winnowing of Common Snipe. The males use this call to attract a female to their nest site.

Continuing on the Stony River Road, you will reach the intersection with FS 11, approximately 20 miles from Rte. 1. Turn right onto FS 11 (west) and drive 1.5 miles to County Road (CR) 2. Turn right on CR 2 and go 2 miles to the White Pine Picnic

Area on your right. Look and listen here for Cape May, Pine, and Bay-breasted warblers, as well as Solitary Vireo. In fall and winter, this is a good place for grosbeaks and crossbills. Next, continue north on CR 2 for about 21 miles to its junction with Rte. 1. The last 4 miles of CR 2 are good for Spruce Grouse; watch for them in the forest understory. The best time to see these elusive birds, however, is at dawn in winter, when they come to the roads for gravel.

Turn left on Rte. 1 toward Ely, and you will come to another prime location for Spruce Grouse; a population of birds has been observed regularly along the road in the vicinity of Milepost 301. Rte. 1 even-tually enters the town of Ely, 27 miles west of the CR 2 junction.

If you have time, a trip along Echo Trail is worthwhile. To reach this magnificent wildland area from Ely, turn right at the junction of Rte. 1 and Minnesota Rte. 169 and drive east for 1.2 miles to CR 88. Turn left onto CR 88, go 2 miles, and turn right (north) onto Echo Trail (CR 116). The road meanders northwestward for 50 miles across the Forest, through stretches of coniferous woods, passing several lakes, campgrounds, and Boundary Waters Canoe Area Wilderness entry-points, eventually ending at the intersection of CR 24 near Echo Lake. Virtually all of the birds described above can be found here, including Boreal Owl.

Turn left onto CR 24 and drive south, first along the Vermilion River and eventually around the west end of Vermilion Lake to the town of Cook on U.S. Route 53, 35 miles from Echo Lake. In the area where CR 24 follows the Vermilion River, there are thriving wild-rice beds and a wide floodplain, utilized by a host of breeding and migrant waterfowl and other aquatic birds. Watch for Double-crested Cormorant. Vermilion Lake hosts 24 to 25 breeding pairs of Osprey and a dozen pairs of breeding Bald Eagle, the largest concentrations on the Forest. Duluth is about 96 miles south of Cook on U.S. 53.

ACCOMMODATIONS ◆ WEATHER ◆ OTHER ATTRACTIONS

When to visit. The best time to visit the Forest is November to March for winter finches and Spruce Grouse; early March to mid-April for owls; and late May to early July for warblers and other passerines.

Where to stay. Many campgrounds on the Forest. Lodging facilities and resorts throughout the area with concentrations near Duluth, Two Harbors, Silver Bay, Tofte, Grand Marais, Ely, Cook, Virginia, and (limited) Isabella.

Weather and attire. In summer, temperatures range from the 60s on the shore of Lake Superior to an occasional 90° F inland. Winter temperatures can dip down to the minus 40s. From May into July, wear long sleeves for protection against biting insects, and be prepared for clouds of mosquitoes and black flies..

What else to do. On the Forest: Canoe, boat, or fish in the multitude of lakes and streams; hike the Superior Hiking Trail; cross-country ski, snowmobile from lodge to lodge (canoes and skis are available for rent from area businesses). The route along Lake Superior's North Shore is dotted with state parks and scenic waysides. In Duluth, Hawk Ridge is considered one of the best raptor-watching spots in the nation; on the average, more than fifty thousand birds funnel through here each fall. Ely is home to the International Wolf Center with a marvelous timber wolf interpretive display. The Boundary Waters Canoe Area Wilderness, more than a million acres of interconnected lakes, lies entirely within the Forest along its northern border with Canada. In Grand Rapids is the Forest History Center with its living history of the logging era. And the Tower-Soudan Mine, now a state park, offers tours into the half-mile-deep hard-rock iron mine.

If you have time for a side trip, the Sax-Zim Bog, which lies outside the Forest, is a favorite spot for Northern Hawk Owl, Great Gray Owl, and Boreal Chickadee in winter, Sharp-tailed Grouse in April (Minnesota Department of Natural Resources maintains blinds to observe leks—call 218/749-7748 for more information), and Connecticut Warbler and Le Conte's Sparrow in summer. The bog is southwest of the town of Eveleth and just west of U.S. Route 53. It is roughly the area bounded by County Road (CR) 27 on the north, U.S. 53 on the east, CR 133 on the south, and CR 5 on the west. The best birding road is CR 7, which runs north-south from CR 133 to CR 27, about 5 miles west of U.S. 53.

For more information. Campground, general information, District Office addresses, maps, bird list: Superior National Forest, P.O. Box 338, Duluth, Minnesota 55801; telephone 218/720-5324.

WILD RICE

HIAWATHA FOREST
Michigan

Hiawatha National Forest

Sault Ste Marie

Munising
Rapid River

MICHIGAN

Cadillac

Detroit

HOW TO GET THERE. *From the Lower Peninsula follow Interstate 75 north of the Mackinac Bridge into the eastern portion of the Forest. For the Munising Route, take U.S. Route 2 west at the north end of the bridge for 65 miles to Michigan Route 77, go north for 17 miles to Michigan Route 28, then west for 35 miles to Munising. To reach Rapid River, take U.S. 2 west, but do not turn north at County Road M-77; instead continue west on U.S. 2 for another 62 miles. Rapid River can also be reached from northeastern Wisconsin, via U.S. Route 41 or Michigan Route 35 and is about 70 miles north of the state line at Marinette-Menominee.*

HIAWATHA NATIONAL FOREST, located in the east–central portion of Michigan's Upper Peninsula, is the only National Forest adjacent to three of the Great Lakes: Superior, Michigan, and Huron. Among the treasures of this 879,000-acre domain are upland boreal forests, northern hardwoods, rocky cliffs on the Great Lakes shorelines, beaches, grasslands, and wetlands that encompass almost 50 percent of the total acreage.

Nestled between the Great Lakes, this sea of trees is home to the greatest variety of nesting warblers in the country. The vast watersheds within the Forest contain plant life ranging from sedges to swamp conifers and swamp hardwoods. In the wetlands, the orchids, grass pink, dragon's mouth, and gentians color the landscape. Concerts of spring peepers and wood, mink, and leopard frogs will entertain you in spring. Here, too, are red-bellied and northern water snakes, snapping and wood turtles, and four-toed and spotted salamanders. All told, at least twenty-five species of amphibians and reptiles re-

JULIE ZICKEFOOSE, DRAWING

SANDHILL CRANES

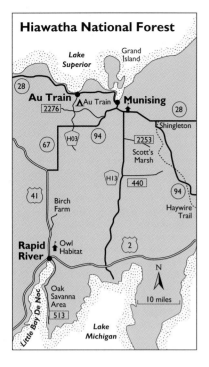

Hiawatha National Forest

side on the Forest. Mammals include white-tailed deer, moose, black bear, pine marten, fisher, and an occasional timber wolf.

Bird Life

Each of Hiawatha's communities offers a different assortment of birds, with more than 200 species recorded overall. The boreal forest harbors woodpeckers, flycatchers, chickadees, kinglets, and warblers. The rocky cliffs are utilized by numerous Herring Gulls, while Killdeer, Spotted Sandpiper, and Common and Caspian terns breed on the islands in Lake Michigan. The grasslands in the northern portion of the Stonington Peninsula (south of U.S. Route 2) support various breeding raptors, Sharp-tailed Grouse, Upland Sandpiper, and Savannah Sparrow. Large flocks of Sandhill Cranes gather in September and October near the villages of Fibre and Pickford in the eastern section of the Forest. Forest wetlands, such as the 10,000-acre Scott's Marsh, are home to bitterns, herons, rails, waterfowl, and various passerines.

Birding Routes

Five key birding locations can be reached by two routes. The Munising route includes the Au Train Lake area, Grand Island, and Scott's Marsh to the west, north, and southeast of Munising; the three sites can be done in any order. The Peninsula route takes in the Rapid River area and Stonington Peninsula south to Peninsula Point.

Munising Route. Begin in Munising and follow Michigan Route 28 west for 10 miles to the village of Au Train. From there, turn south onto County Road (CR) H-03 and drive six miles along the west shore of Au Train Lake to Forest Service Road (FR) 2276. Turn left and follow the signs to the Au Train Campground on Au Train Lake. At Campsite 11, you will find a viewing-platform that overlooks a shallow bay and an extensive marsh.

Scope the bay and the surrounding wetland for water birds. You should get Great Blue Heron, nesting Killdeer and Spotted Sandpiper, migrant Greater Yellowlegs, Solitary and Least sandpipers, and, if you are lucky, American Bittern. Also look for Common Loon, Double-breasted Cormorant, Wood Duck, American Black Duck, Mallard, Common Merganser, and Bald Eagle.

Next, walk the 2-mile-long Songbird Trail that begins at the viewing-platform. As the trail skirts along a riparian area,

one can hear Northern Waterthrush and see Ruby-crowned Kinglet. Farther along the trail, in an eastern hemlock inclusion, Blackburnian Warbler and Brown Creeper make their presence known. A feature of the Forest is an interpretive kit (cassette and player, ID pamphlet, binoculars) to help people locate and enjoy the twenty bird species found along the Songbird Trail. The kits can be rented for a nominal fee at the A and L Grocery, Au Train Grocery, or the Friends and Food Restaurant in Au Train. While the kits are intended mainly for tourists, birders may find the pamphlet and interpretive cassette interesting.

The Au Train Campground can be very good for migrant warblers. In late May and early June, a diligent birder can log more than fifteen species in a morning. Possibilities include Nashville, Yellow, Chestnut-sided, Magnolia, Black-throated Blue, Yellow-rumped, Black-throated Green, Blackburnian, Bay-breasted, Black-and-white, Connecticut, Mourning, Wilson's, and Canada; also Northern Parula, American Redstart, and Common Yellowthroat.

On your return to Munising, follow the signs to Pictured Rock Cruises, Inc., located at the Munising City Dock on the northwest edge of Munising on

South Bay. Take the boat-tour to Grand Island and Pictured Rocks National Lakeshore; times, prices, and reservations can be obtained by calling 906/387-2379.

The Grand Island trip will give you a fine chance for Common Loon, Double-crested Cormorant, Hooded, Common, and Red-breasted mergansers, Osprey, and Bald Eagle. Numerous nesting Herring Gulls swarm around the cliffs, and a lingering Glaucous Gull might be encountered. In late spring and early summer, migrant Bonaparte Gulls are still present. You also should find Common Tern, Belted Kingfisher, and Northern Rough-winged and Cliff swallows. Watch, too, for Peregrine Falcon. In summer 1992, captive-bred Peregrines were released at a site on the cliffs of the northwest side of the island.

Upon returning to Munising, drive southeast on Rte. 28 for 3 miles to Wetmore and turn right onto CR H-13. Continue south for 6.5 miles to FR 2253 and turn left. Cautiously follow FR 2253 east for 2.5 miles. This is the best place to search for Spruce Grouse. Another 2 miles down FR 2253, you will find Scott's Marsh Trailhead and parking area (in front of a gate). This road is minimally maintained to reduce disturbance at the marsh and may require a high-clearance vehicle. The Scott's

SCOTT FALLS, HIAWATHA NATIONAL FOREST

Marsh Trail runs for a mile through the heart of the marsh, providing an opportunity to experience this 5000-acre sedge-meadow community with its fascinating plants and animals. In spring and fall, you can expect migrating Tundra Swan, Snow Goose (rare), Northern Pintail, American Wigeon, Greater and Lesser yellowlegs, and Snow Bunting. Golden Eagles turn up occasionally.

During early summer, while admiring dragon's mouth and blue-eyed grass, you are likely to find American Bittern, Great Blue Heron, Black-crowned Night-Heron, and Sedge and Marsh wrens. There is also a chance of hearing the distinctive click and whinney calls of Yellow Rail and Sora. Osprey and Bald Eagle fish the adjacent pools, and Northern

Harrier and, possibly, Great Gray Owl (late fall to early spring, rare) can be found hunting the marsh. Golden-winged, Chestnut-sided, and Blackburnian warblers and Lincoln's and Swamp sparrows breed here. In fall, Sharp-tailed Grouse, Gray Jay, and Cedar Waxwing feed on winter berries. Sharp-tailed Grouse can be seen in the open sedge meadow off of FR 2253.

If time allows, you may wish to visit a nearby boreal forest. Return to Rte. 28 in Wetmore and turn right for 7 miles to Shingleton. Turn right onto Michigan Route 94 and drive south for 1.7 miles to the Haywire Snowmobile Trail that follows an old railroad bed for miles and crosses the North Branch of the Stutts River and other small streams. In summer, the trail is a narrow dirt road that you can either drive or walk. Turn right onto the trail from Rte. 94; a turnaround is located 1.2 miles down the trail from the highway, but, if you wish, you can follow the trail for about 12 miles until it again crosses Rte. 94.

Spruce and tamarack dominate the area, and there are also pockets of

COMMON TERNS

eared and Northern Saw-whet owls can be seen in the fall flying along the coastline at dusk.

During May and August, major concentrations of warblers feed on insects in the upper canopy of the hardwood forest. Look for Palm and Blackpoll in addition to most of the species listed for Au Trail Campground.

Continue north on CR 513 for about 15 miles, and take a short side-trip east on FR 2374, just north of Schaawe Lake. Follow FR 2374 east for 0.5 mile to the site of the 1988 Stockyard Burn. This is the best area on the Forest for Upland Sandpiper, Vesper Sparrow, and Brewer's Blackbird. Black-backed Woodpecker is seen here from time to time.

Then return to CR 513 and continue north to U.S. 2 and west to Rapid River. Follow the signs in the center of town south to the Rapid River Boat Launch. Many birds are attracted to the abundance of small fishes at this feeding spot where the Whitefish, Rapid, and Tacoosh Rivers all flow into Little Bay De Noc. You may find grebes, Double-crested

alder and cattails along the river banks. This is where you should look for Spruce Grouse (rare), Black-backed Woodpecker, flycatchers (Olive-sided, Yellow-bellied, and Alder), Boreal Chickadee, Golden-crowned Kinglet, warblers (Tennessee, Bay-breasted, and Connecticut), and Red and White-winged crossbills. The preferred habitat for Olive-sided and Yellow-belled flycatchers is along the Haywire route. There are also numerous beaver floodings along the Haywire. The dead or dying swamp conifers are ideal locations for Black-backed Woodpecker.

Peninsula Route. Begin at Peninsula Point, which is 17 miles south of U.S. Route 2 on CR 513, just east of Rapid River and Whitefish Point. The Point is a birder's Shangri-la for spring and fall waterfowl. Green-winged and Blue-winged teal, Northern Pintail, Northern Shoveler, Gadwall, American Wigeon, Canvasback, Redhead, Ring-necked Duck, Greater and Lesser scaups, and Common Goldeneye all migrate in spring and fall past the Point in large numbers. A lucky birder may find Red-necked Grebe, Oldsquaw, scoters (March/April or October/November), and jaegers (early fall). Long-

BLACK-THROATED BLUE WARBLER

Cormorant, Osprey, Bald Eagle, and Common and Caspian terns fishing together. Be alert for Yellow-headed Blackbird along the banks.

There are three additional birding sites to the north of Rapid River: a grassy plain at Birch Farm, a large block of Forest especially good for owls, and a superb warbler-nesting site along FR 2380 (see below). To reach Birch Farm, drive north from Rapid River on U.S. Route 41 (a right turnoff U.S. 2 just west of town) for about 8 miles and turn right onto County Road I-13, just after crossing the Rapid River. After about a mile, you will begin to see grassy openings. This plain supports a wide diversity of birds: Northern Harrier, Red-tailed Hawk, American Kestrel, Upland Sandpiper, Eastern Bluebird, Chipping, Clay-colored, Field, Vesper, and Savannah sparrows, Bobolink, Eastern Meadowlark, and Brewer's Blackbird. In early spring, look for migrating Horned Larks, American Tree Sparrows, and Snow Buntings. And, in winter, Bald Eagles use Birch Farm as a feeding-area.

To reach the owl habitat, return to Rapid River and drive east on U.S. 2 for 4 miles past the CR 513 intersection; turn left onto FR 2235. Go north for about 4 miles, then turn right onto FR 2231. Good habitat exists on both sides of the road for the next 4 miles to the intersection with FR 2233. Great Horned, Barred, Long-eared, and Northern Saw-whet owls can be heard here after dark in spring and early summer. Additional habitat can be found along FR 2233 for 3 miles north to FR 2229, then east for 4 miles to the CR H-13 intersection.

To explore still more excellent warbler country, follow CR H-13 north 11 miles from the junction with FR 2229

(18 miles from the junction of U.S. 2 and CR H-13) to CR 440. Turn right (east) on CR 440, go about 1.3 miles to CR N-3 and turn right again. Drive south on CR N-3 for about a mile to FR 2380, directly across from FR 2225, which is on the left. FR 2380 is a small dirt road suitable only for high-clearance vehicles; you will do much better by birding it on foot. You can find Northern Parula, Magnolia, Black-throated Blue, Blackburnian, and Blackpoll warblers.

The eastern portion of Michigan's Upper Peninsula offers an exceptional opportunity to view Sandhill Cranes on their staging-areas in September. As many as 1000 to 1500 birds pass through, because the nu-

BAY-BREASTED WARBLER

merous farm fields, beaver ponds, and meadows provide food and loafing-grounds. While searching for the cranes, you may also find Canada and Snow geese, Northern Harrier, American Kestrel, Sharp-tailed Grouse, and Eastern Bluebird.

There are two good areas to bird. You can visit the Pickford staging area by taking Interstate 75 north to Michigan Route 48 (28 miles north of the Mackinac Bridge), then driving east for about 9 miles to Michigan Route 129. Turn south on Rte. 129 and go 2 miles to the village of Pickford. Watch for cranes along Rte. 129 for two miles south of town and along local roads for two miles west of town. The Fibre staging area can be visited by returning west on Rte. 48 west about 2 miles beyond the Interstate, then north 3 miles to the village of Rudyard. Turn west (left) on CR H-40 and drive 8 miles to Fiber. Cranes can be observed in the farm fields along CR H-40 for 5 miles east and west of Fibre.

ACCOMMODATIONS ◆ WEATHER ◆ OTHER ATTRACTIONS

When to visit. Late April through June is best for birding, but fall migration, from late August through September is productive as well.

Where to stay. Numerous campgrounds on the Forest; major chain motels in Sault Ste. Marie, St. Ignace, Manistique, and Munising. Other small motels all along U.S. Route 2.

Weather and attire. Temperatures fluctuate from 30 to 60° F in spring and fall. Summertime highs are near 80° F, and lows can drop to almost 40° F. Rain-gear is always advisable. Insect repellent is strongly recommended in spring, summer, and fall.

What else to do. Hiking, biking, fishing, and canoeing. Nearby are Pictured Rocks National Lakeshore with its beaches, towering cliffs, and hiking-trails. Seney National Wildlife Refuge, 30 miles east of Munising, is renowned for its water-bird and especially Yellow Rail populations. Whitefish Point Bird Observatory near Paradise, Michigan, is a super spot in spring and fall migration for waterfowl, hawks, owls, and songbirds (late May); vagrants show up regularly.

For more information. General and campground information, District Office addresses, maps, bird list: Hiawatha National Forest, Rte. 2, 400 E. Munising Ave., Munising, Michigan 49682; telephone 906/387-2512.

TRILLIUM

SHOWY LADY-SLIPPER

HURON-MANISTEE FORESTS
Michigan

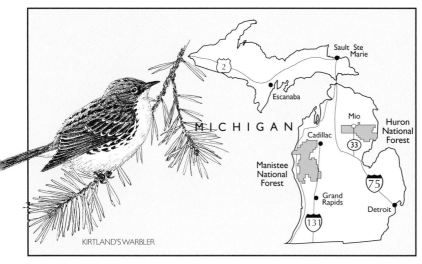

KIRTLAND'S WARBLER

CARL JAMES FREEMAN, DRAWING

HOW TO GET THERE.
For the Huron: From Saginaw, Michigan, take Interstate 75 north about 50 miles to Alger, then from Michigan Route 33 go north 35 miles to Mio.
For the Manistee: From Grand Rapids, take Interstate 131 north about 40 miles toward White Cloud and Baldwin.

TO THE HISTORIANS of the U.S. Forest Service, the 965,000-acre Huron–Manistee National Forests are wryly known as "the lands nobody wanted." That was not so in the beginning, of course. The first settlers thought the immense stands of white pine would last forever. But they were mistaken. By the turn of the century, when President Theodore Roosevelt moved to protect the nation's woodlands, the area had been clearcut, burned over, and farmed out. So poor and cheap was the land that the young Forest Service was able to buy one parcel of 32,504 acres for a mere $77,188.86—or $2.37 an acre. The area was then replanted, mainly in the 1930s by the Depression-era Civilian Conservation Corps. Most of what you see is no more than 50 to 60 years old, and the reforestation continues.

Huron Forest is a riparian environment. Five large rivers—the AuSable, Manistee, Muskegon, Pere Marquette, and the Pine—and many smaller creeks and streams meander through Michigan's Northern Lower Peninsula, nourishing the communities of jack pine, white-cedar, balsam fir, black spruce, white oak, and balsam poplar.

The Forest supports a large herd of white-tailed deer, along with populations of snowshoe hare, raccoon, river otter, mink, beaver, black bear, and bobcat. Wood and painted turtles, five-lined skink, northern water and eastern hognose snakes, and the poisonous eastern massasauga reside here, as well.

The gently flowing rivers are easily accessed by road, but canoeing is the best way to experience the riparian environment. Canoe rentals are

ICE FISHERMAN'S TRACKS, HURON NATIONAL FOREST

THERESA THOMPSON, PHOTOGRAPH

available in most towns in and around the Forest.

Bird Life

More than 180 species of birds have been recorded within the various habitats on the Forest. Wild Turkeys are abundant and can be found in almost all upland areas. In April and May, the gobblers display for hens along roadsides and in openings.

The extensive riverine communities attract American Bittern, Great Blue Heron, Wood Duck, Hooded Merganser, Osprey, Northern Goshawk, Red-shouldered Hawk, Black-billed Cuckoo, Barred Owl, Ruby-throated Hummingbird, Pileated Woodpecker, Bank Swallow, Cedar Waxwing, and Golden-winged and Black-throated Blue warblers. Eagles, Common Goldeneye, and Common Merganser remain along the ice-free portions of the rivers in winter.

Winter also brings avian visitors from the north. Rough-legged Hawk, Snowy Owl, Northern Shrike, Snow Bunting, Red and White-winged crossbills, and Pine Siskin mix with the year-round residents, such as Common Raven and Evening Grosbeak. Many of the roads on the Forest are open in winter.

The most sought-after bird of the Forest is the endangered Kirtland's Warbler, a bird of the jack pines. The total population is thought to be on the order of 485 nesting pairs, of which two-thirds breed on the Forest. Kirtland's Warbler requires dense, young jack pines that regenerate naturally after large forest fires. But modern fire-control efforts have reduced the amount of suitable habitat. In 1980, the Mack Lake Fire burned 25,000 acres of pines, producing the largest natural block of essential habitat in recent decades. Today, federal and state agencies cooperatively manage the jack-pine ecosystem by harvesting large areas of mature trees and then replanting with jack-pine seedlings to ensure a sustainable supply of habitat.

During the breeding season, access to Kirtland's Warbler habitat is governed by some restrictions to public entry, but tours are conducted from approximately May 15 to July 4 (see box at end for details). Two species closely associated with Kirtland's Warbler habitat that are uncommon farther east are Upland Sandpiper and Clay-colored Sparrow.

Black-backed Woodpeckers (very rare) may be found in areas recently burned by wildfires. Consult Forest Service personnel about known and potential locations for this species. Spruce Grouse can sometimes be seen in the jack pine plains.

Birding Routes

Kirtland's Warbler draws birders to the Huron part of Huron–Manistee National Forests. Several other nearby habitats should be visited to see the greatest variety of birds. The Luzerne–Wakeley Lake Route will produce swamp and open water birds, while the Hoist and Reid lakes Route offers birds of forest, pasture, and wetland communities.

Luzerne–Wakeley Lake. This route begins at Mio and follows Michigan Route 72 west for 8 miles to Deeter Road. Turn left onto Deeter Road for 0.5 mile to Galloway Road and left again for 0.75 mile to the Luzerne Swamp parking area and trailhead. Walk north (left) on the short (0.25 mile) segment of a horse trail that winds through a cool, dark northern white-cedar and balsam swamp to a boardwalk. The boardwalk leads to a wooden bridge that crosses a trout stream. Marsh marigold, sundew, turtlehead, partridge-berry, twinflower, and fringed polygala add color to the moss-covered ground.

Birding this area during the nesting season will likely produce Ruffed Grouse, American Woodcock, Winter Wren, Veery, Hermit Thrush, Cedar Waxwing, Black-

JULIE ZICKEFOOSE, DRAWING

WILD TURKEYS

throated Green and Canada warblers, American Redstart, Ovenbird, and Northern Waterthrush.

Return to Rte. 72 and continue west for 12 miles to the highway sign for Wakeley Lake Foot-Travel Area. At the parking lot you can acquire a map showing the 17 miles of trails through this semi-primitive area.

The cry of Common Loons often echoes across the lake, and Bald Eagles and Ospreys are frequently seen foraging for fish. Check the alder and willow thickets around the lake for Alder Flycatcher and Common Yellowthroat. Look for Wood Duck and American Black Duck, Hooded Merganser, and Common Snipe

at beaver ponds. Virginia Rail and Sora frequent the cattail swamps. Listen for Black-throated Green and Pine warblers in stands of mature red and white pine. Also found in the forested areas are Broad-winged Hawk, Ruffed Grouse, Yellow-bellied Sapsucker, Black-capped Chickadee, Scarlet Tanager, and Evening Grosbeak. After sunset, the hooting of Great Horned, Barred, and Northern Saw-whet owls often can be heard, along with the incessant chanting of the Whip-poor-will.

Hoist and Reid lakes. This route begins in Mio. Go east on Rte. 72 for 23 miles to the junction with Michigan Route 65, then continue south for 7 miles to where the two highways split. Hoist Lake is about 0.5 mile south of this junction on Rte. 65. Reid Lake is 3.5 miles east of the junction on Rte. 72. Trail maps are available at both sites.

These areas offer tranquil forest settings to replenish the spirit as well as

UPLAND SANDPIPER

to enjoy the birds. You are likely to find Northern Goshawk, Ruffed Grouse, Wild Turkey, Red-headed, Downy, and Hairy woodpeckers, Northern Flicker, Olive-sided and Least flycatchers, Eastern Bluebird, Red-eyed Vireo, Chestnut-sided, Black-throated Blue, and Black-throated Green warblers, Eastern Meadowlark, and Bobolink.

From Hoist Lake, continue south on Rte. 65 for about 15 miles to the River Road Scenic Byway. This 22-mile route follows the Au Sable River east to Oscoda, providing glimpses of the area's history. Stop first at Iargo Spring, a mile east of the Rte. 65–River Road junction. Local Indians believed Iargo Springs held mystical powers and used the location for tribal powwows. The birding can be excellent in the mixed forest at the base of the stairway that descends to the springs. Look for such southern species as Red-shouldered Hawk, Yellow-throated Vireo, and Louisiana Waterthrush, among the more northerly Golden-crowned Kinglets, Winter Wrens, and Black-throated Green Warblers. The dammed-up river into which the springs flow supports Pied-billed Grebe, Wood Duck, and Marsh Wren.

One half-mile east of Iargo Springs is Eagle's Nest Overlook. Nowadays, a pair of Bald Eagles nests out of sight in the gorge, but the birds are often seen flying up and down Cooke Dam Basin.

A third stop is the Lumberman's Monument Visitors Center, 2 miles beyond the overlook. The pines around the visitors center and along River Road provide nesting habitat for Pileated Woodpecker, Common Raven, Red-breasted Nuthatch, Hermit Thrush, Solitary Vireo, Yellow-

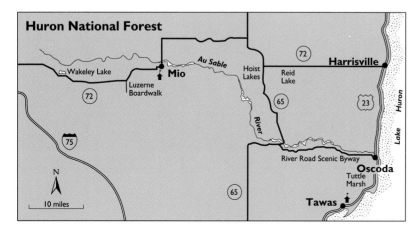

Huron National Forest

Wakeley Lake
Au Sable
Mio
Luzerne Boardwalk
72
75
N
10 miles
Hoist Lakes
Reid Lake
65
River
72
Harrisville
23
Lake Huron
River Road Scenic Byway
Oscoda
Tuttle Marsh
65
Tawas

rumped and Pine warblers, and Scarlet Tanager.

Tuttle Marsh is but a short drive from the Monument and is good for numerous wetland birds. Take River Road 7.5 miles east to Wells Road (Forest Service Road 4496), turn right, and proceed about 3 miles to old U.S. Route 23. Turn left on old U.S. 23 for 2 miles to Tuttle Marsh Road, and turn right. This road extends for only 4 miles, but offers good birding along the entire way. Tuttle Marsh Impoundment is 2 miles beyond the junction.

Scan the marsh and impoundment for Pied-billed Grebe, American and Least bitterns, Great Blue and Green

herons, Wood Duck, Mallard, Blue-winged Teal, Black Tern, Hooded Merganser, Virginia Rail, and Sora. Other breeding species to be found in the neighborhood include Solitary Vireo, Golden-winged and Chestnut-sided warblers, American Redstart, Common Yellowthroat, and Field and Vesper Sparrows. Look for Upland Sandpiper in large, dry openings, Alder and Least flycatchers and Yellow Warbler in willow swamps, Winter Wren in the cedar swamp, Sedge Wren in large, wet sedge openings and Marsh Wren and Swamp Sparrow in cattail marshes.

Continue south another 1.5 miles to the intersection of Tuttle Marsh

BLACK-CAPPED CHICKADEES

and Davidson Road. The open fields to the north often turn up Wild Turkey, Eastern Bluebird, and Clay-colored and Vesper sparrows.

KENN KAUFMAN, DRAWING

ACCOMMODATIONS ◆ WEATHER ◆ OTHER ATTRACTIONS

When to visit. Birding is best from mid-May to the end of June. Winter residents arrive in November and stay until March.

Where to stay. Camping on the Forest; motels and bed-and-breakfast accommodations in Cadillac, Mio, Manistee, and Tawas.

Weather and attire. Spring and summer mornings are cool, and winters are cold with snow. Warm jackets, rain-gear, and insect repellent are recommended.

What else to do. Canoeing, fishing, paddle-wheel cruises (Foote and Five Channels Dam Pond), hiking, horseback riding, morel mushroom hunting (spring), berry-picking, fall-color touring (late September to early October), cross-country skiing, and snowmobiling.

Visit Hartwick Pines State Park, just north of Grayling off Interstate 75. The old-growth pine forest there is good for Pileated Woodpecker, Northern Parula, Black-throated Green, Blackburnian, and Pine warblers, and Evening Grosbeak; Sleeping Bear Dunes National Lakeshore (shorebirds, auto tour, hiking-trails, views of Lake Michigan); Nordhouse Dunes Wilderness Area in the Manistee section of the Forest (shorebirds, Prairie Warbler, hiking-trails, more views of Lake Michigan); Mackinac Bridge and Straits (scenery, Fort Michilimack-

inac, Old Mill Creek sawmill), and Tawas Point and Alabaster (both good traps for migrant songbirds in spring). The Forest Service runs Kirtland's Warbler tours out of Mio during breeding-season. For information contact: Mio Ranger District, 401 Court Street, Mio, Michigan 48647; telephone 517/826-3252. The U.S. Fish and Wildlife Service runs another Kirtland's Warbler tour from Grayling. For information contact: Grayling Field Office, P.O. Box 507, Grayling, Michigan 49738; telephone 517/348-6371. Reservations required for groups of ten or more on either tour.

For more information. General and campground information, District Office addresses, maps, bird list: Huron–Manistee National Forests, 421 South Mitchell St., Cadillac, Michigan 49601; telephone 800/821-6263.

BIRDS FOOT VIOLET

ALLEGHENY FOREST
Pennsylvania

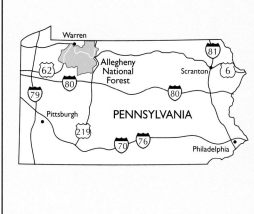

HOW TO GET THERE. The Forest Headquarters and the starting point for the Bean Fields-Hearts Content tour route are in Warren. To reach Warren from the south or west, take Interstate 80 ten miles east of Interstate 79 to Pennsylvania Route 8 (Exit 3), go north on Rte. 8 for 16 miles to Franklin, turn right on U.S. Route 62, and drive north on U.S. 62 for 56 miles. From the east, there are several possible routes from I-80. One scenic route leaves I-80 at Pennsylvania Route 36 (Exit 13), then goes north for 47 miles via Pennsylvania Routes 36, 899, 66, and 948 to the junction with U.S. 6 at Sheffield, 13 miles southeast of Warren. The Tionesta Scenic Area tour begins at Ludlow, 7 miles east of Sheffield. From the north, leave I-90 at Dunkirk and follow New York Route 60 and U.S. 62 south to Warren.

PENNSYLVANIA'S ONLY National Forest spreads across the rugged plateau country dominating the northwestern corner of the state. The area's many creeks and streams cut deeply into the rolling plateau, creating a dissected topography with a 1300-foot relief.

This 513,000-acre Forest is mostly hardwoods with black cherry, white ash, sugar maple, beech, hemlock, yellow poplar, and several species of oaks. More than half the Forest floor is carpeted with New York and hay-scented ferns (see back cover). Common wildflowers include trillium, wood sorrel, spring beauty, black-eyed susan, bee balm, and several violets. Mid-to-late June usually is the best time of year to see mountain laurel in bloom, especially along Pennsylvania Route 59 between the Bradford Ranger Station and the Allegheny Reservoir.

The 4100-acre Tionesta Scenic Area, just west of Kane and south of Ludlow, and the 122-acre Hearts Content Scenic Area south of Warren feature some of the oldest tracts of beech–hemlock–white pine forest in the U.S. The oldest trees in these pristine areas date back to the 1700s.

White-tailed deer, black bear, porcupine, and woodchuck can be seen along the many Forest roads. Among the reptiles and amphibians residing on the Forest are wood and snapping turtles, timber rattlesnake, eastern garter, eastern milk, and northern water snakes, wood and leopard frogs, northern spring peepers, eastern American toad, red-backed and northern dusky salamanders, and red-spotted newts.

Bird Life
More than two hundred species of birds have been found on the Forest.

POND IN MORNING FOG, ALLEGHENY NATIONAL FOREST

JOHN P. GEORGE, PHOTOGRAPH

Ruffed Grouse and Wild Turkey are common. Yellow-bellied Sapsucker, Pileated Woodpecker, Winter Wren, and Hermit Thrush inhabit the hardwood forests. Clearcuts that are regenerating as dense seedlings and saplings are prime spots for Mourning Warbler.

A few southern species are at or near the northern edge of their range here: White-eye Vireo, Yellow-throated Warbler, and Yellow-breasted Chat. Many northern species that nest on the forest are uncommon farther south and along the coast, except in the higher parts of the Appalachian Mountains. These include Swainson's Thrush, Nashville, Magnolia, Black-throated Blue, Yellow-rumped, Blackburnian, and Mourning warblers, White-throated Sparrow, and Dark-eyed Junco.

Warbler migration can be excellent. The best time is during late April and May, before leaf-out obstructs views. Most common are Yellow, Chestnut-sided, Magnolia, Black-throated Blue, Yellow-rumped, Black-throated Green, Blackburnian, Black-and-white, and Canada warblers, Northern Parula, American Redstart, and Common Yellowthroat. Tennessee, Cape May, Bay-breasted, and Blackpoll warblers do not nest here, but may be seen occasionally during migration. Swainson's and Hermit thrushes, Scarlet Tanager, and Rose-breasted Grosbeak add color and song to the spring forest.

Birding Routes

Two of the best spots are the Hearts Content Scenic Area, 10 miles south of Warren, and the Tionesta Scenic Area, 6 miles south of Ludlow. Additional good birding sites include the Allegheny Reservoir, Buzzard Swamp, Owl's Nest, and Tracy Ridge National Recreation Area.

The Bean Fields–Hearts Content Route. Begin at Warren and follow U.S. Routes 6 and 62 west for five miles to where the two highways divide. Turn left on U.S. 62 and drive for less than 0.5 mile. Just before the road crosses the Allegheny River, make a right turn and follow the signs for the Buckaloons Recreation Area. Continue on this road (the old U.S. Route 6) past the Buckaloons Campground and the Forestry Sciences Laboratory, across Brokenstraw Creek, and past a large field on your left. Just beyond the field is a gate marked with a Forest Service sign inviting you to walk in. Accept the invitation. Park near the gate, without blocking access, and follow the old railroad bed for about a mile between the base of the wooded slope on the right and a variety of swamps, brush, cut-over woods, old fields, and marsh on the left.

Watch along this path for Blue-winged and Golden-winged warblers; they like overgrown meadow habitat. Keep an eye out for the two hybrids, Lawrence's and Brewster's warblers, that are often found where the ranges of the two species overlap. Other birds to expect include Green Heron, Wood Duck, Ruby-throated Hummingbird, Downy Woodpecker, Eastern Kingbird, Black-capped Chickadee, Veery, Wood Thrush, Gray Catbird, Cedar Waxwing, Red-eyed Vireo, Yellow and Chestnut-sided warblers, American Redstart, Northern Cardinal, Indigo Bunting, Rufous-sided Towhee, Song Sparrow, and Northern Oriole.

You can either return to your car or turn left after passing the second gate and take the old driveway (blocked by a log) to the river. Turn left and follow the trail past the old Newbold Estate (no buildings remain) with its overgrown fields and woods adjacent to the Allegheny River; this area is known locally as the Bean Fields. It is one of the Forest's best locations for finding a large variety of birds, especially in spring and summer; even in winter, birding can be good here, with a chance to see Red-tailed, Cooper's, and Sharp-shinned hawks, Pileated and Red-bellied woodpeckers, Northern Cardinal, and Song, Tree,

PILEATED WOODPECKER

and White-throated sparrows. Common Goldeneye, Bufflehead, and Common Merganser feed in the river.

When you come to a fork, stay left as the trail passes through a stand of large Norway spruces and past the Pennsylvania champion European larch (39 inches in diameter and 111 feet tall); Northern Parula nests in this habitat. Continue through the old fields with young maples and pines and the cutover woods back to the railroad bed to return to the start. Red-bellied and Pileated woodpeckers reside here year-round, and White-eyed Vireo and Yellow-breasted Chat have been found in spring and summer. Listen for Yellow-throated Vireo in the white oaks. Watch also for Yellow-throated Warbler, which nests at the nearby Buckaloons Campground.

Afterwards, return to Rte. 62 and turn right. Cross the river and go about a mile and take the first paved

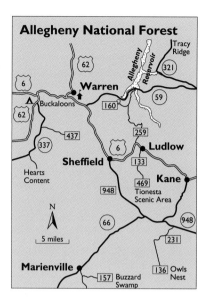

road on the left, Gunderville Road or Pennsylvania Route 202. Drive 0.1 mile to a fork in the road at Forrester Restaurant. Follow this (dirt) road, keeping to a right at the fork, along Lenhart Run for 3.2 miles until it merges with Pennsylvania Route 337.

Turn right on Rte. 337, and after 1.8 miles you will come to Forest Service Road (FR) 437 on the left. This is an excellent place for Barred Owl after dark. You can drive along FR 437 for 4 miles toward Chapman State Park, stopping occasionally to listen for the owl's booming call—a loud *Who cooks for you, who cooks for you all?*

Return to Rte. 337 and continue south. Tree Swallows and Eastern Bluebirds occupy nest-boxes along the road, and, in late summer, Broad-winged Hawks perch on the wires or poles. About 3.5 miles beyond FR 437, Rte. 337 will bear off to the right. You want to go straight ahead on Hearts Content Road, watching for logged areas that are regenerating as dense seedlings and sapling patches; these are where you should look for Mourning Warblers between late May and July. Drive 3.6 miles to the picnic area and hike the short (approximately one mile) loop-trail through the virgin hemlocks and towering white pines. This is one of the best areas in the Forest for Winter Wren, Swainson's Thrush, and a variety of warblers. Yellow-rumped Warbler has nested in the red pines near the picnic area and across the road at the campground entrance.

Additional birds to look for along the forested trail are Hairy and Pileated woodpeckers, Yellow-bellied Sapsucker, Eastern Wood-Pewee, Least Flycatcher, Blue Jay, Black-capped Chickadee, White-breasted Nuthatch, House Wren, Golden-crowned Kinglet, Veery, Hermit and Wood thrushes, Solitary Vireo, Magnolia, Black-throated Blue, Black-throated Green, Blackburnian, and Canada warblers, Ovenbird, Scarlet Tanager, Rose-Breasted Grosbeak, Dark-eyed Junco, and Purple Finch.

RUFFED GROUSE

CARL JAMES FREEMAN, DRAWING

Birdfinding in Forty National Forests and Grasslands

BLACK-THROATED GREEN WARBLER

Tionesta Scenic Area. Drive south from Ludlow (approximately 20 miles southeast of Warren on U.S. 6) on FR 133 for about 6 miles and turn right at the sign for the scenic area. The best way to bird is by hiking the various trails. Tionesta is noted for its raptors, including all three accipiters. Also watch for Common Raven, and Swainson's Hawk. The Interpretive Trail passes through virgin hemlock–beech forest and close to the site of the devastating tornado of May 1985. There is a platform on the parking loop that overlooks the swath of the tornado.

Tionesta Creek is good for Wood Duck and Red-breasted and Hooded mergansers in May and June. Osprey and Bald Eagle are occasionally seen here as well. The best way to experience Tionesta Creek, as well as the Allegheny and Clarion Rivers, is by canoe. Contact the Forest Headquarters for suggestions on where to obtain rentals.

Return to Ludlow and drive west on U.S. 6; go about a mile to unpaved FR 259. Turn right (north) on FR 259 for a pleasant drive through the forest, stopping to bird at the various gated side roads. Look and listen for Yellow-bellied Sapsucker, Veery, and Hermit and Wood thrushes, plus Chestnut-sided, Magnolia, Black-throated Blue, Blackburnian, and Canada warblers among a mix of birds similar to those found at

Heart's Content. Hooded Warbler can be found where there is an understory of saplings or shrubs.

At the junction of FR 259 and FR 160, about 8 miles beyond the junction with U.S. 6, turn left on FR 160 and drive 1.4 miles to the Seneca Pumped Storage Reservoir. During migration, this site can produce a wide variety of waterfowl. Scan for Common Loon, Tundra Swan, Green-winged and Blue-winged teals, Northern Pintail, Ring-necked Duck, Lesser Scaup, Old-squaw, Common Goldeneye, Hooded and Common mergansers, and Ruddy Duck. Osprey and Bald Eagle are sometimes found in this same area. Do not drive these roads without four-wheel drive when there is snow or ice.

Return to the junction with FR 259 and keep left; follow FR 160 north for about 1.5 miles to the Jakes Rocks Road straight ahead. Jakes Rocks provide two overlooks of the Allegheny Reservoir and Kinzua Dam from the top of the ridge. You are almost certain to hear a Hermit Thrush sing in the evening along the trail. This is another good place for mountain laurel. After coming out of the one-way loop, turn left, then right to follow FR 499 and 262 downhill to Pennsylvania Route 59 on the southern edge of the Allegheny Reservoir. Turn left on Rte. 59 toward Warren and drive 3.7 miles to the Kinzua Dam Visitors Center. Park and scope the reservoir for Bald Eagle. When the reservoir freezes over, the eagles often perch along the river just below Kinzua Dam to take advantage of the open water. Sunrise is the best time of day

to view these majestic raptors as they hunt for fish below the dam.

Buzzard Swamp. Another prime birding spot on the Forest is Buzzard Swamp. Access is through Marienville, which is on Pennsylvania Route 66 in the southwestern part of the Forest 30 miles southwest of Kane. From the center of town, take Rte. 27027 (a paved County road) south for 1.2 miles to FR 157. Turn left on FR 157 and drive 2.2 miles to the Buzzard Swamp parking area at the end of the road. Watch for Ruffed Grouse and Wild Turkey along FR 157. From the parking area, take the 1.6-mile Songbird Sojourn Interpretive Trail.

The upland-forest habitat harbors Downy, Hairy, and Pileated woodpeckers, Least and Great

YELLOW-BELLIED SAPSUCKER

Crested flycatchers, Blue Jay, Cedar Waxwing, Yellow-throated and Red-eyed vireos, Chestnut-sided, Magnolia, Black-throated Blue, Black-throated Green, Blackburnian, and Canada warblers, Ovenbird, Northern and Louisiana waterthrushes, American Redstart, Scarlet Tanager, Rose-breasted Grosbeak, Rufous-sided Towhee, Chipping Sparrow, and Northern Oriole. Back at the parking lot, the gated road goes past several impoundments. Common Merganser, Spotted Sandpiper, and Belted Kingfisher nest here, and Great Blue Heron, Canada Goose, Wood Duck, Green-winged Teal, Mallard, and a variety of other waterfowl and shorebirds can often be found. Watch also for Osprey patrolling the impoundments.

Return the same way to the parking lot, or continue ahead past the largest and last impoundment, cross the dam, and follow the little-used road through more open woodland, fields, and planted evergreens, ending at the parking lot. The entire loop is about 3.5 miles. Watch for hawks, Ruffed Grouse, Wild Turkey, Black-billed and Yellow-billed cuckoos, Tree Swallow, Common Raven, Magnolia, Black-throated Green, and Blackburnian warblers, Common Yellowthroat, Dark-eyed Junco, and Eastern Meadowlark.

Owls Nest and Tracy Ridge National Recreation Area. These areas are worth checking in winter. The Owls Nest area is reached by taking Pennsylvania Route 66 east from Marienville town center for 15.3 miles to a fork; bear right for 1.8 miles to Highland Corners. Turn right (south) on FR 231 and go 3.5 miles to the community of Sackett; then turn left on FR 136, a dirt road at the Pennzoil Field office sign, and drive 4.4 miles to Owls Nest. From December throughout February, search the stands of larch for Long-eared Owls .

Tracy Ridge National Recreation Area can be reached by driving east from Warren on Rte. 59 for about 21 miles, past the Allegheny Reservoir and Bradford Ranger Station. Turn left (north) on Pennsylvania Route 321 and drive 10.6 miles to Tracy Ridge Campground. Northern Saw-whet Owls may be found from March through July by searching the conifers along the trails. Cerulean Warblers sing in the oak trees along the Tracy Ridge Trail.

ACCOMMODATIONS ◆ WEATHER ◆ OTHER ATTRACTIONS

When to visit. Late May to early July is best for nesting songbirds, January for Bald Eagles, late June for mountain laurel blooms, and early October for the fall color.

Where to stay. Ten Forest campgrounds and numerous private campgrounds. Motels in Warren, Bradford, Kane, Ridgeway, Marienville, and other towns near the Forest.

Weather and attire. Expect rain any time of year, and snow is possible from November through March. A jacket could be necessary any night of the year, rain-gear is a good idea, and a warm winter coat is needed from November through March.

What else to do. Canoeing, boating, swimming, hunting, mountain-biking, cross-country skiing, and snowmobiling on the Forest. Nearby one can take the scenic train on the Kane Kinzua Railroad from Marienville or Kane to the Kinzua Bridge and return; Pennsylvania's only wild elk herd can be seen near Saint Marys, east of Ridgeway, and the Drake Well Museum in Titusville is the site of the world's first oil-well.

Presque Isle State Park by Lake Erie is a prime birding location in spring; Pymatuning Reservoir and Pymatuning State Park can both be good birding locales in all seasons.

For more information. General and campground information, District Office addresses, maps, bird list: Allegheny National Forest, 222 N. Liberty St., Warren, Pennsylvania 16365; telephone 814/723-5150.

YELLOW LADY'S SLIPPER, TRILLIUM, SPRING BEAUTY, AND FIRE PINK

FINGER LAKES FOREST
New York

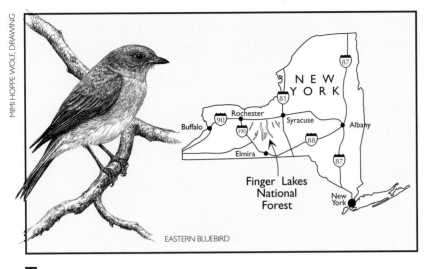

MIMI HOPPE WOLF, DRAWING

EASTERN BLUEBIRD

HOW TO GET THERE. *From the south, take New York Route 17 to Owego, 25 miles west of Binghamton. Go north on New York Route 96 for about 30 miles through Ithaca, and turn left (west) on New York Route 79 toward Mecklenburg. Drive west for 14 miles to the intersection with New York Route 227, turn right, and go 1.3 miles to the junction with Potomac Road in the village of Reynoldsville. From the north, take Exit 42 off the New York Thruway. Turn south on New York Route 14, go a short distance, and turn left onto Rte. 96. Follow Rte. 96 south through Waterloo and Interlaken for about 34 miles to Trumansburg. Turn right on Rte. 227 and follow it through Perry City for about 7 miles to Reynoldsville.*

THIS SMALL NATIONAL FOREST of 13,232 acres is situated in the heart of the Finger Lakes Region of central New York between Cayuga and Seneca Lakes. The area's cultural heritage dates back to the Iroquois Confederacy, whose six nations once ruled a woodland empire that extended for hundreds of miles in all directions. Numbering perhaps 20,000 people at the coming of the white man in the early seventeenth century, the Iroquois were the most advanced of the eastern Indians. They lived in securely palisaded villages, the men hunting deer and other game while the women raised a bounty of corn, squash, and beans. Tribal names such as Cayuga, Seneca, and Taughannock are still used by local communities.

The Forest contains a rich mix of habitats. Following a decades-old tradition of cattle-grazing, about a third of the area, approximately 4000 acres, is maintained in grasslands, shrublands, and pastures. The remainder is forested with northern hardwoods and oaks, plus a combination of pine plantations, native hemlock, and white pine stands.

Gray, red, and northern flying squirrels, red fox, raccoon, and white-tailed deer are some of the many mammals that inhabit the Forest. There also is a variety of reptiles and amphibians, including grass, garter, brown, and milk snakes, painted, snapping, and box turtles, and several salamanders and newts, including red eft, the terrestrial stage of the red-spotted newt. Among the butterflies and moths are the colorful monarch, tiger swallowtail, and mourning cloak butterflies, as well as the exquisite green luna and strongly-patterned cecropia moths.

GAIL DIANE LUCKNER, DRAWING

ROUGH-LEGGED HAWK

HENSLOW'S SPARROW

Bird Life

It is remarkable that 50 percent of New York's 243 breeding birds can be found in this postage-stamp of a place. Look and listen for Henslow's Sparrow in the larger ungrazed fields from May through July. Specific locations vary from year to year depending on mowing and cattle-grazing schedules. Other species range from grassland inhabitants, such as Grasshopper Sparrow, Eastern Bluebird, and Upland Sandpiper, to forest-dwelling Northern Goshawk, Sharp-shinned and Cooper's hawks, Ruffed Grouse, Wild Turkey, and Pileated Woodpecker. Eastern Screech-Owl and Great Horned and Barred owls inhabit the many old woodlots, and, on summer days, Northern Harrier, Red-tailed Hawk, and American Kestrel can be found hunting over the pastures and shrublands.

Finger Lakes National Forest is an important summer refuge for more than seventy breeding species that winter largely in the tropics, including Black-billed and Yellow-billed cuckoos, Ruby-throated Hummingbird, Alder and Willow flycatchers, Veery, Wood Thrush, Solitary, Red-eyed, and Yellow-throated vireos, no fewer than seventeen species of wood warblers, Scarlet Tanager, and Orchard (rare) and Northern orioles. Wintering birds include Rough-legged Hawk, Snow Bunting, and in some winters, Pine Grosbeak, Red and White-winged crossbills, and Common Redpoll.

Birding Route

Potomac, Searsburg, and Seneca Roads. The most rewarding route, a 10-mile tour that takes about four hours, begins at the junction of New York Route 227 and Potomac Road in the village of Reynoldsville. One caution at the start: the Forest contains many private inholdings; be sure to respect No Trespassing signs.

Commence your tour by driving north on Potomac Road for 4 miles to the intersection with Searsburg Road. This leg passes through a mixture of

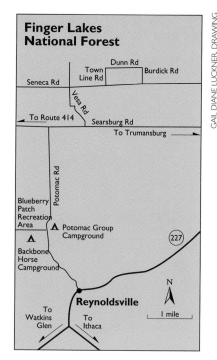

GAIL DIANE LUCKNER, DRAWING

hardwood forest, conifer plantations, shrubs, and pastures, and it is a good place to find migrants. Watch for warblers (Nashville, Magnolia, Chestnut-sided, Black-throated Blue, Black-throated Green, Blackburnian, and Hooded), Solitary and Red-eyed vireos, and Scarlet Tanager.

In the pastures, look for Red-tailed Hawk, American Kestrel, Eastern Bluebird, Eastern Meadowlark, and Bobolink. In spring, evening courtship displays of American Woodcock will reward the diligent observer. A good viewing location is along Picnic Area Road between the Backbone Horse Camp and Blueberry Patch Recreation Area. At the same time, several species of bats can be observed fly-catching over the pastures and shrublands.

At Searsburg Road, turn right and drive 1 mile to Vesa Road, turn left (north) on Vesa Road, and go 1 mile to Seneca Road. If you like, you can take a 2-mile side trip here by continuing north on Vesa Road. The grasslands and pastures along Vesa Road are good for Chipping, Field, Vesper, Savannah, Grasshopper, Henslow's, and Song sparrows, as well as Eastern Meadowlark and

ORANGE SUGAR MAPLES AND FERNS, FINGER LAKES NATIONAL FOREST

JOHN P. GEORGE, PHOTOGRAPH

Birding in Forty National Forests and Grasslands

Bobolink. Henslow's Sparrow is most easily found when it is singing, usually only early or late in the day. Also watch carefully here for Upland Sandpiper, although it does not occur every summer.

Return to the intersection with Seneca Road and turn left (east). Continue 1 mile to the junction with Town Line Road, turn left, drive 0.5 mile to Dunn Road, and turn right. Drive east 0.75 mile to a pond on the south side of the road. This 2.25-mile leg of the route passes through overgrown fields covered with shrubs and wildflowers. Scan for Northern Harrier (which as a breeder is regarded as threatened in New York), as well as Ring-necked Pheasant, Ruby-throated Hummingbird, Eastern Kingbird, and American Goldfinch. At the pond, park and check for Wood Duck, migrant Lesser Yellowlegs (late summer), migrant Solitary, Spotted, and Least sandpipers (late summer), Belted Kingfisher,

Tree, Bank, and Barn swallows, Cedar Waxwing, and Common Yellowthroat.

Continue on Dunn Road to the next corner, turn right on Burdick Road, and go 0.25 mile to Burdick Pond. Check the pond for Great Blue and Green herons, American Black Duck, Hooded Merganser, Alder, Willow, and Least flycatchers, and swallows. Then continue 0.25 mile to Seneca Road, turn left, and follow Seneca Road east out of the Forest to New York Route 96, just north of Trumansburg.

In addition to the many roads, there are numerous trails, especially in the southern part of the Forest. An excellent map is available from the Forest Service. One of the trails ascends 1880-foot Burnt Hill, providing a panoramic view of Seneca Lake to the west and Cayuga Lake to the east. Here may be found Mourning, Chestnut-sided, and Hooded warblers, American Redstart, and Veery.

AMERICAN KESTREL

ACCOMMODATIONS ♦ WEATHER ♦ OTHER ATTRACTIONS

When to visit. Late spring and early summer are best for breeding birds. Late September and early October produce raptor migration and marvelous fall color.

Where to stay. Several campgrounds on the Forest and adjacent state parks; motels and hotels, in Ithaca and Watkins Glen, and a bed-and-breakfast establishment at the southwestern edge of the Forest in Burdett.

Weather and attire. Spring and fall are often foggy and rainy, interspersed with clear, breezy days; temperatures range from 40 to 60° F. Summer temperatures range from 70 to 100° F with a chance of afternoon thunderstorms. Winter temperatures range from 0 to 30° F and can change dramatically and quickly. Waterproof shoes or boots are a necessity regardless of the time of year. Dress in layers with a waterproof outer shell to break the wind.

What else to do. On the Forest: hiking, fishing, horseback riding, picnicking, cross-country skiing. Sapsucker Woods, part of the Cornell University Laboratory of Ornithology, is in nearby Ithaca, at the south end of Cayuga Lake; a visitors center and research library, as well as an observation room overlooking a pond and wetland, are open to the public Monday through Thursday, 11 AM to 3 PM; walking trails are open from dawn to dusk, daily. Montezuma National Wildlife Refuge is at the north end of Cayuga Lake. This refuge has an auto tour and an observation tower and is an excellent place to bird during waterfowl migration and fall shorebird migration. Taughannock State Park, 10 miles north of Ithaca up the west side of Cayuga Lake, has pleasant walking trails and vistas.

For more information. General and campground information, District Office addresses, map, bird list: Finger Lakes National Forest, P.O. Box W, Odessa–Montour Highway, State Route 224, Montour Falls, New York 14865; telephone 607/594-2750.

MONARCH BUTTERFLY ON THISTLE

GREEN MOUNTAIN FOREST
Vermont

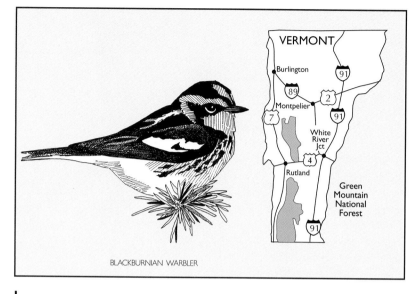

BLACKBURNIAN WARBLER

HOW TO GET THERE. *From Boston, take Massachusetts Route 2 to Interstate 91 north to Interstate 89, and I-89 north to White River Junction, Vermont. The n take U.S. Route 4 west to Rutland, which is Exit 1 after crossing the Connecticut River. From New York City, take Interstate 87 north to Exit 20, just north of Glen Falls. Follow New York Route 149 east to Fort Ann, then U.S. Rte. 4 east to Rutland. From Montreal, take Canadian Route 10 to Quebec Provincial Route 133. Take Rte. 133 south to I-89 at the border, then follow I-89 to Burlington and U.S. Route 7. Follow Rte. 7 south to Rutland. To reach the southern unit of the Forest from New York, take New York Route 7 from Troy to Bennington, then go north on U.S. Route 7 to Manchester; you can reach Manchester from Brattleboro via Vermont Route 30.*

LIKE NEW HAMPSHIRE'S WHITE MOUNTAINS, the Green Mountains of Vermont are justly esteemed for their stunning fall color displays. Located in the southern part of the state, the 350,000-acre Forest not only makes up half of all public lands in Vermont, but also provides a scenic backdrop to rural villages and farms. A visit is an excursion into New England's delightful back country.

Nearly 90 percent of the Forest is northern hardwoods (sugar maple, oak, beech, and yellow and white birches) with an understory of witch hazel, hornbeam, shadbush, blueberry, and hobblebush. The other 10 percent consists of wetlands, spruce and fir forest, and upland openings. Remote areas are home to black bear, fisher, mink, and bobcat. More commonly seen mammals include porcupine, beaver, gray and red squirrels, red fox, raccoon, chipmunk, moose, and white-tailed deer. Among the reptiles and amphibians are garter, brown, and milk snakes, the red eft form of the red-spotted newt, red-backed salamander, painted, snapping, and wood turtles, and the wood frog and spring peeper. Colorful butterflies, such as monarch and swallowtail, feed on the abundant wildflowers.

Bird Life

At least 200 species have been found on the Forest. One unique subspecies, Gray-cheeked (Bicknell's) Thrush, has a breeding-range limited to the northeastern U.S. and eastern Canada. A combination of restricted habitat, acid precipitation, and human intrusion, together with the usual threats to neotropical migrants on their wintering-grounds, makes the future of Bicknell's uncertain. Recent studies may lead to Bicknell's being considered a separate species, which would likely result in its being classified as federally endangered or threatened.

The thrush, which arrives on the forest in late May, is usually found on exposed ridges of stunted red spruce and balsam fir above 3000 feet. It is most vocal at dawn and dusk, but may be heard all day in early summer. Given its inaccessible, restricted breeding-range, little is known about Bicknell's life history. Please report observations to any Forest Service Office, and to the Vermont Institute of Natural Science at Woodstock. Send information to Chris Rimmer, Director of Research.

GRAY-CHEEKED (BICKNELL'S) THRUSH

Among the Forest's other resident and migrant species are Ruffed Grouse, Wild Turkey, Barred Owl, Pileated Woodpecker, Common Raven, Winter Wren, Hermit Thrush, Solitary Vireo, a fine selection of warblers (including Nashville, Chestnut-sided, Magnolia, Black-throated Blue, Yellow-rumped, Black-throated Green, Blackburnian, Blackpoll, Mourning, and Canada warblers, American Redstart, and Ovenbird), plus Scarlet Tanager, Rose-breasted Grosbeak, Northern Oriole, Purple Finch, Pine Siskin, and Evening Grosbeak.

Winter brings an influx of northern species, such as Northern Shrike, American Tree Sparrow, and Red and White-winged crossbills.

Birding Routes

Three areas along the 265-mile Long Trail that stretches from Massachusetts to Canada will give you a full representation of the Forest's bird life. These are Mt. Horrid, Bromley Mountain and Spruce Peak, and Lye Brook Wilderness Area.

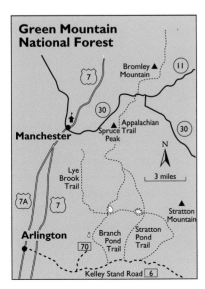

Green Mountain National Forest

Bromley Mountain
Manchester
Spruce Peak
Appalachian Trail
Lye Brook Trail
Arlington
Branch Pond Trail
Stratton Pond Trail
Stratton Mountain
Kelley Stand Road
3 miles
N

Great Cliff of Mt. Horrid. This observation point is not only one of the Forest's best but is also one of the easiest to reach. Access is on Vermont Route 73; drive 7.8 miles east of the intersection with U.S. Route 7 in Brandon, which is 15 miles north of Rutland on U.S. 7. Park in the paved area at the base of the cliff on the right side of the road at Brandon Gap, elevation 2170 feet.

From April to early August, the great attraction at Mt. Horrid is a pair of Peregrine Falcons that court, mate, and rear offspring on the cliff face. Turkey Vulture and Common Raven are regular visitors on Mt. Horrid. In fall, the cliffs are good for migrating hawks: Osprey, Northern Harrier, Northern Goshawk, Sharp-shinned, Cooper's, Red-shouldered, Broad-winged, and Red-tailed hawks, American Kestrel, and Merlin.

Hike the 0.75-mile trail from the parking area to the top of the Great Cliff and another 0.6 mile to Mt. Horrid Summit at 3216 feet. Although the trail rises steeply, it is well-maintained, and the view from the top is superb; you can see New York's Adirondack Mountains to the west and New Hampshire's White Mountains to the east. The side-trail from the summit to the cliff face is closed during the Peregrines' nesting season, but you can still observe the falcons from the parking area with a telescope. The main trail will reward you

PEREGRINE FALCON

with plenty of woodland birds: Ruffed Grouse, Least Flycatcher, Black-billed Cuckoo, Gray-cheeked (Bicknell's) Thrush, Veery, Cedar Waxwing, Red-eyed and Solitary vireos, Golden-crowned Kinglet, and some of the warblers mentioned above, as well as Yellow-rumped, Blackpoll, and Canada.

For those who prefer an easier hike with an excellent view of the Great Cliff, take the Long Trail south from the parking area 0.9 mile along an old logging road to Sunrise Shelter. This climb is only 400 vertical feet. Note that the Long Trail is blazed with white paint and side trails with blue.

For more good birding, turn right and proceed 0.3 mile to another parking lot. Here you can check a beaver pond and surrounding vegetation for Wood Duck, Belted Kingfisher, Tree Swallow, Cedar Waxwing, and Swamp Sparrow. You may also find American Bittern, Spotted Sandpiper, American Woodcock, Virginia Rail, Northern Waterthrush, and

VIEW FROM MT. HORRID TRAIL,
GREEN MOUNTAIN NATIONAL FOREST

Rusty Blackbird. Moose occasionally feed here, as well.

Bromley Mountain and Spruce Peak. The Appalachian Trail passes through the southern part of Vermont, where it uses the Long Trail. There are several trailheads and parking areas maintained by the Forest Service. To reach one of these, which provides convenient access to Bromley Mountain and Spruce Peak, take U.S. 7 south from Rutland for 40 miles to Manchester. Turn left on Vermont Routes 11 and 30, and drive 4.5 miles east to the trailhead parking area, on the left side of the road, just before Rtes. 11 and 30 split.

The 2.8-mile trail to the summit of Bromley Mountain leaves the parking area on the right and climbs slowly from 1800 to 2100 feet in the first 2 miles. It then ascends steeply to the summit at 3260 feet, where the upper station of the Bromley ski-lift is located. Alternatively, you can take the chair-lift, which is open year-round.

The 2.2-mile trail to Spruce Peak begins on the south side of the road, opposite the parking lot, and is a much easier hike, climbing just 240 vertical feet. From the top, you will have a nice view of the Taconic Mountains to the west, along the border with New York.

Breeding birds of the hardwood and coniferous forests likely to be found along the Bromley Mountain and Spruce Peak trails include Ruffed Grouse, Yellow-bellied Sapsucker, Eastern Wood-Pewee, Olive-sided and Great Crested flycatchers, Gray-cheeked (Bicknell's) Thrush, Swainson's and Hermit thrushes, Veery, Scarlet Tanager, and Rose-breasted Grosbeak. Black-throated Blue, Yellow-rumped, Black-throated Green, Canada, and Blackpoll warblers and Ovenbird are common.

Lye Brook Wilderness. Branch Pond and Bourn Pond along the boundary of the Wilderness are rewarding birding locations that require less exertion than the previous two areas. To reach the trailhead to these ponds, take U.S. 7 south from Manchester for 10 miles to the Arlington exit. Turn right onto Warm Brook Road at the sign for East Arlington. Go 1 mile, then turn right on East Arlington Road, and go 0.2 mile. Turn right again onto Old Mill Road by the Chippenhook store, and drive 1.4 miles to the intersection with Forest Service Highway (FH) 6, known locally as

RACCOON

the Kelley Stand Road, which goes uphill straight ahead. Proceed 6.5 miles on FH 6, then turn left on Forest Service Road (FR) 70, the first prominent road you will come to. Drive 2.5 miles north on FR 70 to a parking lot at the edge of the wilderness area. One can also approach this area from West Wardsboro to the east from Vermont Route 100. Birding along FH 6 (Kelley Stand Road) and FR 70 can also be very productive, especially near small ponds such as Beebe Pond and at Kelley Stand itself.

A short trail at the left side of the parking lot leads 0.2 mile to the south end of Branch Pond, a popular canoeing and camping spot. Another trail at the right side of the lot, the Branch Pond Trail, leads north to Bourn Pond (2.6 miles via the east shore of Branch Pond). A side trail at Bourn Pond (Lye Brook Trail) goes 1.8 miles east to Stratton Pond, where it intersects the Appalachian Trail. Despite the distance covered, there is very little variation in altitude; all three ponds are at about 2600 feet.

The birding along this route can be exceptional; in addition to the typical summer residents of the southern Green Mountains mentioned above, the ponds, their marshy edges, and the surrounding coniferous forest usually have nesting Great Blue Heron, American Black Duck, Wood Duck, Common Snipe, Yellow-bellied, Alder, and Olive-sided flycatchers, Veery, Swainson's, and Hermit thrushes, Nashville, Magnolia, Black-throated Blue, Black-throated Green, Blackburnian, Blackpoll, and Canada warblers, Swamp Sparrow, and Rusty Blackbird. Even Black-backed Woodpecker is possible here, although it is rare.

You may see Northern Goshawk and Sharp-shinned and Broad-winged hawks, as well as Barred and Northern Saw-whet owls.

For the hardy birder, the Appalachian Trail departs Stratton Pond to the south and rapidly ascends 3936-foot Stratton Mountain, where there is excellent habitat for Gray-cheeked (Bicknell's) Thrush.

Mount Abraham is also very good for Bicknell's. Skylight Pond, Mooslamoo, and Rattlesnake and White Rocks Mountains are excellent birding; Somerset Reservoir (owned and managed by New England Power Company—certain use-restrictions apply) is good for Common Loons and Bald Eagles.

JULIE ZICKEFOOSE, DRAWING

ACCOMMODATIONS ◆ WEATHER ◆ OTHER ATTRACTIONS

When to visit. Late spring and summer are best for finding breeding birds, and late September to early October are best for raptor migration and fall color.

Where to stay. Campgrounds within the Forest and in nearby state parks. Motels, hotels, bed-and-breakfast facilities, and condominiums close to the National Forest. The Vermont Chamber of Commerce may be reached at Box 37, Granger Road, Montpelier, 05602, (telephone 802/223-3443). The Vermont Travel Division is at 134 State Street, Montpelier, 05602, (telephone 802/828-3236).

Weather and attire. Weather is highly variable and can change quickly, especially at upper elevations. Winter daytime temperatures can be 0° F or below. Spring and fall are often foggy and rainy with temperatures from 25 to 60° F. Summer temperatures range from 60 to 85° F with afternoon thunderstorms possible. From May through July be prepared for biting insects. Dress in layers with a waterproof outer shell that will also break the wind. Good hiking-boots are essential, not only for the paths, but also because of wet ground.

What else to do. Swimming, picnicking, ski-lift rides, cross-country and downhill skiing. The Forest Service Robert Frost interpretive trail is a 1-mile gravel loop, 8 miles east of Middlebury on the right side of Vermont Route 125. Trail and viewing-platforms accessible to all visitors, including those with mobility impairment. The trail from White Rocks Picnic Area (4 miles east of Wallingford on Vermont Route 140) to the top of the White Rocks cliff (for good birding and hawk-watching), to the base of the talus slope, and to the "Ice Beds" south of the talus is a popular day-hike. The Vermont Institute of Natural Science, just off U.S. Route 4 east of Rutland in Woodstock, houses a raptor center where many injured species are brought for recovery and unreleasable birds can be viewed in naturalistic aviary settings. Arts and craft shows in Bennington, Manchester, Rutland, Woodstock, and Middlebury; summer-stock theater is located in Dorset, Killington, and Weston; antiquing, shopping outlet stores, discovering covered bridges, picturesque working farms, and small villages make it fun to explore the back roads.

For more information. General and campground information, District Office addresses, hiking-trail and other maps, bird list: Green Mountain National Forest, 231 North Main St., Rutland, Vermont 05701; telephone 802/747-6700.

JACOB'S LADDER

WHITE MOUNTAIN FOREST
New Hampshire and Maine

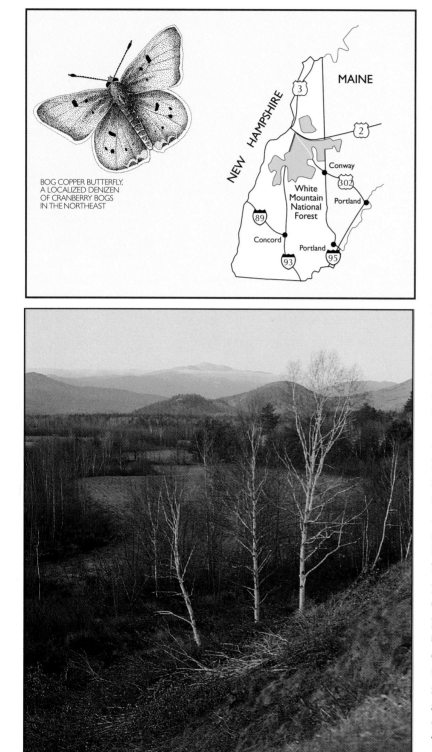

BOG COPPER BUTTERFLY,
A LOCALIZED DENIZEN
OF CRANBERRY BOGS
IN THE NORTHEAST

MAINE

NEW HAMPSHIRE

Conway

White
Mountain
National
Forest

Portland

Concord

Portland

HOW TO GET THERE. *From Boston, take Interstate 93 north to Lincoln, then take the scenic Kancamagus Highway (New Hampshire Route 112) east for 36 miles to Conway. At the intersection with New Hampshire Route 16, turn left and go 5 miles north to North Conway. Alternatively, take Interstate 95 north to Portsmouth, New Hampshire, then follow the Spalding Turnpike north to its end at Rte. 16, 12 miles north of Rochester. Continue on Rte. 16 for about 40 miles to Conway.*

VIEW FROM BACK COUNTRY ROAD, BEAR NOTCH, WHITE MOUNTAIN NATIONAL FOREST

NESTLED IN THE NORTHERN reaches of the Appalachians, White Mountain National Forest spreads over 770,000 acres of forested slopes and windswept alpine ridges. Elevations vary from 440 feet in the Cold River Valley to 6288 feet at the summit of Mt. Washington, highest peak in the northeastern U.S.

There can be no question about who made this place. The White Mountains are world-famed for their northern hardwood forests of red and sugar maples, yellow birch, and American beech that provide God-given displays of autumn color. The landscape literally lights up in breathtaking hues of red, brown, and yellow. At higher elevations the forest remains evergreen, and the air is perfumed with the sweet scent of red spruce and balsam fir. Above the conifers lies the largest alpine area in the U.S. east of the Rockies, a land rich with plants common in Labrador and the Arctic, as well as some varieties unique to the White Mountains. The purple flowers of Lapland rosebay and alpine azalea, as well as the delicate white flowers of diapensia and other alpine species, bloom in early to mid-June.

Forest wildlife ranges from 1200-pound moose to a rare butterfly known as the White Mountain fritillary. White-tailed deer, black bear, fisher, beaver, and numerous other mammals make their homes here. Reptiles and amphibians include the eastern painted turtle, eastern garter snake, spotted salamander, red-spotted newt, American toad, and gray treefrog.

Bird Life

An impressive 218 species have been recorded on the Forest, with late spring and early summer being the best times. Around 40 species can be found on the Forest year-round, and the summer resident population swells to more than 100 species. Another 75 or so species pass through the Forest as migrants heading farther north or as winter visitors; some years there are invasions of Bohemian Waxwing, Red and White-winged crossbills, Pine Grosbeak, and Common Redpoll.

In the lower-elevation hardwood and softwood areas you will find Eastern Wood-Pewee, Olive-sided and Least flycatchers, Red-breasted Nuthatch, Brown Creeper, Winter Wren, Veery, Swainson's, Hermit, and Wood thrushes, Cedar Waxwing, Solitary and Red-eyed vireos, many of the northern warblers, including Mourning, in some of the cutover forest areas, Scarlet Tanager, Rose-breasted Grosbeak, Rusty Blackbird, Purple Finch, and Pine Siskin. Philadelphia Vireo is found in deciduous, mid-elevation forests.

The rare Bicknell's race of the Gray-cheeked Thrush nests in the spruce–fir forests at higher elevations. (See Green Mountain National Forest for more information on this subspecies). In addition to the Gray-cheeked Thrush, the high-elevation coniferous areas on the Forest provide habitat for such specialties as Spruce Grouse, Black-backed Woodpecker, Gray Jay, Yellow-bellied Flycatcher, Boreal Chickadee, and Blackpoll Warbler. Three-toed Woodpecker is extremely rare on the Forest with the last sighting in 1981.

A variety of raptors inhabits the Forest. Peregrine Falcons were reintroduced into New Hampshire in 1976, and seven pairs nested within the state in 1992, including two pairs on the National Forest. In addition, all three accipiters—Sharp-shinned and Cooper's hawks and Northern Goshawk—are year-round residents. Broad-winged Hawk is common in summer, often found adjacent to mature hardwood stands. Red-shouldered Hawk, a less common summer resident, is found near wooded swamps. Osprey, Bald Eagle, and an occasional Northern Harrier may be seen along the major rivers during migration, and Golden Eagles are sighted occasionally in Franconia Notch.

Birding Routes

Two excellent birding hikes offer a good selection of habitats and birds. The Webster–Jackson Trail to Mizpah Hut takes you on a 6.7-mile loop that is considered moderate to difficult; this is a high mountain route, and the hiker should be prepared for harsh weather. The Mountain Pond Trail is a 2.6-mile loop and is less strenuous; it is excellent for spring warblers.

GRAY JAY

Webster–Jackson Trail. This is a route for birders who enjoy a rigorous hike and the chance to explore some of the Forest's boreal communities. To reach the trailhead, take U.S. Route 302/New Hampshire Route 16 north from North Conway for 6 miles to Glen. Follow U.S. 302 west and north for about 20 miles to a paved parking area on the left side of the road, just beyond the 'Leaving Crawford Notch State Park' sign. From the north end of the parking area, cross the road and walk north for 100 feet to the trailhead. The most visible sign facing the road reads Elephant Head Trail. There is also a smaller, less obvious sign for Mt. Webster, Mt. Jackson, and Mizpah Spring Hut.

Take the Mt. Webster–Mt. Jackson Trail that climbs gradually through a primarily evergreen forest of red spruce, balsam fir, and eastern hemlock. After 0.6 mile, you will see a short spur-trail going off right to Bugle Cliff. It offers nice views of Crawford Notch and the exclusive turn-of-the-century Bretton Woods Resort to the north. Watch and listen for Red-breasted Nuthatch, Golden-crowned

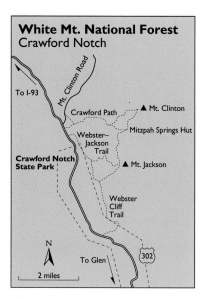

White Mt. National Forest
Crawford Notch

To I-93
Mt. Clinton Road
Crawford Path
▲ Mt. Clinton
Mitzpah Springs Hut
Webster–Jackson Trail
Crawford Notch State Park
▲ Mt. Jackson
Webster Cliff Trail
N
To Glen
302
2 miles

Kinglet, Yellow-rumped and Black-poll warblers, White-throated Sparrow, and Dark-eyed Junco along the way. Common Ravens may be seen soaring overhead. Be careful: the trail can be icy in spring and late fall.

Return to the main trail. In another 0.9 mile you will reach the Mt. Webster–Mt. Jackson fork; take the left fork toward Mt. Jackson. This portion of the trail climbs steeply before reaching the open ledges on Mt. Jackson (again, be careful if it is wet or icy). The 2100-foot summit is 2.6 miles from the trailhead and affords fine views in all directions, especially northeast toward the southern Presidential Range, including Mt. Washington, and west into Crawford Notch. Along the trail, watch for Boreal Chickadee, Winter Wren, Golden-crowned and Ruby-

crowned kinglets, Swainson's Thrush, Magnolia, Yellow-rumped, Black-throated Green, Blackburnian, and other warblers, and Purple Finch. Keep your eyes open for Gray Jay, and, if you are lucky, you may spot a Black-backed Woodpecker.

Continue north from Mt. Jackson on the Webster Cliff Trail toward Mizpah Springs Hut, following a line of cairns (rock piles marking the trail above treeline). The hut is a large structure that can be seen from the summit of Mt. Jackson. This section is part of the Appalachian Trail that runs from Springer Mountain in Georgia to Katahdin in Maine. From Mt. Jackson, the trail descends quickly into scrub vegetation, and then winds through an interesting mountain bog, rich with vibrant purple rhodora that blooms in spring and early summer. Listen here for Yellow-bellied Flycatcher, Nashville Warbler, and White-throated Sparrow.

Just past the bog, about 0.5 mile from the Mt. Jackson summit, a side-trail leads right 40 yards to an overlook. The main trail continues sharply to the left and then drops back into the woods where gregarious Gray Jays reside; they will visit you if you lunch nearby. In another mile the Mizpah cut-off trail leads left to Crawford Path, your return route. But first continue straight ahead for 0.1 mile on the

Webster Cliff Trail to the Mizpah Spring Hut. From June to October, you can dry out in the hut on wet days, or even spend the night (make your reservations well in advance by calling the Appalachian Mountain Club at 603/466-2725). If you do spend the night, listen for the slightly nasal, descending song of the Gray-cheeked Thrush at dusk and dawn. Swainson's Thrush and other boreal species can also be found nearby.

Return to the cutoff and follow the trail 0.7 mile to where it ends at Crawford Path. Go left on Crawford Path. After 1.7 miles, it will return you to Rte. 302, approximately 0.2 mile north of the start of the Webster–Jackson Trail. This final leg of the trail is good Spruce Grouse habitat. In the hardwoods along Crawford Path, look and listen for Pileated Woodpecker, Winter Wren, Wood Thrush, Red-eyed Vireo, Black-throated Blue Warbler, Ovenbird, Scarlet Tanager, Rose-breasted Grosbeak, and many other woodland species.

Mountain Pond Trail. To reach Mountain Pond Trail, follow New Hampshire Route 16/U.S. Route 302 north through North Conway past the junction of River Road. Continue

WHITE-THROATED SPARROWS

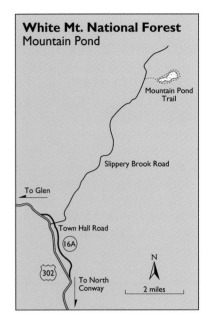

White Mt. National Forest
Mountain Pond

Mountain Pond Trail

Slippery Brook Road

To Glen

Town Hall Road

16A

302

To North Conway

N

2 miles

GAIL DIANE LUCKNER, DRAWING

GREEN HERON

3.7 miles and turn right onto Town Hall Road. At the intersection with New Hampshire 16A (0.1 mile), continue straight onto (unmarked) Slippery Brook Road. In another 2.4 miles, the pavement ends and a small road enters on the right; continue straight. You will see a sign for the White Mountain National Forest in 0.8 mile. Just beyond the sign the road passes through a gate; from here the road is not plowed in winter. Proceed 2.6 miles, stay right at the fork, and go another 0.6 mile to the sign for Mountain Pond Trail Parking on the right.

The trail circles the 80-acre pond tucked into the forest and framed on all sides by wooded peaks. North and South Doublehead, rising to 2938 feet, are visible to the west, and Round Mountain and South Baldface are evident to the north. Walter Mountain bounds the southern section of the pond.

Although situated at only 1500-feet elevation, the pond is surrounded by such a diverse mix of habitats that an amazing eighty-plus species of birds have been found to nest in this one small area. The trail intersects several small streams that may be difficult to cross at high water; sturdy, waterproof hiking-boots are recommended.

At the start of the trail is a wet, swampy area with flooded trees; these provide favored perches for Olive-sided Flycatchers. Watch along

the edges of the swamp for Rusty Blackbird. Other birds likely here include Spotted Sandpiper, Belted Kingfisher, Ruby-throated Hummingbird, Eastern Kingbird, Tree Swallow, Cedar Waxwing, Nashville Warbler, Northern Waterthrush, Common Yellowthroat, and Swamp Sparrow.

Continue straight ahead (clockwise around the pond), passing the return loop-trail on your right and through a mixed habitat of softwood and hardwood trees and openings left by a 1980 windstorm. Be alert for Yellow-bellied Sapsucker, Veery, Hermit Thrush, and Magnolia, Yellow-rumped, and Black-throated Blue

JOHN P. GEORGE, PHOTOGRAPH

SABBADAY BROOK, WHITE MOUNTAIN NATIONAL FOREST

warblers. The beautiful song of Winter Wren or the more emphatic song of Canada Warbler may be heard in the shrubby areas next to the streams. In autumn, Golden-crowned Kinglets and Song and White-throated sparrows abound here.

At about 0.6 mile on the left you will see the Mountain Pond shelter, a welcome respite in case of bad weather. Just north of the pond is one of the few low-elevation hardwood sites on the Forest that survived uncut during the turn-of-the-century logging excess. The huge sugar maple, white ash, yellow birch, and basswood trees in this 132-acre patch are 200 to 250 years old. Here you might find Ruffed Grouse, Hairy Woodpecker, Black-throated Blue, Black-throated Green, and Black-and-white warblers, and Purple Finch.

Follow the trail along the pond. This area is especially lovely in autumn when the fall colors are reflected on the surface of the water. In spring and summer, a pair of Common Loons can usually be found on the pond. Also look for Great Blue and Green herons, Wood and American Black ducks, and Mallard. During migration, Hooded Mergansers often stop here.

Mountain Pond Trail continues around the pond, crossing the outlet (be careful; the footing can be slippery), and in 2.3 miles intersects the loop-trail. Turn left there to return to your vehicle.

ACCOMMODATIONS ◆ WEATHER ◆ OTHER ATTRACTIONS

When to visit. Birding is best in May and June and during fall migration. Winters can be severe, and many of the Forest roads are closed.

Where to stay. Numerous campgrounds around the Forest. A hut system within the Forest operated by the Appalachian Mountain Club provides lodging and meals. Eight mountain hostels located along the Appalachian Trail, which are a day's hike apart. Numerous hotels and inns throughout the region. For information call Mt. Washington Valley Chamber of Commerce 603/356-3171.

Weather and attire. Weather conditions range from warm summers with high temperatures in the 80s to cold winters with mean temperatures in the low 20s in the valleys to minus 10° F at higher elevations. Visitors should be prepared for severe weather conditions at any time of the year. Warm clothing, including a wool cap, rain- and wind-gear (avoid ponchos, which tend to rip in high winds) are necessary, and carry extra food and water, trail map, and flashlight with extra batteries. Also wear sturdy, well broken-in hiking boots. Remember the saying about New England: "If you don't like the weather, wait a minute."

What else to do. On the Forest: hiking, fishing, canoeing. The Kancamagus Scenic Byway (New Hampshire Route 112), as well as other roads through the Forest, is excellent for scenic driving and for fall foliage in early to mid-October. There are covered bridges and other historic sites on the Forest and in the surrounding communities.

Nearby points of interest: Pondicherry Wildlife Refuge, Jefferson and Whitefield, New Hampshire (National Natural Landmarks that provide additional wildlife habitat). Several New Hampshire state parks, including Franconia Notch with its "Old Man of the Mountain" and the nearby Flume, a spectacular, roaring torrent of water. The Science Center of New Hampshire in Holderness, open from May to October featuring interpretive displays of state plants and animals.

For more information. General and campground information, District Office addresses, maps, bird list: White Mountain National Forest, P.O. Box 638, Laconia, New Hampshire 03247; telephone 603/528-8721.

MOUNTAIN AVENS

Birdfinding in Forty National Forests and Grasslands

DAVY CROCKETT FOREST
Texas

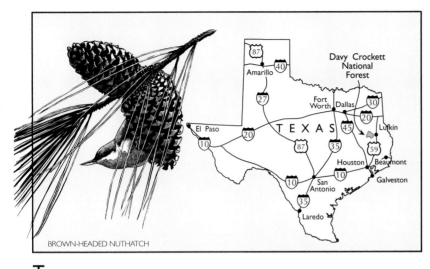

BROWN-HEADED NUTHATCH

HOW TO GET THERE. *From Houston, take U.S. Route 59 north to Farm-to-Market Road (FM) 357, approximately 8 miles north of Corrigan. Take FM 357 west to the junction of FM 2262 at the National Forest boundary.*

THE DAVY CROCKETT National Forest, named after the legendary pioneer, lies in the Trinity and Neches river basins, where the pine forests of the southeastern U.S. join the blackland prairies of central Texas. The result is a marvelous mix of eastern and western species of birds and other wildlife found nowhere else in the state. Here the visitor can expect to see most species of eastern warblers during migration. Many species of reptiles and amphibians, such as the Louisiana pine snake (threatened), northern scarlet snake, spotted salamander, and pickerel frog are at the edge of their range in East Texas, providing unique opportunities for observing these fascinating creatures.

The forest contains habitats ranging from rolling uplands and cypress swamps to vast hardwood bottoms. The upland plant community consists of loblolly and shortleaf pines, sweetgum, hickory, and several species of oaks, such as southern red oak. The understory may be open and grassy, or thick with yaupon holly, hawthorn, and other shrubs. American beauty-berry is abundant. This waist-high shrub produces small whorls of tiny, pale pink flowers in the spring, which often go unnoticed among the other wildflowers. In the fall, however, the clusters of brilliant lavender-colored berries for which the shrub is named are striking and are relished by a variety of birds, such as Northern Mockingbird, Cedar Waxwing, and Northern Cardinal. Several species of woodpecker, including the endangered Red-cockaded, have been observed feeding on the berries. Fall also brings the ripening of the cherry-red, pea-sized, yaupon berries, another favorite of fruit-eating birds. The bottom lands contain a mind-boggling diversity of trees and shrubs. Huge water oaks, towering southern magnolias, and stately American beech are common along major drainages. American holly with its whitish bark and sharply-toothed leaves also is abundant. Watch for American hornbeam, known locally as musclewood because of the resemblance of its smooth, sculpted trunk to an athlete's flexed muscles. River birch with its shaggy bark and bright red twigs grows along the rivers. Two species of silverbells occur in low-lying areas. These shrubs are covered in dainty white blooms during March.

Keep an eye out for beaver, nutria, river otter, mink, raccoon, and white-tailed deer. Areas where the ground has been rooted up are evidence of feral hogs. These 'Piney Woods Rooters,' as they are called locally, are nothing more than domestic hogs gone wild. They are extremely wary and seldom observed; due to their rooting, they can do extensive damage to vegetation.

Herpetologists will find much of interest. More than eighty species of reptiles and amphibians may be found. The frog symphony begins with spring peepers in January and February, followed by chorus frogs, gray, green, and squirrel treefrogs, southern leopard frogs, and Gulf Coast toads. Common snapping turtles, red-eared sliders, and common musk turtles are abundant, and May will find numerous three-toed box turtles crossing the roads.

Because of the variety of habitats, snakes are plentiful. Texas rat snakes are among the most common. Buttermilk racers, several species of water snakes, and eastern hognose snakes are numerous. Ven-

MIMI HOPPE WOLF, DRAWING

omous species are present but seldom seen with the exception of the southern copperhead. The impressive canebrake, or timber, rattlesnake occurs near bottom-land areas. This species is rarely observed because of its cryptic coloration and sedentary habits. The canebrake is listed as a threatened species in Texas, and it is against the law to harm them.

Bird Life

East Texas lies in the path of warblers, vireos, and other species of neotropical migrants, so spring migration can be excellent. If a norther passes through during April or early May, visitors will see hordes of tired, hungry migrants foraging in the hardwood bottoms. Most migrants are attracted to hardwoods, possibly because of the large number of insects among the foliage. Nearly every species of eastern warbler has been found on the Forest. Fall migrants move southward through East Texas, building up fat reserves for their flight across the Gulf. The fall migration is more leisurely, however, and seldom results in large bird concentrations.

Breeding season rings in with a chorus of song beginning in February. Resident species such as Northern Cardinal and Pine Warbler are the first to nest, and the latter may fledge their first broods as early as mid-March. Yet most of the breeding birds arrive in April and early May with the waves of migrants bound for nesting grounds farther north.

Watch for migrating American Swallow-tailed Kites (rare) overhead in mid-April. Mississippi Kite is an abundant spring and fall migrant and can be observed hawking dragonflies above the forest canopy and in residential areas of the local towns.

It begins the southward journey in mid-August. Numbers of Cooper's and Sharp-shinned hawks winter here, and Bald Eagles are occasionally observed flying during the fall and winter.

Woodpeckers are plentiful. The endangered Red-cockaded is a Forest specialty. Red-headed Woodpeckers prefer areas with large snags. Pileated, Red-bellied, Hairy, and Downy woodpeckers are also common nesting species. Northern Flickers nest in small numbers and are joined by large numbers of wintering flickers in the fall. Yellow-bellied Sapsucker is fairly common in winter.

Several species are unique to the southern pine forests. Brown-headed Nuthatches may be found anywhere there are mature pines, although they seldom remain in one area for long. They are often detected first by their squeaky calls, which resemble an infant's squeeze-toy. Once heard they still can be difficult to spot, because they typically remain high in the pines and forage at the tips of the boughs. They vocalize almost continuously and with patience can eventually be seen flying between neighboring pines in small groups. During the breeding season they may be found nesting in broken-off snags as low as 4 to 6 feet above the ground. Bachman's Sparrow is fairly com-

MISSISSIPPI KITE

mon in open pine stands with a grassy understory. Although secretive during most of the year, males sing from conspicuous perches during spring and summer and often allow close approach. Look for the sparrow along Forest Service Road (FS) 541 in and near areas managed for Red-cockaded Woodpecker. Prairie Warblers may be found in recent clearcuts vegetated with young pines interspersed with grass. Some of the best locations for this species are on private timber-company land inside the boundaries of the Forest and along Farm-to-Market Road (FM) 357 between the Forest and U.S. Route 59, where clearcuts of 500 acres or more are common.

While driving through the district, watch for Scissor-tailed Flycatcher, Eastern Kingbird, Blue Grosbeak, and Indigo and Painted buntings in young clearcuts. These openings are good for Eastern Phoebe and sparrows, such as Chipping, Song, Lincoln's, Swamp, and White-throated, during fall and winter. Wintering Dark-eyed Juncos frequent the forest edge. Both the eastern and western forms of Rufous-sided Towhee winter in the

YELLOW-THROATED WARBLER

Forest and often linger into spring. Older plantations, which contain dense young pines and hardwoods 6 to 10 feet high, are good for nesting Yellow-breasted Chat, White-eyed Vireo, and Swainson's Warbler (in wetter areas).

Birding Routes

Holly Bluff Swamp and Neches River. Located in the southeastern corner of the Forest, this swamp and surrounding river bottom lands offer superb birding for everything from waterfowl to warblers and a host of other passerines. Depending on the season, most of the birds described in the preceding section on general bird life can be found here.

To reach the area, start at the junction of FM 357 and FM 2262 at the Forest boundary, and take FM 2262 north for 3.5 miles to the third gravel road on the right. This will be FS 510-A, known locally as Holly Bluff Road. Drive east on FS 510-A for 1.5 miles and watch for the swamp on the south side of the road. Park along the road and unlimber your optics.

If you are visiting in the fall, the ducks can be spectacular. Flights of more than 5000 Wood Duck, Mallard, Gadwall, Green-winged Teal, and American Wigeon have been observed dropping into the swamp at dusk. Large numbers of American Coots gather here as well in October and November. The birds can be observed from the road, or, if you are feeling adventurous, you can wade into the swamp for a short distance along a pipeline right-of-way near the west end of the swamp. Other species to watch for include: resident Red-shouldered Hawk, Wild Turkey, Barred Owl, Great Blue and Little Blue herons, Great Egret, and Belted Kingfisher. In spring and summer, you are likely to find nesting Acadian and Great Crested flycatchers, Red-eyed Vireo, Northern Parula, Yellow-throated, Prothonotary, and Kentucky warblers, along with Louisiana Waterthrush and the eagerly sought-after Swainson's Warbler. Watch overhead for Wood Stork in July and August; this species typically wanders far during post-breeding dispersal.

After birding the swamp, continue on FS 510-A for a short distance until it deadends at Holly Bluff Campground along the Neches River. A spring walk through this mix of bottom-land hardwoods and pines will produce a pleasure of migrant songbirds such as Gray-cheeked and Swainson's thrushes and Veery, Warbling and Philadelphia vireos, numerous warblers, Scarlet Tanager, Rose-breasted Grosbeak, and Northern Oriole. You might flush a Chuck-will's-

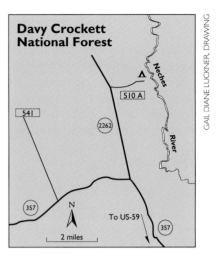

GAIL DIANE LUCKNER, DRAWING

widow from the underbrush as you bird along. In migration, large flocks of Broad-winged Hawks roost in the riverbottom and rise in large kettles on the mid-morning thermals.

If you are visiting in winter, keep an eye out for American Woodcock, Common Snipe, Yellow-bellied Sapsucker, Brown Creeper, Ruby-crowned and Golden-crowned kinglets, Hermit Thrush, Brown Thrasher, and Solitary Vireo.

KENTUCKY WARBLER

DAVID A. SIBLEY, DRAWING

Birdfinding in Forty National Forests and Grasslands

Red-cockaded Woodpecker Route. To reach one site inhabited by this much-desired specialty of the southern forests, take FM 357 west from U.S. 59 8.5 miles to FS 541 (gravel) on the right. Turn right onto FS 541, and watch for the colony site on the left after about 0.75 mile. Cavity trees are marked with a single green painted band at a height of about five feet. The best time to observe the birds is just after dawn when they emerge from their cavities and an hour before dark when they return to roost.

While in the vicinity of the Red-cockaded Woodpecker colony, look for other upland species that benefit from the habitat conditions maintained for the woodpecker. Eastern Wood-Pewee is common in open pine stands, as are Indigo Bunting, Summer Tanager, and Orchard Oriole. American Kestrel is common during the nesting season, and often nests in Red-cockaded Woodpecker cavities that have been enlarged by Pileated Woodpeckers. Yellow-throated Vireos prefer these drier, pine-dominated sites, as opposed to the bottom-land habitat used by Red-eyed Vireo. Most Red-cockaded Woodpecker colony sites have one or more dead cavity trees, which attract Red-headed Woodpeckers. Other cavity-nesters, such as Wood Duck, Eastern Screech-Owl, Carolina Chickadee, Tufted Titmouse, Great Crested Flycatcher, and several species of woodpeckers, also use both live and dead Red-cockaded cavity trees.

RED-COCKADED WOODPECKER

ACCOMMODATIONS ◆ WEATHER ◆ OTHER ATTRACTIONS

When to visit. Spring (late March to mid-May) or fall (late September to November) best for birds. Hunting season runs from November through early January.

Where to stay. Motels in Lufkin. Campgrounds at Holly Bluff as well as Ratcliff Lake between Kennard and Ratcliff. Mission Tejas State Park near Wetches. Primitive camping anywhere in the Forest except during the gun deer season.

Weather and attire. Winters are mild, but may be rainy. Summers hot (upper 90s) and humid. Take plenty of drinking water during the summer. Insect repellent is essential nearly year-round, particularly during spring and summer when chiggers, mosquitoes, and ticks are numerous.

What else to do. Hiking, including many miles of roads closed to motor vehicles, fishing, canoeing, the self-guided dogwood driving-tour (March and April), picking mayhaws (April and May). The Trinity Ranger District is known for its dogwood trail; for maps of the route, and updates on best viewing times, contact the district office.

For more information. For maps and general information, District Office addresses, bird list: Davy Crockett National Forest, P.O. Box 130, Apple Springs, Texas 75926; 409/831-2246; or at the five self-service check-stations at entry points to the Alabama Creek Wildlife Management Area.

PURPLE CONEFLOWER AND INDIAN BLANKET

SAM HOUSTON FOREST
Texas

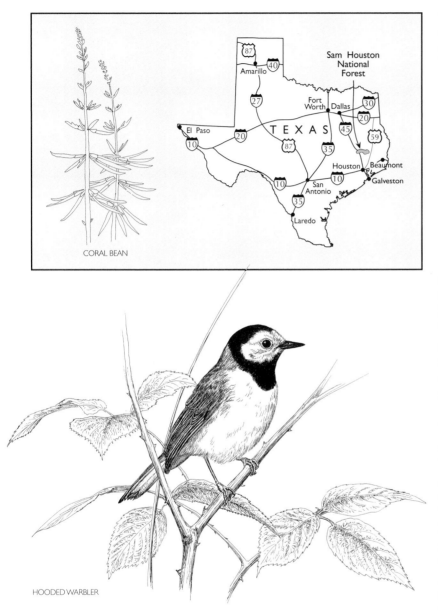

CORAL BEAN

HOODED WARBLER

HOW TO GET THERE. *From Houston, take U.S. Route 59 north for about 45 miles to Cleveland, and exit at Farm-to-Market Road (FM) 2025.*

T HE VAST FORESTS OF THE SOUTH-EAST reach their westernmost extension in the so-called "piney woods" of East Texas. Beyond lie the blackland prairies and post-oak savannahs of central Texas and the coastal plains bordering the Gulf of Mexico.

Named for the great champion of Texas independence, the 158,000-acre Sam Houston National Forest en-compasses huge stands of pines and hardwoods, as well as broad pal-metto flats and quiet bayous that pro-vide habitat for a tremendous array of plants and wildlife. The terrain is relatively flat, and small differences in elevation create noticeable changes in the environment. The uplands are characterized by loblolly and shortleaf pines intermingled with sweet gum, mockernut hickory, and several species of oaks. Lower sites have magnolias and black tupelos. The bottom-land hardwood commu-nity contains American beech, mag-nolia, river birch, American holly, elms, swamp chestnut oak, and many other oaks.

The area owes much of its natural beauty to its abundant wildflowers and flowering vines, shrubs, and trees. The mild climate and long growing-season ensure a palette of color from January through Septem-ber. Violets appear in January, and, by February, yellow jessamine is bloom-ing in profusion, often twining to the tops of trees. The piney woods are famous for dogwood and eastern redbud from late February through March. Spring brings spectacular flo-ral displays that include prairie phlox, rose vervain, Indian blanket, bluebonnet, coreopsis, paintbrush, and pink evening primrose. Orange milkweed, purple coneflower, black-eyed susan, blue-eyed grass, and coral bean appear in early summer. The deep red blooms of standing cy-press may be seen in several locations along Farm-to-Market Road (FM)

MIMI HOPPE WOLF, DRAWING

2025. Moist, shaded sites contain cardinal flower. And the brilliant orange-fringed orchid, which blooms in August, is one of several orchid species found on the Forest.

Bird Life

The most rewarding time to bird the Sam Houston is in spring, when multitudes of neotropical migrants stop to rest and refuel after their perilous flight across the Gulf of Mexico. Hundreds, even thousands, of warblers, vireos, tanagers, orioles, flycatchers, and other passerines can be seen in a single day. During April and again in late September, huge kettles of Broad-winged Hawks occur here; the hawks roost in the bottom lands at night and rise like swarms of bees on the thermals next morning.

Nesting begins early in East Texas. By mid-February, numerous resident White-eyed Vireos and Pine Warblers are singing on territories. The first migrants arrive in early March, including the much-sought-after Swainson's Warbler. They are followed in April by the main contingent of nesters, among them the spectacular Painted Bunting, found in open areas of the Forest.

Brown-headed Nuthatch is abundant on the Forest; listen for that squeaky, chipping call as little parties of these tiny birds forage in the tops of tall pines. Bachman's Sparrows nest

in open pine stands with grassy understory; usually secretive, they are easily located when singing in spring and early summer. The best location is along FM 945, between 3 and 6 miles north of its junction with FM 2025. Greater Roadrunners often dart across the roads. Although uncommon, this large ground-dwelling cuckoo nests throughout the Forest, adapting to habitats that are very different from its more arid surroundings to the west.

Raptors are common, and nesting species include two vultures, four hawks, and four owls. During migration, watch for Osprey, Mississippi and American Swallow-tailed kites, Northern Harrier, and Merlin. Sharp-shinned Hawks winter here, and Bald Eagles frequent the large reservoirs; some of the eagles are of the southern race that nests on the Forest in late winter and fledges young in late March before heading north for the summer.

BROAD-WINGED HAWK

Seven species of woodpeckers are resident: Red-headed, Red-bellied, Downy, Hairy, Pileated, and Red-cockaded woodpeckers, plus Northern Flicker (rare). In winter, large numbers of Yellow-bellied Sapsuckers and Northern Flickers occur here; most of the latter are of the yellow-shafted race, but an occasional red-shafted bird is seen.

Birding Routes

Many birders travel to East Texas to see the endangered Red-cockaded Woodpecker. This species has declined in recent years, but new management techniques show great promise for its recovery. Twenty-six clans or breeding groups of this cooperatively-nesting woodpecker exist on the Forest. One accessible site is 12 miles north from Cleveland on the east side of FM 2025, approximately 150 yards south of the junction of FM 2025 with FM 2666. There is a paved pull-off with benches and an interpretive sign. Cavity trees are located about 75 yards off the road, marked by green painted bands. The birds are most

GREATER ROADRUNNER

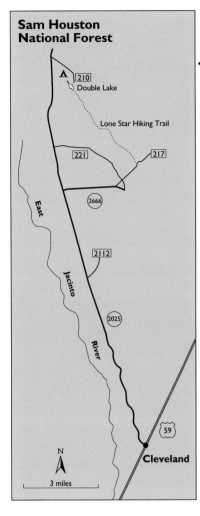

Sam Houston National Forest

▲ 210
Double Lake

Lone Star Hiking Trail

221

217

2666

2112

East

2025

Jacinto

River

59

Cleveland

N

3 miles

F.P. BENNETT, DRAWING

BARRED OWL

easily seen at dawn when they leave their cavity trees, and when they return an hour or two before dark. Contact the Forest Service Office in Cleveland for directions to other sites.

Another much-sought-after bird in East Texas is Swainson's Warbler. This species can be found in wetter pine plantations containing dense, young pines five to fifteen feet tall. Look for them in thick, brushy areas wherever palmettos occur. Locations vary from year to year, since the young plantings become unsuitable habitat after the pines exceed 20 feet in height. To reach one good location, go west from FM 2025 on FM 945 two miles to gravel road FS 274 on the left. The dense thickets of young pines and hardwoods on both sides of FM 945 at this junction are home to several pairs of Swainson's Warblers during the breeding season. They are easily located by their loud song, but can be difficult to spot as they slink through the thick vegetation.

Big Creek Scenic Area. This area is one of the Forest's best overall birding sites. From the junction of FM 2025 and FM 2666, turn right on FM 2666 for 2.5 miles to Forest Service Road (FS) 221. Turn left on the gravel road, drive 0.7 mile to FS 217, turn right, and go 1 mile to a parking area on the left. A network of trails criss-crosses the 1400-acre stand of bottom-land hardwoods and pines. Several species of summer-blooming orchids occur here. In April and May, the towering hardwoods along Big Creek are alive with warblers, vireos, and other migrants. Whip-poor-wills move through in late April.

During the nesting season, look for Red-shouldered Hawk, Barred Owl, Chuck-will's-widow, Red-headed, Downy, and Pileated woodpeckers, Acadian Flycatcher, Wood Thrush, Gray Catbird (rare), Yellow-throated and Red-eyed vireos, Northern

A BIRDING TRAIL, SAM HOUSTON NATIONAL FOREST

Parula, Yellow-throated and Black-and-white warblers, and Louisiana Waterthrush. In winter, you should find American Woodcock, Yellow-bellied Sapsucker, Brown Creeper, Winter Wren, Golden-crowned and Ruby-crowned kinglet, and Solitary Vireo.

At elevated sites with mixed pines and hardwoods, look for nesting Cooper's (rare) and Broad-winged hawks, Yellow-billed Cuckoo, Great Horned Owl, Red-headed, Red-bellied, Downy, Hairy, and Pileated woodpeckers, Eastern Wood-Pewee, Great-crested Fly-catcher, Brown-headed Nuthatch, Blue-gray Gnatcatcher, Kentucky and Hooded warblers, Summer Tanager, Indigo Bunting, and Chipping Sparrow.

Double Lake Recreation Area. To reach this location, which has many of the same species as Big Creek, re-trace your route to the junction of FM 2666 and FM 2025. Turn right (north) onto FM 2025 and go 4 miles to the entrance road on the right, where a sign will announce Double Lake Recreation Area. Below the dam of this 24-acre lake is a beaver pond where Prothonotary Warblers may be found during the breeding season. Also look for Green Heron, Acadian and Great Crested flycatchers, Red-eyed Vireo, and Swainson's and Hooded warblers. An interpretive trail and boardwalk circles the lake; an observation-blind is situated near the upper end. The birds aside, this is a good place to observe beaver; evidence of their activity is all about. The recreation area also provides camping, showers, a small concession-stand, canoe rentals, and fishing.

If time allows, walk the 5-mile section of the Lone Star Hiking Trail that runs between Double Lake and Big Creek Scenic Area. This is an easy ramble over gentle terrain, passing through bottom-land hardwoods and pine forests most of the way. The birding is excellent, and you will want to stop and admire the National Champion black tupelo tree located a short distance down the trail from Double Lake; this giant is 105 feet tall and 5 feet in diameter.

San Jacinto Wildlife Demonstration Area. This area offers a different group of birds. From the junction of FM 2025 and FM 945, 6 miles north of Cleveland, go north on FM 2025 an additional 1.7 miles to FS 2112 on the right. Park at the gate and walk any of the many short roads and trails. The 1600-acre tract was surface-mined for iron ore before its acquisition by the Forest Service. The land was ravaged, but some longleaf pines are still found here, remnants of the westernmost extension of this unique fire-dependent species. Work is underway to restore the longleaf-pine community and its ecosystem.

NORTHERN BOBWHITE

Efforts to increase habitat for Northern Bobwhite have created ideal conditions for wintering sparrows. The open weedy areas support Chipping, Field, Vesper, Savannah, Song, Lincoln's, and Swamp sparrows. Henslow's (rare) and Le Conte's sparrows are possible in wetter areas. Look for the Henslow's in damp grassy openings. Look along the edge of the woods for Rufous-sided Towhee (both eastern and western forms), the abundant White-throated and less common Fox, White-crowned, and Harris's sparrows, Dark-eyed Junco, Pine Siskin, and American Goldfinch. Other species to watch for in winter include Common Snipe, Eastern Phoebe, and Eastern Bluebird. During the breeding season, the area is good for Worm-eating Warbler (along some of the forested drainages), Blue Grosbeak, and Indigo and Painted buntings.

The East Fork of the San Jacinto River provides yet another birding opportunity. A canoe trip through the old-growth bottom-land hardwoods is the best way to enjoy the scenery and to see Green Heron (summer) and Wood Duck. Be sure, also, to watch for river otter along the banks and in the water, as well as bobcat, gray and red foxes, blotched and diamondback water snakes, and western cottonmouths. Canoes may be rented at several locations in Humble, which is on U.S. Route 59 about 25 miles south of Cleveland.

HAIRY WOODPECKER

KENN KAUFMAN, DRAWING

ACCOMMODATIONS ◆ WEATHER ◆ OTHER ATTRACTIONS

CARDINAL FLOWER

When to visit. Spring (late March to May) and fall (late September and October) are best to see the birds. Hunting season runs from November to early January.

Where to stay. Campgrounds, on the Double Lake Recreation Area; motels, in Cleveland and Coldspring.

Weather and attire. Winters are mild with rare freezes; summers, hot (90s) and extremely humid. Lightweight clothing is recommended and insect repellent year-round, but especially in spring and summer (mosquitoes and chiggers). If you are hiking, carry plenty of water.

BLUE-EYED GRASS

What else to do. Entire Forest open to hiking, including many miles of roads closed to motor vehicles. The Lone Star Hiking Trail crosses the entire area. Nearby (approximately 40 miles east) is Big Thicket National Preserve, noted for its unique mixture of ecosystems and great diversity of plants and birds, including fourteen species of nesting warblers.

For more information. General and camping information, District Office addresses, maps, bird list: Sam Houston National Forest, 308 North Belcher, (FM 2025, one block east of U.S. 59) Cleveland, Texas 77327; telephone 713/592-6461.

JEFFERSON FOREST
Virginia

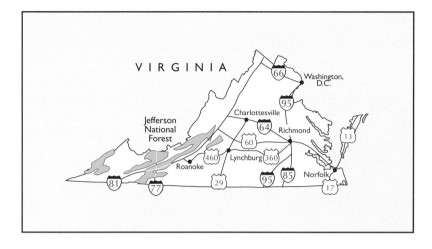

HOW TO GET THERE. *Take Interstate 81 to Exit 45 (Virginia Route 16, Marion), about 100 miles southwest of Roanoke or 155 miles northeast of Knoxville, Tennessee. Go south on Rte. 16 for 7 miles to the Mt. Rogers National Recreation Area Visitor Center.*

DAPHNE GEMMILL, PHOTOGRAPH

HILLSIDE OF BLOOMING RHODODENDRON, JEFFERSON NATIONAL FOREST

THE HEART of the Jefferson National Forest is the 118,000-acre Mount Rogers National Recreational Area (NRA), which extends for 65 miles along the craggy spine of the southern Appalachians and takes up close to one-sixth of the entire 690,000-acre Forest. Elevations in these diverse wild lands range from less than 1000 feet to the 5729-foot summit of Mt. Rogers, the highest peak in the 800-mile stretch from New Hampshire's Mt. Washington to North Carolina's Grandfather Mountain.

The early settlers in the Virginia section of this range extracted enormous bounty from the land. The steep mountainsides were cleared for farming and grazing and by insatiable logging. At the turn of the century, much of the higher mountains and ridges had been scraped bare of the old-growth forests; wild-game populations had been decimated; and repeated fires had swept the ridges. The southern Virginia Appalachians became a wasteland.

As the 1900s progressed, however, programs to halt this ravaging of natural resources gained public and

RUFOUS-SIDED TOWHEE

JULIE ZICKEFOOSE, DRAWING

maple, oak, walnut, poplar, ash, and locust, intermixed with pine stands. In addition, there are 1000 acres of high-country "balds," where native grasses and wildflowers mix with brushy species, such as rhododendrons, blueberries, and blackberries; the balds are reminiscent of the high meadows of the Rocky Mountains.

lied Sapsuckers, Blue Jays, Solitary Vireos, Rose-breasted Grosbeaks, and Cerulean, Kentucky, and many otherwarblers.

The high-elevation spruce–fir community, normally found several hundred miles farther north, offers a variety of birds not normally associated with Virginia: Alder Flycatcher and Hermit and Swainson's thrushes, Chestnut-sided, Magnolia, Black-throated Blue, and Blackburnian warblers, Purple Finch, Red Crossbill, and (possibly) Pine Siskin. Sharp-shinned and Cooper's hawks may also nest near the summit of Mt. Rogers. The rare Northern Saw-whet Owl has been recorded, although it is not known to nest. Golden Eagles are frequent winter visitors.

legislative support, making possible federal purchase of many forest areas. Virginia's southern Appalachians were saved by this program, and in 1936, President Franklin D. Roosevelt dedicated the present National Forest to Thomas Jefferson.

Today, thanks to the restoration of wildlife habitat, visitors may catch glimpses of black bear, white-tailed deer, bobcat, beaver, red squirrel, chipmunk, and the still-endangered northern flying-squirrel. One of the unique features of the Forest is its amazing variety of salamanders; eighteen species have been found, and, in fact, the Forest Service has established a 3000-acre salamander management area. It alone contains fourteen species, some with very limited distribution, such as the black-bellied, seal, green, midland mud, and cave salamanders.

Vegetation types in the NRA vary from cattail swamps along the New River to spruce–fir forests that blanket the highest peaks; the bulk of the trees are eastern hardwoods, such as

Bird Life

More than 160 species of birds have been recorded within the boundaries of the NRA, and 110 of those are known to nest. Breeding birds of the hardwood forests include Ruffed Grouse, Wild Turkeys, Black-billed Cuckoos, Barred Owls, Downy Woodpeckers, Yellow-bel-

Birding Routes

The best birding spots on the Forest are the summits of Mt. Rogers and Whitetop Mountain (the second highest point in Virginia at 5560 feet), several nearby campgrounds, and the New River floodplain. Most birders head first for the summit of Mt. Rogers to find the montane species.

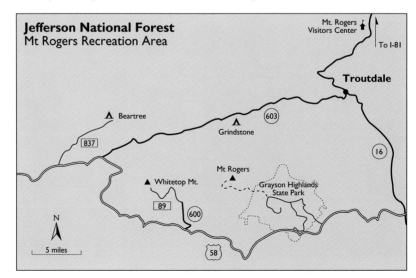

CAROLINA CHICKADEE

Mt. Rogers Summit is best birded from the Massie Gap parking area in Grayson Highlands State Park via Sullivan's Swamp and Rhododendron Gap. The best time to bird here is mid-May through July for breeders, but it is also good year-round for other birds; be on the watch in the winter, however, for harsh and dangerous weather. The Mt. Rogers route involves 4.5 miles (9 miles for a round-trip) of gradual, uphill walking (1080-feet elevation gain) that can easily be accomplished in a day by anyone in reasonably good physical condition. To reach Massie Gap from the Mt. Rogers NRA visitors center, turn right onto Virginia Route 16 and proceed 22 miles, passing through Troutdale and Volney to the junction with U.S. Route 58. Turn right and take U.S. 58 for 8 miles to the state park entrance, on the right; continue into the park for 3.4 miles to the Massie Gap Parking Area.

Begin birding as soon as you park. The surrounding spruce trees are a good place for Cedar Waxwing, Red-eyed Vireo, Chestnut-sided and Black-throated Green warblers, and Dark-eyed Junco. Then take the Rhododendron Gap Trail, marked by blue blazes, for 0.5-mile to where it joins the Appalachian Trail at Sullivan's Swamp. Just after leaving the parking area and passing through a split-rail fence, look and listen for Chipping, Field, Vesper, and Song sparrows as you climb Wilburn Ridge. You are likely to encounter also Northern Bobwhite, Northern Flicker, and Rufous-sided Towhee.

Sullivan's Swamp, just north of the trail junction, is a wet bog of grasses and ferns, rhododendron, mountain-laurel, blueberry, and scattered spruce and eastern hardwoods. This is a good place for Willow and Alder flycatchers, Cedar Waxwing, Chestnut-sided, Magnolia, Blackburnian, and Canada warblers, and Pine Siskin. Also keep an eye skyward for Northern Goshawk and Red-tailed Hawk, as well as Peregrine Falcon that has been reintroduced.

After birding the bog, continue on the Appalachian Trail for 2 miles to Rhododendron Gap, and then another 1.5 miles to the 0.5-mile Mt. Roger Spur Trail to the summit. Birding attractions along this leg of the trail include Veery, Swainson's, Hermit, and Wood thrushes (it is one of the few places in the East where four species of thrushes nest), Magnolia Warbler, and Purple Finch. Northern Saw-whet Owl and Yellow-bellied Flycatcher have been found here, as well.

At the summit, watch for soaring raptors, including Sharp-shinned, Cooper's, Red-shouldered, Broad-winged, and Red-tailed hawks, American Kestrel, and Peregrine Falcon, as well as Chimney Swift and Common Raven. Then retrace your route to the Massie Gap parking area.

Whitetop Mountain offers spectacular scenery and excellent birding. It is recommended for anyone not able or interested in doing much walking. From the Grayson Highlands State Park entrance, turn right on U.S. 58 and drive 7.8 miles to Virginia Route 600. Turn right on Rte. 600, drive 1.7 miles to the junction with Forest Service Road (FS) 89, and turn left. This 3-mile road to the top of Whitetop Mountain is the highest automobile road in Virginia; it is bumpy, but suitable for passenger cars in all but the worst

DARK-EYED JUNCO

GAIL DIANE LUCKNER, DRAWING

DAVID A. SIBLEY, DRAWING

COMMON RAVEN

weather. Numerous pull-outs make it easy to stop to bird.

The first 2 miles pass through a spruce and hardwood forest, where it is possible, but difficult, to find Northern Saw-whet Owl. Best times are from early April to late May. Listen first, then try whistling. Other birds to look for include Common Raven, Red-breasted Nuthatch, Brown Creeper, Golden-crowned Kinglet, Veery, Solitary Vireo, warblers (Chestnut-sided, Black-throated Green, Blackburnian, and American Redstart), Rose-breasted Grosbeak, and Dark-eyed Junco.

The old Balsam Trail on the right, at the sharp hairpin turn at 2.5 miles, runs for 0.6 mile through an old-growth red spruce stand and is another good place to find woodland birds, plus Red Crossbill. And, finally, the summit of Whitetop Mountain offers the same broad selection of raptors as Mt. Rogers.

To resume the birding route, return to U.S. 58 and turn right to continue along this scenic by-way. In approximately 10 miles you will reach the intersection with Virginia Route 603 on the right, but drive on for another 2.9 miles to FS 837 and turn right. This is the road to Beartree Campground and the day-use area, located just east of the town of Damascus. The campground has a number of trails that are popular with birders. A pleasant 0.5-mile trail (partly paved) that extends com-

pletely around 14-acre Beartree Lake (look for Pied-billed Grebe) begins at the Bear Lake Picnic Area, 0.9 mile from U.S. 58. The Beaver Flat Nature Trail, 3.5 miles from U.S. 58, is a little-used one-mile loop through beaver-created meadows.

Summer birds of this area include Acadian Flycatcher, Eastern Phoebe, American Crow, Carolina Chickadee, Cedar Waxwing, Red-eyed Vireo, Golden-winged, Chestnut-sided, Black-throated Blue, Black-and-white, Hooded, and Canada warblers, Northern Parula, Ovenbird, Louisiana Waterthrush, Common Yellowthroat, Scarlet Tanager, and Rose-breasted Grosbeak. Anywhere

WHITE-TAILED DEER

along Straight Branch, which parallels FS 837, listen and look in the rhododendron habitat for Swainson's Warbler, which is uncommon, and Northern Waterthrush. In the evening and early morning, you may encounter a Long-eared Owl.

Afterwards, return to the intersection of U.S. 58 with Rte. 603, turn left, and drive 8 miles to the entrance of Grindstone Campground. This area of beech, cherry, birch, and hemlock woods, is the most reliable place in Virginia to find nesting Least Flycatchers. Look here for Great Horned Owl, Pileated Woodpecker, Wood Thrush, Veery, Solitary and Red-eyed vireos, Black-throated Blue, Black-throated Green, Kentucky, and Canada warblers, and Rose-breasted Grosbeak. Also, watch for Northern and Louisiana waterthrushes; both have been reported nesting.

To return to U.S. 58, you can either retrace your route or continue on FS 603 to Troutdale and turn right on FS 730.

New River Trail extends for more than 30 miles on the eastern end of the NRA, where an abandoned Norfolk & Western Railroad bed has been made into a multiple-use trail. To reach this site, drive northeast on Interstate 81 from Virginia Route 16 for about 34 miles to Exit 79 (U.S. 52), 7 miles past the last exit for Wytheville.

Follow U.S. 52 south for 2 miles to Virginia Route 94 on the right, and take Rte. 94 for 10 miles to the New River where FS 737 forks off to the left. Park anywhere along the road and walk the trail.

Summer birds of this riparian environment include Spotted Sandpiper, Eastern Wood-Pewee, Acadian and Willow flycatchers, Carolina Wren, White-eyed, Yellow-throated, and Red-eyed vireos, Yellow Warbler, American Redstart, Scarlet Tanager, Indigo Bunting, and Northern Oriole. Spring and fall bring many of the eastern migrants.

ACCOMMODATIONS ◆ WEATHER ◆ OTHER ATTRACTIONS

When to visit. April through July is best for breeding birds. Wildflowers are everywhere from May through late July, and rhododendrons are most beautiful around the second or third week of June. Fall colors usually peak in late October or early November.

Where to stay. Numerous campgrounds, on the Forest and state park. Motels along the I-81 corridor as well as in Galax. The Fox Hill Inn in Troutdale is a modern mountaintop lodge with an unsurpassed view (reservations required).

Weather and attire. Spring and fall, generally pleasant but cool with rain possible anytime. Summers, often warm and humid in the lowlands but breezy and pleasant in the highlands. Winters, generally tolerable but can be severe in the mountains. Layers of clothing are recommended for the crest zone at any time of year. Even during summer, a sweater should be carried, and a waterproof windshell is recommended. Insect repellent is advised, especially as a guard against deer ticks, which can transmit Lyme disease.

What else to do. Hike the famous Appalachian National Scenic Trail from a number of points on the Forest; a favorite is Elk Garden off Rte. 600. The Virginia Creeper Trail, a 33-mile-long "rails-to-trails" multiple-use route, runs along an abandoned railroad-bed between Whitetop Community and Abingdon and offers breathtaking views of Mt. Rogers, Whitetop Mountain, and Whitetop Laurel Creek, a fast-flowing trout stream.

Various communities in the region stage summer festivals. Appalachian Trail Days in Damascus, the Mt. Rogers Naturalists Rally in Konnarock, and Ramp Festival in Whitetop are notable.
Other points of interest: Grayson Highlands State Park Visitor Center; the Baxter Theatre in Abingdon, a summer stock-playhouse and the state theater of Virginia; and the Shot Tower located near Wytheville, one of the few remaining Civil War era sites where shotgun pellets were manufactured.

For more information. General and campground information, District Office addresses, maps, bird list: Mt. Rogers National Recreation Area, Route 1, Box 303, Marion, Virginia 24354; telephone 703/783-5196.

RHODODENDRON

CHEROKEE FOREST
Tennessee

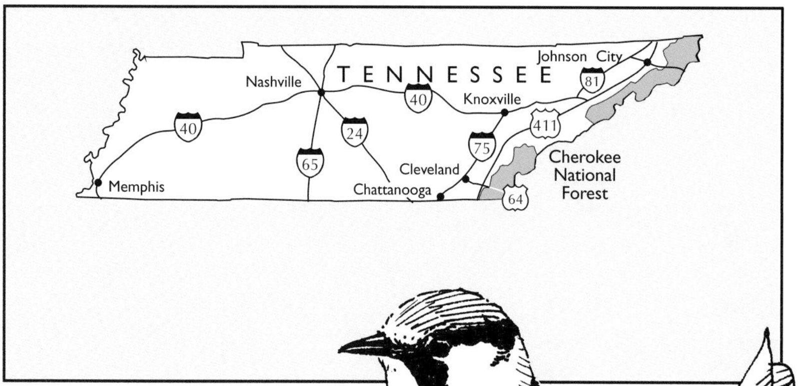

CHESTNUT-SIDED WARBLER

HOW TO GET THERE. *For the first two tour routes, from Knoxville, drive east on Interstate 40 for 28 miles to the junction with Interstate 81. Turn north on I-81 for 56 miles to Interstate 181 South (Johnson City Exit). Then follow I-181 south for 28 miles to Erwin's Main Street (Exit 19). Turn left and follow signs to Tennessee 107 West; the District Office is located at 1205 N. Main Street. The Forest Supervisor's Office is in Cleveland, which is about 80 miles southwest of Knoxville off Interstate 75 and is the starting point for the third tour route.*

THE HIGHLANDS of the southern Blue Ridge Mountains offer cool havens from the sweltering summer heat of the surrounding valleys. Within the 627,000 acres of the Cherokee National Forest, you can visit northern conifer forests, high grassy meadows and rhododendron gardens, clear coldwater streams lined with hemlocks, and a variety of hardwood and pine forests.

Moisture-loving red spruce–fraser fir forests clothe the mountain peaks above 5000 feet, nourished by some of the heaviest rainfall (up to 80 inches annually) in the eastern U.S. These dark, dense stands are relicts of Canadian Zone forests that extended southward during glacial advances.

Where sunlight is able to penetrate the canopy, green carpets of apron moss, shield ferns, and wood sorrel cover the ground.

High-elevation meadows, known locally as "grassy balds," are covered knee-deep with mountain oat and hair grasses and a variety of wildflowers. No one knows exactly how these balds came to be. They may have been created by bison and elk, by Native Americans who burned sections of the woods, by early settlers grazing cattle, or by natural climatic conditions; possibly all four factors played a role.

The endangered Carolina northern flying-squirrel inhabits the ecotone between the spruce–fir and northern hardwood forests. Occasionally, black bears are seen. Here, too, are woodchuck, red squirrel, Eastern chipmunk, and bobcat.

Bird Life

The Forest is host to 262 species in a unique mix of northern and southern forms. Some of the northern birds reach the southern limits of their breeding-range in the spruce-fir forests of the southern Blue Ridge: Northern Saw-whet Owl, Red-breasted Nuthatch, Brown Creeper, Winter Wren, Golden-crowned Kinglet, Veery, Solitary Vireo, Chestnut-sided Warbler (disturbed areas or heath thickets), and Dark-eyed Junco. Here, too, is the Common Raven; listen for its distinct cronk calls as it soars and rolls playfully overhead. Red Crossbills and Pine Siskins may occur anytime; both have nested on Roan Mountain. In winter, northern visitors may include Evening Grosbeak.

JONATHAN ALDERFER, DRAWING

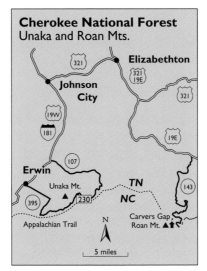

DAVID A. SIBLEY, DRAWING

WORM-EATING WARBLER

Birding Routes

Three routes are suggested. To experience the red spruce forest and a grassy bald, take the 30-mile Unaka Mountain Auto Tour on the north end of the Forest. Roan Mountain, east of Unaka Mountain, gives the visitor a chance to explore spruce-fir forest, grassy balds, and heath balds. In addition, the Tellico Auto Tour on the south end of the Forest offers open water, riparian, and hardwood forest communities.

Unaka Mountain Auto Tour. This route (brochure available from the Ranger Station or from the address listed in *For more information*) begins at the Unaka Ranger Station at 1205 N. Main Street in Erwin on Tennessee Route 107. Go southwest to 10th Street and Tennessee Route 395 and turn left. Drive east on Rte. 395 toward the Tennessee–North Carolina state line for 3.3 miles to Rock Creek Campground. Look and listen here in spring and early summer for Black-throated Green, Worm-eating and Swainson's warblers, Ovenbird, and Louisiana Waterthrush in the dense rhododendron and hemlock thickets. You may also see Ruby-throated Hummingbird, Acadian Flycatcher, Wood Thrush, Solitary and Red-eyed vireos, and Scarlet Tanager.

Continue 3.1 miles on Rte. 395 to the state line at Indian Grave Gap. Turn left onto gravel Forest Service Road (FS) 230. Follow FS 230 for 2.2 miles to Beauty Spot Observation Site (4437 feet); Ruffed Grouse may occur anywhere along this route. You will see a grassy bald beyond the parking area. Search the edges of the bald for Cedar Waxwing, Chestnut-sided Warbler, Rose-breasted Grosbeak, Indigo Bunting, Rufous-sided Towhee, Song Sparrow, and American Goldfinch.

You are likely to see white-tailed deer during the evening hours and might catch a glimpse of a red fox or a bobcat. Also watch for Appalachian cottontail, meadow jumping-mouse, and southern bog lemming. These small mammals attract raptors, so be on the lookout for Sharp-shinned, Cooper's, Broad-winged, and Red-tailed hawks during the daytime, and Great Horned, Barred, and Northern Saw-whet owls after dark. The saw-whet owls call from late March to June, but are very rare and local.

To hike through the red spruce forest, continue on FS 230 another 2.4 miles and park on the roadside at a tight switchback. As you face the rock bluff, the trailhead to the Appalachian Trail will be at the right. You can hike up to Unaka Mountain on the trail from here (it will take 30 to 40 minutes). At high elevations in the Forest (i.e., greater than 3500 ft) there are five species of characteristic high-elevation nesting warblers: Chestnut-sided, Black-throated Green, Black-throated Blue, Canada, and Blackburnian, and their numbers are in that order of prevalence—most to least likely; Blackburnians, in fact, are rare in the north Cherokee. The narrow trail first traverses a hardwood forest at 4600-feet elevation, where you may find Solitary Vireo, and next passes through thickets of blueberry and laurel, a good place for Chestnut-sided Warbler. Once in the higher red spruce forest, watch for Hairy Woodpecker, Red-breasted Nuthatch, Winter Wren, Golden-crowned Kinglet, Veery, Gray Catbird, Rufous-sided Towhee, and Dark-eyed Junco.

Return to your vehicle and continue up FS 230 about 0.7 mile to the Unaka Mountain Overlook; turn left into the parking area. Here you may spot Peregrine Falcon or Common Raven. Young Peregrines have been released at hacking-sites nearby in recent years, and sightings should be reported to the Forest Service. Broad-winged Hawks as well as other migrating raptors pass through in late September.

Continue on FS 230 for 1.1 miles to the Stamping Ground Ridge pull-off. Summering Magnolia Warbler and Northern Saw-whet Owl have been found here in recent years, and towhees and catbirds are common. Also watch carefully for spruce-forest mammals and amphibians. Red-backed voles and cloudland deer mice, and pygmy and Yonahlossee

CAROLINA WREN

DANIEL LANE, DRAWING

salamanders, live among the moss-covered talus slopes and near spring seepages along the roadside.

In another 6 miles, turn west onto Tennessee Route 107 to return to Unicoi and Interstate 181, which will become Interstate 26 in four or five years. To find Grasshopper Sparrows, go west on Rte. 107 for 2 miles, turn right (east) onto Tennessee Route 173, and park in the Community Center parking lot. From early to mid-May through June, listen for the buzzy songs of the Grasshopper Sparrows that nest in the overgrown field and a privately-owned blueberry farm located behind the Community Center. At the U.S. Forest Service's Unicoi Work Center, you may wish to fill a water jug with spring water, tested for drinking quality. Then continue west on Rte. 107 to I-181 to complete the loop.

Roan Mountain Route. Begin at the Roan Mountain State Park Visitors Center. Follow the directions from Knoxville for the Unaka Mountain Auto Tour, but leave I-181 in Johnson City at the exit for U.S. Route 321. Go 7 miles east to Elizabethton,

drive 18 miles south from Elizabethton on U.S. Route 19E, and turn south onto Tennessee Route 143 at the village of Roan Mountain. Go 3 miles to the state park and stop 1.7 miles beyond the visitors center at Picnic Area No. 1. From May through July, the wet willow thicket and old orchard, located between Picnic Area No. 1 and No. 2, are excellent for Cooper's and Red-tailed hawks, Ruffed Grouse (in rhododendron thickets), Acadian Flycatcher, Eastern Wood-Pewee, Carolina Wren, Gray Catbird, Red-eyed Vireo, Golden-winged, Chestnut-sided, and Hooded warblers, Indigo Bunting, American Goldfinch, and Field and Song sparrows.

Continue another 4 miles to the Twin Springs Picnic Area (elevation 4300 feet), located in an older forest of beech, buckeye, and red and striped maples. Stop for Barred Owl, Least Flycatcher, White-breasted Nuthatch, Veery, Solitary Vireo, Black-throated Blue and Black-throated Green warblers, Ovenbird, Scarlet Tanager, and Rose-breasted Grosbeak. As you progress to higher elevations, listen for Winter Wren and Canada Warbler along the roadway.

Carver's Gap, located on the Tennessee–North Carolina border at 5512-feet elevation, is 3.7 miles beyond Twin Springs Picnic Area. The Gap is good for migrant raptors in fall. Possibilities include Osprey, Bald and Golden eagles, Sharp-shinned and Cooper's hawks (fairly common), Northern Goshawk (rare), Mer-

lin, and Peregrine Falcon. The Gap is also an excellent place to observe fall migrant passerines from late August through September. By hiking east along the Appalachian Trail from Carver's Gap, you can experience the longest stretch of grassy balds in the mountains, running 4.8 miles (intermixed with forested areas) from Carver's Gap to Hump Mountain. Cedar Waxwings are attracted to berries and buds along the edge of the grassy balds in spring, summer, and fall. Roan Mountain is the only regular nesting site in Tennessee for Alder Flycatcher, which frequents the alder thickets. Horned Lark and Vesper Sparrow can be found in the tall grass, and Chimney Swifts zip around overhead.

After returning to your vehicle, go right and follow the signs for 1.7 miles to Roan Mountain Gardens. (The road is closed in winter, but visitors may walk or cross-country ski.) Turn left into Gardens Road to reach the parking area for a Forest Service visitors center (open June through September) and wheelchair-accessible nature trail. The trail passes through a red spruce–Fraser fir forest and the largest natural rhododendron garden in the U.S., a 600-acre display of spectacular purple Catawba rhododendrons.

The elevation at Roan High Knob is 6285 feet.

The trail winds through the heath bald, or

ACADIAN FLYCATCHER

GAIL DIANE LUCKNER, DRAWING

"rhododendron garden," where you may see Ruby-throated Hummingbirds visiting the purple flowers at their peak bloom in mid-to-late June. Gray Catbird and Chestnut-sided Warbler are common in the gardens. Where the trail penetrates the spruce–fir forest you are likely to see and hear Red-breasted Nuthatch, Brown Creeper, Winter Wren, Golden-crowned Kinglet, Veery, Hermit Thrush, Canada Warbler, and Dark-eyed Junco. At night, you might hear the whistled toot of the Northern Saw-whet Owl. In winter, a number of northern species are possible: Snow Bunting on the grassy balds and Red and White-winged (very rare) crossbills, Purple Finch, Pine Siskin, and Evening Grosbeak among the surrounding conifers. During years of cone-crop failure in northern states, these finches sometimes move south to winter in the boreal forests of Roan Mountain. Southern "bumper cone-crop" years provide excellent opportunities to see large numbers of these birds.

During the peak rhododendron bloom the main trail may be crowded. If so, there is a gravel road located between the turnoff to Carver's Gap and the Gardens that is less traveled and provides additional spruce–fir birding opportunities.

Tellico Auto Loop. From the junction of U.S. Route 64 and Tennessee Route 40 east of Cleveland, go east on the two routes for 7 miles to U.S. Route 411. Turn left onto U.S. 411 and go about 35 miles north to Rte. 68. Turn right and drive about 16 miles to the town of Tellico Plains. If you are coming from Knoxville, leave Interstate 75 at Exit 60 (County Road (CR) 322, Sweetwater); go east about 2 miles to Rte. 68 and drive 26 miles to Tellico Plains.

Turn left on the Tellico–Robbinsville Road (Tennessee Route 165 East) and after one mile (through town) bear right to stay on Rte. 165E along the Tellico River. Scan the snags for Osprey and Belted Kingfisher.

Oosterneck Creek is 4.3 miles farther on Rte. 165E, where you can bear right on FS 210 to the Tellico Ranger Station for information and maps. Or you can continue east on Rte. 165 for 9 miles to the entrance of Indian Boundary Recreation Area. This was the site of a boundary line between the U.S. and the former Cherokee Indian Nation, imposed by treaty in 1819.

The recreation area includes a campground, picnic area, and a 96-acre lake for swimming and fishing. A 4-mile hiking and bicycling trail encircles the lake and provides good birding opportunities. In spring and summer, watch and listen along the trail for Great Blue and Green herons, Osprey, Black-billed and Yellow-billed cuckoos, Whip-poor-will, Eastern Wood-Pewee, Belted Kingfisher, Acadian and Great Crested flycatchers, Wood Thrush, White-eyed, Yellow-throated and Red-eyed vireos, Northern Parula, Yellow-throated, Black-and-white, and Hooded warblers, Ovenbird, Yellow-breasted Chat, and Scarlet Tanager. A visitor may even spot a brood of Wild Turkeys "bugging" in the orchard grass and clover openings along the trail in summer or hear a male gobbling in spring. Flame azaleas bloom here in early to mid-May.

Continue east on Rte. 165 for another 8.4 miles to a parking area and trail that traverse a northern hardwood forest of American beech, yellow birch, black cherry, and sugar maple at 4000-feet elevation. This for-

SOLITARY VIREO

est has a diverse herb layer of spring wildflowers that bloom from April to June as well as shield ferns and mosses. Look here for such northern birds as Black-billed Cuckoo (on territory), Yellow-bellied Sapsucker, Carolina and Winter wrens, Red-breasted Nuthatch, Veery, Solitary Vireo, Black-throated Blue Warbler, Rose-breasted Grosbeak, and Dark-eyed Junco. The only Tennessee nesting record of the sapsucker is from this area. Other species to watch for are Broad-winged Hawk, Common Raven, Wood Thrush, Gray Catbird, Red-eyed Vireo, Blue-winged (on territory), Golden-winged, Chestnut-sided, Hooded, and Canada warblers, Northern Cardinal, Indigo Bunting, and Rufous-sided Towhee.

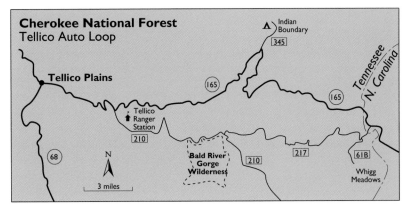

Cherokee National Forest
Tellico Auto Loop

Indian Boundary
345

Tellico Plains

165

Tellico Ranger Station

210

68

N

3 miles

Bald River Gorge Wilderness

210

217

165

61B

Tennessee / N. Carolina

Whigg Meadows

FLOWERS ON WALL AT TRAILHEAD
CHEROKEE NATIONAL FOREST

AILEEN R. LOTZ, PHOTOGRAPH

near the bridge and walk down gravel FS 217 through a forest of Eastern hemlock, Carolina silverbell, and buckeye. Watch for the brilliant orange flash of a male Blackburnian Warbler and look and listen for Red-breasted Nuthatch, nesting Golden-crowned Kinglets, Black-throated Blue and Black-throated Green warblers, and Rose-breasted Grosbeak. The rapid drumming of a male Ruffed Grouse can often be heard in spring or occasionally in fall.

There are two options for travel at this point. If you wish to continue east on Rte. 165 to see Whigg Meadow, a scenic grassy bald, continue 1.8 miles to Mud Gap. You can either park here and walk up FS 61B, or, if you are driving a high-clearance, four-wheel-drive vehicle, you can drive the 1.5 miles to Whigg Meadow (5000 feet). Northern Saw-whet Owl is a possibility here in late April or early May. Keep an eye out for Ruffed Grouse taking dust-baths

in the road. The grassy bald is good for Broad-winged Hawk, American Woodcock, Common Raven, Eastern Bluebird, Gray Catbird, and Chestnut-sided Warbler. In the surrounding northern hardwood forests are Pileated Woodpecker, Winter Wren, Veery, Solitary Vireo, Black-throated Blue Warbler, and Rose-breasted Grosbeak.

The second option from Stratton Gap is to continue southwest on FS 217 for 1.1 miles after you cross under the Rte. 165 bridge. Turn right at this point to stay on FS 217 (North River Road). In 11 miles, turn right onto the paved Tellico River Road and continue to Rte. 165, following signs to return to Tellico Plains. This route crosses several clear coldwater streams lined with mountain-laurel and rhododendron; watch here for Acadian Flycatcher, Black-throated Green and Swainson's warblers, and Louisiana Waterthrush.

Drive east on Rte. 165 for 3.3 miles to Stratton Gap (4500 feet), cross over the bridge, and make an immediate left turn, looping back under the bridge. (Note: between Beech Gap and Mud Gap, the highway crosses into and out of North Carolina.) Park

---

ACCOMMODATIONS ◆ WEATHER ◆ OTHER ATTRACTIONS

FLAME AZALEA

When to visit. There is good birding all year. Nesting season runs from May to early July; April, early and mid-May, and September through early October are best for migration. Fall color peaks in October. Rhododendron bloom is best from mid-to-late June.

Where to stay. Numerous campgrounds on the Forest, in state parks, and in nearby Great Smoky Mountains National Park. Motels in towns surrounding the Forest, including Johnson City, Elizabethton, Sweetwater, and Knoxville. The cabins at Roan Mountain State Park are open year-round; reservations required.

Weather and attire. Some high roads (above Carver's Gap at Roan Mountain, east of Indian Boundary on Rte. 165) close periodically in winter due to snow and ice. Avoid exposed areas at high elevations during lightning-storms. Summers are warm and humid, but high-elevation weather is subject to rapid and frequent change. A warm jacket and rain-gear are recommended all year.

What else to do. Hiking the Appalachian Trail and other trails; whitewater sports on the Tellico, Ocoee, Hiwassee, and Nolichucky Rivers; fishing on the Tellico or North Rivers (daily permit required for Tellico); cross-country skiing, sledding, and snow-shoeing on Roan Mountain some winters. Other points of interest include Great Smoky Mountains National Park, Joyce Kilmer Memorial Forest, near Robbinsville, North Carolina (one of the few remaining old-growth forests in the East), Erwin National Fish Hatchery, and Pheasant Fields Fish Hatchery near Tellico Plains.

For more information. General and campground information, District Office addresses, maps, bird list: Cherokee National Forest, P.O. Box 2010, 2800 N. Ocoee St. Cleveland, Tennessee 37320; telephone 615/476-9700.

CONECUH FOREST
Alabama

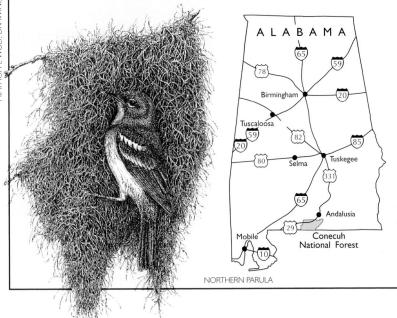

MIMI HOPPE WOLF, DRAWING

ALABAMA

Birmingham

Tuscaloosa

Selma   Tuskegee

Andalusia

Mobile   Conecuh
National Forest

NORTHERN PARULA

HOW TO GET THERE.
*From Mobile, Alabama,
take Interstate 65 north
to the Brewton Exit
and then U.S. Route 29 east
34 miles to Alabama Route 137.
From Pensacola, Florida,
take U.S. 29 to Rte. 137.*

AMONG THE MUSKEGEE INDIANS, the place was known as Conecuh, or land of cane, for the endless stands of switch cane that prevailed before settlement by Europeans. Muskegee artisans used the cane to build their homes, to fashion baskets, and to make weapons. Most of the cane-brakes are gone today, but some patches remain in the 84,000 acres of coastal-plain bottom lands set aside as the Conecuh National Forest.

The habitat on the Forest is characterized by longleaf-pine and a variety of oaks in the upland areas, interspersed with a hardwood bottom-land forest of dogwood, magnolia, and baldcypress. More than two dozen bogs are found on the Forest; they harbor at least twenty species of carnivorous plants, such as pitcher-plant and sun-dew, and a dozen species of wild orchids.

The Forest is also home to numerous mammals, including fox squirrel and white-tailed deer, and a variety of reptiles and amphibians, such as gopher tortoise, American alligator, Florida pine snake, copperhead, eastern diamondback rattlesnake, and pine barrens treefrog

DAPHNE GEMMILL, PHOTOGRAPH

PITCHER PLANTS, CONECUH NATIONAL FOREST

YELLOW-BREASTED CHAT

(one of the rarest amphibians). Numerous butterflies, among them tiger swallowtail and red-spotted purple, feed on a spectrum of wildflowers. One-third of the Forest is set aside as a wildlife management area for the purpose of restoring deer and turkey populations.

Bird Life

Birding is at its best in late spring and early summer, when most of the characteristic breeding birds of the coastal plain are in full song or are busy with nesting activities. A visit to appropriate habitat during April, May, and early June should produce Mississippi Kite, Black Vulture, Red-shouldered and Broad-winged hawks, Wood Duck, Purple Gallinule, Barred Owl, Chuck-will's-widow, Red-headed, Red-bellied, Red-cockaded, and Pileated woodpeckers, Acadian and Great Crested flycatchers, and Eastern Kingbird. You should also find Brown-headed Nuthatch, Wood Thrush, Logger-head Shrike, Yellow-throated Vireo, Northern Parula, Yellow-throated, Pine, Prairie, Prothonotary, Swainson's, Kentucky, and Hooded warblers, Summer Tanager, Blue Grosbeak, Bachman's Sparrow, and Orchard Oriole. Most of these species are present throughout the summer but are harder to find during the hottest time of day.

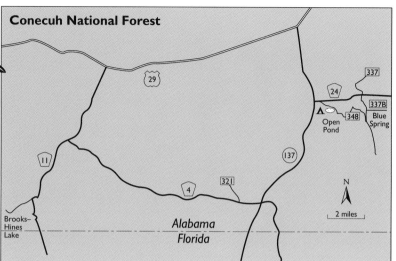

In winter, the many ponds harbor Common Moorhen (permanent resident) and Green Heron; Least Bittern is very rare in winter. American Woodcock forages in the wet woods. Winter visitors include Red-breasted Nuthatch, Winter Wren, Golden-crowned and Ruby-crowned kinglets, Hermit Thrush, Yellow-rumped Warbler, Chipping, Field, Vesper, Savannah, Grasshopper (rare), Henslow's (rare), Fox, Song, Swamp, and White-throated sparrows, and Dark-eyed Junco. Spring and fall migrations bring many of the northern warblers, Scarlet Tanager, Rose-breasted Grosbeak, and Northern Oriole.

Birding Route

Open Pond and Blue Spring.
The following excursion will take you through a variety of habitats, from ponds to longleaf-pine flatwoods and bottom-land hardwood forest. Begin your tour at Open Pond off Alabama Route 137, the main north–south road through the Forest. From the intersection of U.S. Route 29 and Rte. 137, go south

5.5 miles to County Road (CR) 24 and turn left. Drive 0.3 mile east on CR 24 and turn right on Forest Service Road (FS) 336, which leads to Open Pond in about a mile. There is a Red-cockaded Woodpecker observation site on the south side of CR 24, 0.1 mile

DAVID A. SIBLEY, DRAWING

GAIL DIANE LUCKNER, DRAWING

PURPLE GALLINULE

Birdfinding in Forty National Forests and Grasslands

west of the junction with FS 336. This site has two nest trees that went unused in 1992, but forest biologists expect them to be reoccupied.

At the pond, look for Pied-billed Grebe, Great Blue, Little Blue, and Green herons, Great and Snowy egrets, Wood Duck, Purple Gallinule, Common Moorhen, and Red-winged Blackbird. Check the surrounding longleaf pine and scrub oak woods for Red-headed, Red-bellied, and Pileated woodpeckers, Northern Flicker, Great Crested Flycatcher, Carolina Wren, Pine Warbler, Yellow-breasted Chat, and Common Grackle.

If you have time, take the 5-mile south loop of the Conecuh Trail (map available from the Forest Service) to Blue Spring, a large natural spring of clear blue water in the Yellow River hardwood bottom land. The well-marked trail starts at the old Open Pond picnic shelter in the day-use area. The hike will take about three hours. If you prefer, you can drive to Blue Spring and walk a portion of the trail there. Buck Pond, near Open Pond and reached by trail, is another good spot.

To reach the Blue Spring parking area, turn right at the entrance to the Open Pond Recreation Area; proceed approximately 0.1 mile, then turn left onto FS 348 and continue for 1.7 miles to the intersection with FS 337. Turn left onto FS 337 and drive 0.1

LEAST BITTERN

mile to FS 337B, where there is sign for Blue Spring. Turn right onto FS 337B and proceed 0.3 mile to the parking area at the end of the road. By walking the trails you are likely to find Red-tailed, Red-shouldered, and Cooper's (rare) hawks, Acadian and Great Crested flycatchers, Carolina Chickadee, Tufted Titmouse, Brown-headed Nuthatch, Red-eyed and Yellow-throated vireos, and Pine, Prothonotary, and Hooded warblers. In the summer, listen for Swainson's Warbler in the hardwoods in swamps and along any watercourses. Bachman's Sparrow prefers open pine forest with a grassy understory and few bushes. These hard-to-find

SWAINSON'S WARBLER

birds are best located by song. Both Eastern Screech-Owls and Barred Owls are resident here, and might be seen perched in a tree cavity or flying in at dawn or dusk in response to an imitated call. Mississippi Kite can be found in hardwood areas near water in the summer.

A quick way back to Open Pond is to turn right onto FS 337 and drive 1.2 miles to CR 24; turn left and go 2 miles to the Open Pond sign and turn left. To reach the next birding spot, a Red-cockaded Woodpecker colony, return to Rte. 137, turn left, and go 6.7 miles through the town of Wing to CR 4. Turn right onto CR 4 and drive 1.4 miles (look and listen for Bachman's Sparrow along the way) to where FS 321 leads off to the right. From March 10 to October 15, this road, as well as many other roads in the Forest, is closed to vehicles to protect ground-nesting birds from disturbance. The Red-cockaded Woodpecker trees are painted with blue rings. Park on the left (south) side of CR 4 opposite FS 321, where you will have a good view of the painted trees and will not block access to FS 321.

The woodpeckers are easily seen in May when they have young in the nest. Active cavities will have white sap around the entrance-hole. Listen for "squawking" birds, since this species is often noisy while feeding. If you are not there in May, then dawn or dusk is best, though with patience the woodpeckers can be seen at any time of the day. Barred Owl, Northern Flicker, Brown-headed Nuthatch, Eastern Bluebird, Pine Warbler, and Bachman's Sparrow also nest within these woods.

To reach the last stop on the tour, continue west on CR 4 for 11.4 miles to CR 11, where there is a sign for Brooks Hines Lake. This is another good place to search for Bachman's Sparrow. Turn left on CR 11, go 1.4 miles to a dirt road on the right, and follow the signs for the lake. After 0.5 mile take the left road, proceed 0.6 mile, and take a right, still following the signs for the lake. Continue 0.6 mile to the parking lot at the lake.

This recently developed Brooks Hines public fishing lake holds bass, bream, and catfish, which attract many fishermen and a variety of herons and egrets, plus Double-crested Cormorant (winter), Anhinga, Bald Eagle (rare, winter), and Osprey. Wood Duck nests here, and migratory ducks, such as Green-winged Teal, Northern Pintail, Northern Shoveler, American Wigeon, and Bufflehead, visit in winter.

ACCOMMODATIONS ◆ WEATHER ◆ OTHER ATTRACTIONS

When to visit. In early spring (March and April), the dogwood trees are blooming, and the weather is very pleasant, but late April and May are best for breeding birds. *Where to stay.* Camping facilities, in Open Pond Recreation Area; motels and restaurants, in nearby Brewton and Andalusia. *Weather and attire.* Winters mild; summers hot and humid with July being the wettest month. Lightweight clothing appropriate most of the year. In summer, insect repellent, sunscreen, drinking water, hat, and light hiking-boots are advisable. Watch out for poison ivy and venomous snakes. *What else to do.* Photography and other forms of nature study, fishing, hiking and mountain-biking. Adjacent Blackwater River State Forest in Florida offers 183,000 acres of similar habitat. From the town of Wing, go south on Alabama Route 137 for about 18 miles (Rt. 137 becomes Okaloosa CR 189 at the state line). Turn right (west) at the intersection with Florida Route 4, which enters the Forest after a few miles. Environmental center on CR 35, about 8 miles southeast of the town of Munson. *For more information.* General and camping information, District Office addresses, maps: Conecuh National Forest, Rte. 5, Box 157, U.S. Route 29 South, Andalusia, Alabama 36420; 205/222-2555.

DOGWOOD

JASMINE

ROSEBUD ORCHID

APALACHICOLA FOREST
Florida

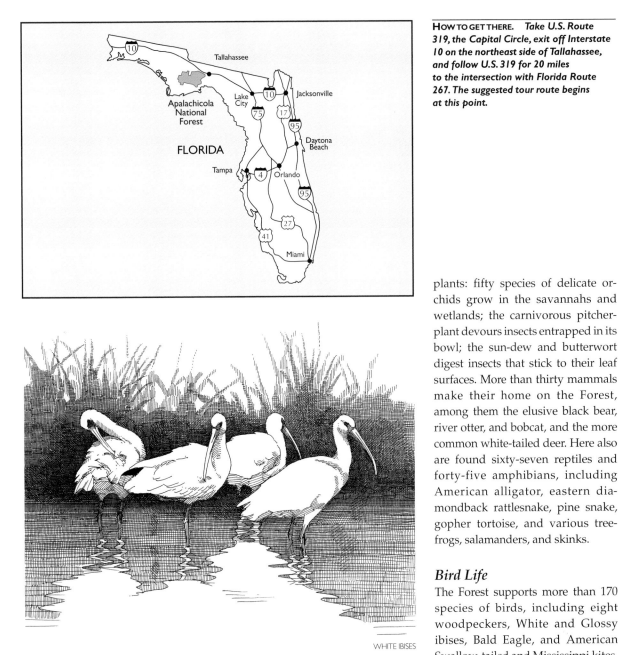

HOW TO GET THERE. *Take U.S. Route 319, the Capital Circle, exit off Interstate 10 on the northeast side of Tallahassee, and follow U.S. 319 for 20 miles to the intersection with Florida Route 267. The suggested tour route begins at this point.*

WHITE IBISES

DAVID A. SIBLEY, DRAWING

AT 563,000 ACRES, or almost 900 square miles, the Apalachicola National Forest near Tallahassee is the largest of Florida's three Federal woodlands. It encompasses six watersheds and a great variety of plant communities, from swamps and treeless savannahs to extensive stands of longleaf pine. Early native Americans found many of the resources necessary for subsistence on the Forest, with burial mounds and various artifacts giving evidence of habitation dating back to 10,000 B.C.

The Apalachicola, established in 1936, is noted for numerous rare plants: fifty species of delicate orchids grow in the savannahs and wetlands; the carnivorous pitcher-plant devours insects entrapped in its bowl; the sun-dew and butterwort digest insects that stick to their leaf surfaces. More than thirty mammals make their home on the Forest, among them the elusive black bear, river otter, and bobcat, and the more common white-tailed deer. Here also are found sixty-seven reptiles and forty-five amphibians, including American alligator, eastern diamondback rattlesnake, pine snake, gopher tortoise, and various tree-frogs, salamanders, and skinks.

Bird Life

The Forest supports more than 170 species of birds, including eight woodpeckers, White and Glossy ibises, Bald Eagle, and American Swallow-tailed and Mississippi kites. The Anhinga is abundant throughout the Forest along its streams and watercourses. No fewer than 21 species of wood warbler have been recorded, of which 10 are known to nest. The greatest avian attraction, however, is the Red-cockaded Woodpecker. More than 680 active clusters exist on the

Forest, resulting in the largest known population—numbering in excess of 2300 individuals—of this endangered species.

The Red-cockaded Woodpecker is the only bird that constructs cavities in live southern pine trees, typically longleaf pines that are ninety to a hundred years old, a foot or more in diameter, and infected with red-heart disease which softens the tree's heartwood, making it easier for the bird to excavate a cavity. The apron of oozing sap that forms below the hole makes the nests easy to spot, but the sticky pine pitch serves as a barrier to snakes and other predators. The birds possess an advanced social order and live in groups numbering up to nine individuals of varying ages. Only one pair in a group breeds in any given year; the rest assist in raising the young, in seeking out sources of food, and in watching for potential predators. The low reproductive rate, however, combined with predation and nest-hole appropriation, makes for a perilous existence. So attractive are the laboriously excavated cavities—despite the pitch—that no fewer than eleven other species of

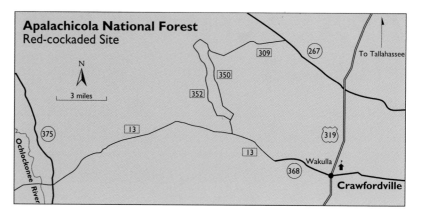

Apalachicola National Forest
Red-cockaded Site

birds (among them Pileated and Red-bellied woodpeckers and Eastern Bluebirds), five mammals, two reptiles, and colonies of bees will oust the original occupants to make a home for themselves if they can.

A second specialty of the Forest is Bachman's Sparrow, which is common throughout, but difficult to find outside the breeding season. In spring and early summer, the sparrow is easily located by its beautiful song, a clear, whistled introductory note followed by a variable trill or warble on a different pitch. It can be devilishly difficult to spot, though, when it sits in a low pine branch, 10 to 20 feet above

the ground, and sings persistently without moving to another perch.

Birding Route

Red-cockaded Site. Although Red-cockaded Woodpecker clusters are well distributed in open mature pine stands across the entire Forest, one of the most accessible sites is along Forest Service Road (FS) 350. To reach FS 350 from the intersection of U.S. Route 319 and Florida Route 267, turn right (west) onto Rte. 267 and drive about 5 miles to FS 309, just beyond the 'Entering Leon County' sign. Turn left (west) on this dirt road (opposite Helen Guard Station Road on the right).

You will want to bird the forested area along FS 309 en route to the woodpeckers. Look in the wooded swamp approximately 1.5 miles from the intersection with Route 267 for Wild Turkey, Barred Owl, Acadian and Great Crested flycatchers, Blue-gray Gnatcatcher, Northern Parula, Swainson's, Kentucky, Prothonotary, and Hooded warblers, and Rufous-sided Towhee.

Continue on FS 309 to the junction with FS 350. It will be on the left, 4.8 miles from Rte. 267. Brown-headed Nuthatch and Bachman's Sparrow can usually be found at this intersection. The nuthatch is abundant throughout the Forest, while the sparrow frequents the same mature pine stands with a low understory of palmetto and scrub oaks that the Red-cockaded Woodpecker prefers. Turn onto FS 350 and go about 0.25

ST. JOHN'S-WORT, APALACHICOLA NATIONAL FOREST

mile to the first Red-cockaded Woodpecker cluster.

Cavity trees are painted with a broad white band. The woodpeckers may be found foraging in and around the clusters all through the daylight hours, although early morning and late afternoon are best. Avoid disturbing the birds by staying at least 300 feet from cavity trees and individual birds.

Continue beyond the first woodpecker cluster on FS 350 to the first stream-crossing with a steel-and-concrete bridge. Look and listen here for Prothonotary Warbler and Summer Tanager. Bear to the right at an intersection, and at 0.2 mile beyond the bridge turn right onto FS 352 and drive about 3 miles to another Red-cockaded Woodpecker cluster and about 4.5 miles (from FS 350) to yet another cluster on the right, opposite a clear-cut. Here you might find six species of woodpeckers: Red-cockaded, Red-headed, Red-bellied, Downy, Hairy, and Pileated. You might also see Yellow-billed Cuckoo, while Brown-headed Nuthatch is almost certain to be present, and Bachman's Sparrow is likely. Check also for Mourning Dove, Common Nighthawk, Chuck-will's-widow, Chimney Swift, Ruby-throated Hummingbird, Eastern Wood-Pewee, Blue Jay, American Crow, Carolina Chickadee, Carolina Wren, Northern Mockingbird, Brown Thrasher, White-eyed and Red-eyed vireos, Yellow-throated and Pine warblers, Summer Tanager, and Northern Cardinal. All are typical of the pine flatwoods of the Florida panhandle.

Another 1.4 miles brings you back to FS 309. Turn right and drive 0.6 mile to a bridge over Lost Creek, a good place (during the mid-mornings and mid-afternoons of March and April) for American Swallow-tailed Kite. This location is only 0.7 mile from the intersection with FS 350 (ahead) where you began this loop drive.

Ochlockonee River. A good place for Mississippi Kite is near the Ochlockonee River. This site can be reached by continuing south from the Red-cockaded Woodpecker colonies on FS 350 to FH 13 (FS 350 ends at FH 13, about 0.8 mile beyond the intersection with FS 352). Turn right on FH 13 and drive about 12 miles to County Road (CR) 375 (first paved road), continue across 375 on FH 13 (now paved) for approximately 1.0 mile, and stop at the bridge over the Ochlockonee River. Look for Mississippi and American Swallow-tailed kites soaring over the water. This site has nesting Prothonotary Warblers and Northern Parulas, and can be very good for passerines during the fall migration.

Apalachee Savannah. The western edge of the Forest, along the Apalachicola River and its tributaries, is excellent for both kites. Such places for kites are usually best mid-morning to mid-afternoon. The Apalachee Savannahs National Forest Scenic Byway, Florida Route 379, provides access to a number of good spots. The most interesting section of the Scenic Byway begins at its junction with Florida Route 12 on the north and runs about 20 miles to the intersection with Florida Route 65.

To reach the junction of Rtes. 12 and 379 from the bridge over the Ochlockonee River, continue west on FH 13 for about 21 miles to the intersection with Rte. 65. Turn right and then immediately left onto Rte. 12, then drive about 6 miles to the junction with Rte. 379, and turn left. If there have been heavy rains, however, do not attempt to reach the junction of Rtes. 12 and 379 via FH 13; it will be impassable. Instead, continue on FH 13 from the Ochlockonee River for about 2.8 miles to Florida Route 67 and turn right. Follow Rte. 67 north and west for about 27 miles, through Telogia, to the intersection with Rte. 12 at the village of Woods. Turn left (south) onto Rte. 12, drive about 8 miles to the intersection with Rte. 379, and turn right.

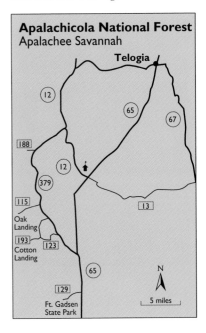

AMERICAN SWALLOW-TAILED KITE

Apalachicola National Forest
Apalachee Savannah

For the next 6 miles, watch over the fields and woods for both species of kite hunting for dragonflies and other large flying insects. Turn right onto FS 188, 6.2 miles from Rte. 12, and drive about 0.8 mile to a private bridge over the Florida River. Scan the skies here for Mississippi Kite and Red-shouldered Hawk. Return to Rte. 379, turn right, and drive 5.2 miles south to FS 115, just before some trailers on the right. Turn right onto FS 115; follow it for 3.5 miles to the end at White Oak Landing on the River Styx, about 1.5 miles from Apalachicola.

The road crosses two streams in the Big Cypress Swamp about 2.5 miles from Rte. 379. A stop at the first bridge in spring and summer should produce Acadian Flycatcher and Hooded Warbler. At the end of the road, scan the skies above the wooded bluffs for raptors, including both kites, Red-shouldered Hawk, and Osprey. Yellow-billed Cuckoo, Acadian Flycatcher, and Prothonotary Warbler nest here. Return to Rte. 379 and turn right; the loop continuation of FS 115 is such a rough road that it is not recommended.

ANHINGA

MIMI HOPPE WOLF: DRAWING

Cotton Landing and Apalachicola River. Another good spot for kites is Cotton Landing, which can be reached by continuing south on Rte. 379 for two miles to FS 123, on the right. Follow the signs, via FS 123 and 193, to the landing in about 4 miles. To view the Apalachicola River and have yet another chance for both kites, take Rte. 379 to Rte. 65, 8.2 miles from FS 115 and turn right. Go 4.5 miles south on Rte. 65 to FS 129 and the sign for Ft. Gadsden State Historical Site. Drive 3 miles to the state park, a 78-acre parcel purchased from the National Forest.

Take the short trail to the site of the former fort, built by the British during the War of 1812. You will have a panoramic view of the river and surrounding woodlands. Even on a hot, humid summer afternoon, when nothing else seems to be moving, the patient observer should obtain excellent views of both Mississippi and American Swallow-tailed kites as they hunt along the river.

ACCOMMODATIONS ◆ WEATHER ◆ OTHER ATTRACTIONS

When to visit. Spring and early fall are best for birds. Wildflowers bloom throughout the year, although late summer generally provides the most spectacular display.

Where to stay. On the Forest: ten campgrounds, open year-round; primitive sites, open at various times of year. Motels, in Tallahassee, Panacea, Lanark Village, and Carrabelle along the Gulf Coast, or the unique Wakulla Springs Lodge in Wakulla Springs State Park, built in 1937 and filled with period furniture (reservations required).

Weather and attire. Summers are hot and humid; winters are generally mild. Lightweight clothing recommended in summer. Insect repellent and snake chaps are advised if walking a lot in the woods.

What else to do. Botanizing and other forms of nature study, hiking, canoeing, and driving. Nearby is Wakulla Springs State Park, with its narrated Jungle Boat Tour, a must for even the most experienced birder. The Park provides unparalleled opportunities to see Anhinga, White Ibis, Wood Duck, Purple Gallinule, and Limpkin at very close range. Also adjacent to the Forest is St. Marks National Wildlife Refuge, noted for its wintering waterfowl, shorebirds, and five species of rails. Torreya State Park, about 15 miles north of Bristol on the Apalachicola River, harbors two rare and endangered trees, the torreya tree and the Florida yew, and offers excellent birding.

For more information. General and campground information, District Office addresses, maps, bird list: National Forests in Florida, Woodcrest Office Park, 325 John Knox Road, Suite F–100, Tallahassee, Florida 32303; telephone 904/942-9300.

SUN-DEW

OSCEOLA FOREST
Florida

MIMI HOPPE WOLF, DRAWING

WOOD STORK

HOW TO GET THERE. *Take Interstate 10 to the Lake City Exit, U.S. Route 441. Go south on Rte. 441 for 3.5 miles and then turn left onto U.S. Route 90. Take U.S. 90 east for 12 miles to the Osceola Ranger District Office. Or, take Interstate 75 to the exit for U.S. 90 at Lake City. Go east on Rte. 90 for about 17 miles to the Forest Service office.*

THE PINE FLATWOODS AND WET-LANDS of this splendid north Florida forest are close enough to Georgia for a finger of the storied Okefenoke Swamp to be included in its 157,000 acres. Stands of longleaf and slash pines cover an understory of saw palmetto, gallberry, and wiregrass. These flatwood expanses are intersected throughout by bay and cypress swamps, where hardwoods, such as sweet gum, red bay, and Virginia willow, often form impenetrable barriers. The boggy terrain and warm, humid climate have discouraged human intrusion. Nevertheless, in 1864, Florida's greatest Civil War battle took place along the southern edge of the Forest, where Confederate forces turned back Union troops marching on Tallahassee.

The Osceola, established in 1931, harbors a particularly impressive array of reptiles and amphibians. This is the domain of eastern diamond-back, canebrake, and dusky pygmy rattlesnakes, of the aggressive Florida cottonmouth and the extremely venomous eastern coral snake, as well as of numerous harmless species. Look for gopher tortoise, for

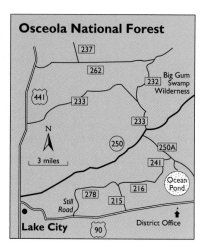

Osceola National Forest

[map showing roads 237, 262, 232, 441, 233, 233, 250, 250A, 241, 216, 278, 215, Big Gum Swamp Wilderness, Ocean Pond, Still Road, Lake City, District Office, 90]

N
3 miles

flatwoods and mole salamanders, and carpenter and bronze frogs. An early-morning drive is likely to provide glimpses of a gray fox or a bobcat. Some of the more secretive residents include Florida black bear, a unique subspecies on the State's threatened list; river otter; beaver; and fox squirrel. Alligators are also denizens of the swamps.

Bird Life

Of 171 bird species known from the Forest, 49 breed there, among them such specialties as American Swallow-tailed Kite, Red-cockaded Woodpecker, and Bachman's Sparrow.

BACHMAN'S SPARROW

Birding Routes

Red-cockaded Sites. Several active clusters of Red-cockaded Woodpecker are scattered along a 5-mile stretch of Forest Service Road (FS) 278 in the southwestern corner of the Forest. The best times for viewing the woodpeckers are early morning and approximately one hour before sundown, when the birds return to roost for the night (see Apalachicola for more details on nesting behavior). As on other National Forests, cavity trees are marked with a painted white band. Active trees are obvious due to fresh pine resin from "wells" maintained by the woodpeckers around the cavities, a defense against predators. Please remember to remain at least 300 feet away from nest trees, especially during April, May, and June. Both Downy and Hairy woodpeckers are found in these woods, so look at the birds carefully. You can reach the area by driving 7.7 miles west on U.S. Route 90 from the District Office to Still Road (FS 236) across from the Lake City Municipal Airport; turn right onto Still Road and go 2 miles to FS 278. Turn right and start your 5-mile drive through the clusters.

Ocean Pond. To bird a somewhat drier, more open expanse of palmetto-flatwoods, continue east on FS 278 for 3.9 miles to the intersection with FS 215. Take a short detour. Drive 0.4 mile straight ahead on FS 215 and park on the right so as not to block the gate to an unimproved road leading west. By walking along this road in spring and summer, even for a short distance, you are likely to find Red-shouldered Hawk, Wild Turkey, Red-headed Woodpecker, Eastern Wood-Pewee, Great Crested Flycatcher, Brown-headed Nuthatch, Eastern Bluebird, Pine Warbler, Summer Tanager, Rufous-sided Towhee, and Bachman's Sparrow. In

spring and summer (to at least July), Bachman's often perches atop the scattered wax-myrtles to whistle and trill its beautiful, intricate song. In winter, Yellow-bellied Sapsuckers frequent these same woods. If you do not find Brown-headed Nuthatches here, look for them on utility poles in the District Office parking area during March and April.

To visit Ocean Pond, return to the junction of FS 278 and FS 215, go east on FS 215 for 0.5 mile, and then bear right onto FS 216. Take this road for 2.4 miles until it ends at

PINE WARBLER

FS 241 and turn left (north). Follow winding FS 241 for 2.9 miles to its end at paved County Road (CR) 250A. Turn right onto 250A and take the first paved road on the right (about 0.3 mile) to Ocean Pond Campground. Just after you turn onto the campground road you will see a 'Florida National Scenic Trail' sign on the right. Park there and walk north on the trail for several hundred yards to a boardwalk into an imposing cypress swamp, a highlight of this Forest. Here you can expect to find Pileated Woodpecker, Carolina Chickadee, Tufted Titmouse, Blue-gray Gnatcatcher, and several species of warblers: Yellow-throated and Black-and-white warblers and Northern Parula are present all year, and Prothonotary and Hooded warblers occur in spring and summer.

GAIL DIANE LUCKNER, DRAWING

DANIEL LANE, DRAWING

PROTHONOTARY WARBLER

JONATHAN ALDERFER, DRAWING

Big Gum Swamp. After birding Ocean Pond, retrace your route to FS 250A. If you wish to return to the District Office, turn right on FS 250A and drive south for 4 miles to U.S. Route 90; then turn right; the office is about 2 miles west. If you turn left (north) on FS 250A and cross over Interstate 10, numerous water birds can usually be found in ponds along the road. Watch for Little Blue Heron, Wood Stork, Wood, Mottled, and Ring-necked ducks, Mallard, and Hooded Merganser, as well as migratory waterfowl. This stretch of road is also good for finding Pileated Woodpecker flying across the roadway.

Continue 3.5 miles on FS 250A until it ends at Florida Route 250. Turn right and drive 0.5 mile to FS 233. The open area along Rte. 250 provides a good vantage-point in spring (late February) and fall (mid-to-late November) to watch for migrant Sandhill Cranes flying over. Turn left onto FS 233, go 2.5 miles to FS 232, and turn right. FS 232 runs for about 7.5 miles along the western border of the Big Gum Swamp Wilderness, a relatively undisturbed cypress gum swamp area with pine flatwoods on

the perimeter. Watch and listen for Eastern Screech-Owl, Barred Owl, Yellow-billed Cuckoo, Acadian Flycatcher, Yellow-throated and Red-eyed vireos, and Prothonotary and Hooded warblers in spring and summer. In winter, check the hardwood thickets for Eastern Phoebe, Solitary Vireo, and Orange-crowned Warbler.

Hardwood Bottom Land. The final section of Osceola's birding route is reached by turning west at the junction of FS 232 to FS 262, about 3 miles north of FS 233. In spring and summer, stop here to scan the skies for American Swallow-tailed Kite; these graceful raptors nest nearby and often can be found soaring over the open forest and wetlands. The next mile takes you through hardwood bottom-land, which is worth a stop.

Then, drive west on FS 262 for 7.2 miles and turn right onto FS 237; 0.25 mile north, Deep Creek crosses the road. The bridge has been washed away, so you cannot continue, but the low shrubby creek banks are utilized by White-eyed Vireos and Prairie Warblers in spring and summer and Palm Warblers in winter. Return to FS 262 and continue west for about 2 miles to U.S. Route 441. Lake City is 11.2 miles south of this junction.

ACCOMMODATIONS ◆ WEATHER ◆ OTHER ATTRACTIONS

When to visit. The greatest variety of birds can be found in spring and fall; winters are productive as well.

Where to stay. Four campgrounds open all year on the Forest; primitive camping allowed, except during hunting season. Motels in Lake City, west of the Forest.

Weather and attire. Summers are hot, humid, and buggy; winters are mild; spring and fall are usually pleasant. Lightweight clothing is recommended for most of the year, although a light jacket may be necessary in winter. Insect repellent and snake chaps are advised if you plan to do a lot of walking in the woods.

What else to do. Boating, fishing, and swimming are available at Ocean Pond Campground. The Olustee Battlefield State Historic Site, commemorating Florida's major Civil War battle, is located on U.S. 90, 2.5 miles east of Olustee. Each February, the battlefield comes alive during a reenactment of this historic event. A 23-mile segment of the Florida National Scenic Trail traverses the Forest; trailheads are located at Olustee Battlefield and on SR Route 250. O'Leno State Park and Ichetucknee Springs State Park, south of Lake City, have river-bottom habitat with nesting Mississippi Kites.

For more information. General and camping information, District Office addresses, maps, bird list: National Forests in Florida, Woodcrest Office Park, 325 John Knox Road, Suite F–100, Tallahassee, Forida 32303; telephone 904/942-9300, or Osceola Ranger District, Rte. 90 (located on the southside, approximately equal distance from east and west Forest boundaries), P.O. Box 70, Olustee, Florida, 32072; telephone 904/752-2577.

CRESTED FRINGED ORCHID

OCALA FOREST
Florida

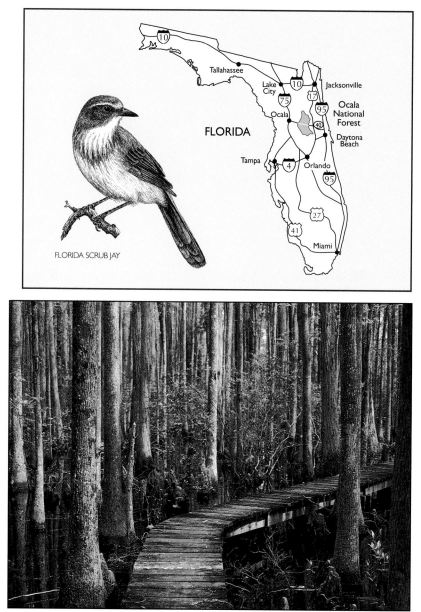

FLORIDA SCRUB JAY

FLORIDA

HOW TO GET THERE. *Exit Interstate 75 at Ocala onto Florida Route 40 and take Rte. 40 east 15 miles to the Ocala National Forest Visitor Center, at the junction with County Road 314. Or, from the east, exit I-95 just north of Daytona Beach onto Rte. 40 and drive about 40 miles west to the Visitor Center.*

MIMI HOPPE WOLF, DRAWING

BOARDWALK TRAIL, OCALA NATIONAL FOREST

AILEEN R. LOTZ, PHOTOGRAPH

OUR SOUTHERNMOST NATIONAL Forest in the continental United States extends over 383,000 acres of central Florida and embraces four distinct environments: scrub, sandhill, hardwood, and aquatic. The scrub community dominates all; it covers nearly sixty percent of the total acreage, and is the greatest such expanse in the country. The vegetation there is characterized by sand pine—the only tree that will achieve moderate size in the extremely dry, sandy soil—along with several types of low-growing evergreen oaks known collectively as scrub oak. This unique ecosystem harbors many endangered or threatened plants, animals, and insects.

The Ocala National Forest's sandhill environment is not quite so dry and often occurs as islands within the expanse of scrub. Here, longleaf pine is the common tree, with a turkey oak mid-story and wiregrass understory. The hardwood areas are climax forests resulting from favorable moisture conditions and the absence of frequent fires; the hardwoods thrive mainly in zones around aquatic communities, such as rivers, lakes, ponds, and springs.

History has left its imprint on the region. The earliest habitation goes back at least 10,000 years to prehistoric peoples who lived mainly in large villages along watercourses and left behind huge middens of shellfish remains. The modern era began in the sixteenth century, with European intrusion and settlement, culminating in the Seminole War of 1835–1842, during which the U.S. government forcibly removed the native inhabitants. (The name 'Ocala' belatedly honors one of the early Seminole chiefs.) The way was then

SHORT-TAILED HAWK

DAVID A. SIBLEY DRAWING

open for intensive exploitation by citrus farmers, turpentine refiners, and timber cutters, whose abandoned homesteads, railroad embarkments, turpentine distilleries, and sawmills still dot the landscape.

Nevertheless, the Forest, established in 1908, provides a sanctuary for a tremendous variety of wildlife. Among the common mammals are opossum, spotted and striped skunks, bobcat, white-tailed deer, raccoon, and the interesting and imperturbable armadillo; black bear is present but infrequently seen. A long list of reptiles and amphibians includes more than two dozen snakes; some of them, such as hog-nosed snake, Florida pine snake, crowned snake, and the endemic Florida short-tailed snake, are limited to dry, sandy soils typical of the Ocala. Venomous snakes occurring on the Forest are eastern diamondbacked and pygmy rattlesnakes, eastern coral snake, and cottonmouth. Gopher tortoise and American alligator are uncommon-to-rare. The threatened sand skink and scrub lizard are denizens of the scrub lands.

Bird Life

One of the Forest's more interesting birds is the Florida Scrub Jay. At present, the jay is considered to be an identifiable eastern race of the western Scrub Jay, but it is expected to become a full species when it will be called Florida Jay. Though listed

KENN KAUFMAN, DRAWING

as threatened overall, it is commonly found in young stands of scrub pine, where the canopy is just closing over. Historically, the jay's habitat was perpetuated by fires that set portions of the forest back to an early successional seedling stage. The jay's population has declined from 20,000 to 10,000 in the past 100 years. Today, conservation management practices are necessary to maintain suitable habitat for the Scrub Jay.

The islands of long-leafed pine provide prime habitat for Red-cockaded Woodpecker, Pine Warbler, Brown-headed Nuthatch, and Bachman's Sparrow, while the hardwood prairies harbor Wild Turkey and Chuck-will's-widow. Birds associated with the aquatic habitat of lake edges, streams, and rivers include Osprey, American Swallow-tailed Kite, and Bald Eagle, as well as herons, egrets, and a variety of waterfowl; four Southern specialties are Wood Stork, Sandhill Crane, Limpkin, and Short-tailed Hawk.

Birding Routes

Two excursions are recommended: The Scrub-Sandhill-Hardwood tour will introduce upland communities, and the Lakes Route covers the wetlands. A word of warning: always keep your vehicle on the roadbed; do not take a chance of getting stuck in the sandy road shoulders.

The Scrub–Sandhill–Hardwood Route. This route begins at the Forest visitor center on Florida Route 40. From the visitor center, drive east on

Rte. 40 for 13 miles to Forest Service Road (FS) 88 and turn left. Drive north for 5.3 miles to a dirt road marked "10," watching along the way for parties of Scrub Jays among the stands of young sand pines less than 10 feet high. The jays frequently post an easily-seen sentry along the roadside. White-eyed Vireo and Rufous-sided Towhee are common here, as well.

Turn right on 10 and enter a sandhill area locally known as "Hughes Island." Look for American Kestrel (now listed as a "sensitive" species in the southeast), Wild Turkey, Northern Bobwhite, Eastern Screech-Owl,

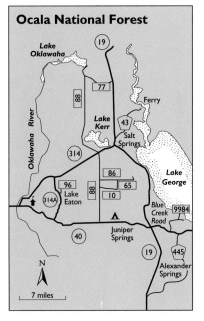

BROWN THRASHER

Ocala National Forest

Red-headed, Red-bellied, Downy, Red-cockaded, and Pileated woodpeckers, Great Crested Flycatcher, Brown-headed Nuthatch, Yellow-throated and Pine warblers, Northern Parula, Common Yellowthroat, Summer Tanager, Northern Cardinal, Rufous-sided Towhee, and Bachman's Sparrow. One mile beyond the junction of FS 88 and 10, keep an eye out for three long-needled pine trees, painted with white bands; these are active Red-cockaded Woodpecker nest sites (See Apalachicola National Forest for information about this endangered species). Remain 300 feet or so from the nest trees, so as not to disturb the birds.

Continue east on 10 for 1.7 miles to FS 65, turn left (north), and go 1.4 miles to FS 86. Turn right onto FS 86 and drive east for 2.5 miles to FS 86F and turn left. You are now in a hardwood community known as "Hopkins Prairie." The rich bird life here includes Osprey, Red-shouldered Hawk, Wild Turkey, Sandhill Crane, Chuck-will's-widow, Red-bellied, Downy, and Pileated woodpeckers, Blue Jay, Carolina Chickadee, Carolina Wren, Brown Thrasher, Common Yellowthroat, and Northern Cardinal. This is a good spot for migrants in spring and fall.

After birding Hopkins Prairie, return to FS 86, turn right, and drive 5.2 miles west to rejoin FS 88. Turn right on FS 88 and go north 3.9 miles to the intersection with County Road (CR) 314. To your left is Salt Springs Island, another example of sandhill environment and an excellent spot for Red-cockaded Woodpecker. Forest biologists are experimenting with artificial cavities in suitable trees in hopes of boosting the woodpeckers' breeding success. So far, so good; nearly half of Ocala's 13 active clusters roost in these cavities. Look for a white painted band on a tree 15 to 20 feet from the right side of the road, 100 yards before the intersection. This is an active nesting cavity; the hole is in clear view from your vehicle. In general, you will find the same species here as at Hughes Island.

A second excellent hardwood location is at Lake Eaton Campground, which you can reach by turning left on CR 314 and driving southwest for 7.8 miles to CR 314A. Turn left (south) on CR 314A and go 2.5 miles to FS 96. Turn left on FS 96. The campground entrance is on the north side of the road after 0.4 mile.

To return to the start of the Prairie–Hardwood Route, turn left on CR 314A and go about 4 miles to Highway 40. Turn right, and drive about 5.5 miles west to the visitor center.

The Lakes Route. Several lakes and streams in widely separated parts of the Forest comprise the Lakes Route. You can visit them individually or as side trips off the Prairie–Hardwood tour.

Lake Oklawaha, a large reservoir created by the Rodman Dam on the Oklawaha River, serves as the northwestern boundary of the Forest. The lake has numerous nesting Bald

Eagles, and is a good spot for observing American Swallow-tailed Kite. Parts of the reservoir can be viewed from County Roads 315 and 310, outside the Forest, but one good spot to look for kites is at the dam. To reach the dam from the visitor center, take CR 314 northeast for about 18 miles to the junction with Florida Route 19. Turn left and drive north for about a mile to the town of Salt Springs, then continue on Rte. 19 for 8 miles to FS 77, turn left, and go 4 miles to FS 88. Turn right onto FS 88 and proceed north for 1.0 mile to the dam. Scan the treeline for kites and eagles and the lake for waterfowl in winter. Regular visitors at that season are Green-winged and Blue-winged teals, Mallard, Northern Pintail, Northern Shoveler, American Wigeon, Ring-necked Duck, Lesser Scaup, and Hooded Merganser.

Lake George, which actually is a wide spot in the St. John's River, marks the eastern boundary of the Forest. It has many Bald Eagle and Osprey nests and wading-bird rookeries along its shorelines. Here you should see Anhinga, Great Blue, Little Blue, and Tricolored herons, Cattle, Great, and Snowy egrets, Black-crowned and Yellow-crowned night-herons, Limpkin, and Glossy and White ibises. Much of the access to Lake George is private, but two good places to visit are the Fort Gates Ferry, northeast of Salt Springs, and Blue Creek Road (FS 9883 on the map), at the southern end. For the ferry, retrace your route to Salt Springs, then turn left onto CR 43 and follow the signs 7 miles northeast to the ferry terminal at the lakeshore. To reach Blue Creek Road, take Rte. 19 south from Salt Springs to the junction with Highway 40, then turn left and drive 3 miles to Blue Creek Road on the left. Follow the road about 2.5 miles, then turn left onto FS 9984 (no sign), which ends at the lake in about one mile.

One of the best birding areas on the Forest, and the most popular

TRICOLORED HERON

Birdfinding in Forty National Forests and Grasslands

SHAWNEEN FINNEGAN, DRAWING

campground, is at Alexander Springs, where 80 million gallons of crystal clear fresh water gush forth everyday. From the intersection of Blue Creek Road and Highway 40, go east of Rte. 40 about one mile to CR 445, on the right. Take CR 445 south for 6 miles to the campground. The best birding is along the Timucum Nature Trail by the swimming hole. A one-mile loop highlights local vegetation used by early Native Americans. In summer watch for Limpkin, American Swallow-tailed Kite, Acadian Flycatcher, Prothonotary Warbler, and Summer Tanager; if you are fortunate, you might even see a Short-tailed Hawk. Canoes are available for rent at the campground, and a trip down Alexander Springs Creek will provide even better opportunities for seeing Anhinga, Limpkin, Purple Gallinule, and Pileated Woodpecker.

A canoe rental concession is also located at Juniper Springs, on the north side of Highway 40, about 4 miles west of the junction with Rte. 19. The leisurely trip down the meandering Juniper Creek through the Juniper Prairie Wilderness covers about seven miles to the takeout point on Rte. 19, 3 miles north of the junction with Route 40. Here, too, you might find Limpkin and Anhinga. If you have your own canoe, or can find a private concession off the Forest, the 20-mile stretch of the Oklawaha River between Highway 40 and CR 316 at Eureka offers excellent chances for finding Limpkin and would greatly increase your chances to find Short-tailed Hawk. Canoes can put in at either highway crossing; this dark-water river, which forms the western boundary of the Forest, flows north through a wide floodplain swamp, so CR 316 is downstream from Highway 40.

LIMPKIN

ACCOMMODATIONS ◆ WEATHER ◆ OTHER ATTRACTIONS

When to visit. Birding is best during the cooler period of the year, fall through spring.

Where to stay. On the Forest: eighteen campgrounds open year-round. Motels in Ocala and Silver Springs.

Weather and attire. Summers are hot and humid with daily afternoon thunderstorms; winters are mild. Rain-gear is recommended in summer, and insect repellent is useful year-round.

What else to do. Hiking on the 66-mile Florida Trail, fishing for panfish and bass, horseback riding (livery at Umatilla), and canoeing. Blue Springs State Park, a few miles to the southeast near the town of Orange City, is a great place to get good views of manatees throughout the colder months when they leave the ocean and swim up rivers to the constant-temperature springs. Silver Springs, between Ocala and the Forest, features glass-bottom-boat rides over many beautiful springs; Limpkin, all the waders, and American alligator can be seen up close. Walt Disney World is 35 miles south of the Forest, west of Kissimmee. Lake Woodruff National Wildlife Refuge borders the Forest on the southeast. When the marshes are wet enough, Black Rail may be found here. The Kennedy Space Center is 40 miles east of Orlando, and Merritt Island National Wildlife Refuge and Canaveral National Seashore, adjoining the Space Center, harbor a number of endangered and threatened species, such as manatee and sea turtles. Manatee are most often seen in the summer in the Atlantic Ocean. Three species of sea turtles are known to nest on the beaches of Brevard County. June is the best month to observe sea turtles. Walking the beach after dark gives opportunities to observe the adult females as they crawl up the beach to lay their eggs, but do not shine lights in their eyes. The Atlantic loggerhead is the most common of the three species, with thousands nesting each summer. Hundreds of Atlantic green turtles nest here, and there are a few records of Atlantic leatherbacks nesting. Atlantic Hawksbill and Atlantic Ridley have nested in very small numbers in other parts of Florida and may someday be found nesting in the Canaveral area.

The Turtle Mound area of Canaveral National Seashore is a great place to watch for pelagic birds when there is a strong east wind blowing.

For more information. General and camping information, District Office addresses, maps, bird list: National Forests in Florida, Woodcrest Office Park, 325 John Knox Road, Suite F–100, Tallahassee, Florida 32303; telephone 904/942-9300.

PASSION FLOWER

CARIBBEAN FOREST
Puerto Rico

PUERTO RICAN PARROT

HOW TO GET THERE. *Take Puerto Rico Route 3, a four-lane road for most of the route, east from San Juan for about 20 miles. Turn right onto Puerto Rico Route 191 at the large El Yunque sign, pass through Palmer, and you will enter the Forest about 1.9 miles from Rte. 3.*

SHAWNEEN FINNEGAN, DRAWING

Hurricanes, which periodically sweep over the island, are a major disturbance. Hurricane Hugo caused widespread tree blow-down and defoliation in September 1989. Shade-intolerant trees, vines, and other plants rapidly filled the openings, however, and today the principal evidence of the storm's fury are the remnants of trees that were snapped in two by the sustained 140-mph winds and 200-mph gusts.

Plant diversity on the Caribbean National Forest, although not comparable to that of a continental tropical forest, is greater than in any other similarly sized area in the U.S. Five plant zones have been identified: subtropical wet forest, subtropical rain forest, lower montane wet forest, lower montane, and a small area of subtropical moist forest. Native vegetation includes 225 tree species, about 80 orchids, and more than 150 ferns, including immense tree ferns that grow 40 feet tall. The forest floor and woody plants support a profusion of vines, shrubs, bromeliads, ferns, and other plants. Except for non-native plants that have been introduced along roads and in plantations at

EL YUNQUE, AS THIS 28,000-ACRE Forest is known to Puerto Ricans, is one of the smallest but most interesting of our National Forests. The only tropical rain forest in the system, it will transport you to a world of fascinating topography, cascading streams, and awesomely luxuriant vegetation.

Located in the Luquillo Mountains of northeastern Puerto Rico, the Forest catches the prevailing northeast tradewinds off the Atlantic. Clouds often cover the 3000-foot peaks, releasing 200 inches of rainfall annu-

ally. Solar radiation on the Forest is only 60 percent of that for the coast, scarcely 6 miles away. Daily temperatures average 80° F at the lowest elevation (300 feet) and 65° F above 3000 feet.

The Spanish Crown was first to recognize the wonder of El Yunque, designating it a "forest reserve" in 1876. It became a National Forest Reserve in 1903 after Puerto Rico became a U.S. Territory following the Spanish American War of 1898, and a National Forest in 1907.

lower elevations, much of the Forest remains in the same general condition as it was when Columbus first landed on the island in 1493.

As with its neighbors in the Greater and Lesser Antilles, Puerto Rico conforms to the concept in biogeography that islands far from continents have a limited fauna with a high proportion of endemic species. Bats, lizards, and birds comprise the majority of the 120 vertebrate species present. The 11 species of bats found on the Forest are the area's only native mammals. Forest streams provide habitat for 6 species of fishes, 9 freshwater shrimps, and 1 freshwater crab. Fifteen species of amphibians occur on the Forest, including 12 frogs. Most of these belong to a group locally known as "coqui," after their habit of loudly and insistently pronouncing their name, especially at sundown and after rain showers. The only snake present is the non-poisonous Puerto Rican boa, which may grow to a length of 8 feet.

Bird Life

Sixty-six species of birds have occurred on the Forest, including nine species unique to the island: Puerto Rican Parrot, Puerto Rican Lizard-Cuckoo, Green Mango, Puerto Rican Emerald, Puerto Rican Tody, Puerto Rican Woodpecker, Elfin Woods Warbler, Puerto Rican Tanager, and Puerto Rican Bullfinch. The Puerto Rican Screech-Owl and Puerto Rican Flycatcher occur elsewhere only in the adjacent Virgin Islands.

Wintering migrants are primarily warblers; seventeen species regularly occur on the Forest. Four species are common: Northern Parula, Black-throated Blue Warbler, American Redstart, and Louisiana Waterthrush.

Due to the Forest's lush vegetation, birds in the rain forest are more often heard than seen. The ubiquitous Bananaquit with its colorful black, white, and yellow plumage is an exception; so is the Pearly-eyed Thrasher. Puerto Rican Todies are fairly common throughout the Forest, but, because of their tiny size, they are easily overlooked, at least until you tune in to their vocalizations. Related to kingfishers, todies nest in banks along the roads and trails. They are special to the West Indies, occurring only on Puerto Rico, Jamaica, Cuba, and Hispaniola. The much sought-after Elfin Woods Warbler is a dwarf-forest ('elfin woods') habitat specialist. This Black-and-white Warbler look-alike escaped scientific recognition as a distinct species until 1971.

Birding Route

El Yunque Forest Road. The best birding is easily accessible off Puerto Rico Route 191. Known as the El Yunque Forest Road, it is the main route through the Forest. The road is narrow with tight curves, and on summer weekends it carries heavy traffic.

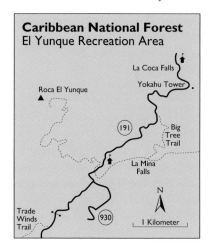

Caribbean National Forest
El Yunque Recreation Area

Roca El Yunque ▲

La Coca Falls

Yokahu Tower

(191)

Big Tree Trail

La Mina Falls

N

Trade Winds Trail

(930)

1 Kilometer

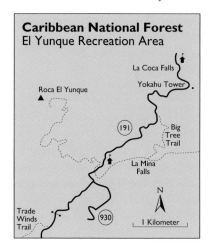
PEARLY-EYED THRASHER

Begin your birding at La Coca Falls (kilometer marker K8 H1), the largest falls on the Forest. Look for Green Mango and Puerto Rican Emerald among the bright red flowers of the African tulip-trees along the road. Watch the roadsides, especially in early morning, for Red-legged Thrush and Black-faced Grassquit. Todies are here; look for them in the lower canopy.

Stop next at Yokahua Tower at K8 H9. The tower was built in the 1950s in the same architectural style as famed El Morro Fort in Old San Juan. Parking, restrooms, books, postcards, and Forest Service guides are available here. Climb the winding stairway to the observation area at the top of the tower. This is a fine vantage-point from which to see the Forest and its bird life. It is, in fact, your best chance for the rare and endangered Puerto Rican Parrot, of which only forty to fifty birds were known to exist in the wild before Hurricane Hugo; forty of them had been accounted for by 1992. Try to get there early in the morning and scan for the parrots as they fly from their overnight roosts or nests to foraging-areas. Since the hurricane, the parrots have relocated to new nesting sites with the result that their population is now more spread out. Most are found in the Upper Luquillo Tropical Rain Forest, between 650- and 2000-ft elevation.

BANANAQUIT AND HIBISCUS

MIMI HOPPE WOLF, DRAWING (RIGHT)

ELFIN WOODS WARBLER

F. P. BENNETT, DRAWING (LEFT)

Also from the tower, you may see Puerto Rico's Sharp-shinned and Broad-winged hawks (both distinct subspecies) as they take advantage of rising thermals. In the surrounding canopy, watch for some of the forest specialties: Scaly-naped Pigeon, the raucous Puerto Rican Lizard-Cuckoo, Stripe-headed Tanager, and Puerto Rican Bullfinch. The forest edge around the parking area is a good place for Puerto Rican Tody, Puerto Rican Woodpecker, Black-whiskered Vireo, and Antillean Euphonia.

The trail-head parking area for Big Tree Trail to La Mina Falls is 0.7 mile above Yokahu Tower (K10 H2). This well-maintained paved trail (3 miles round-trip) includes interpretive signs in English and Spanish for 0.3 mile. It winds through huge tabonuco trees to La Mina Falls. The best place for parrots is near the Interpretive Center in the early morning hours. After 7 AM it is hard to find them, so observers probably need to "stake out" an area from 6:30 AM onward. Most of the same birds possible at the tower can be found along this trail.

The upper slopes of the Forest are covered by a dwarf forest, or "cloud forest," that usually is bathed in mist and clouds; it receives rain on virtually every day of the year. The dense stands of stunted and contorted shrubs and small trees reach a height of barely 15 to 20 feet. The trees and the forest floor are festooned with mosses, vines, lianas, and bromeliads. As might be expected in such a dark environment, there are relatively few vertebrate species, but here is where you will find Elfin Woods Warbler.

The best route into the dwarf forest is the El Toro/Trade Winds Trail (K13 H3), just beyond a locked gate across Rte. 191. Limited parking is available at the junction of Rte. 191 and Forest Road 930, within 100 feet

of the gate. This little-used 6-mile (one way) trail takes the hiker into the Forest's most remote region. The excursion is likely to be an all-day affair but is well worth the effort. The trail traverses a ridge of dwarf forest for much of its length to 3524-foot El Toro Peak, where you just might get a splendid view of El Yunque's Caribbean and Atlantic slopes if the clouds part for a few minutes.

The forest near the junction is ex-

MIMI HOPPE WOLF, DRAWING

PUERTO RICAN TODY

cellent for Puerto Rican Screech-Owl at dawn and dusk. Ruddy Quail-Doves also frequent this area, and their low, mournful calls help locate these elusive ground-dwellers. Other birds to look for while walking along the roadway between the gate and trailhead: Puerto Rican Emerald,

EL TORO TRAIL, REST STOP NO. 3, ELFIN WOODS WARBLER HABITAT, EL YUNQUE

LEE F. SNYDER, PHOTOGRAPH

Puerto Rican Tody, Puerto Rican Woodpecker, Pearly-eyed Thrasher, Bananaquit, Black-whiskered Vireo, Stripe-headed and Puerto Rican tanagers, and Puerto Rican Bullfinch. Also, keep an eye out for Red-tailed Hawk and Caribbean Martin, passing Scaly-naped Pigeons, and fast-flying Black Swifts.

Patience. We are getting to the Elfin Woods Warbler. The first mile of the El Toro/Trade Winds Trail is a well-maintained rocky path with shelters approximately ten minutes apart—handy in escaping from the frequent but brief downpours. Beyond Shelter 4 the trail is poorly maintained; it is narrow, and muddy with occasional washouts and downed trees; hiking-boots are recommended. Fortunately, your target bird, the Elfin Woods Warbler, is most likely to be seen between the second and third shelters and between Shelters 3 and 4. This is on the El Toro Trail before the first extensive area of dwarf forest is found. Check at the La Mina Recreation area for directions after you have seen your parrots. The warbler joins mixed feeding-flocks of Puerto Rican Todys, Puerto Rican Woodpeckers, Bananaquits, and Stripe-headed and Puerto Rican tanagers. In winter, various North American warblers, including Northern Parula, Black-throated Blue, Black-and-white, and American Redstart, join these foraging-parties. And overflights of Puerto Rican Parrots are always possible.

ACCOMMODATIONS ◆ WEATHER ◆ OTHER ATTRACTIONS

When to visit. The Forest is open year-round. Resident breeding birds are most active in March, April, and May.

Where to stay. Campgrounds on the Forest. Many hotels in San Juan and in Fajardo, and several government-licensed guest houses (*paradores*). For information on accommodations, call the Puerto Rico Tourism Company in New York City: 212/541-6630.

Weather and attire. The lowlands are warm and humid year-round, but the mountains are cooler and usually cloudy with rain in the dwarf forest at the highest elevations. Carry a sweater if you are going to visit the dwarf forest, it can be quite cool. Also, carry a change of clothes if you are planning more than a short hike; you are likely to get wet from rain and perspiration. Carry water on the long hikes.

What else to do. The Forest is a garden of delights for the botanist and contains a variety of trails for the hiker. The quiet beaches of the nearby small island of Vieques offer a bird list of over one hundred species and snorkeling in a bioluminescent bay. Another nearby island, Culebra, has seabird colonies with Red-billed and White-tailed tropicbirds and Bridled, Sooty, and Noddy terns. Luquillo Balneario, located on Puerto Rico Route 3 between Palmer and Luquillo, is one of Puerto Rico's most popular public beaches. Puerto Rico Routes 187/188 through the towns of Loiza and the Pinones area is an alternate route for part of the trip between the airport and El Yunque; it has fine views of Puerto Rico's Atlantic Coast. El Faro (or Cabezas de San Juan) is a wildlife reserve–interpretive center of the Puerto Rico Conservation Foundation on Road 987, next to the Seven Seas Recreation Area north of Fajardo on the east coast; reservations are required, 809/772-5882.

For more information. General information, District Office addresses, maps, bird list: Caribbean National Forest, P.O. Box B, Palmer, Puerto Rico 00721; telephone 809/887-2875.

ORCHID TREE

BIRDING ETHICS

Code of the American Birding Association

WE, THE MEMBERSHIP of the American Birding Association, believe that all birders have an obligation at all times to protect wildlife, the natural environment, and the rights of others. We therefore pledge ourselves to provide leadership in meeting this obligation by adhering to the following general guidelines of good birding behavior.

I.   Birders must always act in ways that do not endanger the welfare of birds or other wildlife.
In keeping with this principle, we will
- Observe and photograph birds without knowingly disturbing them in any significant way.
- Avoid chasing or repeatedly flushing birds.
- We will only sparingly use recordings and similar methods of attracting birds and not use these methods in heavily birded areas.
- Keep an appropriate distance from nests and nesting colonies so as not to disturb the birds or expose them to danger.
- Refrain from handling birds or eggs unless engaged in recognized research activities.

II.   Birders must always act in ways that do not harm the natural environment.
In keeping with this principle, we will
- Stay on existing roads, trails, and pathways whenever possible to avoid trampling or otherwise disturbing fragile habitat.
- Leave all habitat as it was found.

III.   Birders must always respect the rights of others.
In keeping with this principle, we will
- Respect the privacy and property of others by observing 'No Trespassing' signs and by asking permission to enter private or posted lands.
- Observe all laws and the rules and regulations that govern public use of birding areas.
- Practice common courtesy in our contacts with others. For example, limit requests for information, and make them at reasonable hours of the day.
- Always behave in a manner that will enhance the image of the birding community in the eyes of the public.

IV.   Birders in groups should assume special responsibilities.
As group members, we will
- Take special care to alleviate the problems and disturbances that are multiplied when more people are present.
- Act in consideration of the group's interest, as well as our own.
- Support by our actions the responsibility of the group leader(s) for the conduct of the group.

As group leaders, we will
- Assume responsibility for the conduct of the group.
- Learn and inform the group of any special rules, regulations, or conduct applicable to the area, or habitat being visited.
- Limit groups to a size that does not threaten the environment or the peace and tranquillity of others.
- Teach others birding ethics by our words and example.

SHAWNEEN FINNEGAN, DRAWING, TRUMPETER SWANS

Birdfinding in Forty National Forests and Grasslands